Conservation Catalysts

Conservation Catalysts

The Academy as Nature's Agent

Edited by James N. Levitt

With a foreword by Stephen Woodley

LINCOLN INSTITUTE
OF LAND POLICY
CAMBRIDGE, MASSACHUSETTS

Library of Congress Cataloging-in-Publication Data

Conservation catalysts : the academy as nature's agent / edited by James N. Levitt.
    pages cm
  Includes bibliographical references and index.
  ISBN 978-1-55844-301-3 (alk. paper)
  1. Nature conservation—Societies, etc.   2. Nature conservation—International
cooperation.   3. Landscape protection—Societies, etc.   4. Landscape protection—
International cooperation.   I. Levitt, James N., editor of compilation.
  QH75.C6627 2014
  333.72—dc23

                                                                    2014022573

Designed by Dreamit, Inc.

Composed in Janson by Westchester Publishing Services in Danbury, Connecticut.
Printed and bound by Puritan Press Inc., in Hollis, New Hampshire.
The paper is Rolland Enviro 100, an acid-free, 100 percent PCW recycled sheet.

MANUFACTURED IN THE UNITED STATES OF AMERICA

Contents

Foreword

Stephen Woodley

AMONG the pressing environmental issues of our age, two large problems dominate: biodiversity loss and climate change, two interrelated challenges to planetary and human well-being. We are now losing species at a rate that is estimated at a hundred to a thousand times the "background," or average, extinction rate of the evolutionary timescale of planet Earth. While a busy urban society seems not to notice, we are losing insects, amphibians, birds, and even mammals.

The fact that these species are the building blocks of the very ecosystems that keep us alive, however, goes relatively unacknowledged. Ecosystems function because of the intricate relationships of their parts, and these parts are species. It is now well established that losing species degrades fundamental ecological processes like productivity and decomposition that very much keep us all alive. Also, species loss is not just a developing world problem. The richer, so-called "developed" countries, including the United States, Canada, and Australia, have rates of species endangerment that equal or exceed the global average.

Biodiversity loss is a problem that has been with us for a while now; its primary driver is habitat loss, from humans converting ecosystems to cities, roads, farms, and industrial uses. It is important to realize that biodiversity loss has been occurring from other causes, completely independent of climate change. However, as climate change becomes globally significant, it will greatly exacerbate the current species loss problem and create new losses as ecosystems collapse and reform.

There is one common solution to these combined issues: to develop conservation landscapes and seascapes composed of both well-managed conservation lands and production areas that are ecologically connected at local, regional, and continental scales. Such a conservation landscape (or seascape), based on large core representative protected areas, would be the most resilient to changing climates and have the greatest chance of conserving large populations. These core large protected areas need to be complemented by a set of smaller conservation areas that are focused on conserving the rare, unique, and endangered. The final piece of a conservation landscape is to plan for meaningful ecological connectivity between protected units so that individuals of species can move between populations and migrate in response to climate change.

Planning for ecological connectivity will require new considerations of the way we plan and manage our production lands, including farms, forests, and towns. We will need to offer incentives to farmers to conserve riparian corridors and establish forestry practices that ensure connectivity. We will need to restore connectivity to many areas through active restoration, and plan our towns and cities to realize connectivity as a goal. It will be challenging, it will cost money, and it will require active participation from all elements of society. However, physical, on-the-ground conservation networks offer the only real solution to responding to the combined problems of species loss and climate change. We are left with little other choice.

Over the last century, we have largely relied on governments to create and manage our parks and protected areas. While much progress has been made, it has been far too little to ward off a crisis in species loss. It is certainly far too little to deal with climate change. We need, and we are finding, new partners.

Indeed, increasing numbers of new partners are rising to the challenge. A diverse range of citizen groups has seized the agenda and led governments in both vision and practical solutions. Private landowners around the globe are embracing opportunities to be responsible stewards of working lands. Indigenous peoples from every corner of the earth, from Australia to Mongolia, Montana, Patagonia, and the Serengeti are showing the rest of us how traditional land use practices can sustain wildlife, water supplies, woodlands, and the sacred places where we can engage, recreate, and refresh our bodies, our minds, and our spirits.

And, as this book shows us, universities, colleges, and independent field stations can serve as surprisingly powerful catalysts in conceiving, establishing, and sustaining large landscape conservation initiatives. To cite just two examples illustrated in the chapters that follow, the collaborative efforts of the University of Montana, the University of Calgary, and a broad coalition of similarly oriented academic and research sector partners, native peoples, nonprofit groups, and private landowners—as well as national, state, provincial, and local government agencies—have made the binational Crown of the Continent initiative in Montana, Alberta, and British Columbia a highly effective force for conservation across a 19-million-acre catchment area. Similarly, the efforts of the University of Nairobi, in partnership with Colorado State University and local NGOs, are making notable headway in organizing local pastoralists and ranchers to work towards the conservation of spectacular and iconic wildlife populations on the Serengeti.

We can gain encouragement from the coalition of groups that have rallied together to promote conservation and embrace connectivity: universities, environmental groups, land trusts, churches, and private corporations are leading the way. To succeed in conserving our natural heritage for many generations to come, we need them all. This book is about the need for new solutions and the groups that are making solutions happen. It is a message of hope.

Acknowledgments

James N. Levitt

A GREAT MANY PEOPLE have helped us assemble the scholars who have written the chapters and vetted the ideas in this book. I have done my best to express my gratitude to them all. Several deserve special mention here.

At the Lincoln Institute, thanks to Greg Ingram, our recently retired president, who guided us through years of productive labor; George McCarthy, our new leader, who champions initiative and innovation in our work; Armando Carbonell, chair of the Department of Planning and Urban Form and a particularly patient and thoughtful collaborator who has strongly supported this project throughout its multiyear life; Maureen Clarke, the Lincoln Institute's editorial chief, herself a passionate conservationist, who guided this book around one set of rapids after another; Lisa Cloutier, senior department administrator, who with gentle persistence offered insight into large-landscape conservation; Anthony Flint, who has shined media light onto our efforts; Emily Schweitzer, the Department of Planning and Urban Form's outstanding research assistant; Susan Pace, who handled every working paper meticulously; Ellen Cremens and Ruth Terry, who have made every single visitor to Lincoln House feel like a special guest; Brooke Burgess and Melissa Anthony, who have handled logistical requests with precision and good humor; and Tom Thurston, who made sure that every traveler to every convening found the way "there and back again."

Further assistance has come from Isabella Gambill, who has patiently and with good humor helped bring the working papers that led to each of the chapters in this book into elegant shape and who has offered keen editorial insight; Joan Powell, our remarkably efficient and effective copy editor; Jennifer Bossert, our painstakingly attentive production editor; and David Drummond, who composed the book's beautiful cover.

The heart of the enterprise has been the group of participants in the Conservation Catalyst meetings in Petersham, Boulder, and Cambridge; thanks to them for their enthusiasm, constructive criticism, and insight. The group includes the following individuals.

- In Petersham, Massachusetts, in September 2011: Perry Brown, Armando Carbonell, Lisa Cloutier, Susan Culp, Larry Fisher, Karl Flessa, David Foster, Brad Gentry, James N. Levitt, Rob Lilieholm, Matt McKinney, Lynn Scarlett, and Gary Tabor.
- In Boulder, Colorado, in May 2012: Emily Bateson, Fletcher Beaudoin, Perry Brown, Armando Carbonell, Lisa Cloutier, Chip Collins, Susan Culp, Susan Daggett, Tom Daniels, Karl Flessa, David Foster (by phone), Douglas Givens, Stephanie Gripne, Walt Hecox, Chuck Hutchinson, Shawn Johnson, James N. Levitt, Rob Lilieholm, David Mason, Nancy McLaughlin, Doug Meffert, Wendy Millet, David Nkedianye, Peter Pollock, Kim Skyelander, Robin Reid, Peter Stein, Hilary Swain, Gary Tabor, Mary Tyrrell, Dongying Wei, and Geoff Wescott.
- In Cambridge, Massachusetts, in May 2013: Emily Bateson, Bruce Beard, Blair Braverman, Armando Carbonell, Federico Cheever, Charles Chester, Story Clark, Lisa Cloutier, Chip Collins, Guillermo Donoso, Joe Figel, Murray Fisher, Anthony Flint, David Foster, Isabella Gambill, Doug Givens, Caroline Harvey, Laura Johnson, Shawn Johnson, Kathy Lambert, James N. Levitt, Rob Lilieholm, Roel Lopez, Karena Mahung, Robert McIntosh, Nancy McLaughlin, Brent Mitchell, Philip Nyhus, Robin Reid, Fiona Schmiegelow, Catherine Schmitt, Jason Sohigian, Michael Soukup, Peter Stein, Henry Tepper, Geoff Wescott, Stephen Woodley, and Francisco Zamora.

This book is dedicated to two individuals who took particular interest in the progress of conservation innovation work at the Lincoln Institute and the Harvard Forest:

- Neal Birnberg, whose unflagging courage, love of life, and passion for learning serve as an inspiration to his loving family and many friends, and
- Bill Gold, an intrepid entrepreneur, unsinkable adventurer, family pillar, and fearless leader of a great trip down the Colorado River. May we all take the opportunity to live life so fully.

Introduction

James N. Levitt

. . . And I believe
These are the days of lasers in the jungle
Lasers in the jungle somewhere
Staccato signals of constant information
A loose affiliation of millionaires
And billionaires and baby
These are the days of miracle and wonder
This is the long distance call
The way the camera follows us in slo-mo
The way we look to us all
The way we look to a distant constellation
That's dying in a corner of the sky
These are the days of miracle and wonder
And don't cry baby, don't cry
Don't cry . . .

PAUL SIMON, "THE BOY IN THE BUBBLE," 1986

MIRACLES and wonders, indeed. We associate the emergence of new technologies and cultural movements with dramatic change on a global scale. These transformations can be beneficial and productive as well as disruptive and destructive.

Countless gloomy scenarios and alarming outcomes related to accelerating climate change, ongoing landscape fragmentation, and growing human populations have been projected for the coming century. Such scenarios, typically grounded in sound science and a clear understanding of the many ongoing trends measured by natural and social scientists, warn of a degraded future for protected wildlands and productive landscapes and seascapes as well as a dramatic decline in diverse animal and plant populations by the end of the 21st century. These visions of where the world is headed need not, however, be our destiny.

More hopeful scenarios are not only plausible, but also within our reach. With exceptional human talent, highly advanced technology, and inventive organizational and financial tools, we may well be able to provide our children—and their children—with a sustainable economy, improving social conditions, and plentiful open lands that are accessible to people on every continent. But we will only be able to do so with an all-hands-on-deck approach that engages the power of the public, private, academic, and nonprofit sectors around the world.

Consider, for example, an analogous set of developments in the field of electric power production. We are, in 2014, experiencing the more-rapid-than-expected advent of cost-competitive and low-carbon renewable sources of electricity. In markets from Massachusetts to Mongolia, wind and solar electric technologies are rapidly approaching, and in some cases even achieving, cost parity with coal and nuclear (O'Brian 2013). Well-informed analysts from such hard-nosed institutions as Citibank (Parkinson 2013) and Bloomberg New Energy Finance (Caldecott 2013) are questioning whether any new coal plants will ever be built in the U.S. Even economic forecasts of an ever-skyrocketing boom in Chinese coal consumption are now being revised downward (LeVine 2013, Krauss 2013). With the cost of silicon photovoltaic (PV) cells dropping one hundredfold in real dollars in less than 40 years (The Economist 2012), and with wind power on offer to UK consumers at retail prices lower than those for conventional sources of electricity (Ecotricity 2013), the prospect of a low-carbon future in both the developed and developing world is entirely feasible.

This remarkable technological and market evolution is the result of a complex set of interactions among private companies, government decision makers, and nongovernmental organization–based advocates from the United Kingdom to Korea to California. However, what sometimes goes underappreciated in the excitement over the emergence of renewables is the catalytic role of academic institutions in the long trek toward the global proliferation of these technologies. Colleges, universities, and research organizations—ranging from the National Renewable Energy Laboratory (NREL) and the Lawrence Berkeley National Laboratory (LBNL) managed by the University of California at Berkeley in the United States, to Denmark's Risø National Laboratory for Sustainable Energy (now part of the Technical University of Denmark)—have been and continue to be essential players in the research, development, demonstration, and early deployment of these now-competitive renewable energy technologies.

By *catalyst*, I mean "an agent that provokes or speeds significant change or action" (Merriam-Webster 2014). Risø and its staff were vital to the early validation and use of world-class Danish wind turbines, including those manufactured by Vestas, a pioneering wind turbine manufacturer. With steady growth catalyzed by Risø and propelled by Vestas and others, wind as a percentage of the national electric supply in Denmark has grown from 0 percent in 1976 to 33 percent in 2013 (Vittrup 2014).

Both NREL and LBNL have been crucial to the relentless improvement of photovoltaic technology and its deployment in novel contexts. Working with industry players and policy makers from around the globe, NREL has, for example, racked up dozens of R&D 100 awards related to photovoltaic technology (NREL 2014a) and been a key partner in the increase in the best research cell efficiencies, from between 1 and 10 percent efficient in 1976 to more than 40 percent efficient in 2013 (NREL 2014b). Exceptional talent; highly advanced technology; and a globalized research, manufacturing, and financing community have brought the renewable power industry a huge distance over the past 40 years, and the momentum shows few signs of slowing down.

As demonstrated in the field of renewable energy technology, the large-landscape conservation community is similarly benefiting from the catalytic power found in academic institutions. On every continent on earth, land, water, and biodiversity conservationists from the public, private, and nonprofit sectors are collaborating with academic conservationists to solve the challenges facing ecological systems at the local, regional, national, and global levels. Out of necessity or choice, they are forming innovative and enduring conservation partnerships that are proving measurably effective, strategically significant, and transferable to neighboring jurisdictions as well as across hemispheres.

Furthermore, colleges, universities, independent field stations, and research organizations, often working quietly in the background, are now being recognized as essential catalysts in the realization of large-scale, cross-boundary, cross-sectoral, and cross-disciplinary conservation projects that are protecting working and wild landscapes and waterscapes from Canada's boreal forest to the tropical rainforests and reefs of the Caribbean. By applying their knowledge beyond the classroom and the laboratory bench, these entities are serving as agents of change—positive change for large landscape conservation, with beneficial impacts that may endure for centuries.

The essays in this book, developed through a series of meetings organized by the Lincoln Institute of Land Policy, illustrate in clear and accessible language the catalytic role of selected universities, colleges, and research stations in advancing large-scale conservation initiatives. The profiles make evident how we can leverage the logic, passion, and trust that infuse our academic institutions to protect an expansive and diverse range of ecosystems. The Lincoln Institute itself has a long and distinguished history of serving as a catalyst for land conservation; in the early 1980s, it hosted a series of consultations and gatherings led by Lincoln Fellow Kingsbury Browne that led to the creation of what is now known as the Land Trust Alliance, the national umbrella group leading some 1,700 land trusts that exist in every one of America's 50 states.

The first of these gatherings on academic institutions as conservation catalysts arose from a series of conversations between Matt McKinney, director of the Center for Natural Resources and Environmental Policy (CNREP) at the University of Montana, and James N. Levitt, director of the Program on Conservation Innovation at the Harvard Forest and a fellow in the Department of Planning and Urban Form at the Lincoln Institute of Land Policy (and the author of this essay).

Levitt and McKinney agreed that the large-landscape conservation initiatives spearheaded by university-based conservation innovators were of exceptional value, seldom recognized by the broader academic community and only sporadically noticed by society at large. They began to imagine a meeting at which academics who focus on land conservation at Harvard and Montana could meet with similarly motivated colleagues from other institutions to share stories of their work, learn from one another, and inspire other institutions to launch similar efforts. With organizational assistance from the Lincoln Institute, the gathering began to take shape. Initially known as PARCC (short for the Program on Academic and Research Institutions as Conservation Catalysts) and later simply referred to as the organizational meeting of the Conservation Catalysts group, the meeting was held in late September 2011 at the Harvard Forest, a Harvard University facility based in the classic New England village of Petersham, Massachusetts.

Once the group convened, it became apparent that the participants were onto some powerful ideas. The narratives that set the stage for the discussion were related, among others, by David Foster and Bill Labich from Harvard; McKinney, Provost Perry Brown, and their distinguished associate Gary Tabor from the University of Montana; Karl Flessa, a world-class paleontologist and dean of the School of Natural Resources at the University of Arizona; and Hilary Swain, the energetic and effective director of the Archbold Research Station in central Florida. Each story enhanced participant awareness of the remarkably creative, enduring, and cross-disciplinary pathways that were being developed to bring institutional resources to the service of large-landscape conservation. It is fitting, therefore, that the first four chapters of this book, devoted to academic and research organizations as conservation catalysts at multijurisdictional regional scales, has been prepared by Foster, Tabor, Flessa, and Swain, focusing on their respective initiatives in the six-state New England region; the Crown of the Continent region that spreads across Montana, Alberta, and British Columbia; the Colorado River Delta that crosses the border of the United States and Mexico; and the multistakeholder mosaic that now covers the Lake Wales Ridge in Central Florida.

By the end of the day's meeting in Petersham, the group had enthusiastically endorsed the idea of holding a larger meeting in the western United States the following spring, with the ultimate aim of producing a book—this book—that would relate these narratives in a consistent and compelling way. In addition, the group expressed the hope that a network of some kind might make the achievements of the most outstanding conservation catalysts known to one another and to a broader community-of-practice through a widely accessible website. That website, hosted by the Conservation Catalysts Network, is now live online at www.ConservationCatalysts.org.

The second Conservation Catalysts meeting took place in the spring of 2012 at the Colorado Chautauqua Association in Boulder—an exceptional setting at the foot of the spectacular Flatiron Range. Special thanks go to David Mason, Colorado's poet laureate and a professor at Colorado College, who gave us rare insight into "what it means to be human" in the region where the Great Plains meet the Rocky Mountains.

The third meeting, held at Lincoln House in Cambridge, Massachusetts, in the spring of 2013, offered us an opportunity to explore, at a lunchtime break, the backyard garden of Henry Wadsworth Longfellow and so gain a better understanding of the 19th-century roots of the conservation movement. Following outstanding presentations that are the basis for chapters in this book, we were fortunate to hear from Caroline Harvey, who teaches slam poetry at the Berklee College of Music in Boston. Caroline literally brought some of us to tears with an after-dinner performance that illuminated how a backyard beech tree could shape her adult consciousness of and passion for the earth. All three meetings brought together a diverse set of collaborators who vetted, challenged, and helped refine each of the narratives presented here.

Why did we bring poets, tree pollen analysts, and policy wonks together to work with one another? Just as large-landscape conservation initiatives require a multiplicity of talents to realize their objectives, the authors of this book collectively span the range of academic disciplines from the natural sciences to social sciences to professional and policy studies to the humanities. Joe Figel, an intrepid field biologist from the University of Central Florida whose work involves tracking jaguars across Latin America, found common purpose with Blair Braverman, an exceptionally talented nonfiction essayist from the University of Iowa. And the team of Nancy McLaughlin and Fred Cheever, law professors from the University of Utah and the University of Denver respectively, found no communication barriers when sharing their impressive portfolio of conservation-related initiatives to colleagues with expertise in hydrology, ornithology, geography, community development, and filmmaking. With each meeting, it became clearer that the boundary-spanning nature of large-landscape conservation efforts in academia is a strength and necessity in pursuing enduring, significant, and measurably effective change.

You will find, in the essays of this book—introduced individually at the beginning of each of the book's sections—exemplary miracles and wonders, large and small. Just as the slow progress made by scientists in the renewable energy industry has gained formidable momentum in the early 21st century, the work of conservationists working in universities, colleges, and independent research stations around the globe is an opening to what we hope to be historically significant large-landscape conservation achievements over the balance of the century. The light that the pioneers featured in this book are directing to the path ahead signals the beginning of a long and productive journey towards effective large-landscape conservation across the globe.

REFERENCES

Caldecott, C. 2013. "Caldecott: Will Old King Coal Continue to Be a Merry Old Soul?" *Bloomberg New Energy Finance*, August 29, online. *http://about.bnef.com/blog/calde cott-will-old-king-coal-continue-to-be-a-merry-old-soul/*

The Economist. 2012. "Pricing Sunshine: The Rise of Solar Energy." December 28. *www.economist.com/blogs/graphicdetail/2012/12/daily-chart-19*

Ecotricity. 2013. "Ecotricity Announces Price Breakthrough for Green Electricity." Press Release. September 23. *www.ecotricity.co.uk/news/news-archive/2013/ecotricity -announces-price-breakthrough-for-green-electricity*

Krauss, C. 2013. "U.S. Coal Companies Scale Back Export Goals." *New York Times*, September 13. *www.nytimes.com/2013/09/14/business/energy-environment/us-coal -companies-scale-back-export-goals.html*

LeVine, S. 2013. "China May Get Over Its Addiction to Coal Sooner Than Anyone Thought." *Quartz*, September 5, online. *http://qz.com/121608/china-may-get-over -its-addiction-to-coal-sooner-than-anyone-thought/*

Merriam-Webster. 2014. "Definition: Catalyst." Merriam-Webster, Inc., web page. *www .merriam-webster.com/dictionary/catalyst*

National Renewable Energy Laboratory (NREL). 2014a. "Awards & Honors: R&D 100 Awards." Golden, CO: National Renewable Energy Laboratory, web page. *www.nrel.gov/awards/rd_awards.html*

———. 2014b. "National Center for Photovoltaics: Research Cell Efficiency Records." Golden, CO: National Renewable Energy Laboratory, web page. *www.nrel.gov /ncpv/*

O'Brian, H. 2013. "EBRD to Invest in Mongolian Wind." *Windpower Monthly*, June 21. *www.windpowermonthly.com/article/1187270/ebrd-invest-mongolian-wind*

Parkinson, G. 2013. "Obama Slams Door Shut on Coal, and Opens the Gate for Solar." *RenewEconomy*, September 24, online. *http://reneweconomy.com.au/2013/obama-slams -door-shut-on-coal-and-opens-the-gate-for-solar-29257*

Vittrup, C. 2014. "2013 Was a Record-Setting Year for Danish Wind Power." Energinet .dk, January 15, online. *http://energinet.dk/EN/El/Nyheder/Sider/2013-var-et -rekordaar-for-dansk-vindkraft.aspx*

Conservation Catalysts

PART
I

Regional Conservation Initiatives

THROUGH VISIONARY INITIATIVES, conservation action around the world is beginning to coalesce across regional landscapes. Motivated by the need to address complex land and water problems at suitable scale and in ways that consider their socioeconomic contexts, these efforts can span from thousands to millions of acres in geographic extent. They often transcend borders and boundaries, giving rise to new forms of multijurisdictional, multistakeholder, and multipurpose collaboration.

The variety and sophistication of large landscape-scale conservation initiatives has grown considerably since the period of early efforts pioneered by environmental groups that were primarily concerned with safeguarding wildlife corridors and habitat networks. In many respects, today's regional conservation initiatives represent a new and unique breed of conservation action, crafted to address the interdisciplinary nature of the problems we face. Informed by modern science and the world's growing complexity, conservation action is now increasingly understood as a multidimensional project addressing intricately intertwined challenges.

The Wildlands and Woodlands Initiative described by David Foster of the Harvard Forest in Chapter 1 is just such an effort. Even its name signals that it is simultaneously trying to protect working woodlands alongside the prime wildlife habitats and few patches of old-growth forest that remain from Connecticut and Rhode Island in the southern part of the region to the expansive forests of Massachusetts, Vermont, New Hampshire, and Maine that extend to the north. Despite its complexity, the project has captured the imagination of citizens, policy makers, private foresters, and nonprofit conservation organizations across the region. The Wildlands and Woodlands Initiative has united a diverse set of stakeholders in the pursuit of a remarkable and ambitious vision—that some 70 percent of the region's landscape can be sustained as forest for many generations to come. The vision came from a group of university-based scientists that Foster convened in about 2004, and the group is still working together in a variety of ways a decade later.

Gary Tabor's chapter on the Crown of the Continent discusses an even more expansive and long-lived project, spanning the U.S.-Canada border from Montana to Alberta and British Columbia. Across a catchment area of more than 19 million acres (over 7.7 million hectares), a group that encompasses university researchers, tribal leaders, ranchers, civic organizations, and public officials from the federal, state, provincial, and local levels has united around a set of common objectives. They are working in concert to corral invasive species, provide measurably effective public education, keep migratory corridors open for such charismatic megafauna as grizzly bears and gray wolves, and promote sustainable tourism for anyone with sufficient sense of wonder to be awed by the view along Going-to-the-Sun Road in Glacier National Park on the U.S. side, or the spectacular lake vistas in Waterton Lakes National Park in Canada. The success of the Crown of the Continent Initiative has proven to be an important national and international model, studied by conservation practitioners from Kansas to Kenya.

The third chapter of this section, in concise, admirably modest prose, tells the story of how a research network organized by Karl Flessa at the University of Arizona served to catalyze a landmark project spanning the U.S.-Mexico border. The effort was a key factor in the recent initiative to revitalize the desiccated Colorado River delta between the international border and the Sea of Cortez. While the author credits others, the recent treaty amendment allocating new sources of water to the delta very likely would never have happened without the early work of Flessa and his collaborators. In this book, however, credit will go where credit is due. The intellectual curiosity, the generosity of spirit, and the willingness to dream about effective conservation at a regional scale shown by committed groups of academics proved to be key factors in the endurance and vibrancy of the three efforts chronicled in this section, spanning the breadth and width of the North American continent.

1

The Wildlands and Woodlands Initiative of the Harvard Forest, Harvard University

David Foster, David Kittredge, Brian Donahue,
Kathy Fallon Lambert, Clarisse Hart, and James N. Levitt

In late 2003, scholars associated with Harvard University's Harvard Forest gathered to discuss a novel venture: writing a widely distributed argument for the preservation of large forest reserves in Massachusetts embedded in an expansive landscape of actively managed forests. Together, it was reasoned, these wild and harvested tracts would yield major benefits for humans and nature. Vigorous forest protection would complement efforts to protect farmland, advance smart growth in towns and cities, develop an energy efficient economy, increase the production of local resources, and conserve the region's biodiversity. One major impetus for the Harvard group's decision to publish their vision for the region's future was the belief that an independent academic voice grounded in science and history might galvanize conservation and aid advocates for sustainable use of land, resources, and energy.

Ten years later, the Wildlands and Woodlands (W&W) effort has grown into a regional conservation force through release of the reports *Wildlands and Woodlands: A Vision for the Forests of Massachusetts* in 2005 and *Wildlands and Woodlands: A Vision for the New England Landscape* in 2010 (Foster et al. 2005, 2010) (figures 1.1 and 1.2). The vision's implementation is being championed regionally by an independent partner of the Harvard Forest—Highstead Foundation and its eight-member staff and nine-member board—and draws from the energy of countless conservation organizations, land trusts, state and federal agencies, landowners, and academics seeking to conserve the New England landscape.

Much has transpired in a decade. In Massachusetts, conservation directions have been reframed through a public Forest Futures Visioning Process for state-owned lands (Massachusetts Department of Conservation and Recreation 2010, Lambert 2012); the governor has promoted increased conservation funding through novel programs for

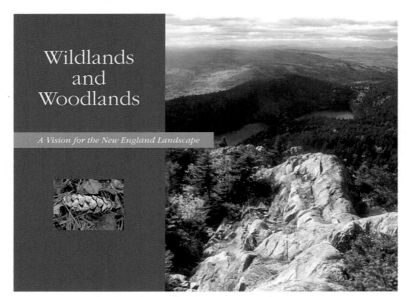

FIGURE 1.1. Wildlands and Woodlands Report, 2010.

FIGURE 1.2. Wildlands and Woodlands Report, 2005.

conservation easements and landscape-scale conservation that were informed by a legislative committee assisted by a W&W author (Levitt and Youngblood 2011); public–private partnerships are achieving record levels of land conservation; and 10 large wildland reserves have been designated on state land. The model organization for collaborative conservation championed by W&W—the North Quabbin Regional Landscape Partnership (NQRLP), headed by the Mount Grace Land Conservation Trust—is a national leader in U.S. Forest Service Forest Legacy projects with multiple landowners. NQRLP has helped to conserve 30 percent of its 510,640-acre region (Leigh Youngblood, pers. comm.).

In New England, more than 38 Regional Conservation Partnerships of collaborating land trusts and agencies now cover more than 55 percent of the region (figure 1.3). The New England Forest Policy Group—a regional collaborative convened after the release of the 2010 W&W report—is advancing major conservation initiatives as well (Wildlands and Woodlands 2013, Labich et al. 2013). Inspired by key W&W collaborator Henry Foster and his edited volume on New England conservation (Foster 2008), the New England Governors' Conference (NEGC) has issued a report calling for greatly increased regional conservation

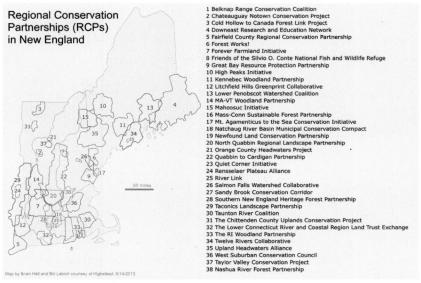

FIGURE 1.3. A map of 38 Regional Conservation Partnerships within New England, covering more than 55% of the region.
Source: Map used with permission from Highstead Foundation.

of forests, farms, and waters (NEGC 2009). A recent assessment of long-term conservation trends in the three northern New England states documents tremendous recent progress in land protection and asserts that the W&W goals can be reached with a historically feasible increase in the pace of conservation (Meyer et al. 2014). And another W&W collaborator, Brian Donahue from Brandeis University, is lead author on a new report calling for the region to produce at least 50 percent of its food by the year 2060 (Donahue et al. 2014).

Over this time, W&W authors have continued integrating new insights from science into the on-the-ground work of conservation planning. Harvard Forest's recent report, *Changes to the Land: Four Scenarios for the Future of the Massachusetts Landscape*, evaluates the benefits of land protection, clustered development, and environmentally sound harvesting to climate mitigation, water quality, wildlife habitat, and related ecosystem services; it was released with strong media coverage and support of conservation, policy, and agency stakeholders (Thompson et al. 2014). With funding from the National Science Foundation (NSF) and private foundations, colleagues from all six states are joining Harvard Forest scientists to form the Science and Policy Exchange, a consortium that will evaluate future land use and climate change scenarios for the entire New England region, among other projects. As Wildlands and Woodlands has grown beyond the scope of standard academic enterprises, the synergies developing among academics, professionals, decision makers, landowners, and other conservation stakeholders have been beneficial to all.

In this chapter we explore the origins of W&W; factors fueling its positive reception and early traction; challenges and opportunities that confront its ambitious goals; and the clear benefits to conservation and academia that have emerged through this effort.

DEEP ORIGINS: BRIEF BACKGROUND ON CONSERVATION RESEARCH AND EDUCATION AT THE HARVARD FOREST

The roots of the Wildlands and Woodlands effort begin with the founding of the Harvard Forest in 1907 and draw from an even longer history of conservation thought. As the first professor in the School of Forestry at Harvard University, Richard Fisher was charged by Dean Nathaniel

Southgate Shaler, a national leader in conservation (Livingstone 1980, 2003), to establish an institutional home in rural New England where faculty, students, and staff would be immersed in studies on the natural and cultural landscape. With university and alumni support, Fisher purchased 2,000 acres of farm woodlots, fields, and successional white pine in the central Massachusetts town of Petersham, including a colonial farmhouse that served as dormitory, classrooms, offices, and laboratory (Fisher Memorial Committee 1935). By the time of his death in 1934, Fisher had trained a number of future conservationists, including Benton MacKaye, Bob Marshall, and Neil Hosley, and through strategic acquisitions had increased the land base to 2,500 acres. He had also established three enduring traditions: (1) a mission to conduct research and provide training, education, and demonstrations of good stewardship; (2) an approach to forest management based on an understanding of the historical and ecological processes that had shaped the land; and (3) an emphasis on learning from nature that encouraged the permanent conservation of the Pisgah old-growth forest in southern New Hampshire and the establishment of forest reserves at the Harvard Forest for ecological studies to guide the active management of surrounding woodlands (Fisher 1933; cf. Foster and Aber 2004; Foster 2014).

The core elements of Fisher's approach remain intact. The Harvard Forest has grown to 3,750 acres through collaborations with landowners, land trusts, and state and federal agencies. The forest's educational and research mission engages more than one hundred scientists and graduate students nationwide with support from endowments and federal grants, including the NSF-funded Long-Term Ecological Research (LTER) program, the National Ecological Observation Network (NEON), the Smithsonian Institution's Global Environmental Observatory (SIGEO), and the Climate Change Research program of the Department of Energy. The educational mission embraces graduate students, a large summer undergraduate research program, and a Schoolyard LTER program that reaches teachers and 5,000 K–12 students in 50 schools. Distinctive among academic ecology programs in constituting a separate "campus" of its governing institution, the forest has 40 full-time staff, including faculty, senior scientists, and students. Fisher's work with private landowners, silvicultural experiments, and local, state, and national forest policy continued into the 1980s with leadership by Al Cline, Steve Spurr, Hugh

Raup, and Ernie Gould. Since then, conservation, management, and policy efforts have expanded with the appointment of David Kittredge as forest policy analyst, Henry Foster as associate, and Brian Donahue as environmental historian, as well as with the creation of the new Program on Conservation Innovation, headed by James N. Levitt, and the Science and Policy Integration Project, directed by Kathy Fallon Lambert.

RECENT HISTORY: INSPIRATION BY INNOVATIVE STUDENTS

The modern origins of the Harvard Forest's vision to conserve 70 percent of New England lies partly in the catalyzing impact of student theses by two undergraduates.

Regional Visions and Partnerships. Alisa Golodetz sought a senior thesis topic at an opportune time. The evening before her initial visit to the Harvard Forest in 1992, David Foster had attended his first board meeting at the Mount Grace Land Conservation Trust (MGLCT), a young regional organization with a growing reputation. He had left the meeting, chaired by Mount Grace founder Keith Ross, concerned that the group lacked a regional map of conservation lands to use in prioritizing its efforts. When Golodetz arrived the following day seeking a project that combined conservation, training, and practical application, Ross responded by asking if she would like to produce such a map as the centerpiece of an evaluation of conservation patterns and trends. The product of her efforts still covers the Harvard Forest's central hallway: U.S. Geological Survey topographic maps on which 239 parcels of conservation land, totaling more than 153,000 acres or 37 percent of the then-415,486-acre Mount Grace region, are color-coded by conservation status and landowner. Golodetz's thesis records the date and motivation of every land transaction since 1900 and reveals a disconcertingly haphazard, but historically understandable, pattern of conservation. Her aspiration to have an impact was achieved: once digitized, the map became a key tool in planning and grant applications by Mount Grace and its emergence as a nationally recognized regional land trust. Meanwhile, her published work helped trigger the formation of the North Quabbin Regional Landscape Partnership.

Golodetz's paper in *Conservation Biology* (Golodetz and Foster 1997) advanced actionable conclusions.

Although the haphazard historical approach to land protection has produced unique and important conservation opportunities, enhanced development and the real threat of landscape fragmentation and parcelization suggests that a comprehensive vision and conservation plan for the North Quabbin Region is now needed (p. 234).

Increased collaboration and exchange of information among groups is necessary if a comprehensive management strategy is to be developed (p. 234).

[To achieve] a balance of economic and conservation goals . . . local involvement in landscape-level planning is critical (p. 234).

The paper called for a broad vision grounded in local action and partnership among the region's 28 conservation entities. Remarkably, the groups responded. The resulting North Quabbin Regional Landscape Partnership and MGLCT, its lead organization, have advanced several major conservation projects (Nudel 2003):

- Tully Initiative (104 parcels, 9,100 acres);
- Quabbin Corridor Forest Legacy Project (20 parcels, 2,100 acres);
- Metacomet–Monadnock Forest Legacy Project (15 parcels, 1,875 acres); and
- Quabbin to Wachusett (Q2W) Forest Legacy Project (23 parcels, 3,000 acres).

Fittingly, the Q2W project advances a proposal promoted two decades earlier by University of Massachusetts professor Jack Ahearn (1995) that informed Golodetz's work.

For academics at the Harvard Forest accustomed to a muted scholarly response to science publications, the reception of Golodetz's work was transformative. We learned that strong, salient research can translate into action when stakeholders are engaged and results are delivered with concrete recommendations. We also recognized that regional coordination enhances conservation by helping to bridge the gap between local landowners and regional vision.

The Illusion of Preservation. In 1999, Mary Berlik's senior thesis explored a question posed in David Foster's ecology course: In suburbanizing landscapes such as southern New England, could more active forest harvesting increase conservation benefits? The question was motivated by the hypothesis that a strong connection between residents and local forests might lead to recognition of the finite nature of these natural resources, reduction in their consumption, and increased interest in forest conservation. While suburbanites often oppose harvesting in the belief that they are conserving nature, global lands that produce wood for consumption in New England are often severely mismanaged. Could both local and global environmental benefits be realized through increased harvesting of our own woods?

Berlik reached out extensively to forest economists and planners nationwide for information, forging connections that would benefit W&W years later. Ideas germane to the W&W project emerged in her thesis: that a regional and global perspective could motivate local action, that local wood production could stimulate forest conservation, and that conservation and preservation must be balanced.

> There is great need for broad-scale conservation of all remaining forests followed by regional planning and strategic selection of areas for intensive management, wildland protection, diverse recreation, and other attributes (p. 1,565).

> We now have the opportunity to cut trees locally, in a heavily forested and ecologically resilient landscape, in order to reduce the impact on often more fragile and globally threatened forests (p. 1,565).

When published in a leading international journal, Berlik's work (Berlik et al. 2002) entered national forestry discussions and became a local rallying point for foresters and conservationists. From Berlik, as from Golodetz, we learned that engagement with practitioners and real-world issues can enrich research and lead to tangible results.

THE PROCESS: ACADEMICS CONVENE

The group that coalesced to write the 2005 W&W report shared three traits: academic association with the Harvard Forest; personal commitment to and experience with land conservation; and belief that an academically based vision for the region could yield new and useful perspectives on conservation. The authors convened over many months, rapidly embracing the balanced approach of widespread forest management on expansive woodlands adjoining and enclosing large wildlands. The writing was invigorating, with give-and-take, compromise, and new thinking injected by authors, colleagues, kibitzers, and more than one hundred scientists and professionals who reviewed drafts through the process.

The resulting vision (Foster et al. 2005) argues for a major initiative in forest conservation and preservation based on the importance of forests to local, regional, and global environments and human populations. The 2005 Massachusetts report proposes the permanent protection of forests covering half of the state, rising from 1 million acres in 2005 to 2.5 million acres by 2060. The report argues that, although passively managed wildlands and actively managed woodlands could conceivably be competing goals, they provide a full range of benefits if carefully combined. The substantial increase in conserved land is expected to occur predominantly through easements from willing landowners paired with strategic conservation acquisitions and economic incentives for conservation. The report highlights the importance of private landowners (85% of land is privately held) and the expansion of the public–private collaborations that have aided land conservation, landowner outreach, and management for decades.

One collaborative mechanism proposed to advance land protection and forest stewardship was the woodland council, an informal group of organizations, agencies, town representatives, and landowners that define a region of shared interest and cooperation. Patterned after the successful North Quabbin Regional Landscape Partnership in Harvard Forest's backyard, the woodland council model was immediately championed by Keith Ross (LandVest) in western Massachusetts and along the border with Connecticut (Ross 2010). Ross also advocated for conservation aggregation projects in which the parcels from many landowners are bundled into a single land protection project, thereby reducing transaction costs and creating a more attractive effort for funding. As the need for larger-scale conservation efforts was recognized, the role of collaborations greatly expanded through the efforts of Highstead and its regional conservationist Bill Labich and conservation director

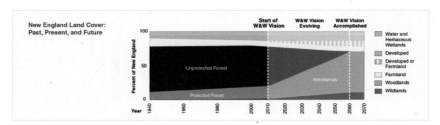

FIGURE 1.4. Proposed Allocation of Land Conserved Under the W&W Vision.
Source: Chart used with permission from Wildlands and Woodlands (2013).

Emily Bateson (Labich et al. 2013). In the process, Regional Conservation Partnerships (RCPs) replaced the original woodland council nomenclature, and a thriving regional network of RCPs emerged.

Encouraged by the response in Massachusetts and across the region, the authors engaged academic colleagues from other states to release the New England–wide W&W report in 2010 (Foster et al. 2010). For this larger, more heavily forested region, the second report advocated a more ambitious land protection goal of 70 percent, with a similar balance of actively managed woodlands and large wildlands (figure 1.4).

THE PROCESS: STAKEHOLDER ENGAGEMENT AND PUBLIC OUTREACH

The authors' regard for models of effective collaboration between scientists and policy makers—such as the Science Links program of the Hubbard Brook Research Foundation (HBRF; Driscoll et al. 2011)—led to an investment of considerable time and resources in communications spearheaded by Kathy Fallon Lambert, former director of HBRF, and Clarisse Hart, outreach manager at the Harvard Forest. To aid this effort, the draft of the 2010 report was circulated to academics, conservationists, land managers, funders, and landowners for review; dozens of discussions were held with agency staff and conservation organizations; meetings were organized with newspaper editorial boards; and a polished report and communications strategy were developed. As a result of this groundwork, the report was improved, stakeholders joined in planning its release, and momentum built rapidly thereafter. Among the notable effects of the report's publication were the following:

- Members of the conservation and funding community embraced the concept as a statewide and regional campaign with potential national importance. Critical momentum was built through organizational meetings convened by the Kendall Foundation, The Trustees of Reservations, The Nature Conservancy, Massachusetts Audubon, Fine Family Foundation, Blue Hills Foundation, and other groups;
- Endorsements from leading regional newspapers (e.g., *The Boston Globe* and *The Providence Journal*) and coverage by national media (e.g., *The Wall Street Journal*, *The New York Times*, MSNBC, *Forbes*);
- Interest from outside the region (Save The Redwood League, Pacific Forest Trust, Ecological Society of America, Wormsloe Plantation and Foundation) that confirmed the sense of broader applicability;
- Independent collaborators (e.g., Keith Ross, C. H. W. Foster, Perry Hagenstein, Kathy Lambert, James N. Levitt) and organizations (Highstead, New England Natural Resources Center, New England Forestry Foundation) lent critical expertise and joined with authors in a steering group to chart a path forward;
- Highstead Foundation reoriented its mission to support W&W, develop relevant staffing (regional conservationist, conservation director, communications manager, operations manager, administrative assistant, internships, two senior fellows), advance the Regional Conservation Partnership effort, and coordinate the W&W partnership of organizations and the New England Forest Policy Group;
- Authors engaged audiences throughout New England and beyond; and
- Harvard Forest collaborators launched new research endeavors to address science and policy questions emerging from the expanded scope of W&W.

Questions and criticisms did arise. One observation made in 2004–2005 was that our timing was atrocious. The Romney administration in Massachusetts had gutted state land protection funding, and the Bush administration at the federal level was cutting conservation funding. We responded by saying that our vision for preservation of the land in perpetuity should circulate at that time for advancement when the environment became more supportive. Questions arose from the beleaguered conservation community: Who would lead this effort, and where would the money come from? Our response: The vision would succeed only if it attracted landowner and grassroots support.

Fortunately, dozens of conservation groups agreed to advance the effort. Jim Levitt and Kathy Lambert tackled the funding question through a conservation finance roundtable and white paper, and a state legislative study committee proposed numerous avenues that were subsequently followed (cf. Levitt and Youngblood 2011, Buglione et al. 2013). Many readers questioned whether enough private landowners would want to protect their land; Dave Kittredge's research on landowner attitudes and motivations (e.g., Kittredge 2009, Rickenbach and Kittredge 2009, Van Fleet et al. 2012) and the land trust community unequivocally confirmed that most do. An influential libertarian argued that the vision undermined private rights and increased public control of land. That voice quieted considerably after she accepted public funds for a conservation easement on her land, the largest land protection deal (3,486 acres, $8.8 million) in state history (Ebbert 2011). A few scientific peers suggested that it was inappropriate for academics to advocate for a conservation vision. We dismissed that concern following a heartfelt discussion; we felt too strongly to stop.

The strong positive response to the release was gratifying. A *Boston Globe* editorial of May 29, 2005, provided a succinct description and forceful endorsement of the vision:

> Harvard University's Harvard Forest research and education center called for a public–private effort to protect woodlands in Massachusetts better. Its goals include designation of 250,000 acres of mostly state-owned forest land as "wildland" reserves, with no logging; the protection of 2.25 million private and public woodland acres—about half the state—for recreation, sustainable timbering, and wildlife habitat; and the establishment of regional woodland councils that could assist land owners and organizations in the management of forest land. [This is] . . . . an ambitious vision, but it should guide public policies even if it cannot be realized quickly . . .

Maintaining woodlands is an effort that must engage everyone from small land owners to town-meeting voters considering zoning issues to state officials setting bond-issue priorities. Without this engagement, asphalt will win (Boston Globe 2005).

Key conservation leaders organized a half-dozen meetings with statewide groups to evaluate the vision and create a horizontal partnership to mobilize action. Notes from one early meeting state that the 40 to 50 participants were at "near, but not complete consensus" concerning the vision's feasibility and that Wes Ward, an eminent conservation leader from The Trustees of Reservations, challenged the assembled group with these words: "If we come up with an approach to this that is eminently feasible, financially doable, and marketable to wide audiences—is there anyone here who thinks their organization would have reluctance in signing on to supporting this vision?" No hands were raised.

The early meetings brought strategic thinking and momentum. Missing or weak elements were highlighted for additional research: early participants pointed to the need for greater attention to farmland and freshwater systems, economic and community development plans, financing for land protection, and a partnership model for W&W. A process emerged for moving forward: a short-term work plan found buy-in from all organizations; meetings of a statewide partnership were convened by a neutral partner (a rotating conservation leader and, by 2006, Highstead's regional conservationist Bill Labich); and subgroups were created on finance and policy, communications and coordination, land protection, woodland councils, mapping, and science. The meetings built cohesion and highlighted W&W as a rallying point for independent groups with different missions: many organizations and individuals could see their own interests in the vision, but all could coalesce around the need to protect more land.

Two sage natural resource professionals (Henry Foster and Perry Hagenstein; Foster and Foster 1999, Foster et al. 2004) joined this group and worked with Ross, Lambert, and Levitt as well as authors Kittredge, Donahue, and Foster to coordinate the behind-the-scenes effort, using their nonprofit New England Natural Resources Center (NENRC) to solicit and receive funding.

In this formative period, which occurred during the first term of Governor Deval Patrick's administration (2006–2010), the Commonwealth of Massachusetts evolved from a skeptical sideline player to an active participant in W&W, promoting policies and funding that aligned well with mutual goals. Robert O'Connor, forest and land policy director for the Executive Office of Energy & Environmental Affairs, joined many meetings and offered strong support for W&W, as evidenced by his letter of December 1, 2005, that accompanied a proposal for funding to a private foundation:

> The Woodlands and Wildlands forest vision involves a balance between working forests and forest reserves. This is a critical concept as it will help build support, understanding, and cooperation among groups that have traditionally been at odds—forest industry, professional foresters, and conservation organizations. The Wildlands and Woodlands vision also includes the formation of local woodland councils [RCPs]. This is an innovative concept that will link the large forest vision to the local level and build support and cooperation for sustainable forestry and the conservation of private forest land (Robert O' Connor, pers. comm.).

In 2006, the Commissioner of the Department of Conservation and Recreation (DCR) invited a W&W author to chair an agency visioning process to chart broad management goals for its 308,000 acres of forest lands. The Harvard Forest hosted the inaugural meeting of the visioning process, where a session by authors Jim Levitt and David Foster set forth major issues in forest history, ecology, and policy. The state Forest Futures Visioning Process regularly referenced W&W and led to DCR lands being designated as reserves, managed woodlands, and parks (Massachusetts DCR 2010, Lambert 2012).

Early proponents of W&W emerged from unlikely places. The Save the Redwood League invited Foster to join a three-day board retreat to share ideas viewed as relevant to the league's shift from a historically protectionist stance to one also embracing restoration and active management of redwood forests. The event revealed a notable historical connection: in 1903, Harvard Forest founder R. T. Fisher wrote the first scientific evaluation of redwood forests and their management (Fisher et al. 1903). On the Georgia coast, Foster was hosted by the 13th-generation owner of the Wormsloe Plantation, where he spoke to 40 plantation owners and friends. Anticipating resistance to the W&W goal of expansive land protection, he instead witnessed deep passion for the land and a desire for enhanced conservation in the face of the relentless sprawl affecting the southeast. From San Francisco, Laurie Wayburn, president of the Pacific Forest Trust, lent strong support: "[W&W] is a visionary way of recognizing the inevitability of development but not the uncontrollability of where and how this development takes place" (Sullivan 2009).

Media exposure lent momentum and broadened interest beyond conservation circles. Reporter Jim Sterba (2005) wrote a front-page *Wall Street Journal* piece on forest management and conservation in suburban Massachusetts that referenced the work of W&W collaborators, including Berlik, Kittredge, and Foster's paper "The Illusion of Preservation," as well as Brian Donahue's suburban forest stewardship projects. "The Working Forest," a *New York Times Magazine* piece by writer Robert Sullivan, explored the surprising boldness and impact of the vision: "Wildlands and Woodlands, or W&W, has been moving through conservation circles like an aggressive invasive species. . . . As opposed to a lot of papers that fall like trees in a forest, this one has ended up being a blueprint" (Sullivan 2009). In the 2010 Green Issue of the *Boston Globe Magazine*, Tom Horton captured the arguments and prognosis for W&W:

> While its ambitions are large and deeply green, the report envisions anything but a "lock it up" approach. It calls for stepped-up use of most forests, including timbering. And it depends on hundreds of thousands of private landowners . . . [who] account for more than half of New England forests. The report also focuses new attention on forests as "green infrastructure," supplying billions of dollars' worth of services to the region, from protecting clean water to absorbing the carbon that would exacerbate climate change.
>
> In Massachusetts, local land trusts are already broadening their forestland protection ambitions. The Patrick administration has pledged to spend $50 million a year from environmental bonds for more land protection. Between 1999 and 2005, the state actually protected substantially more

open space than it lost, about 110,000 acres versus 47,600 claimed by development, according to Mass Audubon's recent "Losing Ground" study. Even so, it will take 85 years to meet the 50-year goals of the Wildlands and Woodlands report, the Audubon study concludes (Horton 2010).

In September 2010, the growing impact of the W&W vision was formally recognized with the Charles Eliot Award from The Trustees of Reservations, the world's oldest regional land trust and a national leader in natural and cultural conservation. The statement by then-Trustees president Andrew Kendall that accompanied the award read in part:

> Wildlands and Woodlands . . . has raised consciousness among policy-makers and the public at large, stimulated strong grassroots activism . . . and contributed to important, ecologically informed changes in forest policy in Massachusetts.

PROVIDING AMMUNITION FOR OTHERS TO USE

The intent of the W&W reports was to advance the land protection success of existing organizations and agencies rather than to build a stand-alone W&W enterprise, and it has been gratifying to see W&W employed in this way. In her organization's newsletter *Forest Notes*, Jane Difley, president of the Society for the Protection of New Hampshire Forests (SPNHF), hailed W&W as she applied its arguments to reignite SPNHF's equally bold and visionary New Hampshire Everlasting Campaign. The New England Forestry Foundation (NEFF) recognized the congruence of W&W with its own messages on forest conservation and stewardship and, under the leadership of executive directors Lynn Lyford and Bob Perschel, has emerged as a champion of W&W. NEFF has featured W&W in its newsletter, embraced its goals, advocated for RCPs, cosponsored a major conference with SPNHF to celebrate and advance the New England vision, and developed its Heart of New England campaign to promote forestry and increase the pace of forest conservation. Across the conservation spectrum, the Northeast Wilderness Trust strongly echoed W&W arguments for large reserves that support landscape-scale natural processes. Many other groups—Vermont Land Trust, Kennebec Land Trust, Mount Grace Land Conservation Trust,

East Quabbin Land Trust, Rensselaer Plateau Alliance, and Kestrel Land Trust—have used the W&W report and goals to advance their own missions.

W&W has also inspired private landowners to redouble their effort at land protection and management. Under George Lovejoy's leadership, the Blue Hills Foundation in southeastern New Hampshire has protected more than 5,000 acres of actively managed forests and 100 acres of farm fields, and has designated a 1,200-acre wildland reserve. In northeastern Vermont, the Jerry Lund Mountain Trust has conserved 650 acres of managed forest with the Vermont Land Trust and has partnered with the state of Vermont to protect the entire watershed of Levi Pond in reserves that total more than 300 acres. Farther south, Highstead Foundation and the Harvard Forest have committed to managing their own lands as a combination of wildlands and woodlands.

REASONS FOR SUCCESS

Although it is still early in the 50-year W&W effort, we can see that early traction has resulted from many factors both anticipated and unforeseen.

Framing of the Message

The W&W authors employed arguments for aggressive land protection that resonate with a broad audience across and beyond New England.

(1) Regional history provides a model of the second chance for conservation. The history of deforestation and reforestation in the northeastern United States is a compelling environmental narrative (McKibben 1995) that offers a second chance to determine the fate of the region's forests. Recent forest declines from haphazard development in every New England state add urgency to conservation (figure 1.5). Applying the historical narrative, W&W authors distinguish between earlier "soft" deforestation for agriculture and modern "hard" deforestation for buildings and roads.

(2) Conservation as investment in natural infrastructure. The W&W reports emphasize broad societal values and argue for a financial investment in conservation equivalent to great public works efforts. Employing the phrase *natural infrastructure*, the authors outline the billions of

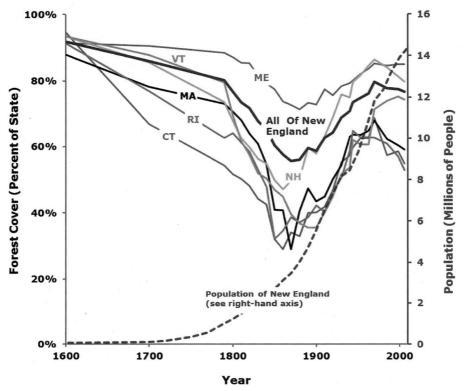

FIGURE 1.5. The historical recovery of forests and recent trend of deforestation motivate widespread conservation in New England.

dollars provided by forests in ecosystem resources and services such as clean water, wildlife, renewable wood products, natural climate buffering, forest jobs, tourism, and recreation.

(3) Wildlands and woodlands as mutually supporting and established conservation goals. While late 20th-century conflicts highlighted tensions between the conservation of resources and the preservation of nature, early conservation visionaries such as Henry Thoreau, Aldo Leopold, and Teddy Roosevelt embraced the approaches as complementary. *All* forests yield many shared benefits simply by being forests. Actively managed woodlands provide wood resources, while wildlands offer contrasting habitat characteristics and human experiences. At the Harvard Forest, Richard Fisher advanced forest management regionally and na-

tionally while leading the successful effort to protect one of the great virgin forests in New England—the Pisgah Forest in Winchester, New Hampshire. His approach to silviculture based on natural processes, called "ecological forestry" (Spurr and Cline 1942), presaged approaches considered innovative today. Bob Marshall fulfilled his own lifetime dream of becoming a forester by working on a forest harvesting study with Fisher and yet went on to found the Wilderness Society. Like the W&W authors, Marshall recognized that wilderness can only thrive when surrounded by well-managed forests that are generating valuable benefits for society (Foster 2014). Both have value; both are needed.

(4) Advancing the good work of others. W&W openly acknowledged its debt to the work of many scholars and organizations and sought to support other groups' efforts through the regionally supportive conservation enterprises led by Highstead (e.g., the Regional Conservation Partnership Network, the New England Forest Policy Group, and the Stewardship Science project). The fact that W&W is a vision rather than a prescriptive plan reinforces this message.

(5) Effective communications. The response to W&W has highlighted the value of broad engagement, outreach, and communications, including the following specific measures:

(a) Prerelease engagement for the 2005 and 2010 Wildlands and Woodlands reports
  - Fundraising from private foundations
  - Media training for coauthors and presentations of embargoed content at conferences and to local stakeholders
  - Website with papers, updates, links to organizations, media outreach, and highlights
  - Press release collaboration with NGOs, the National Science Foundation, and university communications offices
(b) Press outreach
  - Live press webinar featuring authors and stakeholder respondents
  - Press releases to national, state, and local media lists with author contacts
  - 42 national stories and 66 regional stories (25% unique features, 75% AP)

- Positive editorials in every New England state; 31 blog entries; 8 alumni highlights; 9 radio spots, 1 video spot; 9 NGO newsletter features
(c) Public release events
  - Academic keynote hosted by Kennedy School of Government at Harvard University; 150 invited guests from academia, NGOs, and agencies; keynote by Theodore Roosevelt IV
  - Public/NGO conference with more than 250 attendees from the public and private sectors, plenary speakers, and four afternoon workshops
  - Author presentations at 30 regional and national conferences
(d) Ongoing activities
  - Regular digital outreach through websites, e-newsletters, and social media
  - Annual print updates
  - Robust work in conservation, policy, and science (e.g., New England Forest Policy Group, RCP Network, Changes to the Land, and Stewardship Science) to introduce more individuals, organizations, policymakers, and agencies to the vision

Engaging Strong, Credible, and Salient Science

Despite its strong base in ecological and historical research, W&W is not mired in scientific details and debate: it engages science to advance the vision rather than for science's sake. Nonetheless, as W&W grew, it pursued new research to address questions and uncertainties raised by the reports. These investigations have ranged from examining the motivations and decision-making processes of private landowners (Rickenbach and Kittredge 2009, LeVert et al. 2009, Van Fleet et al. 2012, Kittredge et al. 2013) and assessing the impacts of climate change and land use history on regional forest conditions (Thompson et al. 2011) to evaluating the effectiveness of regional conservation partnerships (Labich et al. 2013). Subsequent work evaluating four plausible land-use and climate futures for the region (*Changes to the Land*; Thompson et al. 2014) showed that benefits to wildlife, climate mitigation, clean water, timber harvesting, and resiliency to environmental change increase as land conservation is paralleled by concentrated development and improved timber harvesting practices.

Seeking Critical Institutional Support: The Partnership with Highstead

Although conservation advances gain public notice with major milestones—the completion of big land protection deals, receipt of large grants, or passage of new legislation—the business of conservation is a never-ending daily enterprise. Landowners must be engaged, deals need to be brokered, conservation partnerships must be forged and develop expertise and resources, the groundwork must be laid for new policies, and organizational efforts must be sustained. Consequently, moving W&W from a vision to a growing movement required resources and the persistent energy of an independent "honest broker," a conservation entity with credibility that could work seamlessly with the academic authors and bring new capacity to its efforts. Initially that role was served by the partnership of Massachusetts conservation groups working with the Kendall Foundation. Subsequently, the New England Natural Resources Center stepped in, aided with foundation funding. But the critical step towards a solid W&W trajectory occurred when the founder of the Highstead Foundation chose to make advancing W&W one of its central missions.

A critical ally with independent resources, Highstead brought many strengths: a commitment to science and academic traditions, dedication to the conservation of nature and its resources, a seasoned and insightful board, and willingness to collaborate with the Harvard Forest and other W&W partners while strategically adding talented staff to fill critical roles as required by the growing regional enterprise. No public agency or conservation group could fill the niche of an independent and committed champion of a regional conservation vision. And no academic institution could work at the interface of advocacy, public–private partnerships, and fundraising in the manner needed to advance the W&W vision. As a small, nimble, and innovative nonprofit, Highstead has been able to fill these essential roles while keeping the day-to-day and long-term focus squarely on the W&W goal of conserving the New England landscape. The result is an effective collaboration between an academic institution and a small nonprofit that has grown the Wildlands and Woodlands enterprise while providing the young foundation with a regional and national role that matched its own aspirations.

THE ROLE OF THE ACADEMIC INSTITUTION

Critical to the success of W&W has been its academic origins, which signal a measure of independence from the typical champions of conservation causes, lend credibility to the effort, and allow many different groups and perspectives to join in the initiative. Harvard University has played an ongoing role in hosting key discussions, workshops, and public lectures in support of the launch of the New England vision and in providing outreach to students, alumni, faculty, and the larger community.

The Harvard Forest has also played multiple roles. Through its participation in the NSF-funded LTER program, it contributes scientific insight, conducts key regional analyses, and works at the interface of scholarship and societal need. Institutionally, the Forest maintains strong relationships with diverse constituencies at local, state, regional, and national levels, and its open-door policy to visitors, meetings, and conferences has served a broad user group for decades. As an academic setting, the Forest epitomizes neutral space where groups can share ideas freely; as a reserve, the Forest is a living laboratory in which real-world practices can be designed and tested. The Forest is actively engaged in forest harvesting, cattle grazing, reserve designation, and land acquisition and protection, following a land management plan that is congruent with *wildlands*, *woodlands*, and *farmlands* thinking.

At the same time, we must work to counter the image of ivory tower–bound scholars preaching from a well-endowed nonprofit base. Land management and conservation activities at the Harvard Forest are a crucial part of the W&W mission, and W&W authors themselves own land that they pay taxes on, manage, conserve, and care for while devoting energy to local boards and organizations and epitomizing W&W values.

Given our experience, we see a clear and growing role for colleges and universities in catalyzing conservation. We believe these efforts may be strongest when the following factors are in place:

- The efforts align with the mission, history, and strengths of the academic entity.
- The university leads by example and serves as a model for the ideas it promotes.

- The work is attuned to, but independent from, regional conservation interests.
- The university communicates with a range of stakeholder and interest groups.
- There is a partnering entity to fill roles outside the purview of academia.

At a Harvard Forest workshop in January 2014, W&W authors began exploring the potential for a collaborative of academic institutions advancing conservation, tentatively titled ALPINE (Academics for Land Protection In New England).

THE BENEFITS TO THE ACADEMIC INSTITUTION

Over the years, some skeptical academics have asked what the Harvard Forest and Harvard University gain by releasing and advancing the W&W vision. Initially, we also had misgivings concerning how this activity would be received throughout the university. But we have been delighted by the benefits that have come to our research and educational endeavors, to our engagement across the university, and to the larger mission.

Increased University Engagement

Increased visibility of the Harvard Forest throughout and beyond the university has come through internal and external media, participation in related administrative and academic activities, the active process of finalizing land protection deals with university deans and attorneys, and collaborations with university museums. The latter has included a new permanent exhibit at the Harvard Museum of Natural History titled "New England Forests" and programming of public lectures and gatherings with donors and alumni groups. W&W, like the physical operation of the Harvard Forest—accounting for our 3,750-acre carbon sink, heating efficiently with wood biomass, erecting solar arrays, and significantly reducing greenhouse gas (GHG) emissions—is consistent with the environmental themes and goals of President Drew Faust's Green Initiative. Academic offerings available at both the Forest and in Cambridge include an expanding number of courses on conservation, conservation policy, land use, and climate change.

Enhanced Research

The most surprising outcome of the W&W initiative has been new directions and strengths in Harvard Forest research. The report's discussion of the concept of natural infrastructure has initiated study of the processes underlying specific ecosystem services, including the carbon dynamics of forest development and the role of forested watersheds in mitigating flooding and producing clean water for human consumption. W&W has become integral to the new LTER theme of New Science, Synthesis, Scholarship, and Strategic Vision for Society.

Another activity galvanized by W&W has been long-sought collaboration through the Science–Policy Exchange (SPE) among major ecological research institutions in the northeast: Harvard Forest, Hubbard Brook, the Cary Institute of Ecosystem Studies, the Ecosystems Center at the Marine Biological Laboratory in Woods Hole, the University of New Hampshire, and Syracuse University. SPE currently addresses climate change, land use, water, and energy.

Enhanced Conservation/Partner Engagement

Locally, we are advancing land protection to buffer the boundaries of the Harvard Forest, diversify our research opportunities, and safeguard the quality of our science and viability of our research and educational mission. We have assisted abutting landowners in placing conservation easements on their land and acquired land and buildings through a two-step process in which the land is pre-acquired by a local land trust (e.g., Mount Grace Land Conservation Trust or East Quabbin Land Trust), a conservation easement is placed on it using state and private funding, and the conserved property is acquired by Harvard. This process reduces costs, ensures that the lands are conserved in perpetuity, and has facilitated the placement of conservation restrictions on our existing property.

CONCLUSION

After a decade in action, W&W has accomplished much, but completing the central challenge of conserving the region's forests and farmlands remains (Meyer et al. 2014). The effort has led to effective partnerships to advance this effort and has brought solid rewards to all participants. Importantly, it has highlighted the significant role that academic institutions can play in catalyzing conservation as well as the benefits that can return to academia through such work.

ACKNOWLEDGMENTS

The Wildlands and Woodlands initiative was the brainchild of Harvard Forest colleagues willing to spend long but enjoyable hours around a Harvard Forest–built cherry table in Shaler Hall to hash out a vision that drew from their collective experience in conservation: Betsy Colburn, Tony D'Amato, Brian Donahue, Aaron Ellison, Brian Hall, Dave Kittredge, Glenn Motzkin, Dave Orwig, and David Foster. The vision gained traction due to the energies of Hank Foster, Kathy Lambert, Keith Ross, Perry Hagenstein, James N. Levitt, Bill Labich, and Clarisse Hart and the support of Henry Lee, Ted Smith, Wayne Klockner, Wes Ward, Bob O'Connor, Leigh Youngblood, Rich Hubbard, Bernie McHugh, and many others. It grew to a New England–wide initiative through the added wisdom and energy of authors John Aber, Charlie Cogbill, Charley Driscoll, Tim Fahey, Clarisse Hart, Mac Hunter, Lloyd Irland, Bill Keeton, Rob Lilieholm, and Jonathan Thompson. The work and accomplishments of W&W are advanced by Emily Bateson (conservation director), Bill Labich (regional conservationist), and staff at Highstead (Jody Cologgi, Geordie Elkins, Ed Faison, and Kathleen Kitka) with strong support from its board (Peter Ashton, Mary Ashton, Susan Clark, Elisabeth Dudley, Henry Dudley, David Foster, Kathy Lambert, Sarah Dudley Plimpton, and Peter Del Tredici) in collaboration with partners at many conservation organizations and agencies. We acknowledge support from the Highstead Foundation, Fine Family Foundation, Jessie B. Cox Trust, Cardinal Brook Trust, Blue Hills Foundation, New England Natural Resources Center, Sweet Water Trust, U.S. Forest Service, and the National Science Foundation through the Long-Term Ecological Research program and the Directorate for Biological Sciences.

REFERENCES

Ahern, J. 1995. "Greenways As a Planning Strategy." *Landscape and Urban Planning* 33:131–155.

Berlik, M. M., D. B. Kittredge, and D. R. Foster. 2002. "The Illusion of Preservation: A Global Environmental Argument for the Local Production of Natural Resources." *Journal of Biogeography* 29:1557–1568.

Boston Globe. 2005. "Saving the Woods." Editorial, May 29, D10.

Buglione, A., J. N. Levitt, J. Rasku, and L. Youngblood. 2013. *Greater Quabbin Conservation Investment Zone Assessment*. Petersham, MA: The Program on Conservation Innovation at the Harvard Forest, Harvard University.

Donahue, B., J. Burke, M. Anderson, A. Beal, T. Kelly, M. Lapping, H. Ramer, R. Libby, and L. Berlin. 2014. *A New England Food Vision: Healthy Food for All, Sustainable Farming and Fishing, Thriving Communities.* Durham, NH: Food Solutions New England, University of New Hampshire Sustainability Institute.

Driscoll, C. T., K. F. Lambert, and K. C. Weathers. 2011. "Integrating Science and Policy: A Case Study of the Hubbard Brook Research Foundation Science Links Program." *BioScience* 61:791–801.

Ebbert, S. 2011. "Deal Keeps Parcel of Forest Protected." *Boston Globe*, December 24, B1.

Fisher, R. T. 1933. "New England Forests: Biological Factors. New England's Prospect: 1933." *American Geographical Society Special Publication* 16:213–223.

Fisher, R. T., H. von Schrenk, and A. D. Hopkins. 1903. *The Redwood: A Study of the Redwood.* Washington, DC: U.S. Department of Agriculture, Bureau of Forestry Bulletin No. 38.

Fisher Memorial Committee. 1935. *The Harvard Forest 1907–1934: A Memorial to Its First Director Richard Thornton Fisher.* Cornwall, NY: Cornwall Press.

Foster, C. H. W., ed. 2008. *Twentieth-Century New England Land Conservation: A Heritage of Civic Engagement.* Cambridge, MA: Harvard University Press.

Foster, C. H. W., and D. R. Foster. 1999. *Thinking in Forest Time: A Strategy for the Massachusetts Forest.* Harvard Forest Paper No. 24. Petersham, MA: Harvard Forest, Harvard University.

Foster, C. H. W., P. R. Hagenstein, and D. R. Foster. 2004. "Forest Conservation and Stewardship in Massachusetts." In *Forest Conservation and Stewardship in Massachusetts*, ed. C. H. W. Foster and P. R. Hagenstein. Petersham, MA: Harvard Forest, Harvard University.

Foster, D. R. 2014. *Hemlock. A Forest Giant on the Edge.* New Haven, CT: Yale University Press.

Foster, D. R., and J. D. Aber. 2004. *Forests in Time: The Environmental Consequences of 1000 Years of Change in New England.* New Haven, CT: Yale University Press.

Foster, D. R., B. M. Donahue, D. B. Kittredge, K. F. Lambert, M. L. Hunter, B. R. Hall, L. C. Irland, R. J. Lilieholm, D. A. Orwig, A. W. D'Amato, E. A. Colburn, J. R. Thompson, J. N. Levitt, A. M. Ellison, W. S. Keeton, J. D. Aber, C. V. Cogbill, C. T. Driscoll, T. J. Fahey, and C. M. Hart. 2010. *Wildlands and Woodlands: A Vision for the New England Landscape.* Cambridge, MA: Harvard University Press.

Foster, D. R., D. B. Kittredge, B. Donahue, G. Motzkin, D. A. Orwig, A. M. Ellison, B. Hall, E. A. Colburn, and A. D'Amato. 2005. *Wildlands and Woodlands: A Vision for the Forests of Massachusetts.* Harvard Forest Paper No. 27. Petersham, MA: Harvard Forest, Harvard University.

Golodetz, A., and D. R. Foster. 1997. "History and Importance of Land Use and Protection in the North Quabbin Region of Massachusetts." *Conservation Biology* 11:227–235.

Horton, T. 2010. "Speaking for the Trees." *Boston Globe*, October 10.

Kittredge, D. B. 2009. "The Fire in the East." *Journal of Forestry* (April/May): 162–163.

Kittredge, D. B., M. G. Rickenbach, T. Knoot, E. Snellings, and A. Erazo. 2013. "It's the Network: How Personal Connections Shape Decisions About Private Forest Use." *Northern Journal of Applied Forestry* 30 (2): 67–74.

Labich, W. G., E. M. Hamin, and S. Record. 2013. "Regional Conservation Partnerships in New England." *Journal of Forestry* 111 (5): 326–334.

Lambert, E. 2012. *Landscape Designations for DCR Parks and Forests: Selection Criteria and Management Guidelines.* Boston: Massachusetts Department of Conservation and Recreation (DCR). *www.mass.gov/eea/docs/dcr/ld/management-guidelines.pdf*

LeVert, M., T. Stevens, and D. Kittredge. 2009. "Willingness to Sell Conservation Easements: A Case Study of Private Forestland Owners in Southern New England." *Journal of Forest Economics* 15:261–275.

Levitt, J. N., and L. Youngblood. 2011. *Report of the Massachusetts Commission on Financing Forest Conservation.* Petersham, MA: The Program on Conservation Innovation at the Harvard Forest, Harvard University.

Livingstone, D. N. 1980. "Nature and Man in America: Nathaniel Southgate Shaler and the Conservation of Natural Resources." *Transactions of the Institute of British Geographers* 5:369–382.

———. 2003. *Nathaniel Southgate Shaler and the Culture of American Science.* Tuscaloosa: University of Alabama Press.

Massachusetts Department of Conservation and Recreation. 2010. "Forest Futures Visioning Process Project Summary." Boston: Massachusetts Department of Conservation and Recreation. *www.umb.edu/mopc/projects/ffvp*

McKibben, W. 1995. "An Explosion of Green." *Atlantic Monthly* (April): 61–83.

Meyer, S. R., C. S. Cronan, R. J. Lilieholm, M. L. Johnson, and D. R. Foster. 2014. "Land Conservation in Northern New England: Historic Trends and Alternative Conservation Futures." *Biological Conservation* 174:152–160.

Mount Grace Land Conservation Trust. 2013. "Landscape Conservation." *Views from Mount Grace* 24 (3): 4.

New England Governors' Conference. 2009. *Report of the Blue Ribbon Commission on Land Conservation.* Boston, MA: New England Governors' Conference, Inc. *http://negc.org/uploads/file/Reports/NEGC%20CLC%20Report%209-09.pdf*

Nudel, M. 2003. "Better Conservation Through Partnerships." *Exchange: The Journal of the Land Trust Alliance* (Spring) 22:17–21.

Rickenbach, M. G., and D. B. Kittredge. 2009. "Time and Distance: Comparing Motivations Among Forest Landowners in New England." *Small-Scale Forestry* 8:95–108.

Ross, K. 2010. "Conserve More Land Today Through Parcel Aggregation." *Northern Woodlands* 66:7–8.

Spurr, S. H., and A. C. Cline. 1942. "Ecological Forestry in Central New England." *Journal of Forestry* 40:418–420.

Sterba, J. 2005. "To Preserve Forests, Supporters Suggest Cutting Some Trees." *Wall Street Journal*, May 5.

Sullivan, R. 2009. "The Working Forest." *New York Times Magazine*, Sunday, April 16.

Thompson, J. R., D. R. Foster, R. Scheller, and D. B. Kittredge. 2011. "The Influence of Land Use and Climate Change on Forest Biomass and Composition in Massachusetts, USA." *Ecological Applications* 21:2425–2444.

Thompson, J., K. F. Lambert, D. Foster, M. Blumstein, E. Broadbent, and A. A. Zambrano. 2014. *Changes to the Land: Four Scenarios for the Future of the Massachusetts Landscape*. Petersham, MA: Harvard Forest, Harvard University.

Van Fleet, T. E., D. B. Kittredge, B. J. Butler, and P. Catanzaro. 2012. "Reimagining Family Forest Conservation: Estimating Landowner Awareness and Their Preparedness to Act with the Conservation Awareness Index." *Journal of Forestry* 110 (4): 207–215.

Wildlands and Woodlands. 2013. A Policy Agenda for Conserving New England's Forests. *http://wildlandsandwoodlands.org/sites/default/files/A%20Policy%20Agenda-FY13.pdf*

2

The University of Montana, Missoula: A Campus with an Ecosystem

Gary M. Tabor, Matthew McKinney, and Perry Brown

> Far away in Montana, hidden from view by clustering mountain peaks, lies an unmapped northwestern corner—the Crown of the Continent.
>
> —George Bird Grinnell (1901)

The University of Montana's main campus in Missoula, founded in 1893, lies at the southern entrance of the Rattlesnake Wilderness that extends north to the Crown of the Continent ecosystem (figure 2.1) and the vast extent of the Yellowstone wildlands to the Yukon bioregion in Canada (figure 2.2). Once known as a "Campus with a Mountain," the University of Montana is working toward the notion of becoming a "Campus with an Ecosystem." The 18-million-acre Crown of the Continent landscape, often simply referred to as the Crown, is a rare and special place, an ecological crossroads where plant and animal communities from the moist Pacific Northwest, windswept eastern prairies, arid southern Rockies, and cool boreal forests mingle. In this spine of glacier-carved mountains are the headwaters for three North American continental river basins that flow to the Pacific Ocean, the Gulf of Mexico, and Hudson Bay. No other landscape within the contiguous United States retains its full complement of native habitat and native predators— wolves, grizzly and black bears, cougar, coyote, fox, wolverine, bobcat, and lynx—as well as large populations of moose, elk, bighorn sheep, pronghorn, mountain goat, and deer. Only small populations of bison remain confined within a few special management areas.

At the core of the region are Waterton Lakes National Park in Canada and Glacier National Park in the United States. In the late 1890s, noted natural historian George Bird Grinnell and others lobbied the U.S. Congress to establish Glacier National Park. It was Grinnell who first referred to the region as the Crown of the Continent, and the name has

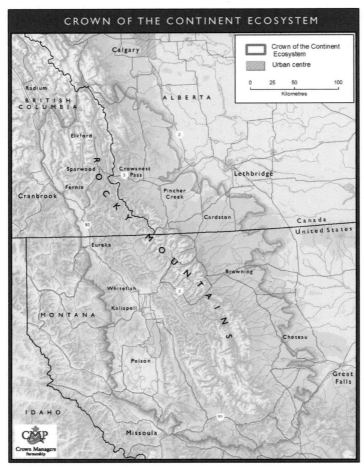

FIGURE 2.1. The Crown of the Continent.
Source: Map used with permission from Crown Managers Partnership.

remained since. An inseparable unit, the contiguous parks were designated by the U.S. Congress and Canadian Parliament in 1932 as the
world's first international peace park. The United Nations Education,
Scientific, and Cultural Organization (UNESCO) granted Biosphere Reserve status to Glacier National Park in 1976 and to Waterton Lakes in
1979. Both parks were named a World Heritage Site in 1995 in recognition
of the area's rich ecological and cultural values. Together these parks
cover about 1.3 million acres, or 13 percent, of all lands in the Crown.

In Montana, the Bob Marshall Wilderness expanded the Crown's inventory of protected lands under the Wilderness Act of 1964. The Scapegoat and Great Bear wildernesses were joined to "the Bob" in 1972 and 1978 respectively. Along with the Mission Mountains Wilderness and the Rattlesnake Wilderness, these stateside protected areas encompass about 1.6 million acres. Today, a remarkable 83 percent of land within the 10-million-acre Crown region is managed in the public trust.

FIGURE 2.2. National Parks and Wilderness Areas within the Crown of the Continent Ecosystem.
Source: Map used with permission from Karen Minot.

Across this vast region, indigenous cultures have thrived for centuries. Those who preceded the Blackfeet, Kainaiwa, Ktunaxa, Salish, and Kootenai peoples were among the first to hunt, fish, and gather food here, making their homes on the plains, in the forests, and along the rivers. Clovis-era spear points and arrowheads, along with other evidence, show that the first people explored the Crown more than 10,000 years ago, after the last great ice sheets retreated. This landscape was sacred to native peoples and remains so today, as First Nations continue to rely on "the Backbone of the World" for its wildlife, plants, rivers, lakes, and spirit (Bates 2010). These first inhabitants interacted with the landscape in many ways: using fire to replenish grasslands, funneling bison over cliffs (buffalo jumps) as a hunting method, wearing trails and roads into the earth, and establishing camps and villages on favorable sites. By the early 1800s, when the first white explorers and trappers arrived, much of the Crown region was already settled, with well-established tribal territories, hunting grounds, and travel routes.

Today, more than 21 federal, tribal, First Nations, state, and provincial agencies strive to cooperatively manage the Crown's wildlands, wildlife, timber, minerals, oil and gas, and other resources. Increasingly, the region's rural communities are diversifying, blending amenity- and knowledge-based economies with agriculture, logging, and energy development. All of these factors make the Crown a rare and special place, a vibrant home for people held here by a quality of life not found outside the region. It is a magical landscape worthy of long-term public–private stewardship for present and future generations.

However, the Crown of the Continent is considered one of the poster landscapes exhibiting the impacts of climate change. The visible retreat of the region's glaciers bears witness to a changing climate. By 2030, climatologists and glaciologists predict that most or all of the 25 glaciers remaining in Glacier National Park will disappear (Hall and Fagre 2003). As a result, the Crown's diminishing cryosphere will transform from a more permanent feature to a seasonal and less climate-tempering presence. The loss of glaciers represents the most obvious impact on the landscape; other changes, manifested in more subtle ways, will play out in no fewer than 21 watersheds shared by the United States and Canada.

The Crown of the Continent is well positioned to serve as a laboratory for observing and predicting climate change impacts. The region encompasses the intersection of four major climate zones and a broad array of microclimates. This unique topography presents a distinct opportunity for researchers in the Crown to play a leading role in global efforts to investigate climate change impacts across a range of climate types and at differing elevations. Significant efforts to understand these dynamics are already underway.

The natural boundaries of the Crown of the Continent provide useful delineations for discussion of river basins, wildlife habitat, and cultural influences. But an assessment of the economic forces currently at work and how they will influence the region in the future must rely on different parameters. Historically, much of the region's economic growth depended on the Crown's abundant natural resources. Communities formed around timber mills, rich farmland, mineral resources, and recreational destinations. Faced with the growing influence of global market forces, some of these commodities lost their competitive advantage, and the engines of economic development shifted and diversified.

Today, the region's economic opportunities relate largely to tourism, energy development, and a growing professional services sector. Nonlabor income sources such as investments, pensions, and public benefits now account for approximately 40 percent of personal income in the counties on the U.S. side of the Crown of the Continent. These and other trends have diversified the Crown's economy and led to demands for a more educated and skilled workforce. In response, local businesses have linked with tribal and two-year colleges to shape curricula and programs, helping both retrain workers and prepare the region's next generation to be competitive in tomorrow's economy.

Over the past several decades, growing communities and shifting land uses have reshaped the ring of human development that surrounds the protected areas at the Crown's core. Three notable trends have strengthened in recent years: (1) larger towns and cities have grown considerably in population over the past 30 years and are projected to experience continued growth; (2) smaller towns and more rural locations have seen little population growth and in many instances have declined in population over the past 30 years; and (3) an increasing number of land use efforts seek to accommodate concentrated growth in and around population centers while preserving important environmental, aesthetic, agricultural, and natural resource values.

Much of the new development has sprawled into surrounding farmland and the woods close to the borders of protected public lands. This growth has been fueled in part by new technology that allows people to conduct business in more remote locations and by a booming market in second homes. For example, Montana's Flathead County, which supports the largest economic center and greatest number of residents in the Crown, grew from 59,218 residents in 1990 to 89,624 in 2009, a 51 percent increase in two decades. The same is true north of the border: Calgary, the closest major city to the Crown, grew by 90.1 percent from 1980 to 2009, and nearby Lethbridge grew by 55 percent over the same period (Bates 2010).

THE ECOLOGY OF GOVERNANCE

> The challenge in . . . collaboration is that each participant has only a limited amount of attention to devote to the collaboration.
> —MICHAEL NIELSEN (2011, 32), *Reinventing Discovery*

In response to this mix of complicated issues, individuals and organizations throughout the Crown are rising to the occasion and creating new forms of democratic practice. In a formal sense, the Crown of the

Continent includes two countries, two provinces, and one state, with more than 20 government agencies exercising some type of jurisdiction over and management of the landscape. While each of these expert-driven institutions plays an important role in managing natural resources, most of the issues facing the Crown present themselves at a spatial scale that crosses legal and cultural boundaries. Although these formal boundaries delineate ownership and management authority, they also act as dividers between disparate cultures, attitudes, goals, and values. Such divisions stymie efforts to address shared challenges in an effective manner.

People who care about the Crown and its future are increasingly looking to bridge these barriers to address the challenges they collectively face at the spatial scale at which they are occurring. What is occurring, in fact, is the development of a nested system of political arrangements within which people with vision, passion, and capacity are creating new opportunities to define issues, frame options, and take action. This nested system is akin, at least in part, to Ostrom's "polycentric systems of governance" (Ostrom 2009). Starting at the smallest geographic scale, at least 20 community-based partnerships have been formed in the Crown, most of them initiated and convened by citizens (figure 2.3). These community-based partnerships create the basic building blocks within the emerging nested system of governance.

Yet with all the vibrancy that comes from these civic and governmental groups, few are sufficiently interconnected to address the problems presented by large-scale threats to the region such as climate change, habitat fragmentation, water management, and invasive species. It is only recently that many local land-based and watershed initiatives have come to grips with the enormity and complexity of these threats. Once recognizing the scale of impacts, these groups are challenged by the costs related to cooperation at larger scales and the diversity of values among stakeholders as they reach further afield. In this mix, universities embody the array of values and interests reflected in these large-scale landscape efforts and can provide the connective tissue and independent facilitation that bring stakeholders together. The enduring institutional presence of universities evident in the map below can also facilitate long-term community engagement in landscapes that require long-term strategies.

FIGURE 2.3. The main hall of the University of Montana, Missoula, at the base of Mount Sentinel.
Source: Photo by Jitze Couperus.

The Crown's ecology of governance—an interconnected web of individuals and organizational actors—illustrates a larger trend in natural resource policy: Citizens and nongovernmental organizations or associations are increasingly taking the lead to convene, coordinate, and implement actions to foster conservation and stewardship. This trend not only suggests a shift from an expert-driven model of politics to more democratic approaches, but also raises some important questions about new models of governance and the roles of citizens, professionals, and communities in these models. The guiding vision of many of these groups is one in which governance is more than government; it is a view that is much more inclusive, engaging both formal and informal actors and institutions. How this proposition develops for large-scale, mixed-ownership landscapes is of course an open question.

From a political perspective, this trend in natural resource policy creates a healthy tension between bottom-up and top-down approaches to governance. In a recent book entitled *Planning with Complexity*, Judith Innes and David Booher (2010) suggest that this tension can be explained—at least in part—by the difference between "instrumental rationality" and "collaborative rationality." Instrumental rationalists tend to approach natural resource and environmental issues as largely technical problems that can be effectively solved by sound science and the separation of politics from decision making (i.e., the expert-driven model of politics).

By contrast, collaborative rationality sees the world as inherently uncertain and assumes that all decisions are necessarily contingent. From this perspective, planning and policy are not about finding the best solution (indeed, it is unlikely there is one best solution), but rather discovering many better ways of proceeding besides following the status quo. Collaborative rational political processes are about engaging with diverse members of a community—including citizens, associations, and experts—to jointly learn and work out how to generate improvements in the face of interpersonal conflict, changing conditions, and divergent sources of information. Such processes—as illustrated by the ecology of governance in the Crown of the Continent—are not only about finding new ways to move forward, but also about helping communities adapt and be resilient in the face of new realities. One ongoing challenge for experts and institutional actors is to realign their activities and expectations in a way that is more conducive to the practices of collaborative rationality.

For a number of reasons, universities are not predisposed to support approaches oriented toward collaborative rationality, especially within the realm of natural resource policy and applied management. First, natural resource policy problems, with few exceptions, require interdisciplinary responses; however, the policy-relevant disciplines are organized (and separated) by departments and dominated by specialized silos that make collaborative research exceedingly difficult. The resulting scholarship typically fails to provide adequate diagnoses or prescriptions for problems as they exist in the world. Second, other academics—not policymakers or citizens—are the primary audience for many academics, who tend to define success as garnering a positive response to one's intellectual agenda rather than solving real-world problems. Good results are measured by gains in knowledge and under-

TABLE 2.1.

A Tale of two cultures

ATTRIBUTE	ACADEMIC COMMUNITY	POLICY COMMUNITY
Objective	Respect of academic peers	Approval of voters
Time horizons	Long	Short
Focus	Internal logic of problem	External logic of setting
Mode of thought	Inductive, generic	Deductive, particular
Mode of work	Solo	Collaborative
Most valued outcome	Original insight	Effective solution
Mode of expression	Abstruse, qualified	Simple, absolute
Preferred form of conclusion	Multiple possibilities; depends on objectives; uncertainties emphasized	One "best solution"; objectives unspecified; uncertainties submerged
Concern for feasibility	Small	Great
Stability of interest	Low	High

Adapted from the work of Szanton (1981).

standing and the use of one's ideas by others pursuing related scientific and policy inquiry.

Given the fact that academics, government officials, and citizens tend to have differing motives, the latter two groups often have limited confidence that universities can help to solve problems related to natural resources and the environment. The professor afflicted with ivory tower syndrome may be a shopworn stereotype, but it still holds sway among people outside academia. Moreover, elected and appointed officials tend to be concerned with politics over policy; partisanship and the effort to get reelected take precedence over the need to solve on-the-ground problems. Citizens and officials will therefore probably be slow to accept the efforts of universities to deepen civic engagement and participate in local decision making on natural resource issues. To overcome these impediments, universities will need to hire leadership and devise institutional mechanisms that reward and support student and faculty participation in policy and management problem solving.

Derived from the work of Peter Szanton (1981), table 2.1 summarizes the different attributes of the academic and policy communities, and suggests the need to build one or more two-way bridges to cross the divide. Acknowledging this dichotomy of cultures, the University of Montana has taken steps to serve as the institutional (and political) bridge between these two worlds.

THE UNIVERSITY OF MONTANA: HISTORICAL CONTEXT

We now have a campus with a mountain.
—UNIVERSITY OF MONTANA PRESIDENT OSCAR CRAIG, 1986

When the University of Montana was created by the Montana state legislature in 1893, four years after statehood, the population of Missoula was approaching 4,000 people. Built on land adjacent to Sentinel Mountain just south of the town, the university was early on referred to as the "Campus with a Mountain" (University of Montana Annual Report 1896) (figure 2.4). By 1889, the school had expanded its reach and established a solid research and educational presence in the nearby Crown of the Continent with the founding of its Flathead Lake Biologi-

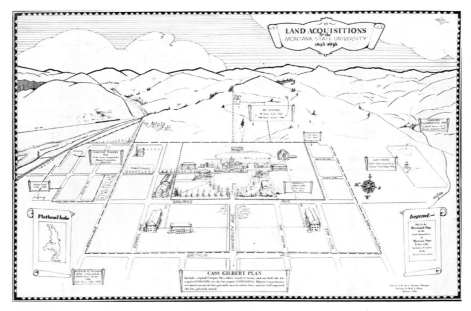

FIGURE 2.4. Map of the University of Montana, 1936
Source: Map by Speer (1936), with permission from University of Montana.

cal Station by Professor Morton J. Elrod. Along with his contemporary Grinnell, Elrod advocated for the creation of Glacier National Park and became the park's first naturalist. Today, the Flathead Lake Biological Station is one of the world's premier freshwater research centers, and the university has more than 40 faculty members in at least five colleges now actively engaged in researching all aspects of the Crown. From Native American studies to geosciences, the Crown is inextricably linked to the university's educational, research, and public service mission.

In 1999, the University of Montana and the University of Calgary established a joint Transboundary Policy, Planning, and Management Initiative to advance conservation across the entire Crown of the Continent. One of the first university-level, landscape-based, transnational research and education collaboratives in the world, the effort served to link the University of Montana's Environmental Studies Program, within the College of Arts and Sciences, with the University of Calgary's Faculty of Environmental Design. As a result, students and faculty have been able to engage broader governmental, tribal, industry, and NGO communities in a variety of solution-oriented processes, and the universities have developed a coordinated framework for U.S. and Canadian collaboration in landscape conservation and management.

THE RISE OF THE ROUNDTABLE OF THE CROWN OF THE CONTINENT

Building from this experience, the University of Montana further strengthened its formal involvement in the conservation of the region. In 2007, then-president George Dennison launched the Crown of the Continent Initiative, which seeks to deepen the university's links to the region through outreach, extension, and synthesis publications. The initiative's community-oriented publications and educational offerings have enhanced the school's presence and image in the context of Crown resource and conservation issues. At about the same time, the university's Center for Natural Resources and Environmental Policy, at the behest of the government interagency collaborative Crown Managers Partnership, launched the Roundtable of the Crown of the Continent to connect all the constituencies, jurisdictions, and interests that support a broad conservation perspective on the ecosystem. The roundtable represents a substantial investment of the university's financial and human resources in shaping the collective conservation agenda in the region.

In partnership with the Lincoln Institute of Land Policy, the University of Montana seeks to create an example of ecosystem-level innovation through strategic participation by institutes of higher education.

An ongoing forum for bringing together people who care about this special place, the roundtable grew out of an awareness that the future of the region is being shaped by more than a hundred government agencies, nongovernmental organizations, and community-based partnerships. Through workshops, forums, policy dialogues, and conferences, the roundtable (1) embraces the 18-million-acre region; (2) includes all perspectives and communities; (3) focuses on connecting people, facilitating communication, and catalyzing action; (4) supplements other activities; and (5) promotes sustainable communities and landscapes. The roundtable has intentionally embraced three broad values in its planning and activities: culture, conservation, and community/sustainable economic development.

The roundtable is not a particular group of people, a government commission, or a new organization. Instead, it provides connective tissue among the diverse individuals, groups, and communities that work and play in this remarkable region. The working assumption of this process is that people are connected to the landscape but not to each other. By connecting people, the roundtable can enhance conservation and sustainable natural resource management to foster economic development across the entire ecosystem. The University of Montana is serving as the independent broker and the facilitator of this process that connects a large-landscape agenda with large-scale human engagement.

Of course, the university is not the only institution of higher education in the Crown; almost a dozen universities, tribal colleges, and community colleges in both the U.S. and Canada have links to this region, and other university interests from around the globe have also participated in the roundtable. As part of its mission to connect people, the roundtable is working to create a network of colleges and universities within the ecosystem, seeking to mobilize and engage this broader community of faculty and students to participate in both regional and subregional initiatives supporting the region's culture, community, and conservation values. Through the roundtable, the University of Montana is providing leadership by connecting its fellow colleges and universities in order to marshal a sufficiently strong response equal to forces that threaten the region.

OTHER SIGNIFICANT UNIVERSITY OF MONTANA PERSPECTIVES

In addition to the university's Crown-specific activities, two of its academic units heavily involved in the Crown have developed strong integrative and practical approaches for much of their work. Both the College of Forestry and Conservation and the Environmental Studies Program within the College of Arts and Sciences engage in instruction and research that transcend disciplinary boundaries and focus on practical problem solving in both the policy and management arenas. These academic units, in short, provide a pool of faculty members and students ideally suited to work with the Crown's officials and citizens.

In addition, as host of the Rocky Mountain Cooperative Ecosystem Studies Unit (RM-CESU)—a federal university partnership that transcends the international boundary of the Crown by including the University of Calgary among its 12 university and multiple U.S. federal agency partners—the university plays a pivotal role, engaging in practical research, technical assistance, and educational projects with federal land managers. The RM-CESU has sponsored and conducted a significant number of projects within the Crown and has brought university faculty members and students into direct contact with land and natural resource managers to help solve management problems or to analyze policy issues for decision making.

THE NEED FOR LARGE-SCALE LANDSCAPE RESPONSE

With the visible impacts of climate change looming over the region and drawing on the resources of the university's Crown activities and capabilities (figure 2.5), the roundtable has become a vehicle for multistakeholder and multisectoral engagement in the work of scaling up adaptation response to climate change. To date, climate adaptation has proved easier to define than to implement, especially amid large landscapes and associated communities. The uncertainty factor in terms of precise climate impacts and ecological responses has stymied many intervention efforts. The risk of unintended consequences or even concern for making a bad situation worse has too often paralyzed implementation action. One of the more vexing challenges to climate adaptation is the issue of spatial scale.

FIGURE 2.5. Grinnell Glacier, 1940 and 2006.
Source: Photo used with permission from U.S. Geological Survey.

While it is true that climate impacts will have variable local manifestations, ecological processes such as hydrology, fire, migration, phenology, and species invasiveness operate at the large-landscape level. Thus, the scale of adaptive action must be commensurate with the scale of the threat, and adaptive management should be implemented at multiple spatial scales through a process of network governance that recognizes socioeconomic and political realities. Fortunately, the Crown is home to an array of collaborative initiatives already identifying and implementing climate adaptation strategies and formulating efforts that can be enhanced and leveraged through more carefully coordinated partnerships.

The Crown of the Continent ecosystem has all the human and natural resource elements to prototype large-scale adaptive management and network governance. The opportunity is at hand to connect the region's capacity to sustain communities and landscapes across all jurisdictions, across all communities, and across all sovereign borders. As the higher education anchor in the Crown of the Continent landscape, the University of Montana is squarely facing the problems laid at its doorstep, in full recognition that the land and the university are intertwined.

REFERENCES

Bates, S. 2010. *Remarkable Beyond Borders: People and Landscapes in the Crown of the Continent.* Tucson, AZ: Sonoran Institute. *http://largelandscapes.org/media/publications /Remarkable-Beyond-Borders.pdf*

Craig, O. J. 1896. *Annual Report of the President, University of Montana.* Missoula: University of Montana, Archives and Special Collections, Maureen and Mike Mansfield Library.

Grinnell, G. B. 1901. "The Crown of the Continent." *Century Magazine* (September): 660–672.

Hall, M. P., and D. B. Fagre. 2003. "Modeled Climate-Induced Glacier Change in Glacier National Park, 1850–2100." *Bioscience* 53 (2): 131–140.

Innes, J. E., and D. E. Booher. 2010. *Planning with Complexity: An Introduction to Collaborative Rationality for Public Policy.* London, U.K.: Routledge.

McKinney, M. 2011. *Realigning Democratic Practices in Natural Resource Policy: From Vision to Action.* Final Report to the Kettering Foundation (June 8). *www.tbpa.net/docs /49_McKinney_KF_Final_Report_6.8.11-small.pdf*

McKinney, M., L. Scarlett, and D. Kemmis. 2010. *Large Landscape Conservation: A Strategic Framework for Policy and Action.* Cambridge, MA: Lincoln Institute of Land Policy. *www.america2050.org/Large%20Landscape%20Conservation%20final .pdf*

Nielsen, M. 2011. *Reinventing Discovery: The New Era of Networked Science.* Princeton, NJ: Princeton University Press.

Ostrom, E. 2009. "Beyond Markets and States: Polycentric Governance of Complex Economic Systems." Nobel Prize lecture, December 8. *www.nobelprize.org/nobel _prizes/economic-sciences/laureates/2009/ostrom_lecture.pdf*

Speer, J. B. 1936. Map drawn by W. Olson. "Illustrated Map of Land Acquisitions of Montana State University, 1893–1936." Archives and Special Collections, Maureen and Mike Mansfield Library. *http://content.lib.umt.edu/omeka/items/show/876*

Szanton, P. 1981. *Not Well Advised: The City As Client: An Illuminating Analysis of Urban Governments and Their Consultants.* New York, NY: Russell Sage Foundation and Ford Foundation.

U.S. Census Bureau. 1976. *The Statistical History of the United States from Colonial Times to the Present.* New York, NY: Basic Books.

———. 2011. *2010 Census of Population and Housing, Demographic Profile.* Summary File: Technical Documentation.

3

Research Networks and Large-Landscape Conservation and Restoration: The Case of the Colorado River Delta

Karl Flessa

In southwestern North America, water transforms landscapes. In the Colorado delta region of the southwestern United States and northwestern Mexico, the diversion of Colorado River water in the early 1900s transformed a dry lake bed and delta plain into agricultural fields. Downstream from this diversion, wetlands and channels dried up—along with their cottonwood trees, willows, and mesquites—creating a bleak landscape of bare dirt and salt flats.

In 1977, another transformation took place: the U.S. sent brackish water down a concrete-lined ditch to a patch of bare dirt and salt flats along the lower delta's eastern margin in Sonora, Mexico. The water, from beneath farm fields in Arizona's Gila Valley, was too salty to send back into the Colorado River; doing so would violate the terms of the 1944 treaty that obligated the U.S. to deliver 1.5 million acre-feet (1,850 million cubic meters) of water to Mexico. In 1974, a new addition to the treaty limited the salinity of the water, but allowed the U.S. to dump it south of the border. It was too salty for crops and too salty to drink, but cattails, bulrush, and common reed thrived on it, giving rise to a new wetland. The open water and vegetation provided a habitat for migratory birds, resident marsh birds, carp, and desert pupfish, and other wildlife.

It was residents of the local *eijidos*, or community farms, who first noticed this unintentional wetland. In 1992, a University of Arizona environmental scientist named it Ciénega de Santa Clara (figure 3.1) (Glenn et al. 1992): *Ciénega* means either spring or wetland, and *Santa Clara* derives from the trace of a nearby former drainage channel, Estero Santa Clara (Sykes 1937). The Ciénega de Santa Clara is also an

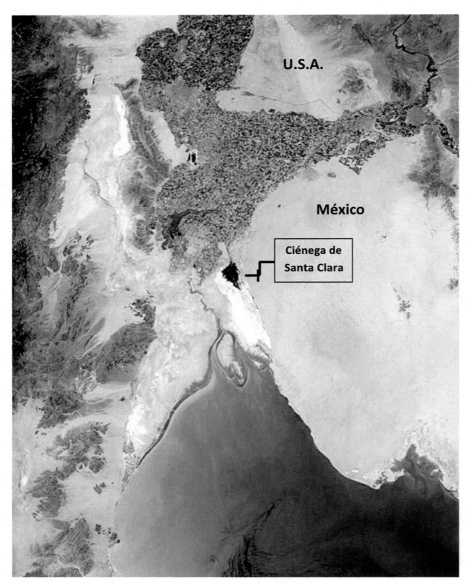

FIGURE 3.1. Colorado River Delta and upper Gulf of California.
Source: NASA.

accidental reincarnation of the green lagoons visited by Aldo Leopold during his travels in the area in 1922. "All this was far away and long ago," he wrote in 1949. "I am told the green lagoons now raise cantaloupes. If so, they should not lack flavor" (Leopold 1949, 157). The green lagoons are now constructs of human activity, not nature, but they are no less valuable for it.

Although it's completely dependent on the delivery of brackish groundwater from the U.S., the Ciénega de Santa Clara became, at 6,000 hectares (15,000 acres), the largest wetland on the Mexican side of the Colorado River delta. A rest stop along the Pacific Flyway for migratory birds, the Ciénega is habitat for species listed as endangered or threatened in both countries, including the Yuma clapper rail (a marsh bird) and desert pupfish. A small ecotourism enterprise catering to birdwatchers, with guides who were trained by U.S. and Mexican environmental organizations, operates in an adjacent farming community. Extensive research efforts, mostly based at the University of Arizona, have established the characteristics and ecological value of the Ciénega (e.g., Glenn et al. 1992, 1995, 1996, 2001, 2013; Hinojosa-Huerta et al. 2001, 2006; Zengel et al. 1995).

In 1993, a presidential decree established Mexico's Reserva de la Biosfera Alto Golfo de California y Delta del Río Colorado (Upper Gulf of California and Colorado River Delta Biosphere Reserve, or biosphere reserve hereafter), a federally protected natural area that encompasses the Colorado River's estuary, delta tidal flats, lowermost channel, and wetlands, including the Ciénega de Santa Clara. The northern part of the Ciénega de Santa Clara lies within a zone—commonly called the buffer zone—that permits the use of natural resources for sustainable purposes, including fishing, tourism, and ecotourism. The southern portion lies within the *zona núcleo* or core region of the biosphere reserve, where only activities such as research, monitoring, restoration, environmental education, and control of introduced species are allowed (SEMARNAT 2007).

In 1997, the wetlands of the Colorado River delta, including the Ciénega de Santa Clara, were added to the list of Wetlands of International Importance under the Ramsar Convention. In 2005, an international group of environmental NGOs (Zamora-Arroyoa et al. 2005) identified the Cienega de Santa Clara as a conservation priority area.

Meanwhile, back in the U.S., the Bureau of Reclamation—the federal agency responsible for the storage, management, and delivery of Colorado River water to U.S. states and to Mexico—completed construction of the Yuma Desalting Plant (YPD), near Yuma, Arizona. The facility would help the U.S. to meet its treaty requirement by ensuring that water delivered to Mexico was equal in quality to the water used on U.S. farms. After a brief trial run, however, the YDP was mothballed, and the U.S. met water quality standards by other, less expensive means, including the release of additional water from Lake Mead, an upstream reservoir.

By 2004, the Colorado River Basin was in a drought. Water levels in the two principal reservoirs, Lake Mead and Lake Powell, had fallen to worrisome levels. As the southwestern cities continued to grow, demand for water continued to increase. In addition, the Metropolitan Water District of Southern California (MWD) was facing limits on the importation of water from northern California because its pumps were affecting an endangered fish.

So, MWD—together with the Southern Nevada Water Authority (SNWA), provider of Colorado River water to Las Vegas, and the Central Arizona Project (CAP), provider of Colorado River water to Phoenix and Tuscon—proposed funding a trial run, at one-third capacity, of the Yuma Desalting Plant, principally at their expense. These agencies wanted to know if the YDP was an economical way to augment existing supplies.

The water for the plant would come from the canal that fed the Ciénega de Santa Clara. One-third of the salty ground water would be diverted to the YDP before it crossed the border into Mexico. All that water belongs to the U.S., which is entitled, by treaty, to use it as it sees fit. The desalted water would then be delivered to Mexico via the river's main channel, helping the U.S. to meet its treaty obligation. A similar volume could then be held in storage in an upstream reservoir for future use. The brine from the desalting process would be directed to the canal that supplies the Ciénega de Santa Clara.

Saltier water would likely harm the Ciénega de Santa Clara, as would lower volumes of water. It would shrink, along with its wet footprint, as saltier water killed or changed the vegetation. A smaller Ciénega would provide less habitat for migratory and resident birds, including endangered species.

NGOs were upset. Legal remedies were not apparent. Courts had earlier held that the U.S. Endangered Species Act did not apply to the consequences of U.S. activities beyond the borders of the U.S.

Seeing protracted conflict ahead, Sid Wilson, then director of the Central Arizona Project, sought a solution that did not involve expensive litigation, public feuds with environmental groups, or the enmity of the Mexican government. He convened an ad hoc working group that included individuals from the major water agencies, the Bureau of Reclamation, and key environmental NGOs. The resulting report (Yuma Desalting Plant/Ciénega de Santa Clara Workgroup 2005) provided the guidelines for what happened next. The group supported operation of the YDP on the condition that no harm would befall the Ciénega de Santa Clara.

Preparations to operate the YDP for a one-year period continued, but now with Mexican representation through the agencies responsible for administering the water treaty, the International Boundary and Water Commission, and its sister agency in Mexico, the Comisión Internacional de Límites y Aguas. Mexican water agencies and Mexican environmental NGOs were also invited to the negotiating table.

The groups avoided conflict in two ways:

1. An agreement to replace the water that would be directed to the YDP. One third of the so-called "arranged" water would come from the U.S., one-third from Mexico, and one-third from a binational collaboration of NGOs. Flow to the Ciénega would not be reduced and its quality would be unchanged.
2. The Ciénega de Santa Clara's hydrology, water quality, vegetation, and bird populations would be monitored before, during, and after the trial operation of the YDP. The water agencies would fund the monitoring effort.

The replacement water and the monitoring program required an addition to the treaty: Minute 316, signed in 2010, marks the first time that water allocated for environmental purposes was allowed to cross the border. Because it was a temporary arrangement, many emphasized that this transboundary flow for environmental purposes was not a precedent for such flows in the future. Of course, whenever people go to great lengths to say that something is not a precedent, it is clearly a precedent.

And finally, the happy ending—for now: The Yuma Desalting Plant ran successfully, the replacement water was delivered to the Ciénega, and the monitoring program did not detect any lasting harm to the Ciénega de Santa Clara. Plant engineers are happy, water agencies are satisfied, environmental NGOs are relieved, and Mexican interests have been respected. This is a good news story about western water and a good news story about transboundary water.

THE ROLE OF RESEARCH NETWORKS

A research network based at the University of Arizona organized the team of scientists that monitored the Ciénega de Santa Clara during the trial run of the YDP. The fact that a binational team could be assembled and deployed on very short notice is the result of a formal Research Coordination Network funded by the U.S. National Science Foundation in 2004, with the author as principal investigator. Research Coordination Networks (RCNs) are intended to stimulate and facilitate interdisciplinary research.

The goal of the Research Coordination Network – Colorado River Delta was to investigate the interaction of the delta's human and natural systems. In less than a hundred years, the water that supported its natural and human-modified ecosystems had passed from short-term control by weather and natural geomorphic processes into control by human activity. How did that happen, and what are the consequences of that shift for the future? This RCN sought to facilitate interdisciplinary, interinstitutional, and international research on those questions. The network hosted binational workshops and field trips that included scientists and other scholars from academic institutions, NGOs, and agencies. It also supported student travel to professional meetings, hosted a website, distributed a newsletter, and provided support for pilot projects and workshops that would enhance the chances for additional funding of research on the Colorado River Delta. As a result of these activities, participants came to know and trust each other better and developed collaborative projects.

When the CAP, acting on behalf of the three major southwestern water agencies, approached me to find out if I could administer a monitoring program for the Ciénega de Santa Clara during its trial operation, I was able to say yes, thanks to the collaborations and mutual trust that had been established by the formal RCN. Frankly, we were not just the best group to do the job; we were the only group that could do the job: a network of scientists who knew the area best and already knew how to work together. Hiring a U.S. consulting firm to do the monitoring was out of the question: Not only would its experts lack knowledge of the area, they could not have gotten the necessary permits from Mexican agencies.

We are proud to have developed trust among individuals from academic institutions, NGOs, and agencies on both sides of the border. And we are proud to have facilitated a new and lasting binational collaboration on environmental protection and restoration.

LESSONS LEARNED FROM THE COLORADO RIVER DELTA ABOUT LARGE LANDSCAPE CONSERVATION

Water transforms landscapes in arid parts of the world. The habitats that support the greatest biodiversity and produce the most ecosystem services are wet or damp ones. Allocating water can be just as important as protecting land. In southwestern North America, water is regulated by a complex and often inflexible legal and physical infrastructure. High-value landscapes in such regions can't depend on water that falls from the sky. Water needs to be delivered and actively managed.

The Colorado River Delta is a binational landscape. Challenges for large landscape conservation across international borders increase greatly when the economies of the affected countries differ greatly in size, when there is no common language, and when there are divergent legal systems and policies regarding water and environmental protection. These differences can also work in favor of conservation efforts. For example, research funding and student support can move across the border more easily than water. Mexican water law is more flexible with regard to allocations of water for nature than the Law of the River that prevails in Colorado River Basin states. Water in Mexico is regulated by national policy, whereas the states play a larger role in the U.S. If an approach doesn't work in one country, it might work in the other.

As in many delta settings (the Sacramento–San Joaquin rivers, the Yellow River, the Rhine–Meuse–Scheldt rivers, and others), most of the Colorado River Delta has already been transformed for human use. Few, if any, natural areas remain. Under these circumstances, large-landscape *restoration* is the challenge that we face.

LESSONS LEARNED ABOUT THE ROLE OF THE UNIVERSITY OF ARIZONA

The University of Arizona is a large public land-grant research university. Its mission statement makes no mention of the importance of large-landscape conservation.

In 2011, the University of Arizona budget exceeded $1.8 billion dollars, with $618 million (33%) coming from state-appropriated funds, including tuition. The remaining funds came from grants, contracts, donations, and proceeds from a relatively small endowment. Most of those grants and contracts resulted from the efforts of individual faculty and research scientists. Indeed, faculty—especially those in the sciences, engineering, and health-related fields—are encouraged to think of themselves as entrepreneurs who bring in, from external sources, the funds needed to support their research, their students, and their scholarly publications, and to convey their cutting-edge knowledge in the classroom. That way, everyone benefits.

To the extent that an individual faculty member—or a team of them—dedicates efforts toward large-landscape conservation, the university can be said to be dedicating such effort. In such a way, universities provide the business services and financial accountability needed for such efforts, some flexibility in how funds are spent, the students who work on such projects, and the office space and research facilities. While this is a substantial contribution, the principle is that the research should pay for itself. The institutional subsidy, if any, is modest.

That said, the role of students in academically based research in large-landscape conservation is vital. Students often end up doing the hard work in the field and lab for relatively little monetary reward. Their long-term contribution can be enormous when they go on to careers in relevant NGOs, agencies, or other academic institutions. The Colorado River Delta has served as a natural laboratory and training ground for dozens of people who are now conservation practitioners and leaders. Indeed, individual faculty advisors and mentors—and the University of Arizona—take great pride in the many graduates of its environmental programs who are now in Mexican universities, agencies, and NGOs. In many cases, their education was supported by funds from the Mexican government as well as grants earned by their advisors or wages earned as teaching assistants supported by the university. Certainly one important mission of a research university is increasing the scientific capacity of institutions that serve society in some way.

One of the ways in which universities serve society is through research that serves state, national, and international needs. Although efforts such as seeking a cure for cancer or increasing fuel efficiency are not controversial, not all research is so universally valued by the public. While large-landscape conservation seems benign, it is not without the potential for conflict. The sagebrush rebellion and its descendant movements asserted the primacy of local control over public lands and their exploitation. One person's protected area is another person's productive land that has been "locked away" from wise use.

The Colorado River is already overallocated—dedicating water for nature in the Colorado River Delta can mean that some existing water user will get less without adequate compensation. The aphorism attributed to Mark Twain is apt here: in the West, whiskey is for drinking; water is for fighting. For example, the University of Arizona's alumni magazine published an article about my work on the value of ecosystem services lost due to large-scale diversions of Colorado River water. The article prompted a letter to the editor in the next issue that stated, "Flessa should go jump in the Colorado River and stay there."

In the case of the Colorado River Delta, the University of Arizona provided neutral ground and funding flexibility. To employ an oft-used metaphor, the university functioned as a neutral Switzerland in such efforts. Precisely because large-landscape conservation is not in the mission statement of the University of Arizona, there is no conflict of interest. The university's success does not depend on the success of a particular effort at large-landscape conservation. Both agencies and NGOs can depend on university scientists to provide objective, or at least independent, analyses of facts. Unlike politicians and attorneys, university scientists are still held in high regard by the general public. When inclined to do so, academic scientists can work with all stakeholders precisely because they are not stakeholders themselves.

The university can also function as a kind of Swiss bank, and although this allusion to Switzerland is less appealing, the role can be just as important. While this characterization can imply financial deals that are hidden from view, such is decidedly not the case with the transparent and highly regulated practices of university business offices. In the case at hand, the University of Arizona could subcontract with NGOs and disburse funds to Mexican institutions, whereas such activities can be difficult or impossible for water agencies.

As valuable as research networks and academic institutions were in facilitating this effort, the initiative and financial support needed to make this a good news story came from farsighted individuals in NGOs and water agencies.

LESSONS LEARNED ON THE ROLE OF ACADEMIC SCIENTISTS

It is hard to imagine academic scientists effectively conserving large-landscapes by acting only within their institutions. One major lesson learned from the case of the Colorado River Delta is that partnerships with NGOs and agencies are vital. As universities and funding agencies seek to speed up the transition from basic research to beneficial application, there is likely no better pathway than collaborations with mission agencies and NGOs.

Scientists and engineers are less expensive than lawyers. Agencies and businesses don't like litigation: It can be expensive and can delay or even stop projects. With some exceptions, NGOs would also prefer to stay out of court. If scientists and engineers can be deployed to find answers, provide options, or devise solutions to avoid or lessen conflict, then the lawyers lose, but money and time are saved.

Not all academic scientists are comfortable dealing with matters of public policy and the attendant risks of conflict. Some consider working with environmental NGOs as a violation of some unstated principle of academic neutrality (though the large corporations that award contracts to university scientists are advocates for their own cause—profitability—and no more disinterested than NGOs).

Roger Pielke (2007) offers a fourfold classification of academic scientists in his book *The Honest Broker: Making Sense of Science in Policy and Politics.* The Pure Scientist likes the isolation of the ivory tower and wishes to be left alone; it is up to others to decide whether his or her work is useful in the public arena. The Science Arbiter responds to the needs of decision makers by providing expert judgment on scientific issues arising in policy debates while attempting to remain above the fray. In contrast, the Issue Advocate aligns himself or herself with a particular position, marshaling or generating scientific data in its support. Some Issue Advocates make their stands known, while others act in stealth mode. Finally, there is Pielke's ideal, the Honest Broker of Policy Alternatives. The Honest Broker works directly with decision makers and often with other such scientists. Honest Brokers both explore the consequences of policy alternatives and actively try to devise new ones or new compromises among existing choices. Pielke contrasts Issue Advocates and Honest Brokers by noting that Honest Brokers seek to expand policy alternatives while Issue Advocates seek to narrow them.

The four categories are, of course, caricatures, and they do not even lie along a single spectrum. To the extent that they exist, there is a place in the academic community for all of them. Pielke's categories are a useful reminder that many, if not most, policy issues involving scientists are controversial to some degree. Issues surrounding conservation and restoration are often fraught with conflict.

Note, however, that in Pielke's taxonomy, it is only the Issue Advocate who has—or is allowed to have—an opinion, or who is allowed to act on a considered judgment. In this way, Pielke comes close to subscribing to the fallacy that scientists lack human emotions, biases, or even points of view and that scientists should simply let the facts speak for themselves. But the facts never speak for themselves. Pielke's book is a compendium of cautionary lessons about the dangers of politicizing science, but there is a danger to not politicizing science as well. If scientists don't put their considered judgments or scientifically informed opinions to work, they risk failing to address significant problems. As society converts more and more land—and water—to direct human use, failure to advocate for an alternative (so-called neutrality) is the same thing as acquiescence.

Most conservation biologists—even those in academic institutions—are Issue Advocates. So be it. We subscribe to Ed Abbey's dictum (1990, 89): "It is not enough to understand the natural world. The point is to defend and preserve it."

ACKNOWLEDGMENTS

I thank the National Science Foundation, the University of Arizona Water Sustainability Program, Australia's Commonwealth Scientific and Industrial Research Organisation, and the Central Arizona Project for support. The opinions expressed here are my own, not theirs. I thank all the participants in the Research Coordination Network–Colorado River Delta and the Ciénega de Santa Clara Monitoring Team for their hard work and inspiration. Thanks to Jim Levitt and Larry Fisher for their comments; special thanks to Francisco Zamora and the Sonoran Institute for teaching me so much.

REFERENCES

Abbey, E. 1990. *A Voice Crying in the Wilderness (Vox Clamantis in Deserto): Notes from a Secret Journal.* New York: St. Martin's Press.

Glenn, E., R. Felger, A. Burquez, and D. Turner. 1992. "Ciénega de Santa Clara: Endangered Wetland in the Colorado River Delta, Sonora, Mexico." *Natural Resources Journal* 32:817–824.

Glenn, E., K. Flessa, and J. Pitt. 2013. "Restoration Potential of the Aquatic Ecosystems of the Colorado River Delta, Mexico: Introduction to Special Issue on 'Wetlands of the Colorado River Delta.'" *Ecological Engineering* 59:1–6.

Glenn, E., C. Lee, R. Felger, and S. Zengel. 1996. "Effects of Water Management on the Wetlands of the Colorado River Delta, Mexico." *Conservation Biology* 10:1175–1186.

Glenn, E., T. Thompson, R. Frye, J. Riley, and D. Baumgartner. 1995. "Effects of Salinity on Growth and Evapotranspiration of *Typha domingensis* Pers." *Aquatic Botany* 52:75–91.

Glenn, E., F. Zamora-Arroyo, P. Nagler, M. Briggs, W. Shaw, and K. Flessa. 2001. "Ecology and Conservation Biology of the Colorado River Delta, Mexico." *Journal of Arid Environments* 49:5–15.

Hinojosa-Huerta, O., S. DeStefano, and W. Shaw. 2001. "Distribution and Abundance of the Yuma Clapper Rail (*Rallus longirostris yumanensis*) in the Colorado River Delta, Mexico." *Journal of Arid Environments* 49:171–182.

Hinojosa-Huerta, O., J. Rivera-Díaz, H. Iturribarría-Rojas, and A. Calvo-Fonseca. 2006. "Population Trends of Yuma Clapper Rails in the Colorado River Delta, Mexico." *Studies in Avian Biology* 37:74–82.

Leopold, A. 1949. *A Sand County Almanac.* Oxford, U.K.: Oxford University Press.

Pielke, R. 2007. *The Honest Broker: Making Sense of Science in Policy and Politics.* Cambridge, U.K.: Cambridge University Press.

SEMARNAT (Secretaría de Medio Ambiente y Recursos Naturales). 2007. Programa de Conservación y Manejo Reserva de la Biosfera Alto Golfo de California y Delta del Río Colorado, México. Mexico City, Mexico: SEMARNAT. *www.conanp .gob.mx/que_hacemos/pdf/programas_manejo/Final_AltoGolfo.pdf*

Sykes, G. 1937. *The Colorado Delta.* American Geographical Society Special Publication No. 19. New York, NY: American Geographical Society.

Yuma Desalting Plant/Ciénega de Santa Clara Workgroup. 2005. *Balancing Water Needs on the Lower Colorado River: Recommendations of the Yuma Desalting Plant/ Ciénega de Santa Clara Workgroup.* Phoenix, AZ: Central Arizona Project. *www .cap-az.com/Portals/1/Skins/cap/files/newfinaldocument.pdf*

Zamora-Arroyo, F., J. Pitt, S. Cornelius, E. Glenn, O. Hinojosa-Huerta, M. Moreno, J. García, P. Nagler, M. de la Garza, and I. Parra. 2005. *Conservation Priorities in the Colorado River Delta: Mexico and the United States.* Tucson, AZ: Sonoran Institute.

Zengel, S., V. Mertetsky, E. Glenn, R. Felger, and D. Ortiz. 1995. "Ciénega de Santa Clara, a Remnant Wetland in the Rio Colorado Delta (Mexico): Vegetation Distribution and the Effects of Water Flow Reduction." *Ecological Engineering* 4:19–36.

PART
II

Biodiversity Conservation
at the Landscape Scale

ALTHOUGH landscape-scale conservation efforts in the 20th century necessarily address a continuum of objectives from sustainable economic development to water quality, biodiversity conservation remains at the heart of many such initiatives. These biodiversity-focused projects are accomplishing durable, measurable results across large expanses, not by attempting to fully "wall off" the wild world from the built environment, but instead by rebalancing the dynamic tension between human culture and native biomes. Given the accelerating pace of habitat fragmentation and species decline around the world, and the intensifying yet often unpredictable challenges of climate change on species and ecosystem resilience, the need for such innovative and comprehensive approaches to biodiversity protection has never been more urgent than it is today.

In their chapter on the achievements of the Archbold Biological Station, The Nature Conservancy, and their partners to protect rare native habitats on the Lake Wales Ridge in central Florida, Hilary Swain and Tricia Martin provide us with a deep look into a genuinely exemplary case. As they explain, the Florida scrub, ranked as the 15th most endangered ecosystem in the nation with one of the highest densities of endemic species in the world, came perilously close to extirpation. Over the last 20 years, an enduring alliance of scientists and conservation partners from 13 local, state, and federal agencies and nonprofits has provided more than $100 million in financial resources to protect more than 34,000 acres of prime habitat and buffer, rescuing these ecological treasures from oblivion, as well as forming the Lake Wales Ridge Ecosystem Working Group to provide the social capital for collaborative land management.

The next chapter, written by Fiona Schmiegelow and her co-authors from institutions across Canada, considers a college- and university-grounded initiative that has had an impact at a continental scale, from British Columbia and the Yukon on the Pacific Rim to Newfoundland in the North Atlantic. The team has established the Canadian BEACONs

(Boreal Ecosystem Analysis for Conservation Networks) Project as a "made in Canada" approach to conservation planning that has played a key role in the protection and sustainable use of many millions of hectares of land controlled by governments, private interests, nongovernmental organizations, and First Nations in the far north.

Innovative conservation at the landscape scale, of course, involves not only the faculty and staff of engaged academic and research institutions. Students with broad imaginations and fresh energy are also an indispensable part of the mix. Joe Figel, a Ph.D. candidate working in the lab led by Reed Noss at the University of Central Florida, describes in his chapter how palm oil plantations now springing up in Central and South America can be designed and productively cultivated to provide cover and help maintain a transit corridor for endangered jaguars and other wide-ranging species. Figel's work is testimony to the fact that large landscape conservation can and ought to span geographic scales, from the very local to the intercontinental. Indeed, this work, together with a growing body of work on wildlife corridors from institutions across the hemisphere, should contribute in important ways to our understanding of how to sustain a wildcat thoroughfare that stretches from the pine-oak woodlands of the southwestern United States through Mexico, Central America, the Amazon, and into the thorn forests of northern Argentina.

4

Saving the Florida Scrub Ecosystem: Translating Science into Conservation Action

Hilary M. Swain and Patricia A. Martin

This is the story of the endeavor to save the Florida scrub, ranked as the 15th most endangered ecosystem in the nation (Noss and Peters 1995). Our focus is on the scrub habitat of the Lake Wales Ridge in central Florida and its associated threatened and endangered plants and animals. This scrub ecosystem came perilously close to extirpation, but has been rescued from oblivion largely by the catalytic partnership forged between an internationally recognized nonprofit research institution, Archbold Biological Station, and the global conservation organization The Nature Conservancy (TNC). By the 1980s, high demand for dry, sandy soils— first for citrus and then for housing—had so diminished the Florida scrub that the remaining habitat was declared globally imperiled (Florida Natural Areas Inventory 1990). Scientists and conservationists rallied to save the scrub. A massive investment by public agencies and nonprofit organizations has tripled the area of protected scrub and reduced the risk of extinction for many species. A broad and enduring alliance of science and conservation partners has coalesced over the last 20 years, providing the social capital to sustain this conservation juggernaut. How did all these efforts come together in the remote heart of rural central Florida? Who were the key people? When were the turning points? Which opportunities were seized or missed? And what are the threats and challenges that must be overcome to maintain success into the future?

THE LAKE WALES RIDGE: A UNIQUE LOCATION AND BIOLOGICAL HISTORY

The ancient sand of the Florida scrub was formed millions of years ago as the southern Appalachian mountains eroded. Rivers carried the quartz sand to the sea, and coastal currents transported the sand south, creating dune islands. Sea levels have risen and fallen many times, with changing

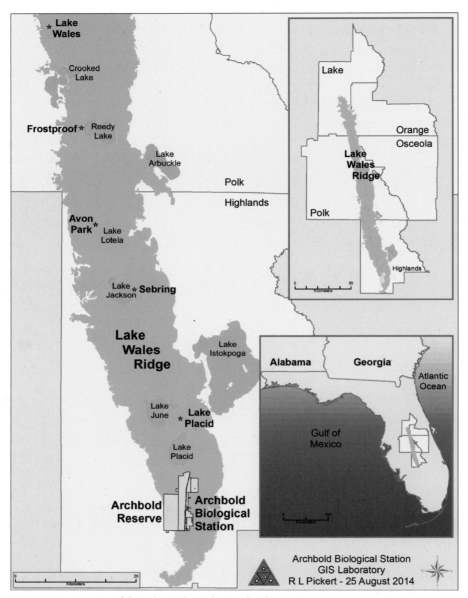

FIGURE 4.1. Location of the Lake Wales Ridge in Florida.
Source: Map used with permission from Archbold Biological Station.

climate and the advance and retreat of global ice sheets. When sea level was low, the shallow margins of the Gulf of Mexico emerged as part of Florida; when sea level was high, much of Florida was isolated or underwater. Whenever the oceans receded, new coastal sand dunes formed, resulting in a series of parallel ridges, running north to south, where a unique ecosystem, the Florida scrub, developed and persists. The Lake Wales Ridge, the largest and oldest of these scrub ridges in central Florida, has stood above sea level for more than a million years (White 1970, McCarten and Moy 1995). Today it lies about 80 miles from both the Atlantic Ocean to the east and the Gulf of Mexico to the west (figure 4.1), occupying an area of 116 miles north to south by 5 to 10 miles east to west (Weekley et al. 2008). Rising 100 to 300 feet above sea level, it is the sandy backbone of central Florida. With its unique ecosystem and distinct geography, the Ridge is a cohesive, identifiable landscape for conservation action.

Millions of years ago, the higher, drier lands of Florida were connected biologically to the terrain of the U.S. West and desert Southwest that extends as far as California and Mexico; as a result, many plants and animals in these disjunct arid ecosystems are near relatives—the Florida scrub-jay (*Aphelocoma coerulescens*) and other scrub-jays found in the west (*Aphelocoma californica* for example), as well as Florida ziziphus (*Ziziphus celata*) and Parry's jujube (*Ziziphus parryi*). Like oceanic islands, the ancient scrub ridges were intermittently isolated by the sea or surrounded by wetlands inhospitable to scrub plants and animals, favoring the rapid evolution of distinct races and species. With strong selection pressures for adaptations to hot wet summers, cool dry winters, droughty nutrient-poor sandy soils, and frequent wildfires, a unique collection of plants and animals evolved in the Florida scrub (Myers 1990, Menges 1998). Given this biogeographical history, it is no surprise that the Florida scrub of the central ridges is rich in endemics, many found nowhere else in the world (Muller et al. 1989). It is a biodiversity hotspot for rare endemic species that would rank comparably with other familiar global hotspots such as the Caribbean Islands (Turner et al. 2006a).

BUILDING THE KNOWLEDGE BASE FOR SCIENCE AND CONSERVATION

The unique flora and fauna of the Florida scrub drew ardent interest from early naturalists and explorers. In the first half of the 20th century, the botanist John Kunkel Small (Austin et al. 1987) and the entomologist Theodore Hubbell (1932) argued for the importance of the scrub habitat. Over the same timespan, chance brought three wealthy philanthropists with an interest in science and conservation to the Ridge. John

A. Roebling II, Richard Archbold, and Edward Bok established the tradition of science and land conservation that would eventually lead to the first efforts to protect the Ridge.

In 1941, wealthy industrialist John A. Roebling gifted his 1,058-acre Red Hill Estate at the southern end of the Ridge to aviator, explorer, and patron of science Richard Archbold (1907–1976), who founded the Archbold Biological Station on the property and lived on site for the next 37 years. The station hosted a veritable who's who of mid-century ecologists; thousands of plants, insects, birds, and mammals were studied, collected, and preserved, building the knowledge of the Florida scrub's biodiversity. James Layne became Archbold's research director in 1967, setting a vision for long-term studies and environmental monitoring. Thomas Eisner, visiting professor from Cornell University, pioneered the field of chemical ecology at Archbold and served as the ecosystem's prominent spokesman for science and conservation on the national stage. He later wrote, "The Archbold Station was to become my primary natural laboratory, and is to this day my favorite outdoor haunt. It is where I made most of my discoveries and where I feel most at home as a naturalist. I fell in love with the Florida scrub on my very first trip in 1958, and have remained in love with that unique habitat ever since, acutely aware of its threatened status" (Eisner 2003, 80). Richard Archbold died in 1976, leaving the land, buildings, and his personal fortune to the nonprofit Archbold Expeditions to continue the station's research, conservation, and education programs.

The station's research programs continue to this day. The study of the Florida scrub-jay initiated at Archbold in 1969 by Glen Woolfenden and now led by Reed Bowman, is the longest-running continuous bird population study in North America. To date, scrub-jay research at Archbold has produced nearly 200 scientific publications, including Woolfenden and John Fitzpatrick's classic book on the subject (Woolfenden and Fitzpatrick 1984). Archbold ornithologists spearheaded conservation planning to save this threatened species, and their work has served as a model for bird conservation projects worldwide. A succession of plant ecologists working at Archbold, from Leonard Brass in the 1940s to Eric Menges now, has produced detailed descriptions of the scrub plant community and its dependence on fire (Abrahamson 1984a, Myers 1990, Menges 1998). Working at Archbold under contract from U.S. Fish and Wildlife Service, Ann Johnson (1981) produced the first systematic inventory of endemic scrub plants at 38 sites on the Ridge. Eric Menges has published widely on the population biology of rare scrub plants, especially in relation to fire, creating detailed, long-term datasets that inform science and guide management and recovery (Menges and Kohfeldt 1995). His research has vital implications for plant conservation studies in fire-driven ecosystems around the world. Mark Deyrup, once described as the "Hubble telescope of the insect world," (Eisner 2001) has personally added more than 150,000 specimens of arthropods to the Archbold natural history collection and published descriptions of 12 new arthropod species from the Ridge in the last 30 years, reminding us that no biodiversity inventory is ever complete. He is the epitome of the naturalist with an engaging style that captivates the public, giving them an appreciation for science and conservation (Deyrup and Eisner 1993).

Described recently by Carlton Ward as the "Smithsonian of the Scrub" (Ward 2011), Archbold, with its geographic focus on the Ridge, has forged and promoted a strong interdisciplinary approach to the scrub ecosystem. The Archbold Board of Trustees, committed to the seamless coupling of rigorous inquiry and effective conservation, has appointed two recent directors, John Fitzpatrick (1987–1995) and Hilary Swain (1995–present), with a passion for both pursuits. Archbold supports a staff of 50, hosts thousands of visiting scientists and students annually, and has provided training for more than 460 research interns since 1968. The generosity and vision established by founder Richard Archbold (Morse 2000), nurtured by his sister Frances Archbold Hufty (who served as chairman of the board from 1976 to 2010), and sustained by the family members who continue to serve on the board, has enabled Archbold to become the scientific powerhouse behind conservation on the Ridge.

Other academics in the state have also made important contributions to scrub conservation. Richard Wunderlin at the University of South Florida (USF) has prepared status reports of endemic scrub plants and compiled numerous herbarium records for scrub species. Henry Mushinsky and Earl McCoy, also at USF, contributed to system-wide understanding of herptile communities (Mushinsky and McCoy 1991). Jack Stout at the University of Central Florida and researchers at Kennedy Space Center—notably Ross Hinkle, Paul Schmalzer, and Dave Breininger—have published many papers making important contributions to our understanding of northern and coastal Florida scrubs.

Florida Natural Areas Inventory (FNAI), the state heritage program established by TNC in 1981, built critical databases for the Florida scrub. In 1983, TNC and FNAI contracted with Gary Schultz at the University of Florida to survey 55 scrub sites (Cooper and Schultz 1984). FNAI continues to systematically track the status of scrub species and protected areas (Schultz et al. 1999). Kris Delaney, a botanist from Avon Park, found and described several new species of scrub plants on the Ridge, including the Avon Park harebells (*Crotalaria avonensis*) in 1989 and the Highlands County goldenaster (*Chrysopsis highlandsensis*) in 2002. And independent consultant Steve Christman recorded many astute observations and site records.

A second research facility was founded on the Ridge in 1986 when Bok Tower Gardens joined the Center for Plant Conservation, an organization of botanical institutions committed to conserving plant species. Curator of Endangered Plants Susan Wallace at Bok Tower Gardens established their endangered plant species program using propagation techniques, reintroductions of plants into the wild, and a collection of both seeds and cuttings (Wallace and McMahon 1988).

However, despite this rich history of study and widespread academic recognition of its conservation value, the Florida scrub was almost lost.

SCRUB ON THE RIDGE SUCCUMBS TO A LITANY OF ASSAULTS

Too dry for most crops and too poor for cattle ranching, the Ridge's scrub habitat remained more or less intact until the early 20th century, when successive losses to logging, citrus, mining, and real estate all but wiped it off the face of Florida.

Timber

During 1920 and 1921, the Consolidated Land Company hired A. E. Little to conduct a timber inventory of its lands throughout Highlands County (Little 1920–1921). He described most trees on scrub soils as "worthless" but documented harvestable pines on Ridge slopes. Logging camps and company towns arrived, and by the 1950s, nearly all the virgin timber on the Ridge had been logged. The remnants of Sherman Mill, one of the original eight logging camps on the Ridge, are preserved on Archbold land.

Oranges

After a series of devastating freezes destroyed orange crops planted north of the Ridge, citrus growers began arriving in the 1920s and 1930s, planted small groves, and founded towns with reassuring names like

Frostproof. Later, these citrus barons, described eloquently in John McPhee's (1966) book *Oranges*, established large groves on the more fertile yellow sands that were often home to sandhill rather than scrub habitat. Initially, the northern half of the Ridge was converted to citrus, with the result that very little scrub or sandhill habitat remains in that area. As late as the mid-1980s, citrus growers were planting large acreages on the white sands and scrub-dominated soils of the southern Ridge.

Development

Some scrub was lost when the resort communities of the 1910s and 1920s—such as Lake Wales, Avon Park, Sebring, and Lake Placid—were built in conjunction with the railroad line. Many of these developments went bankrupt during the Great Depression, and little further population growth ensued until the 1970s, when real estate on the Ridge fell into further cycles of boom and bust development. From 1970 to 2010, Polk County's population trebled to more than 600,000 and that of Highlands County increased fivefold to 100,000 (figure 4.2). High, dry

FIGURE 4.2. Population growth in Polk and Highlands counties (along the Lake Wales Ridge) during the last century.
Source: Bureau of Economic and Business Research (BEBR), *University of Florida. Graph used with permission from Archbold Biological Station.*

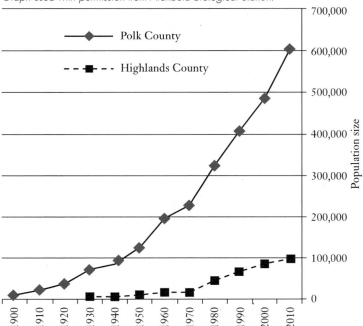

scrubland that had not been converted to citrus became a prime target for development.

Counties permitted huge platted subdivisions up and down the length of the Ridge. As a result, the remaining large areas of scrub were sold worldwide as quarter- and half-acre lots to unsuspecting buyers, often those from overseas or with military backgrounds. The legacy of these ill-conceived planning decisions and disingenuous marketing ploys still haunts modern Ridge conservation. The real estate cycle that reached its zenith from 2004 to 2007 threatened much of the remaining scrub, but the boom collapsed precipitously during the Great Recession in 2008, granting the land a temporary reprieve from further losses.

Sand Mining

In the wake of the rapid development of the 1970s and 1980s, the pockets of coarse quartz sands along the Ridge became attractive to mining companies. Mining, however, was an activity that aroused public concern; in 1988, a public outcry prevented the issuance of a mining permit for approximately 630 acres of a 2,800-acre scrub site northeast of Frostproof and adjacent to TNC's Tiger Creek Preserve. TNC's local attorney explained the potential for environmental impacts at the site as well as the fact that significant sand reserves existed elsewhere, and convinced all five Polk County commissioners to deny the mining request. The state subsequently purchased the land for conservation.

THE RIDGE BECOMES AN EPICENTER FOR THREATENED AND ENDANGERED SPECIES

Researchers have carefully documented the extent of habitat loss and fragmentation on the Ridge, and the number has risen inexorably over the past few decades, from 64 percent lost (Peroni and Abrahamson 1985) to 70 percent (Christman 1988a) to 83 percent (Weekley et al. 2008) (figure 4.3).

Given progressive habitat loss, it was inevitable that scrub plants and animals, notable for endemism and rarity, would be added to state and federal protected species lists (Christman and Judd 1990). The U.S. Fish and Wildlife Service (U.S. FWS) has classified 29 species on the

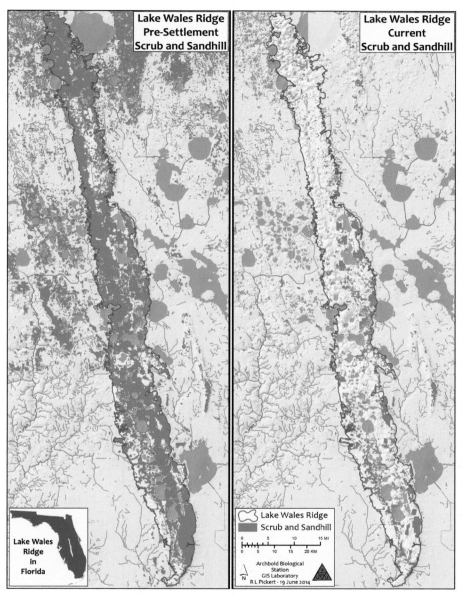

FIGURE 4.3. Extent of loss (83%) of scrub and sandhill habitat on the Lake Wales Ridge from (a) presettlement circa 1900 to (b) 2006.
Source: Weekley et al 2008. Map used with permission from Archbold Biological Station.

Ridge as endangered or threatened (U.S. FWS 1999). Highlands and Polk counties, which support most remaining scrub habitat, rank among the top 11 counties in the U.S. critical to the protection of endangered species (Dobson et al. 1997, Chaplin et al. 2000). Highlands County is the highest-ranked county in the southeastern U.S. for its number of rare endemic plants (Estill and Cruzan 2001).

A database of imperiled Ridge species assembled by Turner et al. (2006a) records 56 species that either have NatureServe ranks of G3 (globally vulnerable) or higher, or are listed by the U.S. FWS as threatened or endangered. Of these 56 species, a subset of 36 plants and animals are endemic or near endemic to the Ridge (i.e., ≥ 80% of all known occurrences are on the Ridge or are restricted to scrub or sandhill habitats in Florida). Other Ridge species may merit listing; for example, Deyrup and Carrel (2011) surveyed the Ridge for 93 scrub arthropod species that are either endemics or specialists dependent on gopher tortoise (*Gopherus polyphemus*) burrows. Of the 93 species, they note that 25 species of arthropods are not of conservation concern, as they occur on 10 or more Ridge sites. However, 66 species of arthropods are known on fewer than 10 sites, or their status is difficult to ascertain because they are hard to catch.

SURVIVAL OF THE SCRUB HANGS IN THE BALANCE

In 1988, Steve Christman (1988b) wrote an impassioned plea to the science and conservation community that "the ancient and unique scrub community of Florida's Central Ridges will soon disappear forever." At the time, only seven Ridge sites were protected; these totaled approximately 30,000 acres but harbored relatively little scrub or sandhill. Archbold had grown from 1,058 acres in 1941 to 3,974 acres in 1988, and was the only protected locality for two plants, Lake Placid scrub balm (*Dicerandra frutescens*) and wedge-leaved button snakeroot (*Eryngium cuneifolium*). Highlands Hammock State Park, gifted earlier to the state by the same Roebling family that donated the land for Archbold, totaled nearly 4,000 acres by 1988 but protected little scrub habitat. Lake Louisa State Park at the north end of the Ridge was established in 1973 after acquisition of nearly 1,800 acres under the state's Environmentally Endangered Lands program, but it is a fairly disturbed site, with virtually no remaining scrub.

TNC had established a toehold on the Ridge in 1971 with its purchase of Tiger Creek Preserve, the story of which has its roots in a much older preservation effort. In the 1920s, author, publisher, and philanthropist Edward Bok established the 58-acre Mountain Lake Sanctuary, which encompassed a small patch of sandhill as well as gardens and a carillon tower. Bok also fell in love with an area on the eastern slope of the Ridge, although he never purchased the land himself. Decades later, Ken Morrison, director of the sanctuary (now called Bok Tower Gardens), and Bok's son, Cary, who was on TNC's Board of Governors, revived the dream. Morrison and philanthropist George Cooley mounted a grassroots fundraising campaign to purchase the eastern slope property. In 1971, TNC purchased 580 acres, to be called Tiger Creek Preserve; by 1988, it totaled 4,700 acres (now 4,862 acres) of mostly sandhill and forested wetlands. In 1989, TNC also began acquisition of the 829-acre Saddle Blanket Scrub Preserve, an exceptional example of Ridge scrub.

Between 1984 and 1986, the state of Florida, with funding from the Conservation and Recreation Lands (CARL) program, purchased 13,746 acres—the largest public area on the Ridge—that harbored some of the best remaining scrub in central Florida. The area became the Lake Arbuckle State Forest and State Park (later combined and renamed the Lake Wales Ridge State Forest).

Just to the east, off the Ridge, a much larger site of high conservation value was also in public ownership, but not with conservation as its primary mission. While WWII war clouds were gathering, the U.S. government purchased extensive land to provide for air-to-ground bombing training. The modern Avon Park Air Force Range (APAFR) is now 106,110-acres in size, encompassing a small scrub ridge called the Bombing Range Ridge and one of the highest numbers of threatened and endangered species of any Department of Defense (DOD) installation in the country, including several scrub species, though none of the rarest Ridge endemics.

Despite the seven protected sites on the Ridge and the APAFR, it was abundantly clear that the scrub and its associated species were "all going extinct" (Christman 1988b). The regulatory provisions of the Endangered Species Act had made scant headway in meeting recovery plan goals. The state listed only three sites as acquisition priorities: Saddle Blanket, Catfish Creek, and an extension of Highlands Hammock

(Florida Department of Natural Resources 1990). Nearly every site displayed "For Sale" signs; time for action was overdue.

SCIENTISTS RALLY TO SAVE THE SCRUB

In 1985, the Florida Game and Freshwater Fish Commission (FGFWFC)—now the Florida Fish and Wildlife Conservation Commission (FFWCC)—engaged scientist and conservationist Steve Christman to conduct a three-year statewide assessment of scrub plants and animals. In conjunction with Dennis Hardin at FNAI, he used aerial photography to identify more than 250 Ridge scrub and sandhill parcels for survey. His report (Christman 1988a) documented the status of 35 plants and two lizards, combining earlier data with his own survey results. The report crystallized the degree of endangerment for scrub species and provided a rallying call for conservation on the Ridge.

In response to this report and others, a workshop was convened at Archbold on November 29 and 30, 1989, with participants from Archbold, TNC, and federal, state, and local agencies as well as other scientists and conservationists to review potential plans for saving the Ridge ecosystem (Fitzpatrick 2012). Based on data, expert knowledge, and rudimentary mapping, the resultant white paper entitled *Biological Priorities for a Network of Scrub Preserves on the Lake Wales Ridge* (Archbold Biological Station 1989) established the goal of "provid[ing] for the long-term persistence and continued biological health of all species and natural communities native to the upland habitats on the Ridge, and to preserve their original geographic extent." The report included maps of sites proposed for protection—24 in Highlands County and 25 in Polk County—that had not yet been included in any other land acquisition proposal. Decades of scientific knowledge were distilled into a single document, and the design of a network of conservation sites was proposed. At last, a large, ambitious, and cohesive plan for preserving Ridge habitat had been formulated and was finding an audience.

State Land Acquisition: The Lake Wales Ridge Project

The 1989 Biological Priorities Report was timely. John Fitzpatrick, Archbold director and board member of the Florida chapter of TNC, argued passionately for the supreme importance of protecting the remaining scrub of the Ridge. Emboldened by strong public support for conservation, John Flicker, then-director of the Florida chapter of TNC, had conceived of a far-reaching strategy for state land acquisition. TNC promoted the cause; recruited allies in other conservation organizations and in state, county, and municipal governments; and formed alliances with supportive legislators (Willson 2012). In 1989, Governor Bob Martinez appointed a commission to examine threats to the future of Florida's environment. The commission recommended that the state sell long-term bonds to fund needed land acquisition rather than relying on the established mechanism of year-to-year collection of documentary stamp taxes (Farr and Brock 2006). (The attraction of the "doc stamp tax," generally levied on documents that transfer an interest in real property, was that it targeted state newcomers and real estate developers as an appropriate source of funds for conservation.) The Florida legislature responded in 1990 with passage of the landmark Preservation 2000 Act, authorizing the sale of $3 billion in bonds from 1991 to 2000. This was a voluntary seller program with only willing landowners participating. Preservation 2000 (P2000) was a phenomenal success; Florida preserved almost two million acres for conservation and resource-based recreation through the programs it funded (Farr and Brock 2006).

As soon as the P2000 legislation passed, TNC, FNAI, and Archbold jointly submitted the *Lake Wales/Highlands Ridge Ecosystem CARL Project Proposal* to the state for consideration (TNC 1991). Drawing from the 1989 workshop, the authors targeted 21 scrub sites in Highlands and Polk counties to complement existing conservation lands. The proposal incorporated enough sites to protect a complete portfolio of scrub endemics and contain examples of each distinctive mix of scrub microhabitats. The spatial configuration allowed for sufficient sites along the linear north–south axis of the Ridge to protect the full geographic range of species. Multiple tracts connected by smaller habitat islands would serve as stepping stones for better dispersal of species. Other conservation attributes, like the protection of aquifer recharge, were also woven into the plan. The 21 sites encompassed everything from large single ownerships of scrub that had miraculously escaped clearance to the eight so-called megaparcel sites: large areas of scrub that had been subdivided and sold as quarter- and half-acre lots—many to foreign owners—but never developed and still retaining valuable scrub. Involving more than 20,000 lots, the megaparcel sites targeted for state acquisition were a challenging legacy of earlier flawed planning. No one in real estate would envisage, never mind choose to assemble, such a complex acquisition strategy, except that these were the last, best, and often the only remaining areas of scrub.

After P2000 was launched, TNC convened a statewide planning charrette in 1991 to flesh out details for an acquisition strategy (Wilson 2012). Steve Gatewood led a group of approximately 50 well-known scientists and conservationists from nonprofit organizations and state agencies to determine Florida's areas of greatest need in the field of biodiversity preservation. The Lake Wales Ridge Project ranked among the top priorities at this planning charrette and, over the next two decades, would always rank at or near the top of the state's priority list for land acquisition.

The state contracted with TNC to serve as the acquisition partner and agent for most of the proposed Lake Wales Ridge Project sites. Early purchases included large single ownerships—an 800-acre extension to Highlands Hammock in 1990, the Placid Lakes Scrub (3,188 acres) in 1993, more than 4,000 acres for Allen David Broussard Catfish Creek Preserve State Park (1991 and 1994), the 9,995-acre Walk in the Water Tract (1995 and 1996) that was added to the Lake Wales Ridge State Forest (site of the proposed former sand mine that was refused planning permission), Lake June Scrub (897 acres in 1996), Gould Road (156 acres in 1996), and the major ownership in Silver Lake (2,020 acres). In 1998, TNC decided to retain ownership of the Saddle Blanket site. Bob Burns, Keith Fountain, Richard Hilsenbeck, and Mike Izzarone with TNC's protection department successfully closed many of these deals on behalf of the state. They also started purchasing the megaparcel lots—a grueling process, as it can be as difficult to purchase a single quarter-acre lot as a 4,000-acre parcel.

In 1999, following a 72 percent vote in favor of Amendment 5, the Florida constitutional revision provision to continue funding conservation land acquisition, the legislature passed a successor program to P2000, the Florida Forever Act. It authorized bonding $300 million annually for up to 10 years, starting in 2000, and thus land acquisition on the Ridge continued. From 2000 to 2006, Hilary Swain, Archbold's executive director, served as the gubernatorial appointment on the nine-member Acquisition and Restoration Council, with responsibility to recommend acquisitions under Florida Forever as well as oversight of land management on all state-owned lands. Her participation gave the science community unrivaled access to and insight about the state process of identifying and selecting lands for preservation. Under Florida Forever, TNC made extraordinary progress in purchasing lots on behalf of the state in the megaparcels, managing to close on 5,800 acres, or nearly 14,000 lots (out of a total of approximately 24,500 lots). Several changes were made over the years to the Lake Wales Ridge Project; some megaparcel sites were never started, a few less viable sites were dropped because of encroaching development, and three new sites and many boundary amendments were added. Overall, conservation progress under P2000 and Florida Forever was transformational; 15 of the original 21 sites proposed have been acquired or partially acquired, and 34,926 acres on the Ridge have been purchased (figure 4.4).

In the same timeframe, Archbold itself raised private funding, expanding to nearly 9,000 acres, and now lies nestled within a contiguous network of state- and federally-protected conservation lands totaling 53,000 acres.

State acquisition brought five major new players to the table for scrub conservation on the Ridge, contributing tremendous knowledge and greatly expanding capacity. Three agencies—Florida Department of Environmental Protection (FL DEP), Florida Forest Service (FFS, formerly the Florida Division of Forestry), and FFWCC—assumed management responsibility for state land acquisitions. The South Florida and Southwest Florida Water Management Districts (SFWMD and SWFWMD) also purchased and managed sites, with their major acquisitions being Horse Creek (1,325 acres) and Henscratch/Jack Creek (1,309 acres) respectively.

Following the financial crises of 2008, funding for the Florida Forever program and state for acquisition stalled. Few acres have been acquired since then. The Ridge was among 14 state conservation sites still targeted, although funds could only purchase a very small number of the 24,237 acres remaining, most of which are lots in the megaparcel sites.

Establishing the Federal Lake Wales Ridge National Wildlife Refuge
In response to the large number of federally listed species in jeopardy, the federal government joined the state government in land acquisition on the Ridge. In 1993, the U.S. FWS proposed establishment of the Lake Wales Ridge National Wildlife Refuge (U.S. FWS 1993); its goal was to enhance the recovery of four listed vertebrates as well as 26 listed or list-candidate plants. FWS employee Dave Martin took a passionate

interest in protecting Ridge plants, describing them as a national "treasure trove of biodiversity" (Martin 1993, 3). Although the refuge—the first designated to protect endangered plants—was authorized by Congress in 1994, little money was allocated for acquisition. Of the 19,630 acres proposed, only four tracts were acquired, although the state eventually purchased some proposed sites. The U.S. FWS now owns and manages a total of 1,843 acres on the Ridge, including Flamingo Villas (1,039 acres), Carter Creek South (626 acres), Snell Creek (Lake Marion) (139 acres), and Lake McLeod (38 acres) (figure 4.4).

Local Government Becomes Engaged: Polk County
Much of the Ridge's biodiversity resides in two counties: Polk and Highlands. Of the two, Polk is larger and more urban. Thanks to a grassroots effort in 1994, a majority of voters in Polk County voted to increase their ad valorem taxes for the purchase of environmentally sensitive land. This county program attracted matching state funds to leverage its dollars, purchasing four Ridge sites that totaled 804 acres (figure 4.6). In 2008, a few local Highlands County champions also thought about mounting a local ballot, but times were tough, and the measure never made the ballot.

SCIENTIFIC EVALUATION: STATE OF THE SCRUB

Through a combination of nonprofit, local, state, and federal efforts, more than $100 million has been spent for land acquisition on the Ridge in the last 25 years, and more than 104,000 acres of land—including approximately half the remaining native xeric upland habitat—has been set aside for preservation. The conservation community, appalled at what has been lost, remains somewhat amazed at what has been saved. But is it enough? Prompted by the question "to what extent has acquisition on the Ridge made a difference for conservation?" Hilary Swain at Archbold partnered with Dave Wilcove and Will Turner from Princeton University to complete the first scientific assessment of the success of land acquisition in reducing threats to rare and endemic Ridge species. Their *State of the Scrub* report (Turner et al. 2006a) synthesized existing data on 36 of the rare and endemic species on the Ridge. The analyses indicated that conservation efforts had contributed greatly to protecting imperiled plants and animals. Using a quantitative approach (figure 4.5), they showed that conservation purchases since 1988 had

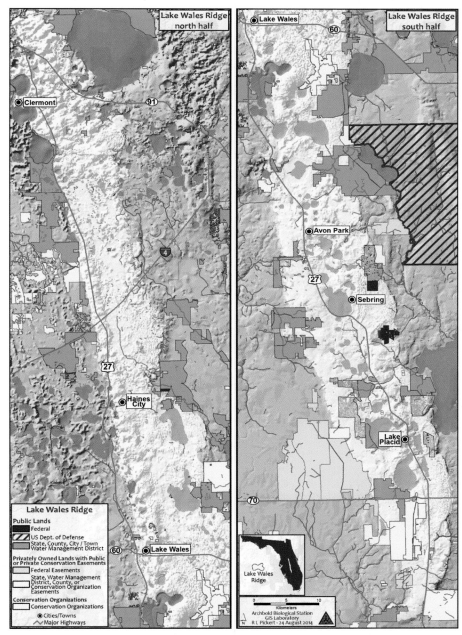

FIGURE 4.4. Land acquisition and easement purchases by federal, state, and local agencies and conservation organizations on the Lake Wales Ridge and surrounding lands.

Source: FNAI and Roberta Pickert, Archbold GIS Laboratory. Map used with permission from Archbold Biological Station.

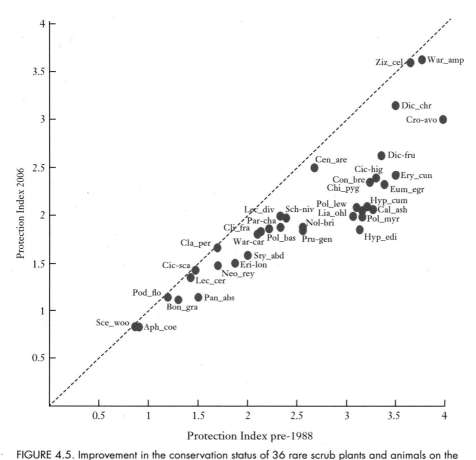

FIGURE 4.5. Improvement in the conservation status of 36 rare scrub plants and animals on the Lake Wales Ridge as a result of land acquisition between 1988 and 2006, as measured by a protection index (very low = 4 to high = 0.5) that integrates the number of populations of a species that are protected, area occupied, and geographic range (based on Figure 7 in Turner et al. 2006a). The status of species lying below the line is improved.

Source: Archbold Biological Station. (Mammals: *Podomys floridanus*; Birds: *Aphelocoma coerulescens*; Reptiles: *Eumeces egregius lividus, Neoseps reynoldsi, Sceloporus woodi*; Arthropods: *Cicindela highlandensis, Cicindela scabrosa*; Plants: *Bonamia grandiflora, Calamintha ashei, Centrosema arenicola, Chionanthus pygmaeus, Cladonia perforata, Clitoria fragrans, Conradina brevifolia, Crotalaria avonensis, Dicerandra christmanii, Dicerandra frutescens, Eriogonum longifolium* var *gnaphalifolium, Eryngium cuneifolium, Hypericum cumulicola, Hypericum edisonianum, Lechea cernua, Lechea divaricata, Liatris ohlingerae, Nolina brittoniana, Panicum abscissum, Paronychia chartacea* ssp *chartacea, Polygala lewtonii, Polygonella basiramia, Polygonella myriophylla, Prunus geniculata, Schizachyrium niveum, Stylisma abdita, Warea amplexifolia, Warea carteri, Ziziphus celata*.)

reduced extinction risk by increasing the proportion of sites at which species are protected and the protected area over which species occur, and by maintaining their geographic range.

Despite this success, most scrub species are likely to remain at risk of extinction primarily because even the most optimistic acquisition scenarios will protect little more than 7 percent of the original Ridge habitats, most having already been destroyed. Turner et al. (2006b) used a reserve-design algorithm to determine which remaining sites should be high priorities for future protection based on their biological value and cost-effectiveness, and then estimated the incremental effectiveness of the reserve network likely to result from planned future acquisitions. They noted that—however successful future acquisition efforts may be—virtually all scrub species will depend upon active management, especially prescribed fire, for their long-term persistence.

AN INCREASING ROLE FOR SCIENCE IN CONSERVATION LAND MANAGEMENT

Recognizing that fire management is critical, TNC and Archbold started to address the management needs of the patchwork of conservation lands and the coordination required among twelve managing agencies (two federal, five state, two county, and three nonprofit). Science was to play a key role in land management planning and implementation. Building the social capital to achieve management coordination was critical for a conservation landscape with multiple sites and multiple agencies.

In 1991, anticipating the long-term need for a collaborative land management approach, TNC called for the creation of a working group for the original agencies managing land around Lake Arbuckle. This group included TNC, the Florida Division of Forestry (now the Florida Forest Service), the Florida Department of Natural Resources (now the Florida Department of Environmental Protection), the Florida Game and Freshwater Fish Commission (now the Florida Fish and Wildlife Conservation Commission), the Avon Park Bombing Range (now Avon Park Air Force Range), Polk County Parks and Recreation, and Polk County Water Resources Division. Soon the geographic scope was expanded, and Archbold was invited to join.

First established as the Greater Arbuckle Working Group, the association is now called the Lake Wales Ridge Ecosystem Working Group

(LWREWG). An interagency steering committee and five subcommittees (invasive species, rare species, GIS, fire, and education) provide the framework for all the partners managing land along the Ridge to work collaboratively. Presentations by scientists at quarterly meetings ensure exposure to current research and management practices. Joint projects and problem-solving allow managers to be more effective and efficient. The institutional brokering mitigates some of the effects of fragmentation.

More than twenty years later, the LWREWG is still going strong. Virtually every land manager participates, as well as nearly all scientists working in the scrub ecosystem. Meetings usually have 50 to 70 attendees, bringing many knowledgeable and innovative agency and scientist minds to the conservation process. The LWREWG has allowed scientists and agencies to share information and resources, to develop a shared vision, and to foster accord between the aims of research and conservation. Research directly translates into conservation action and conservation needs define new research questions. With no charter, bylaws, government oversight, votes, or any kind of formal structuring, the LWREWG has exhibited surprising resiliency, although it is not an advocacy organization. The far-sighted vision of a nonthreatening forum for exchange of information has proven to be a powerful force in conservation. The success of the LWREWG inspired the state to create working groups in other regions and project areas.

Fire as a Vital Tool for Land Management

Although the Ridge conservation community achieved considerable success in land acquisition and the LWREWG established an important forum for collaboration, fire management continued to lag behind. The species-rich xeric upland communities depend on periodic fires to maintain habitat. If the conservation community was going to save this ecosystem, it had to implement fire management more successfully. An initial field assessment conducted by TNC in 1994 revealed that 75 percent of a subset of 18 Ridge scrub sites proposed for acquisition were badly overgrown and at risk of losing their endemic species due to fire exclusion (Huffman 1994).

Decades of research had documented the critical role of fire in the scrub habitat. Warren Abrahamson's widely cited papers on the role of fire in scrub (Abrahamson 1984a, 1984b) represented a paradigm shift

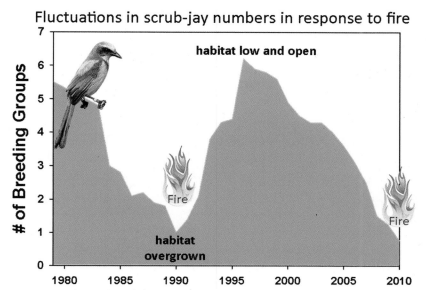

Fluctuations in scrub-jay numbers in response to fire

FIGURE 4.6. The number of Florida scrub-jay groups in relation to time since fire in burn unit 50 at Archbold Biological Station.
Source: Figure by Reed Bowman. Used with permission from Archbold Biological Station.

for both the science and the conservation communities in Florida and nationally. Numerous Florida scrub-jay studies at Archbold confirmed the essential role of fire in creating low, open habitat for this threatened species (figure 4.6).

Guided by research findings, prescribed burns were used after 1979 to mimic fire's natural cycles on Archbold's globally threatened preserve (Main and Menges 1997). Ron Myers, who conducted the early burns at Archbold, went on to a career promoting fire management nationally for TNC. In parallel with Archbold's research-driven approach to fire management, Steve Morrison, TNC's first employee on the Ridge, was experimenting with prescribed fire at the Tiger Creek Preserve and reached many of the same conclusions.

By 1999, despite decades of successful management by TNC and Archbold on their own sites, the partners were deeply concerned that, of 31 Ridge sites in conservation ownership, 19 had not received any fire management since they were purchased (Huffman 1999). Mary Huffman, chair of the LWREWG fire committee, convened a meeting to ask partners to identify the biggest barriers to getting fires completed. This inquiry revealed that managers were hampered largely by a shortage of staff on days when the weather was conducive for burning; adding crew members with accompanying equipment might tip the balance. TNC secured partial funding to provide an innovative approach to increasing fire management: a roving crew initially called the Florida Scrub-Jay Fire Strike Team.

The area burned by the team has increased annually from about 1,000 acres in 2001 to more than 20,000 acres in 2012. Thirteen managing agencies rely on the group, which has evolved into the Central Florida Ecosystem Restoration Team. An excellent example of public–private partnerships and interagency cooperation, the team has become a model for other regions. Despite significant progress, a recent Archbold analysis by Boughton and Bowman (2011) has revealed that Florida scrub-jay populations have declined by as much as 25 percent from 1992–1993 to 2009–2010 on protected public lands statewide. The current number of scrub-jays is less than 50 percent of the estimated carrying capacity on public lands, and the decline is largely attributable to a lack of fire. Obviously much remains to be done.

Another Conundrum: Management of Invasive Species

Invasive plants on the Ridge like cogon grass (*Imperata cylindrica*), Natal grass (*Rhynchelytrum repens*), and Old World climbing fern (*Lygodium microphyllum*) as well as feral hogs (*Sus scrofa*) require constant attention. TNC was able to expand the LWREWG to treat priority invasive species, including those on private lands adjacent to conservation sites. The LWREWG invasives subcommittee became a management springboard to develop Cooperative Invasive Species Management Areas statewide. This collaborative approach has facilitated strategies such as aerial surveys to understand the scope of the threat, and created a forum for exchanging information on effective responses and early detection.

Coordinating Recovery Planning with the U.S. Fish and Wildlife Service and Others

Over the last 30 years, scientists at Archbold and elsewhere have contributed to the development of at least 13 U.S. FWS recovery plans for federally listed scrub species, one for 11 scrub plants (expanded later to 20 plants; U.S. FWS 1995) and others for indigo snakes, sand skinks, blue-tailed mole skinks, and the Florida scrub-jay. This planning culminated in the creation of the comprehensive South Florida Multi-Species Recovery Plan, which includes scrub plant species (U.S. FWS 1999).

In partnership with the Cornell Laboratory of Ornithology, Archbold completed complex analyses of population viability, landscape connectivity, genetic structuring, reintroductions, habitat restoration, and habitat conservation plans for the Florida scrub-jay. These studies brought massive scientific firepower to bear on conservation of the species.

Carl Weekley at Archbold, in partnership with TNC, Bok Tower Gardens, and federal and state agencies, has spearheaded the recovery of *Ziziphus celata*, an extremely rare and genetically depauperate Ridge plant once thought to have been extirpated but now listed as endangered (Weekley et al. 2012). This work involves extensive surveys for new locations, basic ecology, genetics research, plant propagation, and successful reintroductions. For at least six other Ridge scrub plants, scientific assistance for translocation and/or propagation may be necessary to ensure their survival (Turner et al. 2006a).

Adaptation and Mitigation for Climate Change

Florida's climate exhibits high seasonal and annual variability, and many scrub species have marked correlations with variability in rainfall, temperature, and cycles such as El Niño–La Niña and the Atlantic Multidecadal Oscillation. To date, we do not have equivocal evidence of responses to long-term climate change in scrub habitats on the Ridge. Climate data at Archbold, like many rural southeastern sites, do not exhibit marked increases in temperatures or changes in rainfall or fire frequency. Von Holle et al. (2010) detected temperature-induced shifts statewide in Florida plant phenology, documenting a trend for delayed seasonal flowering among plants in rural Florida. The climate change adaptation strategy on the Ridge is to focus on continually improving management to ensure that habitat is maintained in optimal condition.

LARGE LANDSCAPES: THINKING AT THE SCALE OF A BEAR

After the Ridge reserve network was established, management organized, and species-specific recovery underway, another threat loomed. The initial reserve network was envisioned within a matrix of agriculture, but by the mid-2000s, a new wave of habitat conversion was turning agricultural land over to development. Former citrus groves and the rural lands bordering the Ridge, much of it used for low-intensity cattle ranching, became a focus of increasing development pressure. Five developments large enough to be categorized as having regional impact were proposed for Highlands County. The alarming *Florida 2060* report showed that Polk and Highlands counties were poised for large landscape-level change (Zwick and Carr 2006). Two major toll roads were proposed that could forever change the character of the region. It became clear that science and conservation partners needed to propose connections and buffer conservation lands to create a functional landscape, allowing the movement of species among sites and limiting encroachment in order to facilitate fire management. The types of land use surrounding conservation areas play a critical role in our ability to preserve their conservation value over time.

In the face of these new challenges, the partners brought in landscape ecologist Tom Hoctor from the University of Florida to develop a spatial analysis of land use on the Ridge. The resulting analysis relied on a collaborative study on the travel patterns of the Florida black bear (*Ursus americanus floridanus*) in Highlands and Glades counties by the University of Kentucky and Archbold (Ulrey 2007, Guthrie 2012) as well as the statewide modeling by Hoctor. The resulting Greater Ridge Conservation Planning Tool (TNC et al. 2007) can be used to give planners guidance about where Ridge communities could continue to grow while simultaneously emphasizing the need to preserve a functional landscape that allows for the movement of wildlife, the continuing application of prescribed fire, the protection of watersheds, and the preservation of rare species. This project in turn served as the springboard for further spatial analyses, including conservation corridor mapping for Highlands County (Swain et al. 2009), a regional Heartland 2060 analysis in conjunction with FNAI (Hoctor et al. 2010), and a regional corridor analysis under the state's Cooperative Conservation Blueprint (FFWCC 2010).

Land managers planning controlled burns are significantly constrained by the proximity of smoke-sensitive land uses such as major highways, airports, and hospitals. The team thus developed a GIS-based tool as a guide for land use planning around conservation lands (Pace-Aldana 2009). The Florida Department of Transportation is considering adoption of this smoke-buffering tool statewide, and the data are being used for local and regional planning.

Facing similar concerns about encroaching development and the incompatibility of growth with military missions, the Department of Defense initiated a joint land use study around APAFR in 2010 (figure 4.7) (APAFR 2010). The purpose of the study was to work collaboratively with local governments to develop compatible land use plans and land development regulations. The use of conservation funding to protect this military site from encroachment using conservation funding has attracted new sources of federal support for planning and conservation, such as a conservation buffer program that includes a portion of the Ridge under the DoD's National Readiness and Environmental Protection Initiative.

THE CHALLENGES OF ENGAGING THE PUBLIC

Scientists and professional conservationists have always been intrigued by the scrub ecosystem; they consider the Florida scrub as one of the most interesting and unusual of habitats, supporting plants and animals that are an almost Dr. Seuss-like collection of delightful oddities (Wilcove 1999). But unlike the grandeur of mountains and canyons, or the verdant luxuriousness of forests and riverine meadows, the Florida scrub has never been a captivating landscape to the novice or public eye. Public opinion nowadays differs little from that offered 80 years ago by the ecologist Maurice Mulvania (1931, 528).

> The vegetation is mostly dwarfed, gnarled and crooked, and presents a tangled scraggly aspect. It . . . display[s] the misery through which it has passed and is passing in its solution of life's grim riddle. Here live the rosemary (*Ceratiola ericoides*), spruce-pine (*Pinus clausa*), poor grub (*Xolisma ferruginea*), and their associates rooted in a bed of silica, to which the term soil is but remotely applicable. Here the sun sheds its glare and takes a toll of the unfit.

Saving this ecosystem has never involved much public grassroots conservation effort. Instead, the scrub's survival has depended mostly on a determined cadre of scientists and professional conservationists who marshaled incontrovertible conservation arguments. Few public champions emerged. This state of affairs may be because most of the remaining

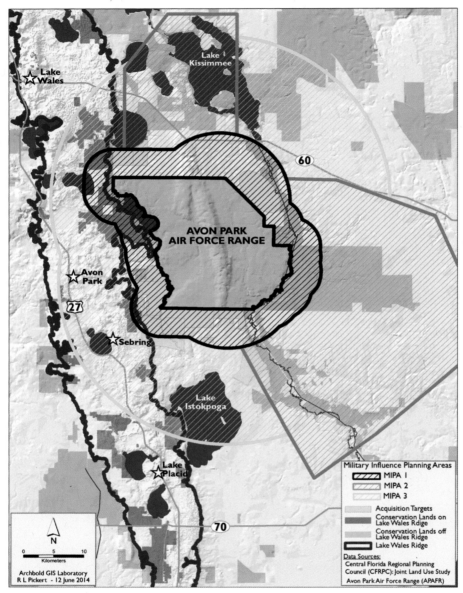

FIGURE 4.7. The location of existing conservation lands on the Lake Wales Ridge and potential land acquisitions targeted to reduce conflicts within the Military Influence Planning Areas (MIPA) around the Avon Park Air Force Range. MIPA 1: 3-mile buffer with moderate noise risk plus low-level flights; MIPA 2: low noise risk plus low-level flights; MIPA 3: low noise risk.
Source: Central Florida Regional Planning Council. Map used with permission from Archbold Biological Station.

scrub on the Ridge is located in a part of Florida that is still relatively rural, where residents are sensitive to any perceived infringement on property rights, elected officials are loath to bypass any "development opportunity," and out-of-state retirees have no sense of place or awareness of the area's history.

Despite these challenges, the partners have made a concerted effort to build a conservation constituency. At the outset, the conservation organizations realized the importance of educating the public. Since 1990, Archbold's K–12 education program has hosted more than 40,000 local schoolchildren at the station and produced an award-winning science curricula based on scrub ecology that is used throughout the state. Archbold's new learning center, opened in 2012, invites the public to explore the scrub and learn about the Ridge. In 2008, Polk County joined with the SWFWMD to create a visitor center just off the Ridge at Circle B Bar. The Center attracts 20,000 visitors annually and offers a variety of environmental education programs. In addition, Highlands Hammock State Park can host 2,000 to 3,000 visitors daily, and many other Ridge sites provide hiking trails and host the public in small visitor centers.

While the reserve network was being assembled, TNC staff tried to get the public involved in caring for the sites to increase awareness about the ecology of the Ridge and develop support for the newly acquired public lands. In 1995, TNC created an interagency volunteer program called Ridge Rangers, engaging citizens in on-the-ground conservation work for nearly all the managing agencies on the Ridge. In 2002, TNC transferred the program to the FFWCC to provide a more stable funding source. The program now has 128 members who volunteer nearly 5,000 hours annually (Parken 2012).

Building on the pioneering work of the Cornell Laboratory of Ornithology in the area of citizen science, TNC and Archbold created a targeted program called Jay Watch that enlisted local residents to monitor the scrub's flagship umbrella species. Scrub-jays are an indicator of scrub habitat condition because the range of optimal conditions for jays is also good for many other rare scrub species (Breininger et al. 2006). The beauty of this approach was that while the public usually hates smoke and fire, they almost instantly fall in love with scrub-jays. Demographic data on scrub-jays are collected annually, and biennial vegetation monitoring tracks habitat condition in relation to scrub-jay presence.

Archbold scientists then evaluate and analyze the data collected. This monitoring informs prescribed fire planning for maintenance of good quality scrub. Jay Watch began surveys on public conservation lands along the Ridge and has since expanded to cover 73 sites in 19 counties, with the assistance of more than 200 volunteers. Now managed by Florida Audubon with scientific support from Archbold, the program has become the baseline scrub-jay monitoring standard for state lands managed by the DEP and FFWCC.

Additional efforts to generate support for conservation over the years have included informing and working with international, national, state, and local media outlets to produce hundreds of articles; creating numerous print and audiovisual materials, among them the 19-minute DVD produced by Bill Kurtis called *Islands in Time* as well as a companion print piece called *Florida's Ancient Islands*, working with artists such as printmaker Mollie Doctrow, creator of *Spirit of the Scrub* and the Wildflower Wayside Shrine Trail; and producing numerous site-specific publications as well as interpretive signage.

SECURING THE FUTURE OF THE FLORIDA SCRUB

Progress to date made in saving the scrub could be viewed as one of North America's great conservation success stories, although it has probably not received the national recognition it deserves. Scientists and conservationists have been working together to save this system for more than 25 years. There has been great strength in focusing a broad ecological research program on the large landscape of the Ridge; always opportunistic, this partnership has taken advantage of every chance. Although all conservation projects have their idiosyncrasies, this one provides the world with many innovative models of science leading to conservation action. Broad impacts with global relevance include work in the areas of fire management, endangered species planning, management planning for scrub habitats, land management working groups, training in hands-on conservation science for the next generation of ecologists, management strike teams, and public science platforms for conservation.

Despite the conservation successes, it is still not enough to have trebled the acreage of protected habitat on the Ridge. The community continues to prioritize remaining scrublands for purchase, but it is harder to finish an acquisition program than to start one. The big, sexy land deals have largely been completed, and it's mostly multiple small challenges that remain. The science community and professional conservationists have to support and pressure the public agencies to persevere with purchases. When the state legislature failed to fund Florida Forever in 2008, they set a depressing tone for acquisition for the next few years. Now TNC, Archbold, and other partners are cultivating new sources of funding. This is an acquisition marathon, and the conservation community can't afford to stall.

In addition to the need for continued engagement in land acquisition and protection, there are pressing demands for scientific input into improved land management, particularly prescribed fire. Although the threat to state and federally listed species has decreased, most need perennial conservation management to survive. Maintaining the 20-year-old LWREWG is vital, as is support for the Central Florida Ecosystem Restoration Team. Money for management has become scarce; funders are attracted to creating new programs, not sustaining ongoing efforts. TNC and Archbold have engaged new partners to administer Ridge-wide programs for the public, including Florida Audubon and FFWCC for Jay Watch and FFWCC for Ridge Rangers. But land managers have more land and fewer resources.

Success in conservation is never a single step; it is always a long journey. At the heart of this particular success story is the rich biodiversity of the Ridge; the ecosystem garnered attention because it is so important to save, and we knew that because of a wealth of earlier science. This story illustrates how conservation success increases demands on scientists' time, as they are asked to provide more input at every incremental step of the conservation journey. Every new step adds to the continuing burdens of earlier steps. But scientists must protect enough of their time to continue the fundamental research and inventory that increases knowledge and justifies conservation.

Although scientists have served as catalysts for conservation, conservation has been a wonderful crucible for science. There is a tight coupling between research and conservation: fundamental and applied research feeds directly into conservation planning; conservation action stems from research findings; conservation needs define new research questions and activities; inventory and monitoring is structured to benefit science; taking advantage of well-planned land management activities creates experimental research opportunities; and adding new conservation sites has greatly expanded the scope and scale of research projects. Conservation has been an avenue to research success; institutions like Archbold that focus on a regional ecosystem have the reward of providing answers to real conservation problems while also advancing general ecological knowledge. Conservation solutions based on sound research have been favored, based on pressure on state and federal agencies to conserve the environment. Local and regional facilities have had the advantage when it comes to grants, based on their history of research focus and enriched by long-term data accumulation. Research findings have led to general goodwill and public support locally.

However we take into account the benefits of conservation-driven research, scientists and conservationists are spread very thin. The Ridge needs a wider base of public support and enthusiasm to prevent institutional fatigue from setting in. Investments to move from a largely professional-driven conservation program to building grassroots public support will be essential. There is a daunting need for people to engage in local planning decisions that directly affect conservation outcomes. We need marketing to increase public awareness of how the Ridge conservation areas provide clean water, enhance their quality of life, give local communities their sense of place, and hold the secrets of sustainability for future generations. The challenge remains to find a way to convey E.O. Wilson's (2000, x) exhortation that:

> To Americans who know natural history, and their numbers are certain to grow with each passing generation, Nevada's Ash Meadows and Florida's Lake Wales scrubland are sacred landmarks, the equivalent of Independence Hall and Gettysburg of original America.

REFERENCES

Abrahamson, W. G. 1984a. "Species Responses to Fire on the Florida Lake Wales Ridge." *American Journal of Botany* 71:35–42.

———.1984b. "Post-Fire Recovery of Florida Lake Wales Ridge Vegetation." *American Journal of Botany* 71:9–21.

Archbold Biological Station. 1989. *Biological Priorities for a Network of Scrub Preserves on the Lake Wales Ridge*. Lake Placid, FL: Archbold Biological Station.

Austin, D. F., A. F. Cholewa, R. B. Lassiter, and B. F. Hansen. 1987. *The Florida of John Kunkel Small: His Species and Types, Collecting Localities, Bibliography and Selected Reprinted Works*. Volume 18: 3. Bronx: New York Botanical Garden Press.

Avon Park Air Force Range. 2010. *Avon Park Air Force Range Joint Land Use Study.* Prepared by Tetra Tech, Inc., Miller Legg, and Central Florida Regional Planning Council. Avon Park, FL: Avon Park Air Force Range.

Boughton, R. K., and R. Bowman. 2011. *State-Wide Assessment of Florida Scrub-Jays on Managed Areas: A Comparison of Current Populations to the Result of the 1992–93 Survey.* Venus, FL: Archbold Biological Station.

Breininger, D. R., B. Toland, D. M. Oddy, and M. L. Legare. 2006. "Landcover Characterizations and Florida Scrub-Jay (*Aphelocoma coerulescens*) Population Dynamics." *Biological Conservation* 128:169–181.

Chaplin, S. J., R. A. Gerrard, H. M. Watson, L. L. Master, and S. R. Flack. 2000. "The Geography of Imperilment: Targeting Conservation Toward Critical Biodiversity Areas." In *Precious Heritage: The Status of Biodiversity in the United States,* ed. B. A. Stein, L. S. Kutner, and J. S. Adams, 159–200. New York, NY: Oxford University Press.

Christman, S. P. 1988a. *Endemism and Florida's Interior Sand Pine Scrub.* Florida Game and Freshwater Fish Commission Nongame Wildlife Section. Report GFC-84–101. Tallahassee: Florida Game and Freshwater Fish Commission.

———.1988b. "Preserving Florida Scrub." Unpublished manuscript. 1988.

Christman, S. P., and W. S Judd. 1990. "Notes on Plants Endemic to Florida Scrub." *Florida Scientist* 33:52–73.

Cooper, S. T., and G. E. Schultz. 1984. "Endangered Plant Species of the Central Florida Ridge, Polk and Highlands Counties." Paper presented at the Florida Academy of Sciences 1984 Annual Meeting. Abstract in *Florida Scientist* 74: Supplement 1.

Deyrup, M., and J. E. Carrel. 2011. *Conservation Status and Management of Lake Wales Ridge Arthropods Restricted to Scrub Habitat.* Final Report, Project T-15-D, on Lake Wales Ridge Scrub Arthropods to the Florida Fish and Wildlife Conservation Commission. Venus, FL: Archbold Biological Station.

Deyrup, M., and T. Eisner. 1993. "A Last Stand in the Sand." *Natural History* 102:42–47.

Dobson, A. P., J. P. Rodriguez, W. M. Roberts, and D. S. Wilcove. 1997. "Geographic Distribution of Endangered Species in the United States." *Science* 275:550–553.

Eisner, T. 2001. Personal communication, January 19.

Eisner, T. 2003. *For Love of Insects.* Cambridge, MA: Belknap Press of Harvard University Press.

Estill, J. C., and M. Cruzan. 2001. "Phytogeography of Rare Plant Species Endemic to the Southeastern United States." *Castanea* 66:3–23.

Farr, J. A., and O. G Brock. 2006. "Florida's Landmark Programs for Conservation and Recreation Land Acquisition." *Sustain: The Kentucky Institute for the Environment and Sustainable Development* 14:35–44.

Fitzpatrick, J. 2012. Personal communication, April 5.

Florida Department of Environmental Protection. 2012. *Florida Forever Five-Year Plan,* April 2012. Tallahassee: Florida Department of Environmental Protection.

Florida Department of Natural Resources and the Land Acquisition Advisory Council. 1990. *Annual Report of the Conservation and Recreation Lands Program.* Tallahassee: Florida Department of Natural Resources.

Florida Fish and Wildlife Conservation Commission. 2010. *Cooperative Conservation Blueprint: 2010 Status Report.* Tallahassee: Florida Fish and Wildlife Conservation Commission.

Florida Natural Areas Inventory. 1990. *Guide to the Natural Communities of Florida.* Tallahassee: Florida Department of Natural Resources.

Guthrie, J. M. 2012. *Modeling Movement Behavior and Road-Crossing Behavior in the Black Bear of South-Central Florida.* Master's thesis, University of Kentucky, Lexington.

Hoctor, T. S., M. O'Brien, and J. B. Oetting. 2010. *Heartland Ecological Assessment Report.* Babson Park, FL: The Nature Conservancy.

Hubell, T. H. 1932. *A Revision of the Puer Group of the North American Genus* Melanopus *with Remarks on the Taxonomic Value of the Concealed Male Genitalia of Cyrtachanthacrinae (Orthoptera, Acrididae).* Miscellaneous publications of the University of Michigan Museum of Zoology 23:1–64.

Huffman, M. R. 1994. *Discussion Paper: The Urgent Need for Fire Management to Save the Florida Scrub-Jay.* Lake Wales, FL: The Nature Conservancy.

———. 1999. *A Fire Strike Team to Save the Florida Scrub-Jay.* Lake Wales, FL: The Nature Conservancy.

Johnson, A. F. 1981. "Scrub Endemics of the Central Ridge, Florida." Unpublished report prepared for the U.S. Fish and Wildlife Service, Jacksonville, FL.

Little, A. E. 1920–1921. Timber Cruise Reports for Sections of Highlands County for the Consolidated Land Company. Available at Archbold Biological Station, Venus, FL.

Main, K. N., and E. S. Menges. 1997. *Archbold Biological Station: Station Fire Management Plan.* Land Management Publication 97-1. Venus, FL: Archbold Biological Station.

Martin, D. 1993. "The Lake Wales Ridge National Wildlife Refuge: Preserving a Treasure Trove of Biodiversity." *Endangered Species Technical Bulletin* 18 (4): 3–4.

McCarten, L., and W. S. Moy. 1995. *Geologic Map of Sarasota and Arcadia, Florida: 30- ×60-Minute Quadrangles.* U.S. Geological Survey Open File Report 95-261. Reston, VA: U.S. Geological Survey.

McPhee, J. 1966. *Oranges.* New York, NY: Farrar, Straus and Giroux.

Menges, E. S. 1998. "Ecology and Conservation of Florida Scrub." In *Savannas, Barrens, and Rock Outcrop Plant Communities of North America,* ed. R. C. Anderson, J. S. Fralish, and J. Baskin, 7–22. Cambridge, U.K.: Cambridge University Press.

Menges, E. S., and N. Kohfeldt. 1995. "Life History Strategies of Florida Scrub Plants in Relation to Fire." *Bulletin of the Torrey Botanical Club* 122:282–297.

Morse, R. A. 2000. *Richard Archbold and the Archbold Biological Station.* Gainesville: University of Florida Press.

Muller, J. W., E. D. Hardin, D. R. Jackson, S. E. Gatewood, and N. Claire. 1989. *Summary Report on the Vascular Plants, Animals and Plant Communities Endemic to*

Florida. Nongame Wildlife Program Technical Report No. 7. Tallahassee: Florida Game and Freshwater Fish Commission.

Mulvania, M. 1931. "Ecological Survey of a Florida Scrub." *Ecology* 12:528–540.

Mushinsky, H. R., and E. D. McCoy. 1991. *Vertebrate Species Composition of Selected Scrub Islands on the Lake Wales Ridge of Central Florida.* Report NG87-149. Tallahassee: Florida Game and Freshwater Fish Commission, Nongame Wildlife Program.

Myers, R. L. 1990. "Scrub and High Pine." In *Ecosystems of Florida*, ed. R. L. Myers and J. J. Ewel, 150–193. Orlando: University of Central Florida Press.

Noss, R. F., and R. L. Peters. 1995. *Endangered Ecosystems: A Status Report on America's Vanishing Habitat and Wildlife.* Washington, DC: Defenders of Wildlife.

Pace-Aldana, B. 2009. "A GIS Data Layer for Guiding Development Compatible with Fire Management of Neighboring Conservation Sites." In *Proceedings of the 24th Tall Timbers Fire Ecology Conference: The Future of Fire: Public Awareness, Health, and Safety*, ed. K. M. Robertson, R. E. Masters, and K. E. M. Galley. Tallahassee, FL: Tall Timbers Research Station.

Parken, W. 2012. Personal communication, April 5. Florida Fish and Wildlife Conservation Commission.

Peroni, P. A., and W. G. Abrahamson. 1985. "Vegetation Loss on the Southern Lake Wales Ridge." *Palmetto* 5 (3): 6–7.

Schultz, G. E., L. G. Chapin, and S. T. Krupenovich. 1999. *Rare Plant Species and High Quality Natural Communities of Twenty-Six CARL Sites in the Lake Wales Ridge Ecosystem.* Final Report. December 1999. Tallahassee: Florida Natural Areas Inventory.

Swain, H. M., R. L. Pickert, T. S. Hoctor, and J. B. Oetting. 2009. *Highlands County Conservation Lands, Connectivity, and Corridor System: Report, Metadata, and Shapefiles.* Venus, FL: Archbold Biological Station.

Turner, W. R., D. S. Wilcove, and H. M. Swain. 2006a. *State of the Scrub: Conservation Progress, Management Responsibilities, and Land Acquisition Priorities for Imperiled Species of Florida's Lake Wales Ridge.* Venus, FL: Archbold Biological Station.

———. 2006b. "Assessing the Effectiveness of Reserve Acquisition Programs in Protecting Rare and Threatened Species." *Conservation Biology* 20:1657–1669.

Ulrey, W. A. 2007. "Home Range, Habitat Use, and Food Habits of the Black Bear in South-Central Florida." Master's thesis, University of Kentucky, Lexington.

U.S. Fish and Wildlife Service. 1993. *Proposed Establishment of Lake Wales Ridge National Wildlife Refuge.* Atlanta, GA: U.S. Fish and Wildlife Service.

———. 1995. *Draft Recovery Plan for Nineteen Florida Scrub and High Pineland Plant Species (Revision and Expansion of Recovery Plan for Eleven Florida Scrub Plant Species Approved January 20, 1990).* Atlanta, GA: U.S. Fish and Wildlife Service.

———. 1999. *South Florida Multi-Species Recovery Plan.* Atlanta, GA: U.S. Fish and Wildlife Service.

Von Holle, B., Y. Wei, and D. Nickerson. 2010. "Climatic Variability Leads to Later Seasonal Flowering of Floridian Plants." *PLoS ONE* 5 (7): e11500. doi:10.1371/journal.pone.0011500.

Wallace, S. R., and L. R. McMahon. 1988. "A Place in the Sun for the Plants." *Garden* (Jan/Feb): 20–23.

Ward, C. 2011. Keynote speech, Opening ceremony, Frances Archbold Hufty Learning Center, Archbold, December 2.

Weekley, C. W., E. S. Menges, and R. L. Pickert. 2008. "An Ecological Map of Florida's Lake Wales Ridge: A New Boundary Delineation and an Assessment of Post-Columbian Habitat Loss." *Florida Scientist* 71:45–64.

Weekley, C. W., S. A. Smith, S. J. Haller Crate, S. W. McAllister, and E. S. Menges. 2012. *Continuation of Research on the Federally-Listed Lake Wales Ridge Endemic Florida Ziziphus* (Ziziphus celata). Venus, FL: Archbold Biological Station.

White, W. A. 1970. *The Geomorphology of the Florida Peninsula*. Volume 51. Tallahassee: Bureau of Geology, Florida Department of Natural Resources.

Wilcove, D. S. 1999. "A Bounty at the Border." In *The Condor's Shadow: The Loss and Recovery of Wildlife in America*, 170–201. New York, NY: W. H. Freeman and Co.

Willson, G. 2012. Personal communication, April 5.

Wilson, E. O. 2000. Foreword. In *Precious Heritage: The Status of Biodiversity in the United States*. New York, NY: Oxford University Press and The Nature Conservancy and Association for Biodiversity Information.

Woolfenden, G. E., and J. W. Fitzpatrick. 1984. *The Florida Scrub Jay: Demography of a Cooperative-Breeding Bird*. Princeton, NJ: Princeton University Press.

Zwick, P. D., and M. H Carr. 2006. *Florida 2060: A Population Distribution Scenario for the State of Florida*. A research project prepared for the 1,000 Friends of Florida. Gainesville: Geoplan Center, University of Florida.

5

Catalyzing Large Landscape Conservation in Canada's Boreal Systems: The BEACONs Project Experience

Fiona K. A. Schmiegelow, Steven G. Cumming, Kimberly A. Lisgo, Shawn J. Leroux, and Meg A. Krawchuk

Until the late 1990s, it was difficult to garner attention within the conservation community for boreal forest issues. Widely perceived as uninteresting, depauperate systems of homogenous, stunted tree cover with few threats to their persistence, boreal forests met neither the diversity nor vulnerability criteria typically used to highlight areas of concern and prioritize conservation action. Given the lack of empirical data demonstrating the need for protection of these forests, the conversation quickly became one-sided for those trying to increase awareness of conservation concerns in these systems.

A watershed moment in raising this awareness came in 1997 with the release of the World Resources Institute report *The Last Frontier Forests: Ecosystems and Economies on the Edge* (Bryant et al. 1997). Its accompanying world map, the proverbial picture worth a thousand words, depicted where frontier forests had existed 8,000 years ago and, in dark green, where they could be found at the end of the 20th century. Frontier forests were broadly defined as those large enough and sufficiently devoid of human disruption to maintain their native biota without significant intervention (figure 5.1). The dark green mantle cloaking the northern hemisphere stood in stark contrast to the pale tones of lost or altered forests that covered much of the rest of the globe, and the conversation turned to one of opportunities. At the same time, Canada was grappling with increased demands for resource extraction from boreal regions (Senate Subcommittee on the Boreal Forest 1999), and the stage was set for lively debate on the future of these forests.

The past two decades bear witness to a gradual awakening both nationally and internationally to the significance of Canada's boreal

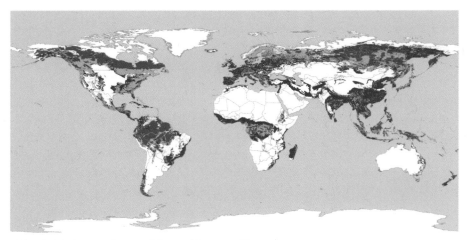

FIGURE 5.1. Frontier forests of the world, circa 1977.

systems. From relative obscurity, the region now occupies an increasingly prominent position in global discourse on biodiversity conservation, carbon sequestration, climate change, and the cumulative impacts of resource extraction on the intimate linkages between economic, ecological, and sociocultural systems.

A group of academic researchers based at institutions across the breadth of Canada, from the Yukon Territories to British Columbia, Alberta, Quebec, and Newfoundland, have contributed to bringing this discourse—and the science at its foundation—to global prominence. Collaborating through the Canadian BEACONs Project (Boreal Ecosystems Analysis for Conservation Networks), the group, which includes the authors of this chapter, has helped to bring its made-in-Canada approach to planners and policy makers now shaping the future of the nation's boreal regions.

Our objective here is to trace the evolution of conservation thinking that is shaping a number of large conservation initiatives in boreal Canada, and to explore the role that academic institutions have played in catalyzing these efforts. Our experience draws from applied research programs that preceded and now transcend much of the current conservation interest in the Canadian boreal (those of Cumming and Schmiegelow), as well as those efforts (on the part of Krawchuk, Lisgo, and Leroux) on the cusp of an increased profile in the region.

CANADA'S BOREAL REGIONS IN BRIEF

Despite the fact that Canada's boreal biome has attracted increased interest both nationally and internationally, it remains a mystery to many, including much of Canada's southern-concentrated population. Spanning the northern reaches of the country, its 552 million hectares (about 1,364 million acres) (Brandt 2009) cover significant portions of seven of the ten provinces and all three northern territories; in total, the boreal biome comprises almost 60 percent of the country (figure 5.2). Across this expanse, vegetation and conditions vary. Boreal regions include over 300 million hectares of forest and wooded lands, but grasslands dominate drier areas, and naturally treeless shrubland and alpine areas abound at the highest latitudes and altitudes. The most ubiquitous feature, however, is the abundant lakes, rivers, and wetlands that are the lifeblood of these northern landscapes and cover over 30 percent of their surface (Schindler and Lee 2010). It is thus a misnomer to refer to the boreal biome of Canada as simply "the boreal forest." The variability across its extent is represented

FIGURE 5.2. Canada contains nearly 30% of the world's boreal biome, with another 4% in the adjacent U.S. state of Alaska.

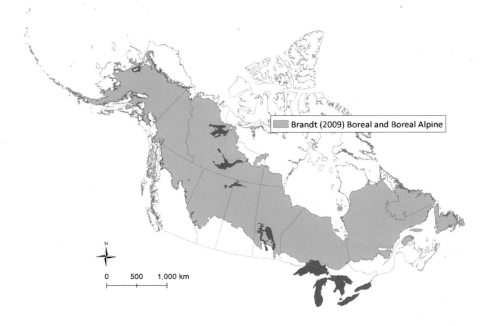

Brandt (2009) Boreal and Boreal Alpine

N

0   500   1,000 km

through various classification schemes. For simplicity, we will generally use the terms *boreal regions* or *boreal systems* to capture this diversity.

Recent analyses have highlighted a number of striking features of Canada's boreal regions. Globally, Canada contains the greatest amount of intact forest, most of it boreal, of any nation (Potapov et al. 2008). Boreal systems are vital for migratory birds, supporting the breeding grounds for more than one-third of North American landbird populations (Blancher 2003) as well as a significant proportion of the continental breeding grounds for migratory waterfowl and shorebirds. They also include some of the last strongholds for a number of North American mammal species that have experienced extensive range contractions throughout their southern distributions (Laliberte and Ripple 2004), and support the largest caribou (*Rangifer tarandus*) populations in the world. Globally, the boreal biome contains more than 60 percent of the world's fresh water (Schindler 2001), and the boreal regions of Canada alone contain 25 percent of the world's wetlands (Natural Resources Canada 2009). Global carbon storage in boreal systems is also greater than in any other biome on earth (Tarnocai et al. 2009), but these regions have been shown to be highly sensitive to climate change (Bergengren et al. 2011). Canada's boreal systems have already experienced significant increases in annual mean temperature (Price et al. 2013), contributing to loss of permafrost among other conspicuous changes.

Northern regions of Canada are not devoid of people, but human settlements are sparsely distributed. Although the boreal regions account for more than 60 percent of the country's landmass, only about 8 percent of the total population, or approximately 2.5 million people, reside in these northern systems. Notably, this number includes about one million First Nations and Métis people in more than 500 communities throughout boreal Canada. Ownership of the vast majority of lands (approximately 95 percent) is public and therefore subject to provincial, territorial, First Nations, or federal government authorities.

THE BACKDROP TO LARGE LANDSCAPE CONSERVATION IN BOREAL CANADA

A growing awareness of the significance of boreal systems and the opportunities they afford has led to a groundswell of interest in their conservation. As recently as the turn of the 21st century, over 70 percent of

Canada's boreal regions consisted of intact forest landscapes (Lee et al. 2003). Similar in concept to frontier forests, intact forest landscapes have been defined as expanses of natural ecosystems that show few conspicuous signs of human activity and are large enough to maintain native biodiversity indefinitely. In contrast to the disintegrating ecosystems in many other regions of the world, these areas are the hinterlands of modern imagination, seemingly secure in their remoteness. (Although this casual view belies the long history of indigenous presence and activities in these landscapes, it can also be interpreted as testimony to the relatively low impact of these activities at the regional scale.) Beneath this tranquil surface, however, advances in technology and expanding world markets were fueling resource interest in Canada's boreal systems, and the increasing national and international attention was in turn creating a demand for conservation planning in advance of widespread development.

In the fall of 2001, a gathering of environmental organizations, First Nations representatives, and a handful of scientists was convened near Thunder Bay, on the edge of the boreal forest of northern Ontario, to discuss the state of knowledge and action in boreal Canada. Precipitated by the Pew Environmental Group, whose interest in boreal Canada had been formalized in 2000, it effectively crystalized what to date had been largely fragmented efforts. This gathering marked the start of the first national initiative in Canada focused on boreal conservation. At that meeting, Fiona Schmiegelow (the lead author of this chapter) was asked to give an overview presentation on Canada's boreal systems and to highlight conservation concerns. At the time, our experience spanned a decade of research addressing various aspects of boreal ecology and management; a significant portion of that time had been spent working with a cross-Canada network of researchers that, along with government, industry, and First Nations partners, formed the Sustainable Forest Management Network (http://www.sfmn.ales.ualberta.ca/). After the talk, a participant remarked with some amusement and an edge of frustration that, while the presentation had highlighted unparalleled conservation opportunities, the only thing we were certain of was high uncertainty. While this latter point was not quite the intended message, there was some truth to this interpretation.

Broadly speaking, the state of scientific knowledge about Canada's boreal systems was woefully incomplete. Despite a surge of research initiated in the 1990s, basic species distribution data were lacking for many areas. Knowledge of system dynamics was limited, but there was recognition that these were inherently variable systems, still largely driven by natural processes, including large-scale natural disturbance. The understanding of responses to anthropogenic drivers of change was in its infancy; however, it was clear that the rate and scale of human-induced change was unprecedented. Anticipated shifts in climate contributed to additional uncertainty in the trajectories of these systems. Far from the data-rich and largely static approach that was guiding conservation planning in more stable and developed systems, it was clear that a different approach was required.

In 2002, the Canadian Boreal Initiative (CBI) was officially launched with a mandate to act as a national convener for conservation in Canada's boreal regions (http://www.borealcanada.ca/). CBI's approach was to work with conservation organizations, First Nations, industry, scientists and other interested parties to identify conservation solutions across the country's boreal systems. As part of the initiative's efforts, a Boreal Leadership Council (BLC) was convened, composed of leading conservation groups, aboriginal communities, resource-based companies, and financial institutions. In December 2003, the BLC released the Canadian Boreal Forest Conservation Framework, which expressed a shared vision for sustaining the ecological and cultural integrity of the Canadian boreal forest in perpetuity, thereby making it the world's best conserved forest ecosystem as well as one that, through the development of leading sustainable management practices, could support northern communities (http://www.borealcanada.ca/framework-e.php). The framework further spoke to a specific commitment to work toward this vision by: 1) establishing a network of large interconnected protected areas and conservation zones over at least half of Canada's boreal forest; and 2) using leading-edge sustainable development practices in remaining areas. This vision was ambitious. Interestingly, the most vocal opposition came from detractors who felt that the first item amounted to "giving away" 50 percent of the boreal.

Amid the launch of the CBI and before the release of the boreal conservation framework, we had been approached to help advance the foundation for conservation planning across the boreal regions. And so began our search for an appropriate scientific framework.

OF PARADIGMS AND POSSIBILITIES

Although there had been a surge of research in Canada's boreal systems over the preceding decade, most of it had been reactive, focused on assessment and mitigation of ongoing or planned development activities in areas where resource allocations had already occurred. The proactive side of the conservation equation remained largely unexplored. Our own research in boreal systems had taught us that adopting conventional scientific paradigms was often inappropriate (e.g., Cumming et al. 1996, Schmiegelow et al. 1997, Cumming et al. 2000, Schmiegelow and Mönkkönen 2002); the same was true of various policy constructs.

We began by revisiting the four objectives of regional conservation identified by Noss and Cooperider (1994). These objectives, stated below, seemed particularly appropriate for the regions we were investigating and came to serve as a guide for evaluating conservation targets, or the amount of a feature or proportion of a region devoted to conservation.

1) Represent, in a system of protected areas, all native ecosystem types and seral stages across their natural range of variation.
2) Maintain viable populations of all native species in natural patterns of abundance and distribution.
3) Maintain ecological and evolutionary processes, such as disturbance regimes, hydrological processes, nutrient cycles, and biotic interactions.
4) Design and manage the system to be resilient to short-term and long-term environmental change.

There are many approaches to establishing conservation targets, all of them subject to uncertainty. The choice of objectives, surrogates, representation criteria, planning units, and spatial extent of analyses will all influence the resultant target levels. However, despite variation in the literature at the time, it was clear that large areas accounting for a significant proportion of the boreal regions would need to be managed with biological conservation as a priority in order to achieve conservation goals. Estimates of individual reserve requirements for mammal assemblages ranged from approximately 5,000 sq km to more than 20,000 sq km (Gurd et al. 2001, Rodrigues and Gaston 2001), the largest of which was still insufficient to ensure maintenance of key processes if considered

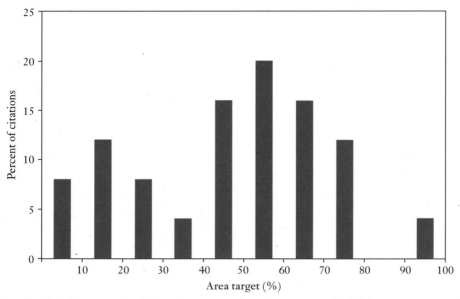

FIGURE 5.3. Frequency distribution of percentage-based area targets (N=24) from quantitative conservation assessments (after Schmiegelow et al. 2004; see Noss et al. 2012 for an updated assessment).

in isolation (Pringle 2001). The frequency distribution of percentage estimates from our literature review was bimodal (figure 5.3), with estimates in the lower range reflecting less ambitious goals, such as the representation of a single occurrence of an element within a region, and the upper range reflecting broader conservation goals. The median area fell above 50 percent, even though large-scale ecological processes and uncertainty had not been considered, except qualitatively in some cases.

As we pondered these results in the context of large landscape conservation in boreal Canada, an epiphany of sorts occurred that triggered a reframing of our perspective. The discipline of conservation science had emerged in response to crisis situations involving species loss and landscape degradation in human-altered systems. Its focus had largely been on the establishment of protected areas after significant conservation concerns had already arisen, and on the management of declining populations. As a result, the classic conservation model is one of patches of remnant natural vegetation embedded in a hostile landscape matrix. The majority of lands within the matrix are not considered to contribute significantly to conservation, and in many instances, protected areas bear the full burden

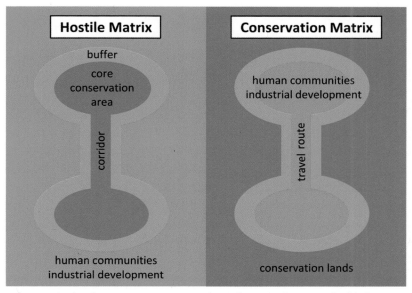

FIGURE 5.4. The classic conservation paradigm of protected areas embedded in a hostile matrix compared with an alternative perspective of a matrix comprised of conservation lands.

of achieving conservation goals. In contrast, in landscapes where the human footprint is light, the reverse is true: the matrix is composed of lands with high conservation value that still support abundant plant and animal life and natural functions, and development activities may be viewed as patches embedded in this supportive environment (figure 5.4).

Our interest was therefore not in managing scarcity but in maintaining integrity. Given this context, the question "how much is enough," or "what percentage of lands must be protected in order to achieve conservation goals," did not, in isolation, address the full range of conservation potential that could be realized in carefully managed systems, particularly those that remained largely intact and supported a high level of ecological integrity. In such systems, including Canada's boreal regions, where the vast majority of lands still maintain high conservation value, it is equally important to ask "how much is too much," or "how much development can be supported without diminishing natural and cultural values or compromising ecological integrity?"

Although our work began with a focus on protected areas, it quickly transitioned to thinking about whole-landscape strategies. To the extent that such a thing was possible, we were interested in a 100-percent conservation solution, and this approach involved planning proactively, not reactively.

A NEW APPROACH TO CONSERVATION PLANNING

We advanced a new approach to conservation planning, which we embodied in a framework we called the Conservation Matrix Model (CMM). This comprehensive strategy integrated the disciplines of conservation and resource management science, and the model acknowledged the valuable contribution that all landscape elements can and must make to achieving landscape sustainability. Our focus was on managing natural patterns of species distribution and abundance and the processes that support them, rather than on maintaining the minimum critical levels necessary to avoid extinction. Recognition of uncertainty and implementation of active adaptive management were central to the CMM, and the overall framework engendered a sense of shared stewardship and encouraged innovation in addressing conservation challenges.

The CMM represents a paradigm shift from reactive conservation planning in highly altered systems to proactive conservation planning in large intact systems. Landscapes are conceptualized as a continuum of conservation opportunities, where the matrix plays a critical role in supporting populations of species, regulating the movement of organisms, buffering sensitive areas and reserves, and maintaining the integrity of aquatic systems (Lindenmayer and Franklin 2002). A key objective of the CMM is to identify activities that are compatible with maintenance of ecological integrity and resilience across large landscapes. This requires a fully integrated approach to planning.

Our model shifts the focus from securing protected areas as the principal instrument for biodiversity conservation to maintaining ecological flows—the movements of organisms, water, and nutrients—across large landscapes. Conservation planning consistent with the CMM requires the identification of landscape elements that play four principal roles. *Ecological benchmarks* are the anchors of an interconnected conservation network and serve as reference sites or controls for understanding the natural dynamics of ecosystems and their response to human activities. They are biodiversity "insurance policies" and buffers to environmental stressors that can compromise ecological integrity. *Site-specific protected areas* capture values that may not be well represented in benchmark areas and may be particularly sensitive to development activities, such as areas of cultural significance, habitats or ecosystems of special scientific or conservation concern, identified special elements (e.g., rare species occurrences), and features that are key to maintaining connectivity across landscapes. *Adaptive management areas and active management sites* experience relatively intense human activity, such as that associated with human settlements, forestry, mining, hydroelectric developments, and the transportation infrastructure linking these activities. These activities are carefully designed, monitored, and evaluated within an adaptive management framework. The *conservation matrix* is the supportive environment within which less intense human activities are also carefully planned and managed in an integrated fashion, in order to avoid the erosion of other values.

Having established a broad conceptual framework to guide conservation-based land-use planning in Canada's boreal systems, we undertook a suite of analyses and developed customized tools to support its implementation. Our initial efforts focused on identifying criteria and candidates for system-level ecological benchmarks, as these were foundational to the framework and represented the most time-limited conservation opportunities, given pressures mounting for resource allocation and development across boreal Canada.

BOREAL CONSERVATION GAINING GROUND

In addition to providing a national vision for conservation in boreal regions of Canada, the launch of the Canadian Boreal Initiative and release of the Boreal Conservation Framework provided cohesiveness and momentum to regional initiatives across Canada. Some of these projects leveraged existing efforts, and others involved the establishment of new partnerships and programs. As part of their participation in the Boreal Leadership Council, each member organization committed to implementing the national vision in its own sphere of activity and developed action plans to facilitate this work. Many of these plans involved partnerships with governments and advanced the critical dialogue and engagement necessary to implement conservation in a lasting way. Common to all these initiatives was the simultaneous consideration of protection and sustainable economic development as key elements of a comprehensive conservation plan, as well as efforts to meaningfully in-clude First Nations and local communities in the planning process. It is paramount to recognize that more than 50 percent of Canada's intact forests occur within settled First Nations land claims, with additional amounts under negotiation, and that First Nations people are leading many of the conservation initiatives in northern boreal regions.

Much needed political capital accumulated both through these ini-tiatives and through several resolutions in support of boreal conserva-tion. In 2004, the International Union for Conservation of Nature (IUCN) passed a recommendation urging Canada and Russia, as pri-mary stewards of northern systems, to take active measures to preserve and protect the ecological processes that sustain these regions in ad-vance of extensive resource allocations (IUCN 2004). In 2007, more than 1,500 scientists from over 50 countries released a letter address-ing all Canadian governments—provincial, territorial, and federal—highlighting the significance of Canada's boreal regions, identifying growing threats to its integrity, and urging action by governments, in-cluding a substantial increase in the amount of formally protected land.

In 2009, the Ontario and Quebec provincial governments an-nounced commitments to protect 50 percent of the boreal systems within their jurisdictions, while identifying opportunities for sustainable development and community-based land-use planning (Ontario MNR 2009; Government of Quebec MNRW 2009). In 2010, Ontario passed the Far North Act, which provides a legislative mandate for this com-mitment (Government of Ontario 2010). Environmental organizations have also promoted improvements to forest management practices through Forest Stewardship Council (FSC) certification. As a result, more than 250,000 sq km of the boreal forest are now managed under FSC-endorsed practices (FSC 2010). In 2010, a far-reaching agreement was struck among 9 environmental organizations and 21 member compa-nies of the Forest Products Association of Canada (FPAC). The Canadian Boreal Forest Agreement, heralded as the world's largest conservation agreement, covers more than 720,000 sq km of the most productive bo-real forest in Canada and commits FPAC members to world-leading environmental standards of forest management and conservation, in-cluding the identification of ecological benchmarks and implementation of active adaptive management (CBFA 2010; http://www.canadianbore-alforestagreement.com/).

In 2012, the federal government released the report *Recovery Strategy for the Woodland Caribou* (Rangifer tarandus caribou), *Boreal Population, in Canada* (Environment Canada 2012). Based on extensive scientific research, the strategy identifies critical habitat across approximately 235,000 sq km of the current distribution of the species and establishes a management approach that applies disturbance thresholds at the scale of local population ranges. Specifically, at least 65 percent of each boreal caribou range must be maintained as undisturbed habitat.

In the first initiative to transcend international boundaries, the Northwest Boreal Landscape Conservation Cooperative (NWB LCC) includes nearly 1.4 million sq km of the boreal biome in south-central and interior Alaska, most of the Yukon Territory, the northern portion of British Columbia, and a small part of Northwest Territories (http://nwblcc.org/). The objective of the NWB LCC is to bring together conservation and resource managers to identify shared interests and pool resources to address landscape-scale stressors, with a vision of maintaining landscapes that sustain functioning, resilient boreal ecosystems and associated cultural resources in perpetuity.

Along with the advances highlighted in earlier sections of this chapter, these initiatives mark significant conservation milestones in boreal Canada and demonstrate substantial progress in advancing conservation planning and implementation consistent with the core principles of the CMM (figure 5.5).

THE ROLE OF UNIVERSITIES AS CONSERVATION CATALYSTS

The BEACONs Project began as a targeted research effort at the University of Alberta, with the engagement of one of us (Schmiegelow) as lead scientific advisor to the Canadian Boreal Initiative. This move provided us with the initial impetus to consider the issues and begin development of an appropriate scientific framework to support comprehensive conservation planning across this vast area. Our core team was modest, comprising primarily graduate students and research associates, with established and emerging expertise in various aspects of boreal ecology and conservation science. Since then, our scope has grown to include many other initiatives and diverse funding sources, and has expanded across institutions as our membership assumes new responsibilities. Our research interests now span the country, with bases in Yukon,

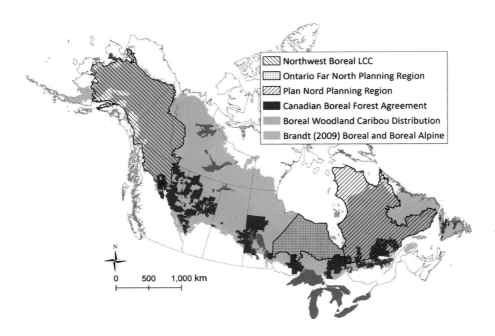

FIGURE 5.5. Landscape conservation initiatives in Canada's boreal regions.

British Columbia, Alberta, Quebec, and Newfoundland. Through our partnerships, we are active in every Canadian jurisdiction with management authority for boreal systems. However, our core team consists of largely the same individuals, and the main investment continues to be our time.

As a group, we spent countless hours assembling background information and databases. When we began, there were essentially no national syntheses of boreal ecology, particularly none that provided quantitative guidance. Similarly, there were few databases that readily permitted analyses at a national scale. Basic concepts necessary to advance a comprehensive and cohesive framework were either poorly developed or unsuitable for the challenge at hand, and so we tuned our minds to a different chorus. Available tools were either inappropriate or inadequate to tackle the spatial extent necessary to address many of the issues, so we designed new ones. Graduate students played a central role in these efforts, and their work crystalized key elements of our research (e.g., Leroux 2007a, 2007b, Anderson 2009).

Within the group, individual investment in outreach has been high. Presentations at a wide variety of nonacademic forums, participation on advisory committees, and direct engagement with partners have involved a substantial commitment of time. Nevertheless, these have been a necessary complement to our research in order to reach the audiences most instrumental to gaining support for conservation in the boreal regions. And these audiences are diverse—environmental organizations, resource companies and industry trade organizations, governments at many levels, First Nations, communities, large foundations, and international bodies. All play a role in affecting the future trajectories of boreal systems in Canada.

Our role has not been to champion a particular initiative but rather to enhance understanding through the provision of a robust and transparent scientific framework for shared learning, built on a foundation of concepts that support constructive dialogue among diverse interests. Our success can be measured by the uptake of our ideas, and the engagement of diverse interests in applying and advancing the framework.

The Canadian Boreal Initiative provided an incubation chamber for the conceptual foundations, and the Boreal Leadership Council acted as an early sounding board for applications of the approach. We refined this work through partnerships with governments on particular issues as well as through broader dialogue with other scientists and practitioners. The Ontario Far North Science Panel recognized the CMM as a principal mechanism for comprehensive conservation planning across northern Ontario. The Quebec government is conducting an evaluation of benchmark areas in support of Quebec's Plan Nord. Implicit in the Canadian Boreal Forest Agreement is recognition of the role of ecological benchmarks as well as a commitment to both their identification and the implementation of active adaptive management. Other jurisdictions and planning processes in boreal Canada are also discussing applications of the CMM, as is the international Northwest Boreal Landscape Conservation Cooperative.

Overall, our work has found a receptive and diverse audience not only among planners and researchers but also in popular print outlets such as the magazines *Bird Conservation* and *Canadian Silviculture*. The

BEACONs project was also recently showcased on the website of the Canadian Foundation for Innovation, a federal funding agency established to support the development of world-class research and technology for the benefit of the Canadian people.

KEY FACTORS IN THE SUCCESS OF THE BEACONS PROJECT TO DATE

We believe that five main factors have been pivotal to the success of the BEACONs Project as a conservation catalyst, although we recognize that the momentum for conservation in boreal Canada has resulted from the efforts of many individuals, organizations, and institutions.

1. Demonstration of a need for change: We described why conventional approaches were unlikely to realize the potential for system-level conservation across large landscapes and demonstrated the need for a new approach.
2. Illustration of an alternative approach: We developed a conceptual framework in which all players could see themselves and established a common currency for objective dialogue. Rather than perpetuating the view of protection as a cost to development, we framed comprehensive conservation as an integral component of sustainability. Recognition of uncertainty and the need for joint learning acted as great equalizers, and the message of shared stewardship resonated broadly.
3. Realization of operational concepts: We conducted analyses and developed tools to support science-based planning and implementation that was transparent and respectful of regional context. A flexible conceptual and analytical framework allowed for customization. There were no black boxes.
4. Persistent investment in partnerships: Understanding perspectives, appreciating constraints, and addressing needs helped us to communicate the relevance of the concepts and approach in a variety of circumstances and to a variety of audiences. We strove to be approachable, responsive, and willing to learn from these partnerships. Partnerships offered reciprocal benefits that improved our work.
5. The advantage of autonomy: The institutional autonomy of academics allows us to play a unique role. We are not beholden to

certain positions except, as scientists, to act as honest brokers of information. We do not have to confer with a caucus, or check with a director, or worry that our employment will be jeopardized by taking a position that conflicts with conventional wisdom.

BARRIERS TO SUCCESS

It must be noted, however, that we remain challenged by the very attributes of this area of study that inspired us to seek new approaches. The paucity of information remains acute in some areas, and the ecological, social, and economic variability across regions makes it difficult to extrapolate conclusions from data. Although the uncertainty inherent in our conclusions can be used to leverage considerable precaution, it can also be used to undermine confidence. Effectively communicating different forms of uncertainty to broad audiences is a daunting task, and we generally do it poorly even in scientific circles. Our institutions and policies are similarly ill equipped to deal with uncertainty and slow to adapt in the face of new knowledge.

These issues are compounded by a highly charged political environment in which rhetoric often reigns over reality. Despite encouraging movement in some jurisdictions, the past decade in Canada has seen a rise in anti-environmental sentiment at the federal level as well as in certain provinces and territories. The rhetorical strategies of many officials and legislators pit the environment against the economy, and—given the prolonged effects of the recession—this perspective has garnered considerable support among voters. Canada's global environmental record has suffered under the current Conservative government as key environmental laws have been dismantled, along with the agencies responsible for their implementation.

Regardless of political persuasion, it is also clear that old paradigms die hard. As so eloquently observed by Forrester (1995, 14), "Old mental models and decision habits are deeply ingrained; they do not change just because of a logical argument." Within the conservation community, longstanding ideas hold powerful sway over how conservation targets should be established and what should be prioritized for protection. Furthermore, as noted by Mackey et al. (2001, 168), ". . . [mapping] values has the potential to be counter-productive by encouraging adoption of reductionist planning and management regimes when the core message is the need for a holistic approach." Although maps are powerful tools, they may not lead to desired outcomes if they are based on incomplete information or too narrow a range of objectives.

An urgency and desire for certainty can pervade planning processes and undermine the careful consideration of alternative strategies and actions. Yet this consideration is a key step in decision analysis and fundamental to implementation of effective adaptive management. Sadly, the trust that is necessary in order to invest in extended deliberations is often absent.

On a more positive note, the demand for our work is great—so great it's a challenge to respond to every opportunity. In this respect, our success is also our downfall. The uptake of our ideas has been significant, but we lack the capacity to meaningfully engage in the many processes unfolding across Canada's boreal regions, and we have not kept step in making our work more directly accessible through various media. We are, however, working to rectify this situation. Delays in the publication of conservation research have repeatedly been lamented by academics and practitioners (Kareiva et al. 2002, O'Donnell et al. 2010), but no one has identified a strikingly obvious reality facing many conservation scientists—we are often so busy applying the work and participating in related processes that we don't have time to write about it.

OPPORTUNITIES GOING FORWARD

Our work has really just begun. Opportunities to refine concepts, improve analyses, and apply results are emerging across Canada's boreal regions. We will hasten progress by engaging and empowering a broader community through outreach and technology transfer. The time is now ripe for broader academic engagement in conservation planning in boreal Canada, and we are hopeful that colleagues will rise to this challenge. Many of these researchers have, of course, been involved in various initiatives, but we need a more consolidated intellectual effort if we are to realize the conservation potential that these systems still hold (e.g., Moen et al. 2014). Expanding the disciplinary focus of this work to include social scientists will help to overcome institutional inertia by addressing broader societal issues (Huntington et al. 2012).

First Nations are gaining a more prominent voice in land-use planning across Canada, resulting from increased recognition of aboriginal title and associated rights. This trend is particularly prevalent in northern regions of the boreal, where modern treaties confer substantial authority to local First Nations over resource management decisions. While we cannot presuppose the outcome of current and anticipated planning processes, a broader range of perspectives around the table is assured—including viewpoints based on a knowledge of these ecosystems that transcends the timeframe studied by conventional science. Incorporating such knowledge into planning presents challenges, but it also offers enormous opportunities to benefit from the experience and diversity of cultural adaptations that have shaped these socioecological systems for millennia.

The scientific knowledge base has been considerably enriched over the past decade, and a recent series of reviews led by federal scientists within Natural Resources Canada provides a synthesis of work conducted in Canada's boreal zone, covering ecosystem processes, health, sustainability, and various environmental issues (see Brandt et al. 2013 for an overview of these contributions). These reviews will help highlight the need and sharpen the focus of conservation planning in these systems.

KEY THREATS TO REALIZING LARGE SCALE CONSERVATION

To date, approximately 30 percent of boreal Canada has been allocated for development and falls under some form of industrial lease or concession (Cheng and Lee 2014). Notably, almost all these lands are public, and some remain under contention due to unsettled land claims by First Nations. By jurisdiction, the proportion of land under development varies enormously, from a low of under 4 percent in the Northwest Territories to a high of nearly 70 percent in Alberta. Historically, clearing for agriculture and hard-rock mining were the dominant land uses across boreal systems. However, forestry is currently the most widespread development activity, accounting for the greatest proportion of all industrial leases on average across provinces (there are no forestry leases in the Northern Territories) and exceeded in magnitude only in Alberta, where oil and gas concessions comprise the majority of land allocated. Many forestry tenures in the boreal are recent, but the rate of harvest is unprecedented. Globally significant oil and gas reserves underlie substantial portions of the western boreal forest, and major hydroelectric projects have altered hydrological regimes in both eastern and western regions.

Most development activities to date have been concentrated in southern portions of the boreal biome (figure 5.6); however, interest is increasing in the rich mineral deposits, oil and gas reserves, and untapped waterways of northern regions. The relatively stable political climate and increasingly favorable regulatory regime in Canada renders it attractive for foreign investment by multinationals. Debate over the extraction of bitumen from the Alberta oil sands and the construction of major new pipelines across northern Canada to link energy reserves to southern markets in the United States further underscore the international context of development pressures.

Preemptive land allocations are eroding the considerable opportunities for proactive conservation in boreal Canada. Certain areas are experiencing rapid change due to the cumulative effects of overlapping

FIGURE 5.6. Development circa 2010 in boreal regions of Canada (adapted by the authors from Cheng and Lee 2014). About 30% of the boreal lands have been allocated for development, although not all have been accessed to date.

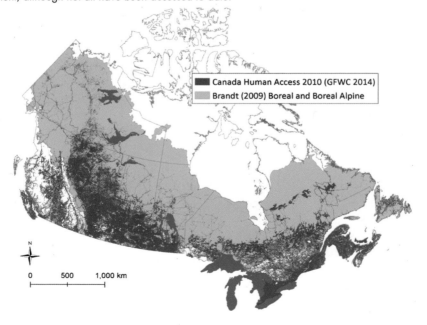

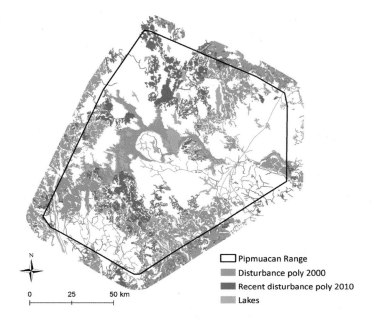

FIGURE 5.7. Satellite extraction of recent, human-caused changes on the Pipmuacan caribou range in central Quebec. Pink and red polygons and lines indicate alterations, which in total represent nearly 50% disturbance of this landscape for caribou.

industrial disturbances, and natural and cultural values have been compromised (figure 5.7).

MAINTAINING MOMENTUM AND ACHIEVING LASTING CONSERVATION

The boreal regions of Canada are now internationally recognized for the broad range of values they support, their conservation potential, and their vulnerability to social and environmental change (e.g., Bradshaw et al. 2009, Chapin et al. 2010, Moen et al. 2014). As of 2013, significant advances have been realized both in the amount of protected lands and in the amount of land under sustainable forest management. A number of jurisdictions have made key commitments to expand these accomplishments. Government leadership is necessary to achieve lasting conservation in boreal systems, but effective outcomes will depend on whether a broad range of interests remain actively engaged in shaping progress. Conservation initiatives in boreal Canada already have considerable momentum; the challenge is to maintain this momentum.

The involvement of universities in boreal conservation initiatives should grow in step with this progress. Conservation scientists, who help to bridge the gap between research and implementation (Arlettaz et al. 2010), are uniquely positioned to provide strong scientific leadership in stakeholder-driven planning processes (Rassweiler et al. 2014). University-based scientists also lend continuity to research programs that support the full cycle of adaptive management, from identifying key uncertainties to modeling management options, developing robust monitoring programs, assisting with interpretation of resultant data relative to initial hypotheses and objectives, and revisiting strategies. Scientists can increase awareness and enhance decision making at multiple levels of conservation planning and resource management by providing guidance to community-based monitoring programs and "citizen science" efforts (Danielsen et al. 2014). Academic institutions foster innovative thinking in students. These students are the next generation of environmentalists, resource managers, policy makers, scientists, and citizens; their experience while in college or university will, in part, shape how they view the world. Encouraging interdisciplinary studies, more direct exposure to current issues, and better problem-solving skills—particularly in the face of uncertainty—will enhance their ability to see the potential of what could be achieved in boreal Canada with vision and commitment, and to lead future endeavors in true sustainability.

An important driver of immediate outcomes will also be the continued evolution of relationships among the diverse interests that are currently leading a number of the large conservation initiatives in Canada. These relationships have the potential to be transformational given their levels of engagement, scope of activities, and cocreation of value and innovation (Austin and Seitanidi 2012), but they remain fragile and subject to significant scrutiny and skepticism from external parties. They are also being closely watched by others as a potential model to emulate. What we have personally observed is tremendous commitment to making these novel partnerships work and significant growth in the respect and trust necessary to collaborate toward shared goals, with science as a foundation for their deliberations. Regardless of near-term outcomes, they are forging important connections that will advance conservation over the long term.

ACKNOWLEDGMENTS

Many researchers across Canada have contributed to the advancement of knowledge that supports conservation of boreal systems. We count ourselves fortunate to be working at the interface of science, policy, and practice, at a unique time in the trajectory of these systems, and with many partners committed to charting a new course for conservation.

REFERENCES

Anderson, L. G. 2009. *Quantitative Methods for Identifying Ecological Benchmarks in Canada's Boreal Forest*. Master's thesis, University of Alberta, Edmonton.

Arlettaz, R., M. Schaub, J. Fournier, T. S. Reichlin, A. Sierro, J. E. M. Watson, and V. Braunisch. 2010. "From Publications to Public Actions: When Conservation Biologists Bridge the Gap Between Research and Implementation." *BioScience* 60:835–842.

Austin, J. E., and M. M. Seitanidi. 2012. "Collaborative Value Creation: A Review of Partnering Between Nonprofits and Businesses. Part 2: Partnership Processes and Outcomes." *Nonprofit and Voluntary Sector Quarterly* 41:929–968.

Bergengren, J. C., D. E. Waliser, and Y. L. Yung. 2011. "Ecological Sensitivity: A Biospheric View of Climate Change." *Climatic Change* 107:433–457.

Blancher, P. 2003. *Importance of Canada's Boreal Forest to Landbirds*. Port Rowan, Ontario: Bird Studies Canada. *www.borealcanada.ca/documents/blancher_report_FINAL.pdf*

Boreal Leadership Council. 2013. "Canadian Boreal Forest Conservation Framework." Ottawa, Ontario: Canadian Boreal Initiative. *www.borealcanada.ca/documents/FrameworkEnglish-December2013.pdf*

Bradshaw, C. J. A., I. G. Warkentin, and N. S. Sodhi. 2009. "Urgent Preservation of Boreal Carbon Stocks and Biodiversity." *Trends in Ecology and Evolution* 24:541–548.

Brandt, J. P. 2009. "The Extent of the North American Boreal Zone." *Environmental Reviews* 17 (1): 101–161.

Brandt, J. P., M. D. Flannigan, D. G. Maynard, I. D. Thompson, and W. J. A. Volney. 2013. "An Introduction to Canada's Boreal Zone: Ecosystem Processes, Health, Sustainability, and Environmental Issues." *Environmental Reviews* 21:207–226.

Bryant, D., D. Nielsen, and L. Tangley. 1997. *The Last Frontier Forests: Ecosystems and Economies on the Edge*. Washington, DC: World Resources Institute. *http://pdf.wri.org/lastfrontierforests.pdf*

Canadian Boreal Forest Agreement. 2010. "The Canadian Boreal Forest Agreement." Ottawa, Ontario: Canadian Boreal Forest Agreement. *http://canadianborealforest agreement.com/publications/CBFAAgreement_Full_NewLook.pdf*

Chapin, F. S. III, S. R. Carpenter, G. P. Kofinas, C. Folke, N. Abel, W. C. Clark, and F. J. Swanson. 2010. "Ecosystem Stewardship: Sustainability Strategies for a Rapidly Changing Planet." *Trends in Ecology and Evolution* 25:241–249.

Cheng, R., and P. Lee. 2014. *Canada's Industrial Concessions: A Spatial Analysis*. Edmonton, Alberta: Global Forest Watch Canada. *www.globalforestwatch.ca/pubs/2014 Releases/04Concessions/downloads.htm*

Cumming, S. G., P. J. Burton, and B. Klinkenberg. 1996. "Boreal Mixedwood Forests May Have No 'Representative' Areas: Some Implications for Reserve Design." *Ecography* 19:162–180.

Cumming, S. G., F. K. A. Schmiegelow, and P. J. Burton. 2000. "Gap Dynamics in Boreal Aspen Stands: Is the Forest Older Than We Think?" *Ecological Applications* 10 (3): 744–759.

Danielsen, F., K. Pirhofer-Walzl, T. P. Adrian, D. R. Kapijimpanga, N. D. Burgess, P. M. Jensen, R. Bonney, M. Funder, A. Landa, N. Levermann, and J. Madsen. 2014. "Linking Public Participation in Scientific Research to the Indicators and Needs of International Environmental Agreements." *Conservation Letters* 7:12–24.

Environment Canada. 2012. *Recovery Strategy for the Woodland Caribou* (Rangifer tarandus caribou), *Boreal population, in Canada*. Species at Risk Act Recovery Strategy Series. Ottawa: Environment Canada.

Forrester, J. 1995. "The Beginning of System Dynamics." *McKinsey Quarterly* 4:4–16.

Gurd, D. B., T. D. Nudds, and D. H. Rivard. 2001. "Conservation of Mammals in Eastern North American Wildlife Reserves: How Small Is Too Small?" *Conservation Biology* 15:1355–1363.

International Union for the Conservation of Nature (IUCN). 2004. "Recommendation 3.101: Advancing Boreal Forest Conservation." IUCN Third World Conservation Congress, Bangkok, Thailand; Gland, Switzerland: IUCN. *http://iucn.org/about /work/programmes/global_Policy/gpu_resources/gpu_res_recs/index.cfm*

Kareiva, P., M. Marvier, S. West, and J. Hornisher. 2002. "Slow-Moving Journals Hinder Conservation Efforts." *Nature* 420:15.

Laliberte, A. S., and W. J. Ripple. 2004. "Range Contractions of North American Carnivores and Ungulates." *BioScience* 54:123–138.

Lee, P., D. Aksenov, L. Laestadius, R. Nogueron, and W. Smith. 2003. *Canada's Large Intact Forest Landscapes*. Edmonton, Alberta: Global Forest Watch Canada.

Lee, P., M. Hanneman, D. Hackenbrook, and I. McIvor. 2011. *Mapping Disturbances and Restoration-Protection Opportunities for Woodland Caribou Within the James Bay Region of Northern Québec. Part 1*. Edmonton, Alberta: Global Forest Watch Canada.

Leroux, S. J., F. K. A. Schmiegelow, R. B. Lessard, and S. G. Cumming. 2007a. "Minimum Dynamic Reserves: A Conceptual Framework for Reserve Size." *Biological Conservation* 138:464–473.

Leroux, S. J., F. K. A. Schmiegelow, S. G. Cumming, R. B. Lessard, and J. Nagy. 2007b. "Accounting for System Dynamics in Reserve Design." *Ecological Applications* 17:1954–1966.

Lindenmayer, D. B., and J. F. Franklin. 2002. *Conserving Forest Biodiversity: A Comprehensive Multi-Scaled Approach.* Washington, DC: Island Press.

Mackey, B. G., H. Nix, and P. Hitchcock. 2001. *The Natural Heritage Significance of Cape York Peninsula.* Report commissioned by the Queensland Environmental Protection Agency, Queensland, Australia. Canberra, Australia: Anutech Pty Ltd.

Moen, J., L. Rist, K. Bishop, F. S. Chapin, D. Ellison, T. Kuuluvainen, H. Petersson, K. Puettmann, J. Rayner, I. G. Warkentin, and C. J. A. Bradshaw. 2014. "Eye on the Taiga: Removing Global Policy Impediments to Safeguard the Boreal Forest." *Conservation Letters.* doi:10.1111/conl.12098.

Noss, R. F., and A. Cooperrider. 1994. *Saving Nature's Legacy: Protecting and Restoring Biodiversity.* Washington, DC: Island Press.

Noss, R. F., A. P. Dobson, R. Baldwin, P. Beier, C. R. Davis, D. A. Dellasalla, J. Francis, H. Locke, K. Nowak, R. Lopez, C. Reining, S. C. Trombulak, and G. Tabor. 2012. "Bolder Thinking for Conservation." *Conservation Biology* 26:1–4.

O'Donnell, R. P., S. R. Supp, and S. M. Cobbold. 2010. "Hindrance of Conservation Biology by Delays in the Submission of Manuscripts." *Conservation Biology* 24:615–620.

Potapov, P., A. Yaroshenko, S. Turubanova, M. Dubinin, L. Laestadius, C. Thies, D. Aksenov, E. Egorov, Y. Yesipova, I. Glushkov, M. Karpachevskiy, A. Kostikova, A. Manisha, E. Tsybikova, and I. Zhuravleva. 2008. "Mapping the World's Intact Forest Landscapes by Remote Sensing." *Ecology and Society* 13 (2): 51.

Price, D. T., R. I. Alfaro, K. J. Brown, M. D. Flannigan, R. A. Fleming, E. H. Hogg, M. P. Girardin, T. Lakusta, M. Johnston, D. W. McKenney, J. H. Pedlar, T. Stratton, R. N. Sturrock, I. D. Thompson, J. A. Trofymow, and L. A. Venier. 2013. "Anticipating the Consequences of Climate Change for Canada's Boreal Forest Ecosystems." *Environmental Reviews* 21:322–365.

Pringle, C. M. 2001. "Hydrologic Connectivity and the Management of Biological Reserves: A Global Perspective." *Ecological Applications* 11:981–998.

Rassweiler, A., C. Costello, R. Hilborn, and D. A. Siegel. 2014. "Integrating Scientific Guidance into Marine Spatial Planning." *Proceedings of the Royal Society B: Biological Sciences* 281:1471–2954.

Rodrigues, A. S. L., and K. J. Gaston. 2001. "How Large Do Reserve Networks Need to Be?" *Ecology Letters* 4:602–609.

Schindler, D. W. 2001. "The Cumulative Effects of Climate Warming and Other Human Stresses in Canadian Freshwaters in the New Millennium." *Canadian Journal of Fisheries and Aquatic Sciences* 58:18–29.

Schindler, D. W., and P. Lee. 2010. "Comprehensive Conservation Planning to Protect Biodiversity and Ecosystem Services in Canadian Boreal Regions Under a Warming Climate and Increasing Exploitation." *Biological Conservation* 143:1571–1586.

Schmiegelow, F. K. A., S. G. Cumming, S. Harrison, S. Leroux, K. Lisgo, R. Noss, and B. Olsen. 2004. "Conservation Beyond Crisis Management: A Reverse-Matrix Model." Discussion paper for the Canadian BEACONs Project, Department of Renewable Resources, University of Alberta.

Schmiegelow, F. K. A., C. S. Machtans, and S. J. Hannon. 1997. "Are Boreal Birds Resilient to Fragmentation? An Experimental Study of Short-Term Community Responses." *Ecology* 78:1914–1932.

Schmiegelow, F. K. A., and M. Mönkkönen. 2002. "Habitat Loss and Fragmentation in Dynamic Landscapes: Avian Perspectives from the Boreal Forest." *Ecological Applications* 12:375–389.

Senate Subcommittee on the Boreal Forest. 1999. "Competing Realities: The Boreal Forest at Risk. Report of the Senate Subcommittee on the Boreal Forest of the Standing Senate Committee on Agriculture and Forestry." Ottawa, Ontario: Parliament of Canada. *www.parl.gc.ca/36/1/parlbus/commbus/senate/Com-e/bore-e/rep-e/rep09jun99-e.htm*

Tarnocai, C., J. G. Canadell, E. A. G. Schuur, P. Kuhry, G. Mazhitova, S. Zimov. 2009. "Soil Organic Carbon Pools in the Northern Circumpolar Permafrost Region." *Global Biogeochemical Cycles* 23, GB2023. doi:10.1029/2008GB003327.

6

Working Landscapes and the Western Hemisphere Jaguar Network

Joe Figel

For the past ten years, I have studied jaguars (*Panthera onca*) on private lands and in national parks, community protected areas (PAs), small-scale agroforests, and now oil palm plantations, and this work has slowly shaped my outlook on large-landscape conservation. During my initial stints in Brazil and Bolivia, I bought in to the traditional paradigm of large carnivore conservation: seek out a large, wild area devoid of people and set up camp. The philosophy of the three Cs—cores, corridors, and carnivores (Soulé and Noss 1998)—was my guiding strategy.

From the outset, identifying cores (large protected areas) and carnivores (jaguars) seemed simple enough. But identifying a corridor (travel pathway between cores) was less straightforward. Jaguars inhabit a broad range of habitat types, but the extent to which oil palm plantations could serve as corridors for jaguars remains unknown, and small sample sizes from radiotelemetry studies have limited utility in revealing potential corridor routes. Fortunately, jaguars are unique among large carnivores in that their habitat is still relatively intact and connectible, enabling the implementation of a creative range-wide conservation initiative known as the jaguar corridor (JC).

Extending from the oak woodlands in northern Mexico to the thorn forests some 8,500 km south in northern Argentina, the JC is one of the largest working models for wildlife conservation in the world. Functioning as a conduit for dispersal and gene flow in landscapes with varying degrees of anthropogenic disturbance, the JC encompasses some 90 jaguar populations across the species' entire distribution, connected by 182 potential corridors varying from 3 km to 1,607 km in length (Rabinowitz and Zeller 2010). Although range-wide landscape permeability is still relatively high, key linkages in the JC are in danger of being permanently severed, in part by oil palm plantations and the expansive infrastructure accompanying them.

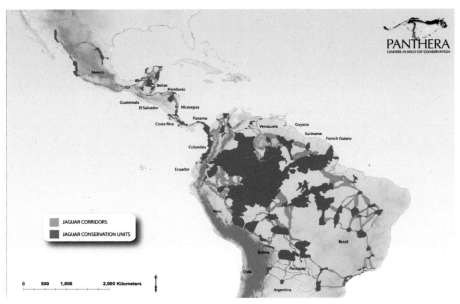

FIGURE 6.1. The jaguar corridor (JC). Field sites are circled.

Two such linkages occur in the Magdalena Medio region of Colombia and the north coast of Honduras, two of my study areas with the highest conservation significance anywhere within the JC (figure 6.1) (Rabinowitz and Zeller 2010). Rapid, ongoing conversion of natural habitat to oil palm plantations is occurring at both sites. At first glance, the plantations appeared to present a puzzling conservation dichotomy: repetitive monocropped rows of nonnative palm shaded by varying levels of cover depending on the age of the plantation. While cover aids a stalking predator (Sunarto et al. 2012), there is less to stalk in transformed, uniform plots isolated from natural habitats. Higher levels of human disturbance (figure 6.2) and homogeneous habitats with fewer seeds, fruits, shrubs, and herbs for foraging prey animals mean less to eat for jaguars.

LASTING IMPACTS OF OIL PALM PLANTATIONS ON THE LANDSCAPE

In contrast to crops such as coffee and cacao, which are generally grown in small patches beneath a forested canopy, most oil palm plantations are monocultures spanning upwards of 1,000 hectares (ha) in areas where

FIGURE 6.2. Photographed by a remote camera, workers move through a plantation accompanied by hunting dogs, in search of the same species preyed upon by jaguars.

FIGURE 6.3. Oil Palm Plantation in Honduras.

tropical forest once stood (figure 6.3). Furthermore, the most desirable locations for oil palm planting are precisely those areas containing the most productive jaguar habitat. Plantation developers target areas that can support some of the highest jaguar densities: well-drained coastal lands and inland alluvial floodplains (Trafton and Washburn 1968, Corley and Tinker 2003). Vast expanses of oil palm monoculture could permanently sever key linkages, although the effects of the plantations on large mammals have not been previously evaluated in Latin America. Faced with rapid plantation development, researchers are racing to collect the requisite data on jaguars in oil palm landscapes, so appropriate land use planning and zoning measures can be implemented.

As the most widely produced vegetable oil in the world (Corley and Tinker 2003), oil palm accounts for almost 10 percent of the world's permanent cropland (Sheil et al. 2009). Nearly 90 percent of all current palm oil production occurs in Indonesia and Malaysia (Danielsen et al. 2008), but neotropical oil palm cultivation is projected to increase exponentially (Butler and Laurance 2008). The biologically depauperate monocultures are invading the lowland neotropics from southeastern Mexico to southern Brazil. Among jaguar range countries, total oil palm plantation area is currently greatest in Ecuador (2,050 sq km), Colombia (1,665 sq km), Honduras (1,170 sq km), and Brazil (1,131 sq km) (FAO 2012).

Because its northern border represents a critical connection between Central and South America, Colombia is one of the most important countries for the long-term viability of the JC. If linkages in Colombia were to be severed, it would effectively cut off gene flow between two continents. The Honduras corridor, another crucial connection, is part of the linkage between two of the most important jaguar conservation units (JCUs) in Central America: the Maya Forest and Río Plátano (Sanderson et al. 2002). The JC in Honduras is increasingly threatened by oil palm and infrastructural development around the industrial port city San Pedro Sula.

Study sites in Honduras and Colombia have contrasting land use histories, an important consideration for large landscape conservation planning (Noss and Daly 2006). Jaguars in Honduras will likely be more dependent on active restoration because the spatial and temporal extent of habitat conversion—and its concomitant impact on fauna—is much greater. More than 80 years ago, American botanist Paul Standley wrote that the fauna of the Lancetilla Valley in northern Honduras included "probably an occasional jaguar" (Standley 1931, 20). Conversely, early explorers in the Magdalena floodplains of Colombia reported that the woods "abounded" with "plentiful" jaguars (Millican 1891, 64, 72).

Honduran Oil Palm Legacy

Oil palm was first introduced to Honduras by the United Fruit Company in 1926 (Trafton and Washburn 1968) and was subsequently cultivated mostly by smallholders; large monocultures were reportedly not in operation until 1971 (Gómez 2010). By 2010, Honduras had 1,250 sq km cultivated with oil palm (Gómez 2010). Most oil palm in Honduras has been planted on degraded lands formerly supporting banana plantations (Soluri 2005), but increasingly palm plantations are encroaching upon forested lands, including the protected areas (PAs) of Jeanette Kawas National Park (782 sq km) and Cuero y Salado Wildlife Refuge (132 sq km). In 2011, survey teams registered five jaguars in Jeanette Kawas (ICF 2011); it is one of the most threatened jaguar populations in Honduras (F. Castañeda, pers. comm.).

There is a long history of extensive deforestation along the coastal plain of Honduras. Beginning in the early 20th century, fruit companies introduced vast operations, planting on previously undeveloped lands and establishing plantations "carved out of jungle and swamp" (United Fruit Company 1949, 19). Advertisements printed by the United Fruit Company in the *New York Herald Tribune* on August 6, 1956, read:

> A wasteland of trees, creeping vines and stagnant lagoons, unchanged for centuries. That was yesterday. Today by the miracle of modern machinery and trained, willing hands, the jungle is a fertile farm, producing in abundance crops needed by the Americas.

This widespread conversion to agriculture is significant not only in terms of habitat loss but because the expansion of plantations can modify seed deposition in the soil and alter the process of secondary succession, as researchers in other tropical agricultural landscapes have described (e.g., Quintana-Ascencio et al. 1996). Paul Standley observed the destruction of the north Honduras coast in the wake of the banana barons. Standley (1931, 12) wrote of the Lancetilla region, "Practically all the land within this area . . . is covered with banana plants . . . which become exceedingly monotonous when massed in plantations many

FIGURE 6.4. Female jaguar photographed in a banana plantation.

miles in extent." Furthermore, the conversion from banana plantations to oil palm is significantly worse for jaguars because the former are usually much smaller and can provide more cover (Figel 2011) (figure 6.4). Oil palm development has left the jaguars of the Honduran north coast with refuge only in areas unsuitable for agriculture; the lands that are now Jeanette Kawas National Park and Cuero y Salado Wildlife Refuge were too swampy for drainage and the coastal mountain range too rugged for mechanized crop production.

Colombian Oil Palm Legacy

In Colombia, most oil palm plantations have been established only within the last few decades, and the majority have replaced former pasturelands. Plantations at my study sites in Colombia have existed for only a fraction of the time that those in Honduras have been in operation. Colombia, however, has the second largest land area under palm cultivation in jaguar range (FAO 2010) and has ambitious plans for industry, targeting a sixfold increase in palm oil production by 2020 (Rincón et al. 2012). Currently 360,500 ha of land are planted with oil palm, but 730,000 ha would be required to meet the 2020 goal (Garcia-Ulloa et al. 2012). There is significant overlap between areas targeted for palm oil expansion and the most critical JC sites in Colombia.

The plantations have homogenized vast landscapes in the flood-plains and lowland valleys in Honduras and Colombia, creating impoverished habitats not unlike those observed in North America by the naturalist Joel A. Allen (1876, 794) well over a century ago:

> While the progress the century has wrought in respect to the development of the resources of our country is justly receiving so much attention, it may not be unfitting to notice briefly other attendant changes that are far less obvious, though no less real, than the transformation of hundreds of thousands of square miles of wilderness into "fruited fields," dotted with towns and cities, and intersected by a network of railways and telegraph lines. With the removal of a vast area of forest that has rendered possible the existence of millions of people where only a few thousand rude savages lived before, there has taken place a revolution in respect to the native animals and plants of this great region as great as has occurred in respect to the general aspect of the country. Not only has indigenous vegetation given place largely to introduced species, but the larger native animals have been in like manner supplanted by exotic ones. While these changes do not pass unnoticed by the naturalist, they are less apparent to the general observer.

Due to the ecological characteristics of the oil palm, plantations are dependent on expansive infrastructural networks, thereby escalating their environmental impact as "fruited fields" in the landscape. Palm fruit spoils within 48 hours of harvest, so it must be quickly transported to a processing mill (Clay 2004).

To date, most biodiversity studies in oil palm plantations have been conducted on invertebrates, many of which use oil palm as primary habitat and do not require additional habitat to survive (Mayfield 2005). Vertebrates, on the other hand, are more prone to endangerment from plantations. For example, Glor et al. (2001) found oil palm plantations provided suitable habitat for fewer than 40 percent of lizards in the

Dominican Republic. A meta-analysis conducted by Danielsen et al. (2008) found that of studies targeting species in both forests and plantations, only 23 percent of the vertebrate species recorded in forests were also present in plantations. However, none of the studies examined by Danielsen et al. (2008) were from jaguar-range countries. To the best of my knowledge, my study is the first to systematically estimate occurrence of mammalian species in neotropical oil palm plantations, which I will accomplish through occupancy modeling.

THE ROLE FOR OCCUPANCY MODELING IN JAGUAR CONSERVATION

Although it has only recently been applied to camera-trap data, occupancy modeling has shown promise for monitoring rare species occurring at vast spatial scales (e.g., Zeller et al. 2011). To estimate occurrence and habitat use of jaguars and their prey, I am conducting presence/absence (detection/nondetection) camera-trap surveys in 25 plantations ranging in size from 80 to 2,100 hectares (ha) ($\overline{X}=600$ ha ± 530 SD). The plantations are my sampling units.

The oil palm plantations are divided into a continuous distribution of age classes; each plantation age class (e.g. clear-cut, mature) offers unique habitat types for the jaguar prey base. During the clear-cut phase, monocultures are vast expanses of open degraded land with little cover or floral diversity. At the intermediate stage, the palms are growing and left in a fallow state in which the abundant rainfall and alluvial soils can support higher floral diversity beneath the palms. During the mature stage, the oil palm fruit is harvested and the understory is cleared, eliminating cover and additional food sources for prey species such as collared peccaries (*Pecari tajacu*) (figure 6.5) and brocket deer (*Mazama americana*). Capable of attaining the largest biomass density—over 370 kg/km^2—among terrestrial neotropical mammals (Eisenberg 1980), peccaries are an especially important prey item for jaguars (Aranda 1994). Peccaries feed on the fruits from 46 palm species, including oil palm, and palm seeds can account for more than 60 percent of their diet (Beck 2006).

Occupancy modeling is based on the premise that changes in the proportion of area (POA) occupied by a species may be correlated with changes in its population size (MacKenzie et al. 2002). The occupancy method uses presence/absence (detection/nondetection) data to estimate

FIGURE 6.5. Collared peccaries—seen here feeding on oil palm fruit inside a plantation—are an important prey item for jaguars.

the probability of occurrence by incorporating an additional parameter of detection probability (MacKenzie et al. 2006). Since it is often not possible to monitor absolute abundance and/or vital rates across large spatial scales, occupancy can be a better option than measuring absolute abundance or population size (Linkie et al. 2007). It is also replicable and takes into account that jaguars may go undetected in a survey of a sampling unit even when they are actually present within that unit. Since monitoring is unlikely to perfectly detect rare and elusive species such as jaguars (i.e., the probability is 1.0), occupancy estimates will be biased unless detection probability is explicitly considered. MacKenzie et al. (2006) proposed that through repeated surveying of the sites, the detection probability of the target species can be estimated, which then enables unbiased estimation of POA. Inference about detection probability is required to draw inference on unsurveyed sites.

The occupancy approach is particularly useful for drawing inferences about habitat use at the landscape scale as well as for monitoring changes in occurrence over time. Although camera-trap rates may not reflect the true absolute abundance of animals, standardized monitoring of long-term trends will be useful for detecting changes in patterns of population size and structure during the development of the oil palm industry.

To further analyze jaguar occupancy and as a complement to camera-trap data, I am carrying out semistructured interviews in communities. Through snowball sampling, I have identified reliable reports of people who have experienced interactions involving jaguars and established a history of sightings. I have recorded the type of interaction (sighting, depredation, vocalization), date, place, and time. I have classified interviewee responses into four subcategorical variables after Zeller et al. (2011): undetected (not seen), rare (observed once/year), moderate/sometimes (seen twice per year to once per month), and frequent (observed more than once per month).

The objectives of my study are threefold: 1) to evaluate how occupancy rates vary across plantations of different size and age classes; 2) to assess differences in habitat use by prey species inside compared to outside plantations among native vegetation, oil palm monoculture, and riparian forest; and 3) to determine the correlation between jaguar occurrence, prey occurrence, and distance to the nearest PA.

FUTURE DIRECTIONS AND CONSERVATION IMPACTS

Although oil palm plantations will never be wildlife sanctuaries, much can be learned about their contribution to conservation at the landscape scale. Landscape-level conservation is not black and white; there is no binary system of whether a certain land use type represents a corridor. Rather, each plantation has the potential to make varying contributions to connectivity, depending on factors such as size, geographic location, and management system.

In 2010, Brazilian president Luiz Inácio Lula da Silva announced Presidential Declaration No. 7172 (2010), promoting sustainable palm oil production in Brazil. A key conservation measure of the 2010 declaration is a proposed bill forbidding the cultivation of palm oil in any area with native vegetation, including the Amazon region. That same year, 4.3 million hectares of previously deforested lands were converted to oil palm plantations in the northern state of Pará (Osava 2010). Unfortunately, enforcement and incentive programs have not yet been passed, severely limiting the effectiveness of the initiative toward preventing further deforestation.

Ultimately, I expect my project to result in the identification of best practices for oil palm growers that can be implemented by managers without sacrificing gains in production. If, as predicted, jaguar occupancy is higher near forest and freshwater, then riparian buffers could be enforced with minimal offsets on palm oil production. Likewise, Quigley and Crawshaw (1992) called for the protection of riverine forests to serve as corridors for interrefuge movement of jaguars in the Brazilian Pantanal.

Preliminary results from my fieldwork highlight the importance of retaining forested patches in and around plantations. After sampling with camera traps for 4,400 nights, I have not yet detected jaguars in oil palm monoculture; instead, all records of the seven jaguars I have photographed thus far are from native habitats on the plantation/forest border or in riparian forest within plantations, both of which need protection if jaguars are to persist in landscapes dominated by plantations. The extent to which current policies are enforced—unlike the aforementioned declaration in Brazil—will hold tremendous influence in determining the fate of jaguars in oil palm landscapes.

As my focus has transitioned from traditional methods to more creative approaches, I see my research contributing to landscape-level conservation on two main fronts: one, by providing vital insights into jaguar conservation strategies outside PAs on communal and private lands, which is where most jaguars likely occur; and, two, by educating and involving cooperative, conservation-minded private landowners as allies toward achieving conservation goals.

After all, the fight to save jaguars will be won not in PAs, which are of disproportionate importance as keystone sites, but in the human landscape beyond. Thus, any conservation approach on such a scale as the range-wide JC must face agricultural expansion head on. Commercial citrus, pineapple, and oil palm plantations and smallholder agroforests are here to stay; the challenge is to figure out how to make such lands conducive to jaguar passage. It may take only one migrant jaguar—and not more than 10 individuals—per local population per generation to obtain an adequate level of gene flow for maintaining genetic diversity (Mills and Allendorf 1996). Ten years from now, my research will have contributed to a template guiding the continued coexistence of jaguars and agriculture by identifying the habitat characteristics that support jaguar presence in oil palm landscapes.

REFERENCES

Allen, J. A. 1876. "The Extirpation of the Large Indigenous Mammals of the United States." *Penn Monthly* 7:794–806.

Aranda, M. 1994. "Importancia de los Pecaries (*Tayassu* spp.) en la Alimentación del Jaguar." *Acta Zoológica Mexicana* 62:11–22.

Beck, H. 2006. "A Review of Peccary–Palm Interactions and Their Ecological Ramifications Across the Neotropics." *Journal of Mammalogy* 87:519–530.

Clay, J. 2004. *World Agriculture and the Environment: A Commodity-by-Commodity Guide to Impacts and Practices*. Washington, DC: Island Press.

Corley, R. H. V., and P. B. Tinker. 2003. *The Oil Palm*. 4th ed. Oxford, U.K.: Blackwell Science.

Danielsen, F., H. Beukema, N. D. Burgess, F. Parish, C. A. Bruhl, P. F. Donald, D. Murdiyarso, B. Phalan, L. Reijnders, M. Struebig, and E. B. Fitzherbert. 2008. "Biofuel Plantations on Forested Lands: Double Jeopardy for Biodiversity and Climate." *Conservation Biology* 23:348–358.

Eisenberg, J. F. 1980. "The Density and Biomass of Tropical Mammals." In *Conservation Biology: An Evolutionary-Ecological Perspective*, ed. M. E. Soule and B. A. Wilcox, 35–55. Sunderland, MA: Sinauer Associates.

FAO. 2012. "FAOSTAT." Online statistical service. Rome, Italy: Statistics Division, Food and Agriculture Organization of the United Nations (FAO). *http://faostat.fao.org/*

Figel, J. J. 2011. "Oil Palm and *Tigres*." *Wild Felid Monitor* 4 (1): 17.

Garcia-Ulloa, J., S. Sloan, P. Pacheco, J. Ghazoul, and L. P. Koh. 2012. "Lowering Environmental Costs of Oil-Palm Expansion in Colombia." *Conservation Letters* 5:366–375.

Glor, R. E., A. S. Flecker, M. F. Benard, and A. G. Power. 2001. "Lizard Diversity and Agricultural Disturbance in a Caribbean Forest Landscape." *Biodiversity and Conservation* 10:711–723.

Gómez, A. 2010. *Honduras: Biofuels Annual*. Washington, DC: Foreign Agricultural Service, U.S. Department of Agriculture.

ICF. 2011. "Plan Nacional para la Conservación del Jaguar (*Panthera onca*)." Tegucigalpa, Honduras: Departamento de Vida Silvestre, Instituto Nacional de Conservación y Desarrollo Forestal, Áreas Protegidas y Vida Silvestre; Proyecto Ecosistemas; Fundación Panthera.

Linkie, M., Y. Dinata, A. Nugroho, and I. A. Haidir. 2007. "Estimating Occupancy of a Data Deficient Mammalian Species Living in Tropical Rainforests: Sun Bears in the Kerinci Seblat Region, Sumatra." *Biological Conservation* 137:20–27.

MacKenzie, D. I., J. D. Nichols, G. B. Lachman, S. Droege, J. A. Royle, and C. A. Langtimm. 2002. "Estimating Site Occupancy Rates When Detection Probabilities Are Less Than One." *Ecology* 83:2248–2255.

MacKenzie, D. I., J. D. Nichols, J. A. Royle, K. H. Pollock, L. L. Bailey, and J. E. Hines. 2006. *Occupancy Estimation and Modeling: Inferring Patterns and Dynamics of Species Occurrence.* Burlington, MA: Academic Press.

Mayfield, M. M. 2005. "The Importance of Nearby Forest to Known and Potential Pollinators of Oil Palm in Southern Costa Rica." *Economic Botany* 59:190–196.

Millican, A. 1891. *Travels and Adventures of an Orchid Hunter: An Account of Canoe and Camp Life in Columbia, While Collecting Orchids in the Northern Andes.* London, U.K.: Cassell and Company.

Mills, L. S., and F. W. Allendorf. 1996. "The One-Migrant-Per-Generation Rule in Conservation and Management." *Conservation Biology* 10:1509–1518.

Noss, R. F., and K. M. Daly. 2006. "Incorporating Connectivity into Broad-Scale Conservation Planning." In *Connectivity Conservation*, ed. K. R. Crooks and M. Sanjayan, 587–620. Cambridge, U.K.: Cambridge University Press.

Osava, M. 2010. "Brazil: Oil Palm Plantations Expand on Degraded Lands in Amazon." Inter Press Service News Agency. *www.ipsnews.net/2010/12/brazil-oil-palm-plantations-expand-on-degraded-land-in-amazon/*

Quigley, H. B., and P. G. Crawshaw Jr. 1992. "A Conservation Plan for the Jaguar *Panthera onca* in the Pantanal Region of Brazil." *Biological Conservation* 61:149–157.

Quintana-Ascencio, P. F., M. González Espinosa, N. Ramírez Marcial, G. Domínguez-Vázquez, and M. Martínez-Icó. 1996. "Soil Seed Banks and Regeneration of Tropical Rain Forest from Milpa Fields at the Selva Lacandona, Chiapas, Mexico." *Biotropica* 28:192–209.

Rabinowitz, A., and K. Zeller. 2010. "A Range-Wide Model of Landscape Connectivity and Conservation for the Jaguar, *Panthera onca.*" *Biological Conservation* 143:939–945.

Rincón, L., A. Cuesta, and E. Felix. 2012. "Calculo del Cambio en Emisiones Generadas Asociadas a la Expansión de Cultivos de Palma Aceitera en Colombia." Rome, Italy: Food and Agriculture Organization of the United Nations. *www.fao.org/fileadmin/templates/ex_act/pdf/ex-act_applications/Report-biofuel-colombia.pdf*

Sanderson, E. W., K. H. Redford, C. B. Chetkiewicz, R. A. Medellin, A. R. Rabinowitz, J. G. Robinson, and A. B. Taber. 2002. "Planning to Save a Species: The Jaguar as a Model." *Conservation Biology* 16:58–72.

Sheil, D., A. Casson, E. Meijaard, M. van Noordwijk, J. Gaskell, J. Sunderland-Groves, K. Wertz, and M. Kanninen. 2009. *The Impacts and Opportunities of Oil Palm in Southeast Asia: What Do We Know and What Do We Need to Know?* Bogor, Indonesia: Center for International Forestry Research.

Soluri, J. 2005. *Banana Cultures: Agriculture, Consumption, and Environmental Change in Honduras and the United States.* Austin: University of Texas Press.

Soulé, M., and R. Noss. 1998. "Complementary Goals for Continental Conservation." *Wild Earth* 22:1–11.

Standley, P. 1931. *Flora of the Lancetilla Valley, Honduras*. Botanical Series, volume 10, publication 283. Chicago, IL: Field Museum of Natural History.

Sunarto, S., M. J. Kelly, K. Parakkasi, S. Klenzendorf, E. Septayuda, and H. Kurniawan. 2012. "Tigers Need Cover: Multi-Scale Occupancy Study of the Big Cat in Sumatran Forest and Plantation Landscapes." *PLOS ONE* 7 (1): e30859. doi: 10.1371/journal.pone.0030859.

Trafton, M., and R. A. Washburn. 1968. *The African Oil Palm in Honduras*. New Orleans, LA: United Fruit Company.

United Fruit Company. 1949. Annual Report. New Orleans, LA: United Fruit Company.

Zeller, K., S. Nijhawan, R. Salom-Pérez, S. Potosme, and J. Hines. 2011. "Integrating Occupancy Modeling and Interview Data for Corridor Identification: A Case Study for Jaguars in Nicaragua." *Biological Conservation* 144:892–901.

PART

III

Sustainable Development and Land Conservation

FOR LARGE landscape conservation initiatives to take hold and endure, they must be sustainable in multiple senses of the word. As these four case studies illustrate, coordinated regional action can draw its strength, stability, traction, and inspiration from the meaningful engagement of local stakeholders and local knowledge.

Fortunately, colleges, universities, and research institutions that are well grounded in their local communities can earn a level of trust that allows their staff, faculty, and students to catalyze such meaningful engagement. It is often within the power of active local communities to determine the viability of a given large landscape initiative. They are likely to do so, in part, by ensuring that their own livelihoods and quality of life are sustained alongside measures of ecosystem services, which may be analytically conceived.

In his inspired essay, Doug Givens describes how patient engagement with local farmers and community leaders has been key to the success of the Philander Chase Corporation, a land trust affiliated with Kenyon College, which has made great strides in protecting the largely agrarian landscape around Gambier, Ohio. The college, which has been based in the area since the early 1800s, continues to work with its civic partners to maintain a distinctively bucolic quality of life. Taking a further step, motivated by the success of these efforts, leaders at Kenyon are presently moving ahead with plans to help replicate its program by sharing what they have learned about the value of local engagement and land conservation with colleges across the country.

Mary Tyrrell and her co-authors articulate in the chapter that follows how the Yale School of Forestry and Environmental Studies has recently embarked on an ambitious effort to conserve the forested landscape of northeastern Connecticut—dubbed the Quiet Corner—by engaging private landowners in stewardship and conservation actions. By joining a Woodland Partnership, these landowners become part of a long-term research and management project aimed at maintaining ecosystem health and connectivity and contributing to the viability of rural communities through participation in ecosystem services markets, renewable energy projects, and sustainable agriculture.

At a considerably larger scale, Rob Lilieholm and his associates at the University of Maine have engaged community stakeholders across the 2.5-million-acre (one-million-hectare) Lower Penobscot River Watershed (LPRW) in an alternative futures modeling effort. Designed to devise on-the-ground solutions to complex sustainability challenges, the computer modeling methodology helps to map out areas of future conflict—by, for example, identifying subwatershed locations where future development may degrade water quality and transgress regulatory thresholds for urban-impaired streams, a problem that would result in significant mitigation and compliance costs for municipalities. With areas of potential conflict identified, the team is working to educate local land use and zoning authorities to direct development in more suitable locations and simultaneously protect more sensitive acreage, ultimately fostering greater collaboration and improved land use across the LPRW. Notably, a group of U.S. and international students who reviewed and evaluated the futures modeling effort at the 2013 Acadian Program in Regional Conservation and Stewardship presented recommendations urging that a new conservation and development vision be created for the Penobscot River watershed. Accordingly, in 2014, the Bay-to-Baxter Initiative is being crafted at the University of Maine as a multipronged effort to promote conservation and economic development in the region.

To conclude this section, Robin Reid, Dickson Kaelo, David Nkedianye, and their co-authors emphasize that the conservation of wildlife in many large savanna landscapes in Africa depends on simultaneously meeting the needs of large wildlife and local people. Once included in these efforts as an afterthought, local communities are now major stakeholders and should remain at the core of future conservation initiatives. Through their Reto-o-Reto Initiative, the authors have worked with local pastoralists in the Serengeti Mara of southwestern Kenya through new wildlife conservancies that are largely designed by local pastoral leaders in cooperation with their partners. More than a story documenting innovative ways of doing conservation business, the development of Reto-o-Reto is the story of building local institutions and supporting local leaders to work broadly across large landscapes and experiment with new models of conservation that support local livelihoods and wildlife at the same time. It is also the story of how conservation science—in this case carried out largely in association with the University of Nairobi and the International Livestock Research Institute—can support and sometimes catalyze these efforts, if scientists coproduce new knowledge with local communities, integrating both local and scientific knowledge.

From Kenya to Connecticut, the work of building community support for land and biodiversity conservation continues. New technologies and networks are bound to change the scope and scale of community interaction to promote sustainability and land protection in the 21st century. But, as all the essays in this section demonstrate, there are few if any better ways to build community support for large landscape conservation than a face-to-face meeting around a kitchen table or a campfire. The hope is that the colleges, universities, and research institutions will not in some future day forget the significance of breaking bread or sharing barbecue with neighbors.

7

The Kenyon College Land Conservation Initiative

Douglas L. Givens

It is no accident that Kenyon College, in Gambier, Ohio, appears on so many lists of America's most beautiful campuses. When Episcopal bishop Philander Chase founded the college on a wooded hilltop in 1824, he envisioned a serene rural environment that would promote serious thought and good conduct. For 190 years, the college and those who have found their way to it have valued this setting. Integral to the Kenyon experience, this environment captures the interest of prospective students and their parents. Timeless rhythms in the landscape afford views that please the eye and nourish the spirit in every season, and students and faculty members use the rural acres adjacent to the campus for fieldwork in a variety of disciplines ranging from sociology to biology and chemistry. Long after graduation, students remember the campus, the surrounding fields and forests, and the twists and turns of the Kokosing State Scenic River. Amounting to more than beautiful natural assets, these resources represent the past, present, and future for Kenyon (figure 7.1).

Chase originally purchased 4,000 acres for the college and the village of Gambier, plus an additional 4,000 acres as an investment, for a total of $18,000. Within five years of its founding, however, Kenyon began selling the investment acreage in response to financial difficulties. By the early 1970s, the college's land holdings had dwindled to fewer than 750 acres.

By the final decade of the 20th century, it was clear that the college could not take its charmed setting for granted. First, the owner of a property on the Kokosing River and directly across from the entrance to Kenyon announced plans to establish a recreational vehicle park. The college purchased the property for a substantial premium and soon thereafter bought an additional 225 acres contiguous to its holdings to quash proposals to establish a business district along the state highway that leads to Gambier. Concurrently, growth and development were changing the landscape in broad swaths of the rural countryside of

FIGURE 7.1. View of the spires of Old Kenyon and surrounding countryside. Old Kenyon, the college's first building, was constructed in the 1820s and destroyed by fire in 1949. A nearly exact replica was built in 1950 and today serves as a residence hall.
Source: Photo by Jeff Corwin.

Knox County. As farm auctions, land sales, and the growth of pell-mell subdivisions and commercial developments accelerated, it became clear that action was required.

THE FORMATION OF THE PHILANDER CHASE CORPORATION

In 1995, the college embarked on a five-year capital campaign that included a $1 million goal for land acquisition. The first preservation gift came from an alumnus visiting the campus one sunny spring weekend in 1997, after he walked to a hilltop overlooking the Kokosing River valley to see what Kenyon needed to protect. The following Monday, the alumnus wired $1 million to the college. By the end of the campaign in 2000, the college had raised more than $3 million—three times the goal for open space preservation.

The campaign showed that alumni and other donors ranked land conservation high on their charitable giving lists, and that the protection of land around the college would continue to enlist the loyalty and charity of Kenyon alumni. In 2000, the school formed the Philander Chase Corporation (PCC) as a separately incorporated nonprofit entity with a simple mission: "To preserve and maintain the farmland, open spaces, scenic views, and characteristic landscapes surrounding Kenyon College and Gambier, Ohio," in Knox County (PCC 2014). With its own 15-member board of directors, PCC's organizational structure is unique among land trusts: It is a membership 501(c)(3) organization, and Kenyon College is the sole member under provisions of Ohio nonprofit law. Even though the Corporation is a separate entity operating under the direction of its board, Kenyon College is the controlling organization and ratifies the election of the corporation's directors, and the president of Kenyon and chair of PCC are *ex officio* members of one another's boards.

At the time, Ohio and federal programs were beginning to provide meaningful funding for land conservation; because the college was ineligible to receive such assistance, the establishment of a land trust was crucial. The PCC would also prevent future boards from selling off land, as the college's 19th- and 20th-century boards had done when they approved the sale of much of Kenyon's original 8,000 acres. PCC also served to improve town-gown relations. While interactions between Kenyon and the surrounding community were not a major problem, there was some friction; although PCC functioned under the college's auspices, local residents generally perceived it as a separate entity with a clean slate.

AID FROM LOCAL PARTNERS

As suggested above, PCC was lucky to have been founded at an especially opportune time, when its concerns coincided and overlapped with similar initiatives taking shape in the state of Ohio and in Knox County, providing the framework and strategies that would later help PCC carry out its work.

In 1996, then-governor Voinovich commissioned a bipartisan Ohio Farmland Preservation Task Force consisting of representatives from government, business, academia, and agricultural interests. In June 1997, the task force reported that in the previous 45 years, more than seven million acres (roughly 33 percent of Ohio farmland) had been lost to nonagricultural uses. Two specific recommendations set the stage for broader conservation efforts: the creation of an Office of Farmland Preservation within the Ohio Department of Agriculture, and a policy statement declaring the state's commitment to protect its productive agricultural land from irretrievable conversion to nonagricultural uses.

The state also announced a $10,000 Community Development Block Grant program to support local farmland preservation plans, which led to the formation of the Knox County Farmland Preservation Task Force in 1998. I served on the local task force, which was charged with identifying better ways to develop land for residential and commercial purposes, and collaborating to preserve local farmlands when possible.

In 2000, state voters approved The Clean Ohio Fund, a $400 million bond program to preserve natural areas and farmland, protect streams, create outdoor recreational opportunities, and revitalize urban areas by returning contaminated brownfields to productive use. The fund (renewed by voters in 2008) dedicated $25 million, to be spent over a four-year period, to the Ohio Agricultural Easement Purchase Program administered through the Ohio Department of Agriculture.

Another key county-level development at that time was the establishment of the Owl Creek Conservancy in 2000. A nonprofit private land trust, the conservancy works with landowners to conserve farmlands, stream corridors, aquifer- and watershed-protection areas, wildlife habitats, woodlands, and other ecologically sensitive areas of central Ohio including Knox County.

From the beginning, PCC determined that good working partnerships would be essential for success, and so it forged ties with policy makers at the village, township, county, and state levels. From the Knox County Commissioners to the Regional Planning Commission to the Soil and Water Conservation District, PCC established and continued to nurture productive relationships. It was also critical that, as the managing director of PCC, I was an active participant in many of these organizations.

PCC'S PRESERVATION STRATEGIES

Amid this dynamic environment, PCC began its operations. Before its establishment, there were reports and numerous recommendations at the local level, but PCC was an early catalyst for countywide action. In keeping with PCC's philosophy of helping others, the newly established Ohio Agricultural Easement Purchase Program provided the perfect opportunity for PCC to engage with the local farming community to help them protect their land from adverse development.

Under the Ohio Agriculture Easement Purchase Program, landowners could not directly apply for easements; a county, township, municipality, or land trust had to apply on their behalf. Shortly after the guidelines were published in 2001, two local farmers asked PCC to act as their local sponsor. The state rewarded applicants who formed larger blocks with nearby properties, so the farmers recruited their neighbors and rallied many of them to attend workshops hosted by PCC with help from the Office of Farmland Preservation. In the program's first year, PCC was the third largest source of applications statewide. Only 24 applications were funded; PCC received one of the coveted easements.

The following year, PCC ingeniously helped raise local farmers' scores on the essay portion of the application. PCC's applicants scored highly on the objective questions, but most scored lower than other applicants statewide on the five essays. So I asked the chair of Kenyon's English department, renowned as one of the nation's best, to enlist about 20 students to assist farmers in writing their essays. Students met with the farmers in their homes, interviewed them, and helped them craft compelling essays. The effort was a rousing success. The farmers enjoyed getting to know Kenyon students, the students loved visiting the farms and talking with the farmers, and in the following years the farmers earned top essay scores.

Permanently protected property in close proximity to an applicant's farm garnered additional points, so PCC secured a conservation easement from the college on the 380-acre Brown Family Environmental

Center. In a similar manner, PCC asked the Owl Creek Conservancy to apply for Clean Ohio Funds to purchase an easement on PCC-owned land. The result was a threefold win: PCC received cash for selling the easement and continued to own the land, the Owl Creek Conservancy held the easement, and agricultural easement applicants received additional points.

PCC boosted local applicants' scores by increasing its local match of state subsidies as well. Ohio funds only 75 percent of an easement's total value; the remaining 25 percent must come from the landowner or another source. If applicants volunteer to pay more than 25 percent, thus lowering the state's obligation, the state awards "bonus" points to the applicant. By using its own money and persuading the Knox County Commissioners to contribute nearly $300,000 to support the program, PCC ensured more successful applications.

Over the years, PCC also raised the scores of applicants whose property qualified for the Ohio Department of Agriculture's Century Farm designation, honoring families who demonstrated continuous family ownership for at least a hundred years. Century Farms received extra points, and, with encouragement and guidance from PCC, five of Knox County's 18 Century Farms successfully applied for easements and conserved their land.

While helping local farmers protect their properties, PCC helped create a county park along the way. Using money generated by the college's fundraising campaign and subsequent gifts, three properties totaling 202 acres were purchased and then resold subject to deed restrictions. One of these properties, the 168-acre Prescott farm between Gambier and Mount Vernon, was especially important to Kenyon as the source of Wolf Run Creek, which flows into the Kokosing River and through the Brown Family Environmental Center. A development company from Pennsylvania had already purchased land across the road from the Prescott farm and planned to build 225 homes there, increasing the pressure to protect the farm. Before the developer could purchase the farm as well, PCC bought it for $626,000.

A year later, PCC agreed to resell the farm to the Knox County Park District only if the district obtained state subsidies to acquire the property and establish Knox County's first park. Because state funding required matching grants—money the district did not have—PCC helped persuade the Mount Vernon Community Foundation and the

Knox County Commissioners to donate land they owned adjacent to the farm to satisfy the matching fund requirement. The plan worked. The park district got the funding and purchased the property from PCC, Knox County had a new 288-acre Wolf Run Regional Park, and the source of Wolf Run Creek was protected from development.

Although some successes happened without funding, many of the accomplishments directly resulted from the availability of money. In addition to donations from alumni and friends during two college campaigns, PCC secured funding from state, federal, and county sources in excess of $2.1 million. The original notion that alumni and other donors might be interested in preserving the nature of the Kenyon experience proved to be correct again.

HOW CAN COLLEGES AND UNIVERSITIES BECOME CONSERVATION CATALYSTS?

PCC has the tools and legal structure to serve not only as an effective conservation catalyst but as a model for other colleges and universities interested in land preservation. By 2013, PCC had outright purchased 230 acres that it manages and leases to farmers; facilitated the creation of 35 easements encompassing 4,216 acres; and, with the Owl Creek Conservancy, protected a total of 6,746 acres in Knox County. Of the county's 339,000 total acres, those remaining 164,666 unprotected acres provide a tremendous opportunity for the local land conservation community (figure 7.2).

Although large landscape conservation projects are taking place both nationally and internationally, local conservation activities have a valuable role to play and a great deal to contribute to activities on a grander scale. According to the Land Trust Alliance 2010 Census, the 1,723 active land trusts operating in the United States had collectively conserved 47 million acres (Land Trust Alliance 2011). If only 10 percent of the 7,500 postsecondary educational institutions in the United States engaged in land conservation using a model similar to PCC's, it could be a major step forward in the conservation movement.

Each institution at which the PCC model might be adopted would have its own unique environment. Nevertheless, the model is widely applicable; every element that led to the formation of PCC is eminently replicable at any educational institution in the country.

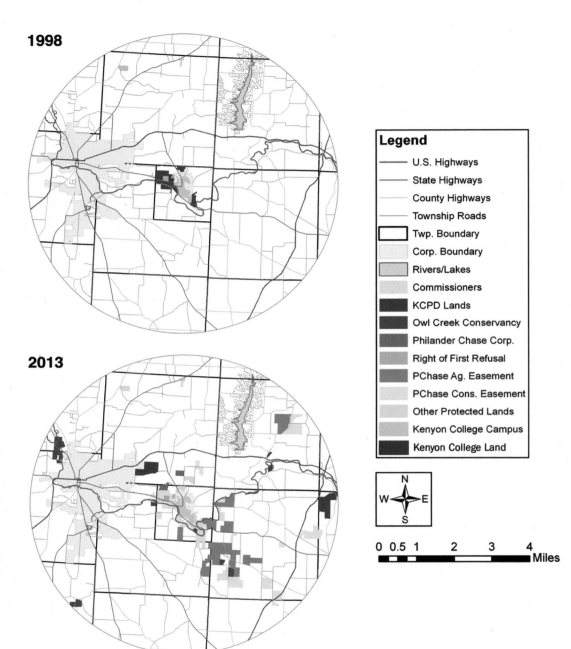

1998

2013

Legend
— U.S. Highways
— State Highways
— County Highways
— Township Roads
☐ Twp. Boundary
Corp. Boundary
Rivers/Lakes
Commissioners
KCPD Lands
Owl Creek Conservancy
Philander Chase Corp.
Right of First Refusal
PChase Ag. Easement
PChase Cons. Easement
Other Protected Lands
Kenyon College Campus
Kenyon College Land

0 0.5 1   2   3   4
Miles

FIGURE 7.2. Expansion of conservation land in Knox County, Ohio: 1998–2013.
Source: Map by Justin Smith, with permission from Knox County Map Office.

The Philander Chase Corporation began at a time when there was growing concern about the deal-by-deal erosion of the rural landscape. The goal was local: It related to Kenyon College and its environs. But PCC's experience and aims were soon shared by overlapping and allied agencies in Knox County and beyond, leading to and suggesting larger possibilities. Our experience demonstrates that what happened here can happen elsewhere.

REFERENCES

Land Trust Alliance. 2011. "2010 National Land Trust Census." Web page. Washington, DC: Land Trust Alliance. *www.landtrustalliance.org/land-trusts/land-trust-census*

Philander Chase Corporation. 2014. "Mission Statement." Home page. Gambier, OH: Philander Chase Corporation. *www.kenyon.edu/directories/offices-services/philander-chase-corporation/*

8

The Quiet Corner Initiative at the Yale School of Forestry & Environmental Studies

Mary Tyrrell, Matthew Fried, Mark Ashton, and Richard Campbell

It may be hard to imagine a Quiet Corner in Connecticut, but a drive along Route 44 in the northeast corner of the state might make you think you were in Vermont rather than suburban southern New England. Woodlands dominate the rolling landscape, interspersed with farms, villages, and country roads (figure 8.1).

Thanks to the efforts of the founders of the Connecticut Forest & Park Association early in the 20th century, large tracts of intact ecosystems in the Quiet Corner are conserved as state forests (Connecticut Forest & Park Association 2012). As in much of New England, however, most forestland is owned by families in relatively small parcels (figure 8.2). A remarkable exception is the 7,860-acre Yale-Myers Forest, owned by Yale University and managed as a working forest since 1930 by the Yale School of Forestry & Environmental Studies (FES). The oldest sustainably managed forest in the region, Yale-Myers has embarked on an ambitious program, the Quiet Corner Initiative (QCI), to create a living laboratory where research and education are used to meet the challenges of fostering healthy and vibrant rural communities and landscape-scale conservation.

The Quiet Corner is part of the Thames River watershed, almost 1,900 square miles of rural and forested land in northeastern Connecticut and south-central Massachusetts. An estimated 13 percent of this land is permanently protected from development, either as public land or in conservation easements (Tyrrell et al. 2005). Nested within the Thames watershed, the Quinebaug–Shetucket Rivers Valley was declared a National Heritage Corridor in 1994 to help with efforts to protect the area's unique history and rural character. Known as the Last Green Valley, it is one of the few remaining large rural areas and forested landscapes in the highly developed east coast corridor between

FIGURE 8.1. The Quiet Corner landscape at the confluence of the Quinebaug and Shetucket rivers.
Source: Photo by Leslie Sweetnam, www.glsweetnam.com.

FIGURE 8.2. Parcel map of the Quiet Corner towns of Ashford, Eastford, Union, and Wood-stock. The large block near the center is the Yale-Myers Forest. The other large blocks are state lands, conservation lands, and private working forests.
Source: Map by Richard Campbell; used with permission from Yale FES.

FIGURE 8.3. NASA night earth image; the Quiet Corner region is circled.
Source: http://visibleearth.nasa.gov/view.php?=55167.

Boston and Washington, D.C.; NASA night earth images show the region as a dark spot nearly surrounded by light (figure 8.3). It is home to the Quinebaug Highlands, a 269-square-mile region of mostly privately owned forestland in Connecticut and Massachusetts, identified as one of Connecticut's Last Great Places by The Nature Conservancy; the privately owned 4,000-acre Norcross Wildlife Sanctuary in Massachusetts; the Yale-Myers Forest; several state forests; and the Pawcatuck Borderlands, a 200-square-mile area of largely contiguous forests along the Connecticut–Rhode Island border. The region is rich with wildlife as well as healthy hardwood and coniferous forests that provide high-value ecosystem services such as wildlife habitat, carbon sequestration, and clean water to downstream communities, including the University of Connecticut's main campus at Storrs.

Although development has abated during the recent economic downturn, this largely forested landscape has in recent decades come under pressure from the sprawling metropolitan areas of Boston, Hartford, and Providence. The smallest towns in this valley experienced an average population growth of 17 percent from 1990 to 2000 (Tyrrell et al. 2005), and development has occurred in a piecemeal, haphazard way that fragments the forest. It is not hard to imagine that this type of suburban development pressure would return in an improving economy (figure 8.4).

FIGURE 8.4. Suburban development in forestland in the Thames Watershed.
Source: Photo by Joel Stocker.

Because so much of the forestland is privately owned, there is no guarantee that unique natural areas like the Quinebaug Highlands will remain intact or immune to development pressures, and therefore a number of conservation organizations have mobilized an effort to protect this region from development (MassConn Sustainable Forest Partnership 2012).

YALE'S QUIET CORNER INITIATIVE

On a cold December day in 2011, seven families, all neighbors along Bigelow Brook, gathered at the Ashford Town Hall to hear about the management plans Yale students had developed for the families' properties. A seemingly small step, this semester-long effort was a catalyst for getting the Quiet Corner Initiative (QCI) off the ground. As one landowner expressed it, "We've gotten to learn what some of our neighbors' goals are. Although I know most of our neighbors, we rarely see each other to discuss land use." Most small landowners don't have the knowledge or resources to sustainably manage their land (Butler et al. 2007), and even if they do, economies of scale work against them. Thinking about neighborhood- or landscape-level management or conservation is well beyond what most landowners can do without significant support and resources, and they often don't understand their conservation options. One of the goals of the Quiet Corner Initiative is to enable landowner cooperation where common goals exist, in order to make individual property management easier and more economical.

Yale's QCI is an effort to integrate the Yale-Myers Forest and the School of Forestry & Environmental Studies more fully into the larger landscape, and to provide opportunities for students and faculty to address real-world conservation and management problems. It is envisioned as an unprecedented living laboratory where research and education meet the challenge of vital current issues and where ideas can be tested and refined on the ground. The initiative establishes Yale as a responsible and forward-thinking land steward with a strong commitment to the local community. It is expected that the project will become a model of how the university can engage with citizens to bring the best science and management to everyday decisions in land use planning and conservation, adaptive land management, and appropriate economic development for rural areas. Ultimately, it aims to assist in creating stable and healthy communities.

As a cornerstone of the initiative, a Woodland Partnership was created for private landowners near the forest. The first goals of the partnership are to create and implement stewardship plans for these landowners, develop regional conservation strategies and assessments, and evaluate the public value of ecosystem services provided by private lands, all through a coordinated set of student courses and projects mentored and overseen by faculty.

The broader objective is to develop the first comprehensive repository of long-term, region-wide research datasets on the biophysical, social, and economic indicators associated with adaptive management, conservation, and the science of place. In so doing, the project team will track performance of specific initiatives across spatial and temporal scales and provide students a way to "learn by doing" while creating a long-term research data warehouse. Programs that may benefit from these datasets include forest management/woodlands conservation, renewable energy and ecosystem services, sustainable agriculture, and open space planning (figure 8.5).

The Yale-Myers Forest is ideally situated to become a hub of research and adaptive management devoted to trying out new ideas and fostering expansion of the ones that work well. As both a rural and urban landowner, Yale is in a unique position to offer a comprehensive

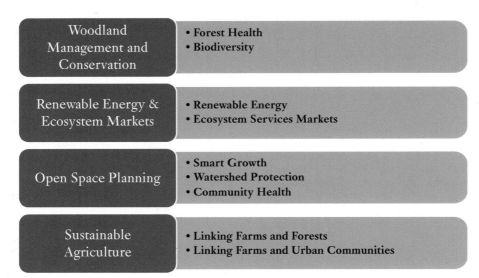

FIGURE 8.5. Programs of the Quiet Corner Initiative.

research facility focused on the biophysical, social, and economic aspects of land conservation and adaptive management. This initiative will provide new education and research opportunities for Yale students and faculty while promoting the visibility, strength, and competitiveness of FES programs; attracting high-quality students with a distinctive program not available elsewhere; and offering new avenues for cultivating alumni and other financial support. It will also mobilize stakeholders in the Quiet Corner region of Connecticut for the benefit of the surrounding communities, bringing more resources to bear than would be otherwise possible. As part of the long-range plan, these efforts can be expanded along the urban–rural continuum in partnership with Yale FES's Hixon Center for Urban Ecology.

STARTING SMALL, THINKING BIG

> Most folks are interested in their specific neighborhoods. We get them to know each other, foster a more cohesive understanding of their different/similar values, and engage them in the idea of a more cohesive plan across the landscape.
>
> —MARK ASHTON, DIRECTOR OF THE YALE FORESTS AND LEADER OF THE QUIET CORNER INITIATIVE

QCI activities are centered on the Yale-Myers Forest and managed by a program called the School Forests. The School Forests' three-pronged mission of management, research, and education guides all work at the forest. Every master's student at the Yale School of Forestry & Environmental Studies spends one week of orientation at the forest, practicing sampling methods and other field skills while bonding with their new classmates. Many continue their relationship with the forest, conducting field research and working as apprentice foresters. The apprentice foresters, about a dozen of whom are hired each summer, gain firsthand skills and knowledge about sustainable forest management techniques. The summer crew learns how to write silvicultural prescriptions and mark timber sales, and proceeds from the annual timber harvest that they design support their apprenticeships and the School Forests budget.

In addition to being a fertile ground for student learning, School Forests' directors and managers have always worked to maintain good relations with neighbors in the towns of Eastford, Ashford, Union, and Woodstock, and to serve as a source of education for them about the region's forests. Several times each year, the School Forests program hosts public workshops, tours, and seminars for individuals and community groups on topics such as forest history, maple sugaring, and conservation. A separate series of workshops, geared specifically to local residents who are Woodland Partnership members, provides a forum in which neighbors can get to know one another and discuss common stewardship interests (figure 8.6).

It was in FES's tradition of engagement with the land and the local community that QCI was conceived. In the spring of 2009, as their clinical project for the Strategies for Land Conservation course, two students conducted a landowner survey and interviewed area residents, teachers, and conservation professionals to gauge sentiment toward the university and to uncover ideas about how Yale could be more engaged in stewardship and education efforts outside the boundaries of its forest. The results of this research showed a strong interest in public workshops. In the summer of 2010, a student funded by the Berkeley Conservation Scholars Program conducted a more in-depth survey of local landowners that illuminated the lack of active management occurring on private property in the area but also reflected local residents' desire to learn more: three-quarters of the survey respondents

FIGURE 8.6. Participants in a field-based workshop at Yale-Myers Forest.
Source: Photo by Angela Orthmeyer.

expressed interest in workshops, and two-thirds indicated they were interested in being part of a Woodland Partnership.

With this encouragement, School Forests proposed the formation of a Woodland Partnership in a meeting at the Ashford town hall in December 2010. The initial goal of the partnership, which has since grown to more than 100 members, is to help small parcel holders to meet economies of scale for management activities and land conservation. Ideally, the partnership will extend the work to other areas, such as payment for ecosystem services, renewable energy, and even sustainable agriculture.

Several faculty members who view practice-based learning as paramount to natural resource management education have guided the initiative's early efforts. Building on the structure of courses they already offer each year, these instructors have been able to incorporate Quiet Corner landowners as project "clients" upon whose needs teams of master's students center their term projects. By using the existing framework of established graduate course offerings, Yale is able to provide professional-quality services to neighbors of the Yale-Myers Forest without requiring additional faculty resources.

PROGRESS THROUGH COORDINATED CLINICAL COURSES

The initiative's building blocks are a coordinated set of clinical courses strategically positioned to engage landowners in perceiving their land as a valuable part of the larger landscape (figure 8.7). Two courses already making an impact in the Quiet Corner are Strategies for Land Conservation and Management Plans for Protected Areas. In Strategies for Land Conservation, taught by Bradford Gentry, students study the legal, financial, and management aspects of conservation tools and

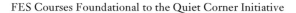

FES Courses Foundational to the Quiet Corner Initiative

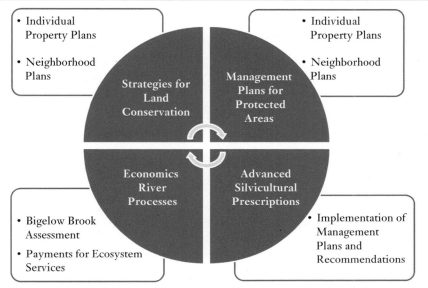

FIGURE 8.7. FES courses foundational to the Quiet Corner Initiative. The blue wedges represent courses or course topics focused on the QCI; the white boxes indicate QCI activities implemented through the courses.

undertake clinical projects with local land conservation organizations. In the spring of 2011, a student team was charged with the task of exploring and promoting potential conservation options available to landowners in the Bigelow Brook subwatershed adjacent to the Yale Forest.

Bigelow Brook was chosen as the first area of concentration for several compelling reasons. The private properties along Bigelow Brook make up a corridor between already protected lands (figure 8.8), so maintaining a well-managed ecosystem in this area can have a large conservation impact. Bigelow Brook is important for downstream water quality and as such has been identified as a conservation priority (Green Valley Institute 2011). And, last but by no means least, one eager and well-connected landowner along the brook was instrumental in pulling his neighbors into the program.

The team produced a conservation options analysis: a two-page document that outlined and explained who key conservation players are in the Quiet Corner and what funding opportunities exist at the private,

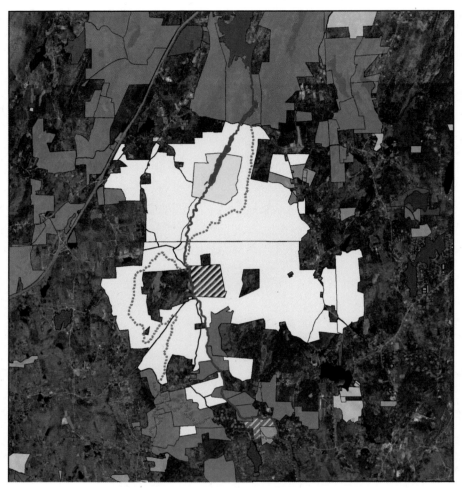

FIGURE 8.8. The Yale-Myers neighborhood. Properties in the Bigelow Brook watershed participating in the first phase of the Quiet Corner Initiative are identified in red; the Yale-Myers forest is in light blue; state lands are in green. The dotted red line represents trails that are part of the Connecticut Blue Trail system.
Source: Map by Shane Hetzler; used with permission from Yale FES.

state, and local levels. The analysis also included suggestions about what Yale's role could be in future conservation efforts and gave a description of various area land trusts that might make good partners for Bigelow Brook landowners.

The conservation options analysis was distributed to the landowners, all of whom expressed interest in one suggestion in particular: a student-written management plan based on their individual properties, with the potential for integrating management recommendations across parcel boundaries at the landscape scale. Through another clinic-based course, Management Plans for Protected Areas taught by Mark Ashton, student teams were assigned the seven Bigelow Brook landowners as clients in the fall semester of 2011. Students worked closely with their clients to ensure that management recommendations were tailored to each landowner's unique objectives, including managing for timber, wildlife, recreation, and maple sugaring. At the conclusion of the term, each landowner received a management plan with detailed information about his property's history, physiography, forest composition, and management options based on existing site characteristics and landowner goals.

Students in Management Plans for Protected Areas report that participation in the course was one of the most comprehensive educational experiences they have had at Yale. To produce a professional-quality management plan for a real client, student teams must draw heavily on the knowledge and skills they've gained through earlier coursework in such areas as silviculture, soils, GIS, hydrology, and social science. This field-based learning complements classroom curriculum and exposes students to challenges common to the professions for which they are training. While students are reaping the benefits of a living laboratory, landowners are receiving, at no charge, a management plan that represents a critical first step toward more thoughtful long-term stewardship.

With each landowner in possession of a management plan for her individual property, a student team from the spring 2012 Strategies for Land Conservation course was tasked with developing the Bigelow Brook Neighborhood Plan as their clinical project. Using the management plans produced in the fall by their peers, the team developed a matrix of landowner objectives and management strategies to determine where commonalities existed among neighbors. The areas of greatest overlapping interest were timber harvesting (to meet various objectives), maple sugaring, and the collective securing of conservation easements for income. Because of the small parcel size of the individual properties, timber-harvesting operations often don't meet economies of scale. With a collective group of contiguous landowners interested in managing timber, harvests can be conducted more efficiently and require construction of fewer logging trails and staging areas.

The spring 2012 team met with each landowner to get personally acquainted and to gauge landowner commitment to the objectives and recommendations stated in the management plans. As it turned out, landowner time constraints had narrowed their interests to the exploration of conservation easement options. Most landowners said they were at least open to the idea of easements on their land if they were to be paid, but few were interested in easements that required public access to qualify. Concerns regarding public access were mostly based on previous experiences with littering, invasion of privacy, and unauthorized ATV use. The student team is now working with the Connecticut Department of Energy and Environmental Protection and local land trusts to determine what funding may be available for conservation easements that protect Bigelow Brook.

Progress has been slow but steady. As of 2013, classes have completed management plans in two other subwatersheds for a total of 14 plans, and students will circle back to Bigelow Brook in the fall of 2014. Five of the plans are currently being implemented, and three more are scheduled for the implementation of harvesting plans in the fall of 2014. The recommendations being followed include small-scale timber harvests, maple sugaring, improved boundaries, trail construction, and potential grants to create a silvopasture operation. The River Processes and Restoration course has completed 10 miles of stream assessments, laying the groundwork for a long-term monitoring program in Bigelow Brook and feeding into Connecticut's regional stream assessment protocol.

THE MAKING OF A MANAGEMENT PLAN: A SNAPSHOT OF QCI IN ACTION

One pair of owners involved in the Quiet Corner Initiative has lived on their 74-acre parcel in Eastford for eighteen years; their family has been stewards of the property along the Bigelow Brook for nearly a century, and respect for this legacy is an important element in how they view the land. Their house was built with timber harvested from the property. They hold dear the rural character of their surroundings and their connection to the land, and they have a strong interest in both limiting excessive development around their property and preserving their land's income-generating merits.

This family was the first of the Quiet Corner landowners to express interest in some form of a partnership, following a chance run-in with Richard Campbell, manager of the Yale-Myers Forest, at a neighborhood farmstand. They mentioned that they were interested in protecting the portion of their land—and that of their neighbors—along Bigelow Brook, but they hadn't had much time to investigate any options. Because they were active in the community, it was fortunate that they became charter members of what became known as the Quiet Corner Woodland Partnership, and they were instrumental in recruiting several other landowners to serve as clients for the Management Plans for Protected Areas class.

Their two principle objectives were sustainable management of the forest for income generation, and maintenance of forest health and wildlife. To meet these objectives, they were interested in timber harvests, maple sugaring, and the potential sale of conservation easements.

The family owns a small portable sawmill and processes timber harvested from its property and that of its neighbors. The timber, primarily white pine, is sold for construction in the Quiet Corner area. While the family regularly harvests 22,000 board feet of white pine annually, the mill has additional capacity, and so the student team was asked to assess the possibility of increasing the annual harvests by about 30 percent.

The students undertook a comprehensive forest inventory, accounting for both current and future timber resources. The harvesting recommendations in the final plan blended the clients' desire for timber with their commitment to protect wildlife habitat and the pristine waters of Bigelow Brook. Although the student team was not able to recommend a harvesting regime yielding the full 30 percent increase, they were able to devise a schedule yielding greater volumes of white pine while allowing for sufficient regeneration of the species into the future by promoting maturation of the existing stock.

The family plans to continue its sawmill operation for the near future, but the work is physically strenuous, and they expressed interest in exploring additional revenue streams that would prove less taxing as they grow older. Their property has a plentiful stock of sugar maples from which they would like to produce maple syrup; however, the trees are not yet of sufficient size to support an economically significant operation. To speed up the process by which these trees could produce large volumes of syrup, the student team proposed a detailed thinning treatment to eliminate competition from non-maple species. Nevertheless, there won't be any sugaring at a useful scale for many decades.

As a final recommendation toward meeting the goal of protecting the Bigelow Brook while generating income, the student team advised more research into the sale of a conservation easement on the portions of the property directly adjacent to the brook. Since this area is only 17 acres, cooperation with adjacent landowners to apply for a collective easement may make the property a more attractive investment to area land trusts. Students in the Strategies for Land Conservation class are working to integrate easement potential across property boundaries to promote greater habitat connectivity and land marketability for conservation funding.

After working closely for four months, the student team presented the family with a professional-quality 60-page management plan. The plan included such information as the property's ownership history; biological assessments of the property's soils, hydrology, and geology; quantitative assessments of the existing vegetation; and full recommendations for future management. The clients were very pleased with the quality of the product they received and are currently working with the land conservation class to put some of their recommendations into action.

BUDGET AND RESOURCES

Most of the initiative's activities thus far have been covered by Yale FES operating budgets. As a graduate school with primary emphasis on a two-year professional master's degree, FES prioritizes applied work through field studies and project classes, and the school's educational model is thus a perfect fit for QCI. Initiative-related faculty teaching and mentoring are part of FES's standard academic work; clinical and field-based classes have shifted emphasis to the Quiet Corner for their projects. Additional funds have been raised to support student internships for specific projects. The total amount of external funds raised to date is $280,000, including a $230,000 three-year grant from the USDA Forest Service Northeastern Area State and Private Forestry Division.

MEASURES OF SUCCESS AND IMPACT

The QCI is a young initiative and a work in progress; it is much too early to say anything about proven results. It is hoped that QCI will encourage an adaptive learning process in landowners, encouraging them to think strategically about the future of their land and the larger region. There is a reluctance to nail down metrics at this early stage, as the team is in a rumination period. Nevertheless, the vision is that over time this initiative will:

- increase collaboration among diverse stakeholders in the Quiet Corner who are currently only organized in small pockets or around single issues;
- create more sustainable communities and better stewardship of landscapes, with implications beyond Connecticut;
- increase the amount of land in the region that is permanently protected from development;
- help improve livelihoods in the region through new avenues for economic development; link rural and urban interests (New Haven to Quiet Corner); and
- protect Yale's own forest assets and expand its future research and educational opportunities.

Possible midterm benchmarks are:

- number of active members in the Quiet Corner Woodland Partnership;
- a periodic assessment of how well management plans are being implemented;
- continuous surveys to evaluate conservation ethics;
- systematic archiving of management plan data and research data; and
- evaluation of changes in values and behaviors over time.

NEXT STEPS: CREATING MOMENTUM FOR LANDSCAPE-SCALE CONSERVATION

Critical to successful landscape-scale conservation is the ability to increase landowner capacity for landscape-level planning in order to reduce costs and enable economies of scale for both management and conservation. By promoting sustainable management of private lands and building the capacity to implement it, the initiative will serve to maintain the biodiversity and health of working forests and the productive capacity of the overall ecosystem. It will also maintain and enhance a sustainable forest-based economy and the multiple socio-economic benefits received by both private landowners and the public in the region. Building upon current efforts, QCI aims to complete work on another three subwatersheds, one per year over the next three years, for which funding has been secured. These areas have been identified as the Still River, Morse Meadow Brook, and Bussey Brook systems.

Specific next steps include:

- expanding capacity to create forest stewardship plans and scale-appropriate forest operations for small private landowners within the greater Quiet Corner region;
- providing greater access to markets for tangible products (timber and non-timber) for small landowners by becoming group-certified by the Forest Stewardship Council (FSC) (piggybacking on the FSC certification of the Yale-Myers Forest);
- developing land conservation strategies for individual landowners and aggregations of landowners, including possible sales of conservation easements along with potential cost-share programs through the USDA Natural Resource Conservation Service;
- assessing the viability of developing payments for ecosystem services (water, carbon, energy, recreation) and, if viable, helping to develop and implement a payments scheme;
- developing an assessment methodology to gauge success over time; and
- sponsoring a Quiet Corner Woodlands Partnership workshop series, an iterative sequence of workshops that become more advanced over time, with topics such as land use history, forest ecol-

ogy, stand dynamics, silviculture, wildlife habitat management, and ecosystem services.

As part of their academic and professional training, graduate students (both master's and doctoral) will develop regional and site-specific conservation plans, assess landowner resources and values, create and help implement forest stewardship plans, and provide workshops and training for landowners in support of these efforts. Faculty as well as professional foresters and conservation planners will mentor and work with the students through courses and research groups with help from the Connecticut Department of Energy and Environmental Protection, Connecticut Forest & Park Association, and Eastern Connecticut Forest Landowners Association.

BARRIERS AND OPPORTUNITIES

As with all such efforts, success will rely on a long-term commitment of people and resources. Local and state conservation organizations and funders; Quiet Corner landowners; and Yale faculty, staff, and students will have to exert steady effort to achieve the initiative's goals over the long haul. Although this is a challenge, the approach of starting small yet within a framework of big ideas and possibilities should provide the momentum necessary to keep the initiative going. QCI fits comfortably within the mission and curriculum of the School of Forestry & Environmental Studies and thus has a good chance of becoming institutionalized. Although the project began as the brainchild of one faculty member, several others are now committed to directing clinical class projects to the Quiet Corner and working within the agreed-upon framework.

Working on a landscape scale requires cooperation among New England neighbors where there is little history of cooperation on what could be perceived as private family matters. By starting small with eager landowners, showing the advantages of participation, and attracting more landowners to the programs over time, QCI hopes to overcome this obstacle.

Bigger ideas (landscape-scale conservation easements, energy, ecosystem services markets) will require bigger investments. Funding will always be a challenge. It may be particularly difficult to obtain funding for purchasing conservation easements in the current economy. The strategy is to build a track record on early successes that will convince funders to make the necessary investment to expand those successes to a larger landscape with more programs.

THE LONG HAUL

QCI is the beginning of a long-term partnership among Yale FES, local private landowners, conservation organizations, local forest industry, and the state to increase the sustainable management of forests in the Quiet Corner region. Over the next three years, it is expected that the initiative will reach at least 40 properties and 4,000 acres with management and conservation actions, including a trial FSC group certification program and the design of a payment for ecosystem services program.

Results from this experience will be published, workshops developed into web-based modules, and the partnership used as a demonstration learning experience for landowners and professionals from other regions. The aim is to work on ten-year cycles between subwatersheds in the Natchaug Basin, and in 2021 to return to the Bigelow Brook subwatershed where the program began in 2011.

Yale FES has the stamina to maintain such a framework by incorporating it into the core of the master's-level professional student education program, which has developed a rich tradition of sustainable forest management over the last 100 years. Using the principles of a continuous forest inventory system, QCI students will compare the information collected at each time step to assess social and biophysical changes and to allow adjustments in management goals and objectives. Such information will serve as a rich data source for analysis and publication. Few such data banks and monitoring protocols exist today to gauge success and failure, even though large amounts of money have been spent on the development of collaborative forest management partnerships throughout the nation.

ACKNOWLEDGMENTS

Yale's Quiet Corner Initiative is the brainchild of Yale School of Forestry & Environmental Studies (FES) faculty members Mark Ashton, Bradford Gentry, and Deborah Spalding, and Yale School Forests manager Richard

Campbell. Nathan Rutenbeck, a student in the 2013 master's class, and Alex Barrett, current manager of the Yale Forests, have made significant contributions through their passionate interest in the project.

REFERENCES

Butler, B. J., M. Tyrrell, G. Feinberg, S. VanManen, L. Wiseman, and S. Wallinger. 2007. "Understanding and Reaching Family Forest Owners: Lessons from Social Marketing Research." *Journal of Forestry* 105 (7): 348–357.

Connecticut Forest and Park Association. 2012. "About Us." Web page. Rockfall, CT: Connecticut Forest and Park Association. *www.ctwoodlands.org/about*

Green Valley Institute. 2011. "Natchaug River Basin Municipal Conservation Compact, April 28, 2011." *www.greenvalleyinstitute.org/NCAP.htm*

MassConn Sustainable Forest Partnership. 2012. "About/What We Are/What We Do/Why a Regional Conservation Partnership?/Who We Are." Web page. *http://www.opacumlt.org/massconn/*

Tyrrell, M. L., M. H. P. Hall, and R. N. Sampson. 2005. "Dynamic Models of Land Use Change in Northeastern USA: Developing Tools, Techniques, and Talents for Effective Conservation Action." In *Emerging Issues Along Urban-Rural Interfaces: Linking Science and Society*, ed. D. N. Laband. Conference proceedings, March 13–16, 2005, Atlanta, Georgia. *http://emergingissues.interfacesouth.org/past conferences/2005proceedings.pdf*

9

Alternative Futures Modeling in Maine's Penobscot River Watershed: Forging a Regional Identity for River Restoration

Robert J. Lilieholm, Christopher S. Cronan, Michelle L. Johnson, Spencer R. Meyer, and Dave Owen

The Penobscot River rises from Maine's North Woods near Mount Katahdin in Baxter State Park and flows more than 350 miles before reaching the state's rugged Downeast coast west of Acadia National Park (figure 9.1). The Penobscot drains 2.2 million hectares (8,610 sq miles)—nearly 25 percent of the state—and throughout its long history has served as both a cultural and an economic mainstay for the people who have inhabited its banks. For the indigenous Wabanaki, the waterway was central to tribal culture, yielding both transport and sustenance. Early European explorers, including Goma in 1525 and Champlain in 1604, navigated Maine's rocky coast and the lower reaches of the Penobscot, their maps supplying military intelligence as France and England vied for control of the region and its resources. Later, these maps would furnish the blueprint for European-American settlement.

English settlement began in earnest after the French and Indian Wars of 1754 to 1763, and the region's vast resources were slowly opened to broader markets along the East Coast, Europe, and the Caribbean. Fisheries of many sorts thrived, including those that harvested abundant shellfish and salmon. Timber from the North Woods was driven downriver to be milled and loaded on ships along Bangor's many wharves. The extensive timber resources attracted the English monarch's attention via the Broad Arrow Policy, which reserved the finest mast trees along major waterways for the Royal Navy. The Broad Arrow Policy was just one of many unpopular edicts that would fuel rebellions such as the 1772 Pine Tree Riot and, ultimately, the American Revolution.

By the mid-1800s, the Penobscot River sent more lumber to market than any other waterway in the world (Wilson 2005), and the logging boom denuded the watershed of its pines. Later markets would exploit

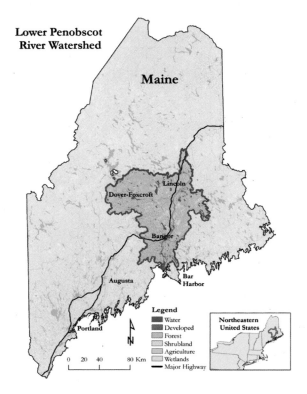

FIGURE 9.1. Maine's Lower Penobscot River Watershed.

the region's other species, including spruce and hemlock. The vast fisheries of the river and Penobscot Bay were also rapidly exploited as the region industrialized, creating a dual assault on the watershed's aquatic and terrestrial systems. Later years saw large integrated pulp and paper mills, textile mills, shipbuilding, and leather tanning operations. Many of these mills harnessed the power of the river as they converted raw materials into finished products. By the mid-20th century, the push for hydroelectric power had begun, and the Great Northern Paper Company both owned vast forest holdings and operated one of the world's largest hydroelectric systems at the time on the Penobscot.

As industry and commerce grew, the Penobscot increasingly served as a source of industrial water, municipal drinking water, and a conduit for wastes of all kinds. During the 1960s, the river's banks supported several pulp and paper mills, 22 leather tanneries, 25 textile plants, and a host of poultry processing facilities, many of which discharged waste directly into the river. In the middle of the 20th century, the river and its tributaries had more than 100 licensed dams. Inevitably, these various uses came into conflict. The city of Bangor discontinued using the river for drinking water in 1959. By 1966, the last major shellfisheries were closed due to contamination, and a 1972 study found the river unable to support most fish species. River communities, once centered on vibrant working waterfronts, saw rail and then highway transport divert attention from the Penobscot as economic activities were reoriented toward new modes of transport.

By the latter half of the 20th century, river communities along the Penobscot and Eastern Seaboard had figuratively and literally turned their backs on their waterfronts. Across Maine and elsewhere, older downtowns near rivers like the Penobscot slipped into decline, a trend exacerbated by urban renewal efforts that obliterated block after block of historic downtowns in Maine (Kunstler 2005).

The decline of the Penobscot and its surrounding communities mirrored that of other major waterways, a process that would eventually give rise to environmental policies designed to reverse the cycle and restore health to America's waterways. On the Penobscot, the Federal Water Pollution Control Act of 1972—better known as the Clean Water Act—played the central role. Across the nation, the Clean Water Act and other environmental statutes like the National Environmental Policy Act of 1969 and the Endangered Species Act (ESA) of 1973 transformed our approach to managing natural resources. On the Penobscot, pollutants dropped an estimated 85 percent. At the state level, Maine's 1971 regulation of shorelands codified setbacks for new development and placed restrictions on the clearing of riparian vegetation. Under these regulations, water and scenic quality improved, and the river's significant bald eagle population saw a dramatic rebound. Nevertheless, some environmental problems remained. In 2000, the National Marine Fisheries Service and U.S. Fish and Wildlife Service listed populations of Atlantic salmon (*Salmo salar*) in several Maine rivers, including the Penobscot, as endangered. The shortnose sturgeon (*Acipenser brevirostrum*) had already been listed as endangered back in 1967 under a predecessor to the ESA. Those designations would further fuel efforts to restore the river.

Today, one can navigate the Penobscot or traverse its banks and see a river that has been repeatedly transformed. In 1604, Champlain's ships sailed amid old-growth forests. By the mid-1800s, those forests were gone, displaced by agricultural fields. In the early 21st century, that pastoral landscape has largely reverted to forest. On the river, additional changes continue to appear. In 2004, the Penobscot River Restoration Trust began planning one of the largest dam removal and river restoration projects in the world. The $63-million project maintains existing hydropower capacity while removing two lower dams and modifying fish passages on another four dams. Begun in 2012, dam removal under the project will reopen 1,000 miles of river habitat to aid in the recovery of 11 sea-run fish species, including Atlantic salmon and shortnose sturgeon, by the end of the decade.

Despite these gains, the Penobscot still faces an uncertain future. Attempts to protect endangered fisheries can collide with renewed calls for alternative energy development, including the creation of hydroelectric power plants. Efforts to assist Maine's struggling paper sector can conflict with efforts to improve water quality and diversify the region's economy though recreation and tourism. And residential and commercial development within the watershed's lower reaches threatens to transform the functioning of both human and natural systems (figure 9.2). Indeed, a 2005 U.S. Forest Service report entitled "Forests on the Edge: Housing Development on America's Private Forests" ranked the Lower Penobscot River Watershed first in the nation based on the projected loss of private forestland to residential development over the next 30 years (Stein et al. 2005). Two nearby Maine watersheds also ranked among the top 15.

The Penobscot River watershed thus provides a compelling opportunity for coordinated efforts to understand and anticipate development and its associated impacts. But realizing a sustainable vision for the Penobscot will require more than a reasonable forecast of development trends. It will require interdisciplinary science and the capacity to work with diverse stakeholders in order to understand and address the social, economic, and biophysical drivers of land use change as well as the complex and coupled nature of human and natural systems. These chal-

FIGURE 9.2. Newly established clearcut and gravel operation on the Penobscot River in a shoreland residential zone in Orrington, Maine.
Source: Photo courtesy of the University of Maine.

lenges are representative of a wide range of emerging and increasingly complex environmental issues facing Maine as well as many other regions around the globe.

This chapter describes one ongoing effort to forge a regional identity for the Penobscot River watershed. We focus on the University of Maine's efforts to realize this goal through an alternative futures modeling research project. That project is part of the five-year, $20-million Sustainability Solutions Initiative (SSI) funded by the National Science Foundation, as well as follow-up activities and initiatives that the project has inspired.

The alternative futures modeling approach described here provides an analytical framework for collaboration in identifying future challenges and opportunities facing the Penobscot River watershed. The approach is designed to provide policy makers and other stakeholders with the tools needed to assess social, economic, and ecological trends, and to develop a range of plausible futures for the region. The process is intended to foster a proactive approach to landscape-level management and planning, and to allow stakeholders to investigate a wide range of issues and policies affecting land use and the long-term sustainability of coupled human and natural systems.

DRIVERS OF LANDSCAPE CHANGE: FOREST MANAGEMENT AND URBANIZATION

Struggling Natural Resource–Based Economies

Few regions in the eastern United States rival Maine for its natural beauty (figure 9.3). Its coasts, forests, and mountains have earned the state a national reputation for high quality of life and have played a formative role in the country's environmental history. In the 1840s, naturalist Henry David Thoreau followed the Penobscot River's banks on his journey to Mount Katahdin, noting the march of settlement as he moved northward himself. Later, the region would inspire young Theodore Roosevelt and help form his conservation ethic, thus influencing the transformative conservation policies of his presidency.

Today, 90 percent of Maine's 8.1 million hectares (20 million acres) are forested—among the highest percentage for any state (McWilliams et al. 2005). And, as Maine is the nation's most rural state, much of this

FIGURE 9.3. Penobscot River, Maine.
Source: Photo by Ian Adams.

land is undeveloped, as can be readily seen from nighttime satellite images (figure 9.4).

But appearances can be misleading. Ninety-five percent of Maine's lands are privately owned, and the unsettled northern reaches of Maine are very much a working landscape traversed by logging roads and dotted with mills. Maine's $8 billion forest products sector is one of the most diversified in the U.S., producing firewood and poles, hardwood and softwood dimensional lumber, wood composites, panel products like plywood and oriented strand board, biomass, and pulp and paper, among other goods. Also important to the region are forest-based recreation and tourism, including hunting, fishing, and recreational camps; guide and outfitting services; support industries for skiing and snowmobiling interests; and a host of nature-based education programs.

Yet these traditional engines of economic growth have faced challenges in recent decades. For example, while the forest sector continues to comprise 25 to 30 percent of total manufacturing jobs, the number of jobs has decreased with overall declines in manufacturing. The greatest decrease in forest sector employment—45 percent since 1990—has occurred in Maine's high-paying pulp and paper sector. Many forms of recreation have also declined from historic highs—especially as measured by visitation at well-known destinations such as Baxter State Park and the popular Allagash River canoe way.

These losses have disproportionately affected Maine's rural communities, already reeling from manufacturing losses over the last several decades (Barkley 1995). Increasingly, younger residents find it difficult to secure meaningful employment, and leave the region in search of better prospects. The results are an aging population and fractured social networks, both of which threaten the long-term vitality of many rural Maine communities. Indeed, the dichotomy between fast-growing southern Maine and the rural north and interior has led to the creation of "Two Maines"—one vibrant and moderately prosperous, the other struggling (figure 9.5).

In Maine and across much of northern New England, the housing boom of the 1990s and early 2000s, coupled with large sales of industrial forestlands, combined to substantially alter public perceptions of natural resources, land use, and development. Indeed, the greater Portland region's rapid growth and low-density development led U.S. Senator Susan

FIGURE 9.4. Satellite image of the U.S. at night, with the state of Maine identified.
Source: Image by S. Meyer; used with permission from NASA.

Collins to dub the city the "Sprawl Capital" of New England. Similar conditions have affected large portions of York, Cumberland, and Knox counties along Maine's southern coast, where—before the 2008 financial crisis—development proposals overwhelmed local planning boards and threatened the economic viability of historic town centers as businesses moved to outlying suburban areas.

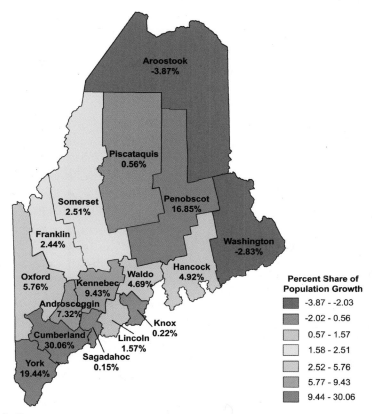

FIGURE 9.5. Census map.
Source: Map by Kara Jacobacci.

Changing Landownership Patterns and Rising Development Pressures

While growth pressures are greatest in the south and along Maine's coast, second home and resort development proposals have the potential to significantly alter land use in virtually every corner of the state, especially along ecologically important streams, ponds, lakes, and waterways.

Maine's abundance of relatively low-priced land and scenic amenities makes it an attractive target for second-home development, but that development also increasingly limits traditional access to the coast, rivers, and lakes (Alig et al. 2004). Foremost on many minds is a recently approved plan by Plum Creek Timber Company to build two resorts with nearly 1,000 house lots in the remote Moosehead Lake region of north-central Maine—the largest development proposal in the state's history. As evidenced by the Plum Creek proposal, large development proposals can now penetrate even far-flung regions of the state.

The stakes in these development controversies are high. An influential 2006 Brookings Institution report identified Maine's natural amenities and quality of life as key components of its economic assets at risk from haphazard growth and development. Indeed, between 1980 and 2000, the report noted, over 320,000 hectares (800,000 acres) of rural land was altered statewide, with 263,000 hectares (650,000 acres) converted during the 1990s alone. And while Maine added just 47,000 new residents during the 1990s, 65,000 new housing units were constructed, each with an average footprint of 4 hectares (10 acres). These findings added credence to the concerns raised in the U.S. Forest Service "Forests on the Edge" report (Stein et al. 2005).

Haphazard development jeopardizes not only Maine's unique reputation for quality of life, but also the long-term viability of its forest products sector and of many types of recreation. Despite an active industry, there has been a massive shift in forest land ownership in the sparsely settled northern half of the state as the forest industry has largely divested itself of timberlands (figure 9.6). This transfer of land has precipitated a number of changes and challenges to forestry and recreational uses (Egan and Luloff 2000, Shelby et al. 2004, Lilieholm et al. 2010), including:

- fragmentation of forest land and forest parcels, along with the conversion of forest to residential and commercial development;
- decreased access to recreational sites and timber for harvests;
- increased taxes as municipal budgets and demands for services rise;
- decreased landowner investment in stand improvement; and
- heightened concerns and regulation over timber harvests and recreational use.

The impacts can be dramatic. For example, the Brookings report documented how low-density residential development cost the state more than $200 million in school construction costs even as overall student enrollments declined (Brookings Institution 2006).

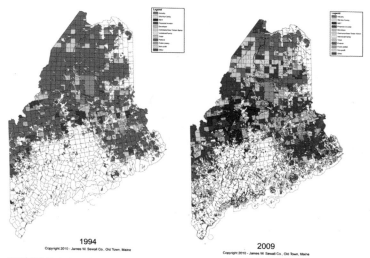

1994

Copyright 2010 - James W. Sewall Co., Old Town, Maine

2009

Copyright 2010 - James W. Sewall Co., Old Town, Maine

FIGURE 9.6. Land ownership change in northern Maine, 1994–2009.
Source: Map by James W. Sewall Co., Old Town, Maine.

Amenity-Based Economic Development

The Brookings report noted that Maine's newfound growth was largely driven by the migration of residents from nearby states seeking improved quality of life, lower living costs, and a variety of scenic and cultural amenities. Such in-migration is critical to the state's economic future given its aging population and limited natural rate of increase. Indeed, Maine has the oldest median population in the country—a ranking exacerbated in part from the significant number of 25- to 34-year-olds that have left the state in recent decades (Brookings Institution 2006).

The Brookings report energized an emerging view in the state: that Maine's primary challenge—and opportunity—was to attract new residents and associated development while protecting the Maine "brand"—the combination of natural and social assets that increasingly attracts both visitors and new residents (Reilly and Renski 2007). The view has some roots in older concepts of environmental protection, which had emphasized the preservation of Maine's natural resources as one method of preserving the state's quality of life. But the Brookings report exemplified a partial shift away from a preservation-based view of environmental protection and toward a view more closely aligned with concepts of sustainable development.

Under this view, the state's working forests and waterfronts, not just its relatively pristine natural areas, could play a central role in defining the state's image and supporting economic growth and development (Fausold and Lilieholm 1999, McConnell and Walls 2005).

Even before 2006, Maine was transitioning toward this strategy. More than 100 land trusts—in partnership with landowners, recreationists, foresters, and state and federal agencies—have in recent decades permanently protected from development roughly 1.6 million hectares (4 million acres)—19.5 percent of the state's area—through means ranging from fee simple acquisition to conservation easements (Cronan et al. 2010, Lilieholm et al. 2010, Meyer et al. 2012). The state itself protected many of these lands, using funding from several successful Land for Maine's Future Program ballot initiatives. The Forest Legacy Program administered by the U.S. Forest Service has allocated more land protection funding to Maine than any other state. Private fundraising also has played a major role. Some of these acquisitions and easements precluded industrial or agricultural use, but many, while precluding future development, guarantee continued production of food and fiber. While agricultural preservation easements are common across the country, the prevalence of working forest easements is largely unique to the Northeast.

Collectively, these protected lands represent one of the nation's most ambitious and successful public–private land conservation partnerships. However, although Maine has invested significant resources in protecting lands for ecosystem function, fiber production, recreation, and tourism, a recent assessment of conserved lands highlighted the need for a more strategic, proactive, and coordinated approach to land conservation (Cronan et al. 2010). Ideally, what is needed is a stakeholder-driven approach that strategically considers both the biophysical and the human dimensions of ecosystem protection. One framework for action—albeit on a larger, New England–wide scale—was offered in the Wildlands and Woodlands vision of protecting 70 percent of the region's forests from development (Foster et al. 2010). These ideas would help guide the University of Maine's efforts to promote a regional, strategic, long-term vision for the Lower Penobscot River Watershed.

THE UNIVERSITY OF MAINE'S SUSTAINABILITY SOLUTIONS INITIATIVE

In 2006, researchers at the University of Maine began thinking about how the university could better direct its efforts to meet stakeholder needs, foster cross-campus collaboration, and effect meaningful change both in Maine and around the globe. These discussions led to the creation of the five-year, $20 million NSF-funded program known as the Maine Sustainability Solutions Initiative (SSI).

SSI's overall goal is to study how forest management, urbanization, and climate change drive landscape transformation in coupled social-ecological systems (SES). SSI's portfolio of nearly 20 independent research projects strives to address integrated ecological, social, and economic systems. The initiative attempts to greatly expand the university's interdisciplinary research, to embrace stakeholder involvement, and to focus on real-world solutions—that is, to cultivate knowledge that leads to action. While pursuing these broad objectives, the project is also studying how SSI's integrated focus affects researchers, students, and the state's colleges and universities—a program called "research on the research."

Through SSI, nearly 100 scientists, 50 graduate students, and roughly 100 undergraduates are working on a wide variety of sustainability science issues in Maine. To provide a few examples, individual projects include research on forest management and urbanization, alternative energy technologies, and efforts to integrate Native American communities into the development of invasive species policies. SSI has also for the first time begun to harness the institutional power represented across the state's major colleges and universities, including the University of Maine's five campuses as well as private colleges such as Colby, Bates, and Bowdoin. SSI's efforts have catalyzed other units on the University of Maine-Orono campus as well. For example, the Center for Research on Sustainable Forests reorganized in 2010 to better address newly identified areas of interest by expanding its traditional focus on industrial timberlands to encompass two new research areas: Family Forests, and Conservation Lands and Public Values.

One of SSI's projects—reported here—explores sociodemographic and land use challenges facing the Lower Penobscot River Watershed (LPRW). Our research approach seeks to understand past, current, and future drivers of landscape change in order to better inform decision making and foster landscapes that sustain both human and natural systems.

ALTERNATIVE FUTURES MODELING IN THE LOWER PENOBSCOT RIVER WATERSHED

Alternative futures modeling is an analytical framework that spatially integrates biophysical, sociodemographic, and economic information into a GIS-based system of simulation models that can be used to assess the impacts of land use policies on a variety of social, cultural, and natural features (Theobold and Hobbs 2002, Hunter et al. 2003, Busch et al. 2005, McCloskey et al. 2011, Gomben et al. 2012). Researchers use these models to generate and evaluate alternative future scenarios depicting how landscapes are likely to develop under varying assumptions and conditions. The models may focus on single components of a landscape, like water resources, or the interaction among multiple components, like urban development and the loss of agricultural lands or sensitive species habitat (Hunter et al. 2003).

We selected the one-million-hectare (2.5-million-acre) LPRW as our focal area for several reasons (figure 9.7). First, the Penobscot is Maine's largest watershed and New England's second largest waterway, draining nearly one-quarter of the state; its central location within the state is also an asset, along with the diversity of cover types and land uses. Focusing on this watershed allows us to study land use change across socioeconomic and environmental gradients. Rising from the heart of Maine's North Woods—one of the most remote and undeveloped regions remaining in the eastern U.S.—the river winds through forests, agricultural lands, communities, and a series of dams on its way to Penobscot Bay. Also important is the river's proximity to the University of Maine's flagship campus in Orono. The campus, which sits on an island in the river, provides an ideal place-based outdoor laboratory for both faculty and students.

The LPRW faces a number of significant challenges and opportunities. On the one hand, major improvements in water quality have transformed the river from a liability to an asset for many communities. As water quality has improved, communities are increasingly reorienting their social and economic life toward the river. The dam removal projects of the Penobscot River Restoration Trust are already accelerating

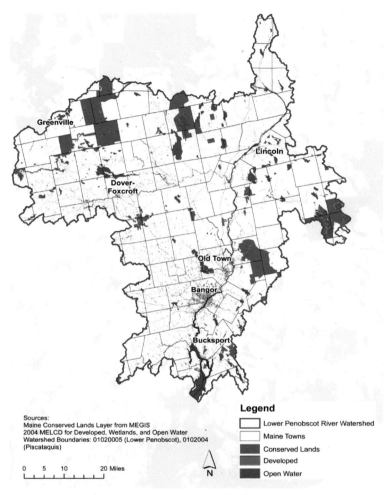

FIGURE 9.7. The Lower Penobscot River Watershed.

this trend. Indeed, communities such as Bangor, Brewer, Hampden, Bucksport, and others have begun to transform their waterfronts with parks and retail development in an effort to attract new growth, aided in part by state funding through a voter-approved Riverfront Community Development Bond.

Beyond the river's banks, the forests and farms that comprise the LPRW's working landscape face rising development pressures. These open space lands—which produce a host of private and public goods and services—are undergoing fragmentation and development at a rapid pace. For example, between 1990 and 2000, the LPRW's population increased just 2 percent while the number of housing units increased 10 percent (White 2005); the number of seasonal homes increased by 14 percent during the same period (White 2005). Moreover, the vast majority of new development was located outside of existing downtowns, thus undermining their economic viability and further challenging the ability of municipalities to provide services in an economically efficient manner (Brookings Institution 2006). Scattered, low-density development also fragments the landscape and challenges the economic viability of working farms and forests.

Study Goals and Objectives

Our research integrates spatial data and stakeholder knowledge to develop a decision-support system for generating and evaluating alternative future landscape scenarios for the LPRW. Our work is intended to foster proactive and strategic land use planning by identifying lands suitable for human development activities as well as those suitable for the conservation of ecosystem services, working forests, and working agricultural lands. Our approach stems from the following hypothesis:

> A collaborative and strategic landscape planning process engaging a diverse range of stakeholder interests can: (1) identify and prioritize the suitability of lands for development and other uses; (2) build broader and more effective partnerships; and (3) result in a landscape that better meets social, economic, and ecological needs for current and future generations.

Our research has three primary objectives:

1. Develop a set of stakeholder-derived models that integrate spatial and expert knowledge of biophysical and socioeconomic variables that can be used to spatially identify land suitability for: (1) development; (2) ecosystem protection; (3) working forests; and (4) working farmlands.
2. Describe how high-value development lands intersect with other competing land uses, and explore the potential for future conflicts and compatibilities.

3. Using stakeholder input, develop and evaluate a set of alternative futures scenarios that reflect a plausible range of demographic trends, land use policies, alternative development patterns, and conservation strategies.

Stakeholder-Derived Land Suitability Modeling with Bayesian Belief Networks

We used Bayesian belief networks (BBNs) to integrate spatial GIS data with expert knowledge across the LPRW (Marcot et al. 2006). Our goal was to identify, on a 30-x-30-meter gridcell basis, lands important for development, ecosystem protection, working forests, and working farmlands.

BBNs are hierarchical, probabilistic models that depict the relationship between random variables and their conditional dependencies. BBNs have been used to model drivers of urban land use change and explore stakeholder-derived alternative planning scenarios (Prato 2005, Kocabas and Dragicevic 2007, Ma et al. 2007, Pourret et al. 2008, Steventon 2008, McCloskey et al. 2011). Several factors have driven the increasing use of this methodology. First, BBNs are well suited for integrating expert knowledge and empirical data— especially spatial data—using the Netica software package (Marcot et al. 2006, Chow and Sadler 2010). Second, as new information becomes available, BBNs are relatively easy to calibrate, validate, and update (Steventon et al. 2008), attributes that make them useful for generating hypotheses and assessing land use alternatives. Third, unlike statistical models that project the future based on past trends, BBNs can anticipate future changes that depart from past practices. In the wake of the 2008 financial crisis and the subsequent transformation of the real estate market, that feature is particularly important, for past data may be poor predictors of future trends.

We began our process by convening a series of four land use–specific focus groups, each composed of stakeholders with expertise in each particular land use type. Our panelists began by identifying biophysical and socioeconomic attributes that make land particularly suitable for each use. For example, the development focus group identified factors such as slope, soils, road access, utility access, and nearby population density as important for residential and commercial development. We then worked with the expert panels to create BBN influence diagrams describing the connections between model variables (figure 9.8). Experts ranked the importance of their chosen variables by completing a set of conditional probability tables (CPTs) based on the influence diagram. We obtained feedback on the CPTs via email surveys with our focus group participants using Likert-scale responses. Through several rounds of communication, we: (1) fine-tuned the influence diagrams; (2) arrived at suitable thresholds for each BBN box or node (figure 9.8); and (3) obtained CPT values.

The process resulted in four land use–specific BBNs designed to spatially identify lands suitable for each land use. We then used the Netica software system to apply each BBN to each 30-x-30-meter gridcell in the LPRW study area. The result was a series of maps depicting the likelihood of suitability for each land use. Once these maps were produced, we reconvened all of our stakeholders as a single group to review models and output maps, and consider potential conflicts and compatibilities among the various land uses.

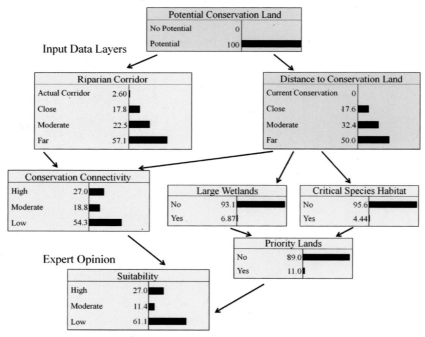

FIGURE 9.8. Sample Bayesian belief network for conservation lands; data from McCloskey et al. 2011.
Source: Diagram by Kara Jacobacci.

Identifying Areas of Potential Conflict and Compatibility
Figure 9.9 shows some early results of our modeling efforts. In the figure, dark green lands portray existing conserved lands, while dark gray areas show lands already developed. Light gray areas show lands that are currently undeveloped but highly suitable for future development. Light green areas show unprotected lands highly suitable for conservation. Areas in red depict lands highly suitable for both future conservation and future development. Given our modeling assumptions, these areas are

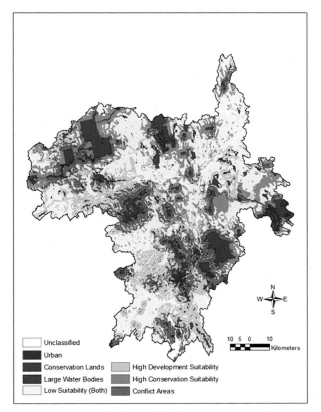

FIGURE 9.9. Areas highly suitable for conservation and development, including potential regions of future conflict; data from McCloskey et al. 2011.
Source: Reprinted from Landscape and Urban Planning, *101/2, Jon T. McCloskey, Robert J. Lilieholm, Christopher Cronan, "Using Bayesian belief networks to identify potential compatibilities and conflicts between development and landscape conservation," Pages 90–203, 2011, with permission from Elsevier.*

where the region is likely to experience future conflicts over land use. As shown in the figure, much of the projected conflict is located near water bodies and existing conservation areas—areas of interest to both developers and conservationists.

Figure 9.10 places the spatial data underlying figure 9.9 in context with current conditions in the LPRW study area. For example, the 279,532 hectares of land highly suitable for development in figure 9.10 represent a sevenfold increase over the actual number of developed hectares in the study area (i.e., 38,550 hectares). Similarly, the region's existing 81,575 hectares of conserved land represent roughly one-quarter of the additional 305,268 hectares of land identified as highly suitable for conservation under our modeling process.

Figure 9.11 further breaks down these two land classes, showing that there are 157,834 hectares that are highly suitable for development but not highly suitable for conservation. Development could be targeted to these lands, where it would be less likely to compromise important ecosystem values. Similarly, 183,570 hectares are highly suitable for conservation and not highly suitable for development; in these areas, conservation is unlikely to displace lands valued for development. Finally, the 121,698 hectares identified as overlapping areas in figure 9.11 represent the red areas in

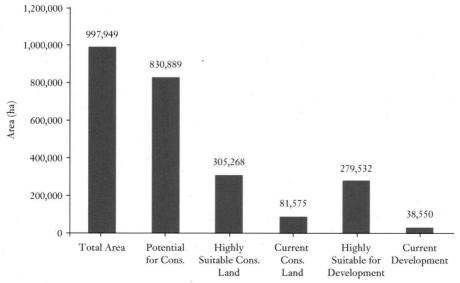

FIGURE 9.10. Areas suitable for conservation and development in the LPRW study area.
Source: Chart by Kara Jacobacci.

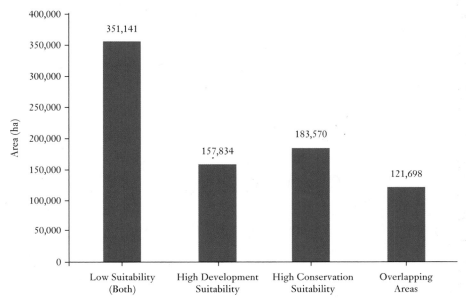

FIGURE 9.11. Areas of potential conflict between conservation and development in the LPRW study area.
Source: Chart by Kara Jacobacci.

figure 9.9—that is, areas of likely future conflict over land use stemming from their high suitability for both conservation and development.

Scenarios of Future Development for the LPRW

The land use suitability maps described above give stakeholders an idea of how areas of future conflict and compatibility among land uses are likely to be distributed across the landscape. Yet not all of the areas we identified as highly suitable for development will experience actual development pressure under reasonable futures scenarios. As a result, we expect only a small portion of the red areas in figure 9.9 to experience actual conversion to development. That finding—that the supply of developable land greatly exceeds future demand—is important because it implies ample room for encouraging development in areas where impacts might be lessened.

Identifying plausible future development scenarios helps researchers and decision makers develop possible future land use policies and evaluate the effects of those policies. Indeed, the pace and location of development-induced land conversion is influenced by a wide range of factors, including population growth and housing demands; zoning and other land use policies; household size and income; the location of employment centers and existing infrastructure; land values; and a host of site-specific features including access, slope, aspect, and drainage (Alberti 2008). These factors often interact in complex and uncertain ways.

To address challenges like these, researchers have developed a wide and expanding range of urban growth models (see, e.g., Wu and Silva 2010). General approaches range from large-scale urban planning models that can assess the regional impacts of population growth and transportation policies (e.g., METROPILUS by Putnam and Shih-Liang 2001, SPARTACUS by Lautso 2003, TRANUS by de la Barra 2001, and UrbanSim by Waddell 2005), to rule-based models (e.g., Landis 2001, Klosterman and Pettit 2005), state-change models (e.g., Landis 2001), and cellular automata models (e.g., Clarke and Gaydos 1998, Battie and Xie 2005).

While modeling capabilities continue to advance and grow in sophistication, these models are not expected to predict with certainty the spatial distribution of future land uses (Ma et al. 2007). Instead, as Irwin (2010, 71–72) notes:

> [T]he goal is not to predict the exact plots of land that will be developed, since such modeling accuracy simply isn't possible. Instead, the goal is to understand how various causal factors influence the qualitative aspects of the observed land use pattern (e.g., the degree of contiguity, fragmentation, concentration, density of various land uses) and changes over time in these pattern measures at a spatially disaggregate scale of analysis.

An important step of our research was to use our land use suitability maps and stakeholder feedback as foundations for generating a range of plausible future development scenarios. Our goal was to identify, under varying projections, which of the areas determined to be highly suitable for development were likely to experience conversion over the next 30 years, and what opportunities and conflicts would arise from those projected changes. To achieve this goal, we "populated" our development suitability maps to arrive at development footprints for 10-year intervals between 2006 and 2036 (figure 9.12).

We constructed five scenarios of land use change between 2006 and 2036. One scenario depicts what things might look like if past trends

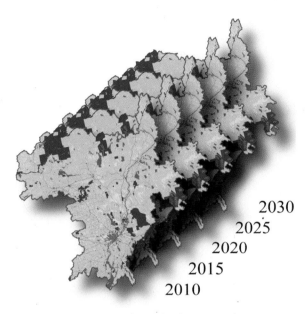

2030
2025
2020
2015
2010

FIGURE 9.12. Projecting future development in the LPRW study area through time.

are simply continued; this is our baseline scenario. Around this baseline, we constructed four additional scenarios that vary according to population growth (high vs. low) and the degree of emphasis placed on environmental protection and economic development choices.

Our five scenarios result in easily understood spatial depictions of future landscapes and are designed to stimulate feedback from stakeholders and ideas for future policies. Our experience in other regions of the country suggests that this approach is effective in informing stakeholders about the potential consequences of alternative land use futures, and that it can help foster proactive land use planning that protects both human and natural systems.

For example, concern over municipal water supplies or flood hazards could lead to the development of scenarios that encourage future development away from these zones. The resulting development footprint would then indicate the displacement of development under the new policies being considered—another important research output because development precluded from one area will often simply relocate to another. To facilitate such comparisons, we have created an online tool—the Maine Futures Community Mapper—that allows anyone to explore our land suitability indices and examine the five stakeholder-derived base scenarios (see http://www.MaineLandUseFutures.org).

NEXT STEPS AND FUTURE DIRECTIONS

Effects of Development on Ecological and Regulatory Thresholds

One important land use conflict, the impairment of urban streams, illustrates the potential applications of our mapping efforts and forms a central focus for our future work. Water is a key feature of the Maine landscape, and one important application of our suitability models and development scenarios will be to assess the implications of future growth scenarios on sensitive aquatic resources.

The negative influence of urbanization on hydrologic systems is well documented, and researchers now conventionally refer to "urban stream syndrome" as a pervasive condition of small watersheds in developed areas. Stream impairment results from a diverse set of physical and chemical drivers that include hydrology, thermal stress, and chemical and nutrient pollution (Meyer et al. 2005). Most of these drivers are closely linked to development, and researchers and regulators now use development levels as powerful, albeit imperfect, predictors of watershed stress.

Despite the close and inverse relationship between development and water quality, urban stream protection efforts generally emerge somewhat haphazardly, often beginning only after development has largely occurred and water quality has been degraded (Owen et al. 2010). But by applying our models at the municipal and watershed levels, we hope to anticipate water quality issues likely to result from future development and to facilitate more proactive efforts to balance communities' development goals with state and federal laws protecting water quality.

Such predictions could be quite valuable because proactive efforts to prevent or manage urban stream degradation are likely to produce positive environmental outcomes at much lower cost than restoration efforts begun after degradation has substantially progressed (Owen et al. 2010).

Fostering Knowledge-to-Action

While researchers and nonprofit groups have pursued many alternative futures modeling projects in recent years, the processes of conveying maps to stakeholders and of turning maps into actual change on the ground are still relatively understudied and undocumented. In response, another extension of our work is exploring how stakeholders and other end-users perceive and react to both models and futures scenarios. We are using a variety of tools, including web-based interactive surveys, to explore how stakeholders perceive models and their utility by varying background information, presentation formats (narratives vs. 2D vs. 3D representations), and other model attributes. We hope to address several specific questions: for example, do stakeholders understand the inherent uncertainty underlying our maps, and do they address that uncertainty in their decision making? Do spatial depictions of future scenarios motivate individuals to take action, and does the magnitude of expected change correlate with individual perceptions and degree of user motivation?

Students as Catalysts: The Penobscot River Bay-to-Baxter Initiative

Finally, we have harnessed the power of students as professionals and stakeholders to help us determine how our research team should progress in the future. This latest research phase dates back to the summer of 2011, when a collaborative effort among the University of Maine, the Quebec-Labrador Foundation, and Acadia National Park launched the Acadian Internship in Large Landscape Conservation and Stewardship. The six-week course, held in Acadia National Park, exposed students from around the world to college-level training in conservation biology, planning, and finance. One week of academic instruction was augmented by a four-week paid internship with local conservation organizations working across Downeast Maine and southeast New Brunswick, Canada. The program concluded with group reports and presentations open to the public.

In 2011 and 2012, some 30 students from more than a dozen countries participated in the Acadian program, working side by side with dozens of conservation groups and projects. Beginning in 2013, with additional support and participation from the Lincoln Institute of Land Policy and Harvard Forest, we revised the program format to focus on student leadership training and place-based problem solving. To meet these goals, we recruited four teams of three students each to prepare and present a collaborative conservation case study to the class.

Student teams from Massachusetts, Pennsylvania, Belize, and Chile were tasked before the beginning of the session to prepare a half-day presentation describing their own work in landscape-scale conservation. They were also asked to prepare to lead program faculty and students from all four sites through an exercise intended to address a pressing challenge that they faced. For example, the team from Belize described their struggles in coordinating cross-border conservation policies with neighboring Guatemala, and worked with students and program faculty to devise collaborative strategies. The Pennsylvania team sought help in dealing with natural gas extraction, which is increasingly degrading water quality along tributaries of the Susquehanna River. The Chilean team brainstormed to identify and refine market-based incentives for conservation, and the Massachusetts team led discussions on methods to achieve large landscape conservation goals across regions composed of small private ownerships. The four teams spent two days on this exercise, gaining experience in both leading discussions and responding to challenges.

For the next two-and-a-half days, the group focused on SSI's LPRW futures work. Members of the LPRW research team first gave an overview of the project and then led students on a day-long field trip across the LPRW, meeting with municipal and tribal officials as well as conservation and agricultural interests. Our question was simple: "Based on our LPRW futures work, what should be our next steps?" In other words, how can we leverage the knowledge gained from our research over the last five years to enact meaningful change across the watershed?

Our interaction with the Acadian program participants proved to be fruitful; indeed, it far exceeded our expectations. Armed with new knowledge of conservation efforts around the world and new skills in complex problem solving, the Acadian interns and the LPRW research team conceived a broad vision for a river-based conservation and economic development strategy. Inspired by this work, we at the University of Maine have launched the Bay-to-Baxter Initiative, which is designed to leverage and expand ongoing conservation and economic development activities across the watershed by forging a broadly shared vision that links economic development with the region's renowned quality of place (see https://bangordailynews.com/2014/07/11/opinion/contributors/bay-to -baxter-as-the-penobscot-river-changes-so-must-we/).

The sweep of this vision—stretching from Penobscot Bay to Baxter State Park and Mount Katahdin in Maine's interior—offers much promise in addressing the social, economic, and environmental challenges facing the region. Indeed, the Penobscot River's recent rebirth has already stimulated significant investment and national attention, including more than $200 million in public–private redevelopment investment along downtown Bangor's waterfront and a $63-million dam removal and river restoration project, which is nearing completion (http://www.penobscotriver.org/).

In the upper reaches of the watershed, interest in both conservation and economic development has heightened. For example, Baxter State Park, located at the headwaters of the Penobscot, is already well known as the home to Mount Katahdin and the terminus of the 2,200-mile Appalachian Trail. The region's long-established reputation as a tourism center is likely to grow in response to a recently announced proposal to create a new 75,000-acre national park adjacent to Baxter, and a new 75,000-acre national recreation area to be located nearby (http://katahdinwoods.org/). Just to the west of the Penobscot watershed, the Plum Creek Timber Company's recently approved plans to develop two amenity-based resorts and nearly 1,000 home sites near Moosehead Lake offer additional recreation and tourism opportunities, bringing the promise of much-needed economic development to one of the poorest regions in the state (Acheson 2010). The challenge for the Bay-to-Baxter Initiative will be to help individuals and institutions that are pushing a variety of efforts across the region, and that are now informed by the LPRW Alternative Futures Modeling work, to collaborate at the landscape scale to achieve common objectives.

LESSONS LEARNED

Communities, planners, businesses, and advocacy groups often lack the time and resources needed to identify and evaluate the impacts of important land use decisions. In many situations, these limitations can mean that important decisions regarding land use are made with incomplete information regarding current and future conditions (Pullin et al. 2004). As a result, approaches that can integrate spatial data with expert knowledge have the potential to improve land use decision-making processes for practitioners, policy makers, and the public.

Our alternative futures modeling approach and online planning tool are designed to help stakeholders with varying land use interests to build relationships, promote transparency, and better understand how land use decisions made today are likely to affect regions in the future (McCloskey et al. 2011, Meyer et al. 2014a, Meyer et al. 2014b). By integrating expert opinion and spatial data, our aim is to engage broad interests and encourage long-term thinking when it comes to how land use policies are developed and implemented. As part of this modeling effort, we have worked with scores of individuals and dozens of agencies and NGOs to better understand existing landscapes and to envision how landscapes may change in the future. Although our modeling process is ongoing, we have already learned several important lessons.

Engaging Stakeholders and Forging Partnerships

Since its inception, the LPRW futures project has engaged a wide range of stakeholders, including governmental agencies at the local, state, and federal levels. Examples include the Maine Department of Agriculture, Conservation, and Forestry and the Department of Inland Fisheries and Wildlife; the Land Use Regulation Commission; the Land Use Planning Commission; the Maine Forest Service; Land for Maine's Future; the U.S. Forest Service; and the USDA Natural Resources Conservation Service. Representatives from major businesses as well as trade associations and nonprofit advocacy groups have participated in our focus groups and workshops. Participants have ranged from the Maine Forest Products Council and Maine Pulp & Paper Association, to the Small Woodland Owners Association of Maine, Maine Coast Heritage Trust, and the Maine Organic Farmers and Gardeners Association.

Through this work, we have learned much about engaging diverse stakeholders and sustaining their interest in the process. The challenges are substantial; time constraints make it difficult to engage thoughtful, energetic, and knowledgeable stakeholders. Sustaining these relationships over time is even more difficult; managing expectations is also challenging. Given the scope of our work, many groups and individuals came forward with a desire to participate, and managing expectations about participation and the resulting end products will always be a concern with projects such as ours.

Nevertheless, we have also learned many positive lessons. Virtually everyone engaged in our focus groups and workshops felt empowered by the experience. They seemed to enjoy working with university researchers, learning new tools, and exploring various futures for the LPRW. Our participants were clearly up to the intellectual challenge and readily grasped the overall intent and value of our work. Perhaps most importantly, they believed that the models accurately reflected their input, opinions, and values.

Fostering Planning in an Anti-Regulatory Environment

Fostering a proactive approach to land use issues can be a challenge anywhere, especially in states such as Maine that have a long-standing deference to local home rule and private property rights (Jacobs 2003). The challenge was heightened in 2010, when control of the executive and legislative branches of state government shifted from Democratic to Republican control. The change soon led to calls for the rollback of many long-standing regulatory programs, expansion of policies intended to strengthen private property rights, and the scaling back of the state's already limited planning capacity. A subset of our participants shared these policy preferences. Nevertheless, while some stakeholders were not supportive of land use planning in concept, their curiosity generally outweighed their concerns over the possibility of increased regulation. In fact, we were surprised to find that many developers were highly supportive of zoning and other land use regulations because of their ability to reduce future uncertainties, especially the potential to avoid future conflicts over incompatible land uses. The preliminary lesson, we think, is that an alternative futures mapping process can divorce planning from some of its ideological overtones and facilitate a more pragmatic dialogue about future land use. A test of that will be the response to the student-conceived Bay-to-Baxter Initiative; also important will be stakeholder adoption of the online Maine Futures Community Mapper. A 30-minute Maine Public Broadcasting Network television documentary, *Preserving Paradise*, described SSI's forecasting tools and their applications (http://www.mpbn.net/Television/LocalTelevisionPrograms/SustainableMaine/PreservingParadise.aspx). How viewers receive the research and act on its message of proactive land use planning will ultimately determine the viability of large landscape conservation in the Penobscot River watershed.

CONCLUSIONS

A core goal of sustainable development policies is to foster sustainable economic activity, vibrant communities, and environmental quality. In Maine, protecting these assets is an important economic development strategy. Understanding landscape change drivers through interdisciplinary research is therefore critical to sustaining human and natural systems (Lilieholm et al. 2013). Equally important is the work of engaging stakeholders in the research process, and of understanding how scientific knowledge can be transformed into meaningful solutions.

Alternative futures modeling is an effective way to foster improved understanding of existing land use and of the intricate and dynamic connections between human and natural systems. In Maine, the approach is particularly relevant given the close economic and social ties between the state's landscape and its people. Ensuring the health of these systems is important not only to quality of life, but to the sustained viability of the tourism and forest products sectors.

Our work has engaged stakeholders across a broad range of interests, including conservation, government, business, and real estate development. This breadth allows us to better understand the factors likely to drive future challenges and opportunities affecting Maine's landscape. Our stakeholder-derived models of land suitability provide the public with quantitative, spatially explicit depictions that not only inform key stakeholders of current land use and suitability, but also allow various interests to design and evaluate the effects of alternative assumptions regarding population growth and development pressures on current and future landscapes. Most important, our modeling is designed to facilitate the identification of locations where compatibilities and conflicts in projected land use are likely to exist across time in response to differing assumptions embodied in future land use scenarios. Creation of the online mapping tool, as well as the 30-minute television documentary, are all important steps in realizing improved land use in the region.

Finally, the Bay-to-Baxter Initiative offers the University of Maine a unique opportunity to leverage its land grant mission of research, education, and service. Indeed, the initiative has the potential to position the university to draw on and foster a host of local and regional conservation and economic development efforts by hundreds of organizations and partnerships. Existing efforts have focused on a host of goals, including biodiversity protection, ecosystem restoration, economic and community development, and the protection of open space and working lands and waterfronts. Together, the collective impact of these diverse and disparate projects will be leveraged under the initiative to attract greater recognition and resources, serving as a national model for how academic institutions can harness the science and practice of large landscape conservation as a tool for economic development and the protection of quality of place.

ACKNOWLEDGMENTS

Support for this research was provided by the Maine Forest and Agricultural Experiment Station, the Center for Research on Sustainable Forests, and the University of Maine's Sustainability Solutions Initiative (NSF grant number EPS-0904155). The authors acknowledge earlier work by Jon McCloskey on portions of this research.

REFERENCES

Acheson, A. W. 2010. *Poverty in Maine 2010*. Orono, ME: Margaret Chase Smith Policy Center, University of Maine.

Alberti, M. 2008. *Advances in Urban Ecology: Integrating Humans and Ecological Processes in Urban Ecosystems*. New York: Springer.

Alig, R. J., J. D. Kline, and M. Lichtenstein. 2004. "Urbanization on the U.S. Landscape: Looking Ahead in the 21st Century." *Urban Planning* 69:219–234.

Barkley, D. L. 1995. "The Economics of Change in Rural America." *American Journal of Agricultural Economics* 77 (12): 1252–1258.

Battie, M., and Y. Xie. 2005. "Urban Growth Using Cellular Automata." In *GIS, Spatial Analysis, and Modeling*, ed. D. Macquire, M. Batty, and M. Goodchild, 151–172. Redlands, CA: ESRI Press.

Brookings Institution Metropolitan Policy Program. 2006. *Charting Maine's Future: An Action Plan for Promoting Sustainable Prosperity and Quality Places*. Washington, DC: The Brookings Institution.

Busch, G., R. J. Lilieholm, R. E. Toth, and T. C. Edwards Jr. 2005. "Alternative Future Growth Scenarios for Utah's Wasatch Front: Assessing the Impacts of Development on the Loss of Prime Agricultural Lands." *Ecology and the Environment* 81:247–256.

Chow, T., and R. Sadler. 2010. "The Consensus of Local Stakeholders and Outside Experts in Suitability Modeling for Future Camp Development." *Landscape and Urban Planning* 94:9–19.

Clarke, K. C., and L. J. Gaydos. 1998. "Loose-Coupling a Cellular Automaton Model and GIS: Long-Term Urban Growth Prediction for San Francisco and Washington/Baltimore." *International Journal of Geographical Information Science* 12:699–714.

Cronan, C. S., R. J. Lilieholm, J. Tremblay, and T. Glidden. 2010. "A Retrospective Assessment of Land Conservation Patterns in Maine Based on Spatial Analysis of Ecological and Socio-Economic Indicators." *Environmental Management* 45 (5): 1076–1095.

de la Barra, T. 2001. "Integrated Land Use and Transport Modeling: The TRANUS Experience." In *Planning Support Systems: Integrating Geographic Information Systems, Models and Visualization Tools*, ed. R. K. Brail and R. E. Klosterman, 129–156. Redlands, CA: ESRI Press.

Egan, A. F., and A. E. Luloff. 2000. "The Exurbanization of America's Forests." *Journal of Forestry* 98 (3): 26–30.

Fausold, C. F., and R. J. Lilieholm. 1999. "The Economic Value of Open Space: A Review and Synthesis." *Environmental Management* 23 (3): 307–320.

Foster, D. R., B. Donahue, D. Kittredge, K. F. Lambert, M. Hunter, B. Hall, L. C. Irland, R. J. Lilieholm, D. A. Orwig, A. D'Amato, E. Colburn, J. Thompson, J. Levitt, A. M. Ellison, J. Aber, C. Cogbill, C. Driscoll, and C. Hart. 2010. *Wildlands and Woodlands: A Vision for the New England Landscape.* Cambridge, MA: Harvard University Press.

Gomben, P. C., R. J. Lilieholm, and M. J. Gonzalez. 2012. "Impact of Demographic Futures on Development Patterns and the Loss of Open Space in the California Mojave Desert." *Environmental Management* 49 (2): 305–324.

Hunter, L. M., M. J. Gonzalez, M. Stevenson, K. S. Karish, R. Toth, T. C. Edwards Jr., R. J. Lilieholm, and M. Cablk. 2003. "Population and Land Use Change in the California Mojave: Natural Habitat Implications of Alternative Futures." *Population Research and Policy Review* 22:373–397.

Irwin, E. G. 2010. "New Directions for Urban Economic Models of Land Use Change: Incorporating Spatial Dynamics and Heterogeneity." *Journal of Regional Science* 50:65–91.

Jacobs, H. M. 2003. "The Politics of Property Rights at the National Level: Signals and Trends." *Journal of the American Planning Association* 69 (2): 181–189.

Klosterman, R. E., and C. J. Pettit. 2005. "An Update on Planning Support Systems." *Environment and Planning B: Planning and Design* 32:477–484.

Kocabas, V., and S. Dragicevic. 2007. "Enhancing a GIS Cellular Automata Model of Land Use Change: Bayesian Networks, Influence Diagrams, and Causality." *Transactions in GIS* 11:81–702.

Kunstler, J. H. 2005. *The Long Emergency: Surviving the Converging Catastrophes of the Twenty-First Century.* New York: Atlantic Monthly Press.

Landis, J. 2001. "CUF, CUF II, and CURBA: A Family of Spatially Explicit Urban Growth and Land-Use Policy Simulation Models." In *Planning Support Systems: Integrating Geographic Information Systems, Models and Visualization Tools*, ed. R. K. Brail and R. E. Klosterman, 157–200. Redlands, CA: ESRI Press.

Lautso, K. 2003. "The SPARTACUS System for Defining and Analyzing Sustainable Land Use and Transport Policies." In *Planning Support Systems in Practice*, ed. S. Geertman and J. Stillwell, 453–463. Heidelberg, Germany: Springer.

Lilieholm, R. J., L. C. Irland, and J. M. Hagan. 2010. "Changing Socio-Economic Conditions for Private Woodland Protection." In *Landscape-Scale Conservation Planning*, ed. S. C. Trombulak and R. F. Baldwin, 67–98. New York: Springer.

Lilieholm, R. J., S. R. Meyer, M. L. Johnson, and C. S. Cronan. 2013. "Land Conservation in the Northeastern United States: An Assessment of Historic Trends and Current Conditions." *Environment* 55 (4): 3–14.

Ma, L., T. Arentze, A. Borgers, and H. Timmermans. 2007. "Modeling Land-Use Decisions Under Conditions of Uncertainty." *Computers, Environment, and Urban Systems* 31:461–476.

Marcot, B., J. Steventon, G. Sutherland, and R. McCann. 2006. "Guidelines for Developing and Updating Bayesian Belief Networks Applied to Ecological Modeling and Conservation." *Canadian Journal of Forest Research* 36:3063–3074.

McCloskey, J. T., R. J. Lilieholm, and C. S. Cronan. 2011. "Using Bayesian Belief Networks to Identify Future Compatibilities and Conflicts Between Development and Landscape Conservation." *Landscape and Urban Planning* 101:190–203.

McConnell, V., and M. Walls. 2005. *The Value of Open Space: Evidence from Studies of Nonmarket Benefits.* Working Paper WP04VM1. Cambridge, MA: Lincoln Institute of Land Policy.

McWilliams, W. H., et al. 2005. *The Forests of Maine: 2003.* USDA Forest Service Resource Bulletin NE-164. Newtown Square, PA: USDA Forest Service.

Meyer, J. L., M. J. Paul, and W. K. Taulbee. 2005. "Stream Ecosystem Function in Urbanizing Landscapes." *Journal of the North American Benthological Society* 24 (3): 602–612.

Meyer, S. R., C. S. Cronan, R. J. Lilieholm, M. L. Johnson, and D. R. Foster. 2014a. "Using the Historical Roots of Land Conservation in Northern New England to Derive Alternative Future Scenarios of Landscape Conservation." *Conservation Biology* (in press).

Meyer, S. R., M. L. Johnson, and R. J. Lilieholm. 2012. "Landscape Conservation in the United States: Evolution and Innovation Across the Urban–Rural Interface." In *Urban–Rural Interfaces: Linking People and Nature*, ed. W. Zipper, D. N. Laband, and B. G. Lockaby, 225–258. Madison, WI: American Society of Agronomy, Crop Science Society of America, Soil Science Society of America.

Meyer, S. R., M. L. Johnson, R. J. Lilieholm, and C. S. Cronan. 2014b. "Development of a Stakeholder-Driven Spatial Modeling Framework for Strategic Landscape Planning Using Bayesian Networks Across Two Urban-Rural Gradients in Maine." *Ecological Modeling* (in press).

Owen, D., C. Bohlen, P. Glaser, Z. Henderson, and C. Kilian. 2010. "Collaboration, Clean Water Act Residual Designation Authority, and Collective Permitting: A Case Study of Long Creek." *Watershed Science Bulletin* (Fall): 25–34.

Pourret, O., P. Naim, and B. Marcot. 2008. *Bayesian Networks: A Practical Guide to Applications.* West Sussex, U.K.: John Wiley and Sons, Ltd.

Prato, T. 2005. "Bayesian Adaptive Management of Ecosystems." *Ecological Modeling* 183:147–156.

Pullin, A. S., T. M. Knight, D. A. Stone, and K. Charman. 2004. "Do Conservation Managers Use Scientific Evidence to Support their Decision-Making?" *Biological Conservation* 119:245–252.

Putnam S. H., and C. Shih-Liang. 2001. "The METROPILUS Planning Support System: Urban Models and GIS." In *Planning Support Systems: Integrating Geographic Information Systems, Models and Visualization Tools*, ed. R. K. Brail and R. E. Klosterman, 99–128. Redlands, CA: ESRI Press.

Reilly, C. J., and H. Renski. 2007. *Place and Prosperity.* Augusta: Maine State Planning Office.

Shelby, B., J. A. Tokarczyk, and R. L. Johnson. 2004. "Timber Harvests and Forest Neighbors." *Journal of Forestry* 102 (1): 8–13.

Stein, S. M., R. E. McRoberts, R. J. Alig, M. D. Nelson, D. M. Theobald, M. Eley, M. Decher, and M. Carr. 2005. *Forests on the Edge: Housing Development on America's Private Forests.* Washington, DC: USDA Forest Service General Technical Report PNW-GTR-636.

Steventon, J. 2008. "Conservation of Marbled Murrelets in British Columbia." In *Bayesian Networks: A Practical Guide to Applications*, ed. O. Pourret, P. Naim, B. Marcot, 127–148. West Sussex, U.K.: John Wiley and Sons.

Theobold, D. M., and N. T. Hobbs. 2002. "A Framework for Evaluating Land Use Planning Alternatives: Protecting Biodiversity on Private Land." *Conservation Ecology* 6:5. *www.consecol.org/vol6/iss1/art5*

Waddell, P. 2005. "Between Politics and Planning: UrbanSim As a Decision-Support System for Metropolitan Planning." In *Planning Support Systems: Integrating Geographic Information Systems, Models, and Visualization Tools*, ed. R. K. Brail and R. E. Klosterman, 201–228. Redlands, CA: ESRI Press.

White, E. M. 2005. *Forests on the Edge: A Case Study of South-Central and Southwest Maine Watersheds.* Portland, OR: USDA Forest Service, Pacific Northwest Research Station.

Wilson, J. S. 2005. "Nineteenth Century Lumber Surveys for Bangor, Maine: Implications for Pre-European Settlement Forest Characteristics in Northern and Eastern Maine." *Journal of Forestry* 103 (5): 218–223.

Wu, N., and E. A. Silva. 2010. "Artificial Intelligence Solutions for Urban Land Dynamics: A Review." *Journal of Planning Literature* 24:246–265.

10

The Mara-Serengeti Ecosystem and Greater Maasailand: Building the Role of Local Leaders, Institutions, and Communities

Robin S. Reid, Dickson Kaelo, David K. Nkedianye,
Patti Kristjanson, Mohammed Y. Said, Kathleen A. Galvin,
and Isabella Gambill

The conservation of wildlife in many large savanna landscapes in Africa depends on meeting the needs of both wildlife and local people (Brockington 2004). This imperative is especially acute when the wild animals to be conserved are large and move long distances, spilling out of core protected areas onto grazing lands where they mix with farmers and livestock. Because grazing lands cover about 40 percent of Africa and 50 percent of east Africa today (Reid et al. 2008, Reid 2012), herding has an outsized importance in that continent's conservation efforts, both because it is so widespread and because the herding lifestyle is often (but not always) compatible with wildlife and other species (Reid 2012). Outside conservation areas, most African rangelands are on land managed by pastoral communities in common, although privatization of land is a growing trend in Africa (Blench 2001).

Much of the effort to include communities in conservation of large landscapes has been driven by interests outside the savannas, either by national governments, NGOs, or foreign conservationists (Neumann 2002, Brockington et al. 2008). Once included in conservation planning only as an afterthought, local communities are now major stakeholders. However, initiatives driven, led, and managed by local leaders, communities, and institutions to meet the needs of both wildlife and people remain rare. The science of community-based conservation rarely answers the questions posed by local communities, integrates local knowledge, or builds the capacity of communities to do their own research. This chapter is the story of our efforts to turn community-based conservation around so that it is driven, led, and managed by local interests, needs, and people in Kenya's northern Serengeti-Mara ecosystem, or the Mara.

To convey the significance of the northern Serengeti-Mara, we will attempt to incorporate the points of view of the region's four predominating types of stakeholders. The first group is conservationists, who include national governments, local and international tourism businesses, local and foreign researchers, and some of the local people. From a conservation perspective, the Serengeti-Mara represents one of the jewels of conservation, an unusual example of an ecosystem relatively undisturbed by people (Sinclair et al. 2002) that we can use as a benchmark to understand how humans are modifying the earth. This ecosystem provides handsome tourism profits for governments (Honey 2008, Norton-Griffiths et al. 2008, Thirgood et al. 2008), the tourism industry (Norton-Griffiths 1995, Osano et al. 2013b), and some local elites (Thompson and Homewood 2002). A second group of stakeholders are pastoralists living within the ecosystem whose livelihoods are sometimes directly threatened by wildlife (Sitati et al. 2003, Kolowski and Holekamp 2006) and who have lost access to their ancestral grazing lands, which are now part of the Maasai Mara National Reserve (Lamprey and Reid 2004). A third group of stakeholders are the farmers who live west and north of the Mara, many of whom arrived in the area after ancient pastoral cultures but before today's Maasai pastoralists (Shetler 2007). Farmers to the north in the Mau Forest and irrigators along the Mara River diminish the flow of this crucial year-round water source for wildlife and pastoralists downstream (Gereta et al. 2002); farmers to the west have conflicts with elephants moving into the Transmara region (Kaelo 2007). The fourth group of stakeholders are the many species of wildlife themselves, which have lived in this ecosystem side by side with hominins for millions of years, far longer than either pastoralists or farmers. We do not hear directly from wildlife, but presumably they are represented by the views of human conservationists.

In this chapter, we describe one effort to work with these stakeholders in Kenya's Mara region through conservancies and other innovative platforms that are largely codesigned by local pastoral leaders with their partners. More than a story about innovative conservation work, this is a narrative about building local institutions and enabling local leaders to work broadly across large landscapes and experiment with new models of conservation that support local livelihoods and wildlife at the same time. It is also the story of how conservation science can support and sometimes catalyze these efforts, if the scientists coproduce new knowledge with local communities that integrates both local and scientific expertise. In telling this story, we will also refer to examples from four other Maasailand ecosystems similar to the Mara, where we worked on supporting local initiatives to build pastoral livelihoods and conserve wildlife.

THE GREATER SERENGETI-MARA WILDLIFE-PASTORAL ECOSYSTEM

Although this chapter will focus principally on the Mara region, we will begin by describing the greater Serengeti-Mara wildlife-pastoral ecosystem because of its status as the site of the migration of wildebeest today and the free flow of people across the area in the past. Today, conservationists define the greater Serengeti-Mara ecosystem as a 25,000 sq km area straddling the border between Kenya and Tanzania and delimited by the savanna grazed by both the million-strong Serengeti wildebeest migration and the much smaller (approximately 30,000) Loita wildebeest migration (Sinclair 1995). While these two migrations mix in the Mara region in the dry season, they are relatively genetically distinct, since the Serengeti population breeds in Tanzania and the Loita population in Kenya. Pastoralists and their livestock also graze much of the Serengeti-Mara, which encompasses two central protected areas, Tanzania's Serengeti National Park and Kenya's Maasai Mara National Reserve; their surrounding game reserves (Maswa, Ikorongo, and Grumeti); Ngorongoro Conservation Area; the Loliondo Game Controlled Area in Tanzania, and the ranches neighboring the Mara Reserve in Kenya (Sinclair and Norton-Griffiths 1979, Thirgood et al. 2008). Although local peoples are excluded from the national parks and reserves, pastoralists and their livestock live and graze in Ngorongoro and Loliondo in Tanzania and the Mara pastoral lands in Kenya.

In the last 50 to 60 years, the Asi, Nata, Ishenya, Ikizu, Ngoreme, Ikoma, Sukuma, Kuria, Tatog, Sikazi, Ndorobo, and Maasai peoples have lost a great deal of their land due to the creation by both colonial and postcolonial governments of the core protected areas that form the heart of the greater Serengeti-Mara ecosystem today (Lamprey and Reid 2004, Shetler 2007). For millions of years, the Serengeti-Mara had been home to humans and their ancestors (Leakey and Hay 1979). In the mid-1900s, colonial governments evicted local people to create new parks and reserves for the conservation of wildlife (Neumann 1995, Shetler 2007), but these herders, hunters, farmers, and fishers still live in the ecosystem, in lands important to them and to wildlife. And, as is the case elsewhere, the vast majority of the costs of these protected areas fall on the shoulders of local people while the vast majority of the benefits flow to more wealthy people living far away from this ecosystem (Thompson and Homewood 2002, Norton-Griffiths et al. 2008).

The greater ecosystem supports the most diverse large wildlife migration in the world (Sinclair 1995), a mass movement of about 1.1 million wildebeest; 360,000 Thomson's gazelles; 200,000 zebras; 7,500 hyenas; 2,800 lions; 850 leopards; 500 cheetahs; and about 350,000 other large animals (Stelfox et al. 1986, Ottichilo et al. 2000, Mduma and Hopcraft 2008, Reid 2012). In addition, there are more than 600 species of birds (two-thirds as many as in all of North America), at least 100 species of dung beetles, 80 grasshopper species, 20 frog species (Sinclair et al. 2008a), and many, many uncounted species.

The Kenyan Mara, the focus of this chapter, makes up only about a quarter of the ecosystem's area (5,934 sq km [Norton-Griffiths 1995]) but assumes outsize importance because it provides crucial sources of food and water for migrating wildlife and pastoral livestock during the dry season and drought (Sinclair and Norton-Griffiths 1979). This productivity is caused by a strong rainfall gradient from Tanzania in the south (500 mm or 20 inches of annual rainfall) to the north (up to 1,340 mm or 53 inches of annual rainfall) (Norton-Griffiths et al. 1975, Ogutu et al. 2011). In the Mara, about 77 percent of the area used by the wildebeest migration is on pastoral land, and loss of their access to this land might result in a 30 percent loss of wildlife (Norton-Griffiths 1995), or perhaps half a million animals.

The way people use the land and the types of boundaries they create on their land determine how freely livestock and wildlife move and how we define this system itself (Reid 2012). Indeed, more than a million people live to the west of the Mara (Campbell and Hofer 1995) in a checkerboard of farming lands and villages reaching from the Mara to Lake Victoria, land use that creates hard boundaries in the former open savanna. But to the north and east of the Mara, the land is relatively open, with a few soft boundaries, and is used by pastoralists for grazing or rented by them to ecotourism businesses for wildlife use. Hard boundaries are physical, like fences or plowed farm fields, or social, like restrictive land use rules on private land or protected areas (Reid 2012). Soft boundaries occur in pastoral lands when people occupy land with their corrals and homesteads (but without fences), or heavily used areas around water points. As people harden boundaries, they fragment the land (Hobbs et al. 2008), which can cause migrations to collapse and deadly conflicts to arise until wildlife are extinguished from these landscapes (Ogutu et al. 2013).

CONFLICTS AND SYNERGIES AMONG PEOPLE AND WILDLIFE IN THE MARA

Pastoralists, wildlife, and livestock have lived side by side in the Mara for thousands of years (Lamprey and Waller 1990, Marshall 1990), sometimes in conflict and sometimes in unexpected synergy. Because the Mara is the most productive part of the ecosystem, it is also in highest demand for other uses by farmers, shopkeepers, tourism businesses, and others. Unlike Serengeti National Park, the Mara Reserve is small and the land used outside the reserve is extensive; thus the challenges for large landscape conservation here are particularly complex and consequential for the entire ecosystem.

First, the unexpected synergies. In the open pastoral land of the Mara, wildlife not only can coexist with livestock and people, but some species appear to prefer to cluster around pastoral settlements (Reid 2012). We think this occurs because of the variation in grass heights that livestock create in this system (Bhola et al. 2012). Smaller wildlife (like small gazelles and warthogs), which have the highest risk of predation (Sinclair et al. 2003), prefer short-grass pastures where predators are visible and grass is nutritious. These short-grass pastures occur around pastoral settlements where livestock graze the grass short. Medium-sized grazers (like wildebeest, topi, and kongoni) prefer pastures with intermediate amounts of forage (Fryxell 1991), where there is a mixture of patches of grass grazed short by livestock for predator visibility as well as longer grass to meet their greater forage intake requirements. The largest wildlife, like elephants and buffalo, are relatively predator-proof and need great amounts of forage, so they often prefer long-grass areas, which occur in the Mara Reserve. Small to medium grazers therefore distribute themselves relatively close to pastoral settlements to take advantage of both predator protection and nutritious pastures nearby, and pastoralists observe these animals (and hyenas) moving close to their settlements, especially at night when predation pressure is highest. Thus, lightly used pastoral areas are richer in wildlife than the reserve when grass is abundant in the wet season, with medium to large wildlife migrating back to the long-grass protected areas in the dry season (Bhola et al. 2012). Topi and warthogs prefer to raise their newborns in the shorter grass areas on pastoral land (Bhola et al. 2012). This scenario demonstrates the value of the Mara's diverse landscape, in which reserve and pastoral lands provide different habitat benefits for the area's diverse wildlife.

Despite these synergies, conflicts are increasing in the Mara, as measured by the overall decline in wildlife populations. Over the last 30 years, some of the pastoral land outside the Mara Reserve has progressively been converted to commercial wheat fields and growing villages (Homewood et al. 2001, Ottichilo et al. 2001, Serneels and Lambin 2001, Ogutu et al. 2009). Illegal hunting of wildlife has been particularly severe along the western side of the Mara, in the areas closest to highly populated farming areas (Ogutu et al. 2009). Dotted with scattered Maasai homesteads, much of the land remained open for both wildlife and livestock over this time. However, even with this open land, resident wildlife populations fell by 82 percent in the pastoral lands and by 74 percent in the reserve between 1977 and 2009 (Ogutu et al. 2011). Strong efforts in the western part of the Mara Reserve to halt poaching have had some effect but do not seem to be stopping the overall decline in wildlife numbers (Ogutu et al. 2011).

In the early 2000s, a new, major threat to the free movement of both wildlife and livestock began in the Mara. To comprehend this threat, it is important to understand what has been called the pastoral paradox. Pastoralists in the Mara, like many around the world, face this paradox when they consider converting their commonly managed pastures into private land parcels (Fernandez-Gimenez 2002). How they solve this paradox deeply affects conservation. On the one hand, herding requires flexible access to land and water, so herders can move their livestock to better pastures as scattered rainfall creates patches of green grass in different parts of the landscape, and especially during the dry season and drought. This flexibility is just what wildlife need too, and largely creates the compatibility of pastoralism with wildlife conservation. On the other hand, many pastoralists also now want secure access to land and water. Thus pastoralists need flexibility but want the guarantee of security—especially in Kenya, which has a history of land grabbing by foreign governments and corporations, a phenomenon common in Africa and

Asia (Rulli et al. 2013). The need for security often encourages pastoralists to stop moving, settle down, and privatize land so they can claim a piece of territory as their own. But settling often creates the hard boundaries that can stop wildlife movement, leads often to greater poaching activity, and is generally incompatible with wildlife conservation (Reid 2012). We will describe in the next section how pastoral communities are resolving this paradox by establishing partnerships with the nonprofit and private sectors in order to create wildlife conservancies.

EXPERIMENTING WITH THE DEVOLUTION OF POWER TO LOCAL STAKEHOLDERS

A History of Experimentation and Research

The Mara and other game reserves in Kenya were some of the first places to experiment with local involvement in conservation. The establishment of Maasai Mara National Reserve (along with several other Kenyan reserves) in the mid-20th century signaled the rise of an innovative model of conservation for east Africa, as these entities were designed from the start to benefit local pastoral governments (Parkipuny 1991). In 1956, as the Maasai lost access to land within the Serengeti, the Kenyan colonial government allowed local district councils to create what were known as African district council (ADC) game reserves (Lamprey and Reid 2004). In 1961, the Mara ADC reserve became the Maasai Mara Game Reserve, and in 1963—under the newly independent Kenyan government—the management of the reserve became the responsibility of the local, Maasai-run council of the Narok district, which then collected profits from gate and camping fees and lodge concessions. Until 2013, the Mara Reserve was run by both the local Transmara and Narok county councils (which joined to become the expanded Narok County Council in 2013), unlike the adjacent Serengeti National Park, which is managed by the central Tanzanian government hundreds of kilometers away.

From devolved management, the devolution of tourism profits followed. In the 1980s, both the Mara Reserve and private tourism businesses began sharing benefits with the ecosystem's people, who bear the costs of living with wildlife (Lamprey and Reid 2004, Thompson et al. 2009, Osano et al. 2013a, Osano et al. 2013b). The Maasai Mara Game Reserve began sharing 10 percent to 20 percent of their annual budgets with surrounding communities, with profits directed to local county councils and some Maasai landowners (Lamprey and Reid 2004). Unfortunately, most of the initial profits flowed into the pockets of wealthy Maasai landowners rather than the majority of poorer Maasai landowners (Thompson and Homewood 2002). In addition, tourism operators created conservation incentive programs and shared some of their profits with local community members in the Mara as well as elsewhere in Kenya and Tanzania (Lamprey and Reid 2004, Schroeder 2008, Thirgood et al. 2008).

At about the same time, a team of researchers at Colorado State University (CSU) began studying pastoral systems, first in northern Kenya and then in the Serengeti-Mara and Ngorongoro. In northern Kenya during the 1980s and 1990s, the South Turkana Ecosystem Project was among the first research endeavors to ask how the social and cultural structures of pastoral people worked, how pastoralists impacted their ecosystems, and how environmental change affected people (Ellis and Swift 1988, Little and Leslie 1999). Although no one asked the Turkana people—the subjects of the study—what questions they needed answered, some did participate in gathering data. For two decades, a group of social scientists and ecologists worked together on the project, crossing disciplinary lines to address complex human and environmental problems.

By the late 1990s, a significant amount of CSU research focused on the Serengeti-Mara ecosystem, with some researchers working in partnership with the International Livestock Research Institute (ILRI) in Nairobi. One project examined the effects of conservation policy on pastoral people in the Ngorongoro Conservation Area compared with those in the Loliondo Game Controlled Area nearby (Galvin et al. 2001, Boone et al. 2002). Another large project used integrated modeling to address human food security, conservation, and ecosystem integrity in the Maasailand ecosystems of both Kenya and Tanzania (Thornton et al. 2003, Galvin et al. 2004). For decades, biologists and ecologists at many institutions collected long-term data on everything from lion behavior to plant dynamics as demonstrated in the well-known books *Serengeti: Dynamics of an Ecosystem* and *Serengeti II: Dynamics, Management, and Conservation of an Ecosystem* (Sinclair and Norton-Griffiths 1979, Sinclair and Arcese 1995) (Broten and Said 1995). In 2002 and 2003, this group partnered with CSU and ILRI researchers, among others, to address research on humans as part of the Serengeti ecosystem, which eventually became part of *Serengeti III: Human Impacts on Ecosystem Dynamics, Serengeti IV: Sustaining Biodiversity in a Coupled Human-Natural System*, and other work on the Mara (Reid et al. 2003, Kaelo 2007, Norton-Griffiths et al. 2008, Ogutu et al. 2008, Sinclair et al. 2008a, Sinclair et al. 2008b, Ogutu et al. 2009, Ogutu et al. 2010, Ogutu et al. 2011, Galvin et al. in press, Reid et al. in press). Some of this work was coproduced with local Maasai in the Mara ecosystem.

These projects helped break new ground in the areas of both research and conservation. On the conservation side, the next logical steps would be local coleadership of initiatives through better training for local leaders and stronger locally led institutions as well as the equal sharing of profits—both government gate fees and private-sector earnings—with local communities. On the research side, a revolution in approach was needed, from expert-driven to community-driven research. The Mara region was transitioning to new forms of both conservation and research about the time the Reto-o-Reto initiative started in 2002.

The Reto-o-Reto Initiative

A team of us started the Reto-o-Reto initiative to build the role of local leaders, institutions, and communities to meet the twin demands of landscape-scale conservation and pastoral development in five ecosystems of Maasailand in northern Tanzania (Longido, Tarangire) and southern Kenya (Mara, Amboseli, and Kitengela) (Reid et al. 2009, Nkedianye and Reid 2012). The overall goal of Reto-o-Reto (which means "you help us, we help you" in Maa, the Maasai language) was to create a new model of local conservation and research that is driven by the needs of local communities and led by them, with the support of others outside their ecosystem as needed. We wanted to turn the power structure upside down, placing local communities in the lead and structuring a supportive role for the outside conservation and research community. In this way, we hoped to empower local action and research so that local needs and desires were at least as powerful as those of outsiders, and hopefully more so. We really had no idea if this would work at the beginning, and neither did our colleagues in local communities. We were far from the only groups pursuing this goal, so we are far from the only ones who should take credit or blame for what then happened. The International Livestock Research Institute led the team, but many community groups held important partnering roles, as did outside institutions such as University College London, University of Louvain, and Colorado State University.

The only way, we thought, to make sure that local voices were dominant in this initiative was to empower those voices to drive the work of the team from the start (Reid et al. 2009). To accomplish this goal, we recruited five respected Maasai leaders from each of the five ecosystems at the heart of our team to act as boundary-spanning leaders of our research and action work. Their role was to be the link among policy makers, scientists, and local communities, and to serve as catalysts for local action and research. A sixth Maasai leader worked directly with policy makers in the Kenyan national government. We took care to select leaders with one foot in their communities and one foot in the wider world. On the community side, they had to be born and raised in their communities, good and humble listeners, articulate speakers, and relatively apolitical so that they could be widely inclusive. In the wider world, they had to be reasonably well connected, so that they could interact with policy makers, and educated in the social or natural sciences, so that they were comfortable interacting with the scientists on our team. Although these requirements would be a tall order in any community, we found six such individuals after a six-month search by a specially selected Maasai search committee.

Cooperating with this group of pastoral facilitators was a transdisciplinary team of researchers: two anthropologists, two veterinarians, three ecologists, one agricultural economist, and one geographer from the International Livestock Research Institute, University College London, the University of Louvain, and Colorado State University. In this context, *transdisciplinary* means researchers who spanned the boundaries among scientific disciplines as well as those between local and scientific knowledge, and between theory and practice. This team was committed to the idea of making their work entirely relevant to local needs so that it was legitimate in the eyes of local stakeholders (Cash et al. 2003). Together, these facilitators and researchers formed the core of the Reto-o-Reto team, and this core worked closely with a wide range of community members, other researchers, government officials, NGO workers, business people, schoolteachers, and others who focused on pastoral development and wildlife conservation.

Propelled by the local leaders, our joint team decided to focus on information gathering, colearning, and empowerment of local voices and action. We quickly realized that this work had to start with the aim of improving local livelihoods and, as we built confidence and trust, could then move to include wildlife conservation. Six primary objectives for our joint work were developed (Nkedianye and Reid 2012):

1. Discover ways to add value to livestock production.
2. Assess the value of alternative land use practices to uncover any incentives or disincentives for conservation.
3. Assess trends in land use, land tenure, and wildlife.
4. Determine the causes of changes to wildlife populations over time.
5. Empower local pastoral communities to be major actors in conservation and ensure that conservation supports their livelihoods and vice versa.
6. Work with local and national policy makers to promote pastoral initiatives that conserve wildlife and support pastoral livelihoods.

LINKING ACTION WITH KNOWLEDGE AND KNOWLEDGE WITH ACTION

The Reto-o-Reto initiative developed a continuous engagement model that empowers local voices; links action with knowledge; and encourages information sharing across disciplines, cultures, languages, and knowledge levels (Reid et al. 2009). In this model, the Maasai community facilitators were assigned to communicate local needs and information to the team, and the researchers were assigned to respond to these needs by finding existing or new information to address reported issues or problems. For example, pastoralists consistently ranked East Coast Fever as a major source of mortality for their livestock. As Reto began, epidemiologists were testing a new vaccine in Tanzania and found it particularly effective. The joint Reto team brought this information to Kenyan pastoralists, who thus had a new option for treating their livestock. This reversed the traditional "loading dock" model of research (Cash et al. 2006) in which scientists find a result and then deliver it to communities; in this case, communities needed information and the research responded by finding existing information that was useful. To ensure that the Reto work was quickly responding to new needs, facilitators worked daily in their communities and then met with the researchers for two days once every two months to discuss progress and new directions.

One particularly effective tool was outcome mapping (Earl et al. 2001), in which we planned our work backwards from the outcomes desired by communities and then built our outputs to satisfy those outcomes. This process encouraged researchers to be more flexible about the questions they asked, the science they conducted, and the ways in which they integrated local and scientific knowledge. Local community members also had to articulate their needs for information from research, which was often a new experience for them.

The Reto team soon found that the information needs of community members and policy makers were far greater than we were able to fulfill. Research is often slow; it can take years to reach a reliable, rigorous answer to any question. We tackled this problem by using research to satisfy information needs only when absolutely needed. Once communities articulated a need for help with an issue, we responded in one of four ways. First, if the facilitators or researchers had no experience with the problem and did not have any information to contribute from their expertise, we told communities that we could not help them. This, however, did not happen often. Second, the facilitators often "traded" knowledge, connecting community members or policy makers to existing knowledge from other community members, other organizations, or sometimes from research. For example, in the Mara, community members were struggling with the pastoral paradox and were not sure if they should privatize their land, since they would then lose the flexibility to move their cattle. The Reto facilitator from the Mara, Dickson Kaelo, took Mara community members to the Kitengela, where communities had privatized their land in the 1980s, to learn about their experiences with using neighborhood agreements to share private grazing lands across property boundaries. This helped Mara communities decide how to solve their own pastoral paradox.

A third approach was knowledge synthesis, in which the facilitator interpreted and combined existing local and scientific knowledge in new ways for community members or policy makers. In the Mara, Kaelo used an economic study (Norton-Griffiths et al. 2008) to learn how much tourism operators needed to pay local pastoral landowners to give them a disincentive to convert land to farming. This amount, eventually set at US$50 per hectare per year, was the profit needed from wildlife tourism to create a real alternative to subdividing and developing land (Norton-Griffiths et al. 2008).

Finally, if there was no information available about an issue identified by community members, the team developed research to generate new knowledge using a collaborative approach. In this approach, community members (and sometimes policy makers) were part of the process from start to finish: joint teams identified the problem or question together and then collected, entered, analyzed, interpreted, and communicated the data together. To cite one example, the pastoral community could not see that livestock grazing harmed wildlife because they observed that the Serengeti wildebeest migration ran north across the Mara Reserve to preferentially graze around their settlements outside the park. This threw open the larger question of whether it made conservation sense to create parks that excluded traditional pastoral livestock grazing. The joint Reto community-researcher team then wrote a proposal to fund work comparing wildlife use in the nearby Mara Reserve (wildlife use only) and the adjacent pastoral lands. As described above in the section on synergies, this research partially supported pastoralist observations that wildlife prefer to use pastoral lands in the wet season but also showed the importance of the reserve for dry season wildlife grazing (as well as dry season livestock grazing in the reserve at night; see Butt et al. 2009, Butt 2011).

In a case similar to the knowledge synthesis example above, the Reto facilitator in the Kitengela, David Nkedianye, and Reto economists Patti Kristjanson and Maren Radeny created information on how much income households received from crop cultivation to help determine fair payments for a land-leasing program that provides pastoral families with incentives to avoid fencing land and to keep land corridors open for wildlife and livestock movements (Kristjanson et al. 2002, Kristjanson et al. 2009, Nkedianye et al. 2009).

Also in Kitengela, a joint community–researcher team mapped 6,741 fencelines to create a fine-resolution land-use map. The map was then presented to the local district commissioner, who worked with the Ministry of Lands to conduct a land-use planning exercise with community groups and county councilors. The resulting land-use map is now the basis for Kenya's first land-use plan for a privatized rangeland (Nkedianye et al. 2009). In 2013, David Nkedianye was elected the first governor of Kajiado County, which includes the Kitengela area. In early 2014, this map became the basis for his six-month moratorium on land development in the area, to slow down the subdivision of land and to give officials time to create a revised land use plan.

In 2009, Reto partnered with CSU to foster community-wide understanding of climate change and other environmental issues. The team facilitated comprehension of the issues and explored local needs for decision making (Galvin et al. 2013). Local people defined the environmental problems, coproduced a number of films to demonstrate their knowledge, and discussed possible solutions (Roque de Pinho 2013).

At the national level, the Reto team has been actively working on policy issues concerning pastoralism and wildlife. In 2013, for example, Reto-o-Reto director Ogeli Ole Makui was a member of the national taskforce on wildlife. Other Reto members (Nkedianye, Kaelo, and Said) worked to empower local community voices about the Wildlife Conservation and Management Bill and were involved in its review with the bill's national commission. Passed in December 2013, the law supports and encourages wildlife conservation and management as a form of land use on public, community, and private land.

RETO OUTCOMES: BUILDING LOCAL LEADERS, INSTITUTIONS, AND COMMUNITIES FOR CONSERVATION AND LIVELIHOODS

It is impossible to separate conservation and livelihood outcomes from the charismatic leaders who helped catalyze them. In the Mara, Reto facilitator Dickson Kaelo was the architect of multiple wildlife conservancies on former group ranch land. These entities are private–private partnerships led jointly by pastoral communities or landowners and tourism businesses. Partners negotiated agreements that allow local communities and landowners to receive significant profits from tourism businesses if they allow free movement of wildlife on their land and move their settlements outside the conservancy (Osano et al. 2013a). Most conservancies also allow pastoral partners to graze their livestock in the conservancies seasonally, some recognizing the benefit of livestock grazing for wildlife. These arrangements clearly benefited pastoral livelihoods, often through monthly payments of profits to the local bank accounts of each landowner.

For those who benefit, these Mara conservancies have big social impacts. The payments made to landowners (also called payments for wildlife conservation, or PWC) are their most equitable income source; these monies promote income diversification and buffer households from livestock income declines during periods of severe drought (Osano et al. 2013b). Local pastoralists earn more than US$3.6 million annually, now paid directly to households on a flat rate based on land holdings. The cobenefits of PWC implementation include the creation of employment opportunities in the conservancy and provision of social services. Likewise, in Kitengela, payments from the land-leasing program can double the incomes of the poorest households in the dry season (Kristjanson et al. 2002) and thus have significant livelihood benefits (Nkedianye et al. 2009).

It is not yet clear, however, if the conservancies are slowing the decades-long decline of wildlife populations, even though wildlife are closely monitored. Certainly the eight conservancies cover a large area of the Mara ecosystem: about 92,000 hectares, which is more than half (61%) of the area of Maasai Mara National Reserve itself (150,000 hectares). As such, the conservancies are benefiting wildlife (and livestock) by maintaining large, connected, fence-free landscapes bordering the Mara Reserve, which is a major accomplishment. Local observations suggest that lion populations are recovering in the Olare Orok Conservancy (R. O'Meara, personal communication), after Maasai moved their settlements and no longer chased lions away from their livestock. But once Maasai moved out of the conservancies, they observed that many small and medium-sized wildlife moved out of the tall (and predator-rich) grass of the conservancy closer to pastoral settlements outside the conservancy (D. Kaelo, personal observation). Some conservancies now try to mimic livestock grazing, creating patches of short and long grass that will be attractive to grazers of different sizes (R. O'Meara, personal communication).

By contrast, in the Kitengela, the land-leasing program may be an example of too little too late. Because of rapid population growth next to the city of Nairobi, payments are not stemming rangeland fragmentation enough and did not restore the wildebeest migration that collapsed in the early 2000s (Ogutu et al. 2013). We conclude that while the programs in the Mara and Kitengela show some promise of slowing the conversion of savannas into villages, maize farms, resort cities, and other conservation-incompatible developments, they must be of sufficient scale to be effective (Greiner 2012, Osano et al. 2013a).

Perhaps the biggest impact of the Reto initiative was how it affected the way all team members—both community members and researchers—approached their work and how their capacity as leaders grew. In late 2013, Dickson Kaelo described a personal change of mind in this way:

"In our universities, we are taught that pastoralism is wrong, it is failing, it is maladaptive. Instead, our Reto work in the Mara, working closely with local community members, created a belief in the community that they can do it, they can make conservation work for their communities." Indeed, Kaelo takes little credit for himself, partly because he saw that our many Mara Reto team members (about 30) grew confident as our research confirmed their observations that livestock and wildlife can benefit each other, convincing them that wildlife conservancies can work if they allowed seasonal livestock grazing. Kaelo also credits his Reto experience for giving him the perspective, experience, and balanced views of livestock and wildlife that enabled him to attain a position as the first CEO of the new Kenya Wildlife Conservancy Association. Governor David Nkedianye concurs about his experience as a Reto facilitator in the Kitengela: "That was the defining period for me, an accelerated, pressurized learning period. I had the opportunity to focus on critical community issues and expose myself to the best science in the world, to travel and build confidence." From the researcher perspective, Robin Reid, now at Colorado State University, says, "This experience completely changed how I think about and do science, and how to link that science to real action on the ground. You really can be a scientist and do work that helps local communities and wildlife at the same time, if you include them every step of the way."

The Reto initiative also helped local communities speak up for themselves. For example, before Reto started, government ministers often arrived in marginalized Maasai communities and made pronouncements about new programs and policies without any consultation or collaboration. Partly as a result of Reto, many communities will no longer participate in government initiatives unless they are consulted at the outset and, often, government officials willingly oblige.

PROJECT TRANSFERABILITY AND ABILITY TO ENDURE

Can this level and intensity of engagement between communities and researchers be replicated elsewhere, or is it just too much work? In fact, our broad team is busy applying different versions of this approach in Africa, Asia, and the United States. The form of the approach is different in each place, but its essential elements are the same: collaborative learning to support local action on critical issues. To do this, it can require redirecting funding to community work and action, sometimes at the expense of deeper research. In our experience, however, the expansion of local residents' capacity to learn and adapt is so great that this redirection is more than worth it. So we say yes: this approach is highly transferable, the impacts on local capacity are highly durable, and these efforts can create positive examples of hope through action on the ground in local communities to promote local livelihoods and large landscape conservation.

ACKNOWLEDGMENTS

The authors thank the members of many communities in Maasailand of Kenya and Tanzania for working closely with our Reto-o-Reto team. We also thank the other members of our boundary-spanning team, including Moses ole Neselle, Ogeli ole Makui, Stephen ole Kiruswa, Leonard ole Onetu, Nicholas ole Kamuaro, Suzanne Serneels, Joseph Ogutu, Maren Radeny, Andrew Muchiru, Mario Herrero, Philip Thornton, Fumi Mizutani, Randy Boone, Shauna BurnSilver, Katherine Homewood, Eric Lambin, Nancy Dickson, William Clark, Mara Goldman, and Jeff Worden. We also thank our Mara team, including John ole Rakwa, James ole Kaigil, Joseph ole Temut, Samson ole Lenjirr, Moses ole Koriata, Daniel ole Naurori, Meole ole Sananka, John ole Siololo, and Charles ole Matankory. We thank the Center for Collaborative Conservation at Colorado State University for support during the writing of this paper and to Jim Levitt and the Lincoln Institute of Land Policy for encouraging us to tell the next chapter of this story.

REFERENCES

Bhola, N., J. O. Ogutu, H. P. Piepho, M. Y. Said, R. S. Reid, N. T. Hobbs, and H. Olff. 2012. "Comparative Changes in Density and Demography of Large Herbivores in the Masai Mara Reserve and Its Surrounding Human-Dominated Pastoral Ranches in Kenya." *Biodiversity and Conservation* 21:1509–1530.

Blench, R. M. 2001. "'You Can't Go Home Again': Pastoralism in the New Millennium." Animal Health and Production Series, No. 50. Rome: Food and Agriculture Organization of the United Nations.

Boone, R. B., M. B. Coughenour, K. A. Galvin, and J. E. Ellis. 2002. "Addressing Management Questions for Ngorongoro Conservation Area, Tanzania, Using the SAVANNA Modelling System." *African Journal of Ecology* 40:138–150.

Brockington, D. 2004. "Community Conservation, Inequality and Injustice: Myths of Power in Protected Area Management." *Conservation and Society* 2:211–232.

Brockington, D., R. Duffy, and J. Igoe. 2008. *Nature Unbound: Conservation, Capitalism and the Future of Protected Areas*. London, U.K.: Earthscan.

Broten, M. D., and M. Said. 1995. "Population Trends of Ungulates In and Around Kenya's Masai Mara Reserve." In *Serengeti: Dynamics, Management and Conservation of an Ecosystem*, ed. A. R. E. Sinclair and P. Arcese, 169–193. Chicago, IL: University of Chicago Press.

Butt, B. 2011. "Coping with Uncertainty and Variability: The Influence of Protected Areas on Pastoral Herding Strategies in East Africa." *Human Ecology* 39:289–307.

Butt, B., A. Shortridge, and A. WinklerPrins. 2009. "Pastoral Herd Management, Drought Coping Strategies, and Cattle Mobility in Southern Kenya." *Annals of the Association of American Geographers* 99:309–334.

Campbell, K., and H. Hofer. 1995. "People and Wildlife: Spatial Dynamics and Zones of Interaction." In *Serengeti: Dynamics, Management and Conservation of an Ecosystem*, ed. A. R. E. Sinclair and P. Arcese, 534–570. Chicago, IL: University of Chicago Press. Cash, D. W., J. C. Borck, and A. G. Patt. 2006. "Countering the Loading-Dock Approach to Linking Science and Decision Making: Comparative Analysis of El Niño/Southern Oscillation (ENSO) Forecasting Systems." *Science Technology and Human Values* 31:465–494.

Cash, D. W., W. C. Clark, F. Alcock, N. M. Dickson, N. Eckley, D. H. Guston, J. Jager, and R. B. Mitchell. 2003. "Knowledge Systems for Sustainable Development." *Proceedings of the National Academy of Sciences* 100:8086–8091.

Earl, S., F. Carden, and T. Smutylo. 2001. *Outcome Mapping: Building Learning and Reflection into Development Programs*. Ottawa, Canada: International Development Research Centre.

Ellis, J. E., and D. M. Swift. 1988. "Stability of African Pastoral Ecosystems: Alternative Paradigms and Implications for Development." *Journal of Range Management* 41:450–459.

Fernandez-Gimenez, M. E. 2002. "Spatial and Social Boundaries and the Paradox of Pastoral Land Tenure: A Case Study from Postsocialist Mongolia." *Human Ecology* 30:49–78.

Fryxell, J. M. 1991. "Forage Quality and Aggregation by Large Herbivores." *American Naturalist* 138:478–498.

Galvin, K. A., R. B. Boone, J. T. McCabe, A. L. Magennis, and T. Beeton. In press. "Transitions in the Ngorongoro Conservation Area: The Story of Cultivation, Human Well-Being, and Conservation." In *Serengeti IV: Sustaining Biodiversity in a Coupled Human-Natural System*, ed. A. J. Sinclair, K. Metzger, and J. Fryxell. Chicago, IL: University of Chicago Press.

Galvin, K. A., R. B. Boone, N. M. Smith, and S. J. Lynn. 2001. "Impacts of Climate Variability on East African Pastoralists: Linking Social Science to Remote Sensing." *Climate Research* 19:161–172.

Galvin, K. A., R. S. Reid, D. Nkedianye, J. Njoka, J. Roque de Pinho, D. Kaelo, and P. K. Thornton. 2013. "Pastoral Transformations to Resilient Futures: Understanding Climate from the Ground Up." Research Brief RB-10-2013. (April). Fort Collins, CO: Feed the Future Innovation Lab for Collaborative Research on Adapting Livestock Systems to Climate Change, Colorado State University. *http://lcccrsp.org/wp-content/uploads/2013/08/RB-10-2013.pdf*

Galvin, K. A., P. K. Thornton, R. B. Boone, and J. Sunderland. 2004. "Climate Variability and Impacts on East African Livestock Herders: The Maasai of Ngorongoro Conservation Area, Tanzania." *African Journal of Range and Forage Science* 21:183–189.

Gereta, E., E. Wolanski, M. Borner, and S. Serneels. 2002. "Use of an Ecohydrology Model to Predict the Impact on the Serengeti Ecosystem of Deforestation, Irrigation and the Proposed Amala Weir Water Diversion Project in Kenya." *Ecohydrology and Hydrobiology* 2:135–142.

Greiner, C. 2012. "Unexpected Consequences: Wildlife Conservation and Territorial Conflict in Northern Kenya." *Human Ecology* 40:415–425.

Hobbs, N. T., K. A. Galvin, C. J. Stokes, J. M. Lackett, A. J. Ash, R. B. Boone, R. S. Reid, and P. K. Thornton. 2008. "Fragmentation of Rangelands: Implications for Humans, Animals, and Landscapes." *Global Environmental Change* 18:776–785.

Homewood, K., E. F. Lambin, E. Coast, A. Kariuki, I. Kikula, J. Kivelia, M. Said, S. Serneels, and M. Thompson. 2001. "Long-Term Changes in Serengeti-Mara Wildebeest and Land Cover: Pastoralism, Population, or Policies?" *Proceedings of the National Academy of Sciences* 98:12544–12549.

Honey, M. 2008. *Ecotourism and Sustainable Development: Who Owns Paradise?* 2nd ed. Washington, DC: Island Press.

Kaelo, D. 2007. "Human-Elephant Conflict in Pastoral Areas North of Maasai Mara National Reserve, Kenya." Master's thesis, Moi University, Eldoret, Kenya.

Kolowski, J. M., and K. E. Holekamp. 2006. "Spatial, Temporal, and Physical Characteristics of Livestock Depredations by Large Carnivores Along a Kenyan Reserve Border." *Biological Conservation* 128:529–541.

Kristjanson, P. M., M. Radeny, D. Nkedianye, R. L. Kruska, R. S. Reid, H. Gichohi, F. Atieno, and R. Sanford. 2002. "Valuing Alternative Land-Use Options in the Kitengela Wildlife Dispersal Area of Kenya." ILRI Impact Assessment Series No. 10. Nairobi, Kenya: International Livestock Research Institute.

Kristjanson, P., R. S. Reid, N. Dickson, W. C. Clark, D. Romney, R. Puskur, S. Mac-Millan, and D. Grace. 2009. "Linking International Agricultural Research Knowledge with Action for Sustainable Development." *Proceedings of the National Academy of Sciences* 106:5047–5052.

Lamprey, R. H., and R. S. Reid. 2004. "Expansion of Human Settlement in Kenya's Maasai Mara: What Future for Pastoralism and Wildlife?" *Journal of Biogeography* 31:997–1032.

Lamprey, R., and R. Waller. 1990. "The Loita-Mara Region in Historical Times: Patterns of Subsistence, Settlement, and Ecological Change." In *Early Pastoralists of South-western Kenya*, ed. P. Robertshaw, 16–35. Nairobi, Kenya: British Institute in Eastern Africa.

Leakey, M. D., and R. L. Hay. 1979. "Pliocene Footprints in the Laetolil Beds at Laetoli, Northern Tanzania." *Nature* 278:317–323.

Little, M. A., and P. W. Leslie. 1999. *Turkana Herders of the Dry Savanna*. Oxford, U.K.: Oxford University Press.

Marshall, F. 1990. "Cattle Herds and Caprine Flocks." In *Early Pastoralists of Southwestern Kenya*, ed. P. Robertshaw, 205–260. Nairobi, Kenya: British Institute of Eastern Africa.

Mduma, S., and G. C. Hopcraft. 2008. "The Main Herbivorous Mammals and Crocodiles in the Greater Serengeti Ecosystem." In *Serengeti III: Human Impacts on Ecosystem Dynamics*, ed. A. R. E. Sinclair, C. Packer, S. A. R. Mduma, and J. M. Fryxell, 497–505. Chicago, IL: University of Chicago Press.

Neumann, R. 1995. "Ways of Seeing Africa: Colonial Recasting of African Society and Landscape in Serengeti National Park." *Ecumene* 2:149–169.

———. 2002. *Imposing Wilderness: Struggles over Livelihood and Nature Preservation in Africa*. Berkeley: University of California Press.

Nkedianye, D., M. Radeny, P. Kristjanson, and M. Herrero. 2009. "Assessing Returns to Land and Changing Livelihood Strategies in Kitengela." In *Staying Maasai? Livelihoods, Conservation and Development in East African Rangelands*, ed. K. Homewood, P. Trench, and P. Kristjanson, 115–150. London, U.K.: Springer-Verlag.

Nkedianye, D., and R. S. Reid. 2012. "International Livestock Institute, The Reto-o-Reto Foundation, Colorado State University/Reto-o-Reto Project." Conservation Catalysts Network, online. *www.conservationcatalysts.net/members/international-live stock-research-institute-reto-o-reto-foundation-colorado-state-university*

Norton-Griffiths, M. 1995. "Economic Incentives to Develop the Rangelands of the Serengeti: Implications for Wildlife Conservation." In *Serengeti: Dynamics, Management, and Conservation of an Ecosystem*, ed. A. R. E. Sinclair and P. Arcese, 588–604. Chicago, IL: University of Chicago Press.

Norton-Griffiths, M., D. Herlocker, and L. Pennycuick. 1975. "The Patterns of Rainfall in the Serengeti Ecosystem, Tanzania." *East African Wildlife Journal* 13:347–374.

Norton-Griffiths, M., M. Y. Said, S. Serneels, D. S. Kaelo, M. B. Coughenour, R. Lamprey, D. M. Thompson, and R. S. Reid. 2008. "Land Use Economics in the Mara Area of the Serengeti Ecosystem." In *Serengeti III: Human Impacts on Ecosystem Dynamics*, ed. A. R. E. Sinclair, C. Packer, S. A. R. Mduma, and J. M. Fryxell, 379–416. Chicago, IL: University of Chicago Press.

Ogutu, J. O., N. Owen-Smith, H.-P. Piepho, and M. Y. Said. 2011. "Continuing Wildlife Population Declines and Range Contraction in the Mara Region of Kenya During 1977–2009." *Journal of Zoology* 285:99–109.

Ogutu, J. O., N. Owen-Smith, H.-P. Piepho, M. Y. Said, S. Kifugo, R. S. Reid, H. Gichohi, P. Kahumbu, and S. Andanje. 2013. "Changing Wildlife Populations in Nairobi National Park and the Adjoining Athi-Kaputiei Plains: Collapse of the Migratory Wildebeest." *Open Conservation Biology Journal* 7:11–26.

Ogutu, J. O., H.-P. Piepho, H. T. Dublin, N. Bhola, and R. S. Reid. 2008. "Rainfall Influences on Ungulate Population Abundance in the Mara-Serengeti Ecosystem." *Journal of Animal Ecology* 77:814–829.

———. 2009. "Dynamics of Mara–Serengeti Ungulates in Relation to Land Use Changes." *Journal of Zoology* 278:1–14.

Ogutu, J. O., H. P. Piepho, R. S. Reid, M. E. Rainy, R. L. Kruska, J. S. Worden, M. Nyabenge, and N. T. Hobbs. 2010. "Large Herbivore Responses to Water and Settlements in Savannas." *Ecological Monographs* 80:241–266.

Osano, P. M., M. Y. Said, J. de Leeuw, S. S. Moiko, D. ole Kaelo, S. Schomers, R. Eimer, and J. O. Ogutu. 2013a. "Pastoralism and Ecosystem-Based Adaptation in Kenyan Masailand." *International Journal of Climate Change Strategies and Management* 5:198–214.

Osano, P. M., M. Y. Said, J. de Leeuw, N. Ndiwa, D. Kaelo, S. Schomers, R. Birner, and J. O. Ogutu. 2013b. "Why Keep Lions Instead of Livestock? Assessing Wildlife-Tourism-Based Payment for Ecosystem Services Involving Herders in the Maasai Mara, Kenya." *Natural Resources Forum* 37:242–256. doi:10.1111/1477-8947 .12027.

Ottichilo, W. K., J. de Leeuw, and H. H. T. Prins. 2001. "Population Trends of Resident Wildebeest (*Connochaetes taurinus hecki* [Neumann]) and Factors Influencing Them in the Masai Mara Ecosystem, Kenya." *Biological Conservation* 97:271–282.

Ottichilo, W. K., J. de Leeuw, A. K. Skidmore, H. H. T. Prins, and M. Y. Said. 2000. "Population Trends of Large Non-Migratory Wild Herbivores and Livestock in the Masai Mara Ecosystem, Kenya, Between 1977 and 1997." *African Journal of Ecology* 38:202–216.

Parkipuny, M. S. 1991. "The Maasai of East Africa: A People Under the Stranglehold of Preservation." Paper presented at "Ethnicity, Equity, and Environment: Confronting a Global Dilemma." A Stanford Centennial Symposium. Stanford Alumni Association, Palo Alto, California.

Reid, R. S. 2012. *Savannas of Our Birth: People, Wildlife, and Change in East Africa.* Berkeley: University of California Press.

Reid, R. S., K. A. Galvin, E. Knapp, J. Ogutu, and D. Kaelo. In press. "Sustainability of the Serengeti-Mara Ecosystem for Wildlife and People." In *Serengeti IV: Sustaining Biodiversity in a Coupled Human-Natural System*, ed. A. R. E. Sinclair and K. Metzger. Chicago, IL: University of Chicago Press.

Reid, R. S., K. A. Galvin, and R. L. Kruska. 2008. "Global Significance of Extensive Grazing Lands and Pastoral Societies: An Introduction." In *Fragmentation in Semi-Arid and Arid Landscapes: Consequences for Human and Natural Systems*, ed. K. A. Galvin, R. S. Reid, R. H. Behnke, and N. T. Hobbs, 1–24. Dordrecht, Netherlands: Springer Verlag.

Reid, R. S., D. Nkedianye, M. Y. Said, D. Kaelo, M. Neselle, O. Makui, L. Onetu, S. Kiruswa, N. ole Kamuaro, P. Kristjanson, S. B. BurnSilver, J. O. Ogutu, M. J. Goldman, R. B. Boone, K. A. Galvin, N. M. Dickson, and W. C. Clark. 2009. "Evolution of Models to Support Community and Policy Action with Science: Balancing Pastoral Livelihoods and Wildlife Conservation in Savannas of East Africa." *Proceedings of the National Academy of Sciences.* Early Edition. doi:10.1073/pnas.0900313106.

Reid, R. S., M. Rainy, J. Ogutu, R. L. Kruska, M. Nyabenge, M. McCartney, K. Kimani, M. Kshatriya, J. Worden, L. N'gan'ga, J. Owuor, J. Kinoti, E. Njuguna, C. J. Wilson, and R. Lamprey. 2003. *Wildlife, People, and Livestock in the Mara*

Ecosystem, Kenya: The Mara Count 2002. Nairobi, Kenya: International Livestock Research Institute.

Roque de Pinho, J. 2013. "Shooting Climate Change in the Maasai Mara: Aesthetics and Expectation in Participatory Film-Making with Kenyan Pastoralists." *Anthropology Now* 5:74–86.

Rulli, M. C., A. Savioris, and P. D'Odorico. 2013. "Global Land and Water Grabbing." *Proceedings of the National Academy of Sciences* 110:892–897.

Schroeder, R. A. 2008. "Environmental Justice and the Market: The Politics of Sharing Wildlife Revenues in Tanzania." *Society and Natural Resources* 21:583–596.

Serneels, S., and E. F. Lambin. 2001. "Impact of Land-Use Changes on the Wildebeest Migration in the Northern Part of the Serengeti-Mara Ecosystem." *Journal of Biogeography* 28:391–407.

Shetler, J. B. 2007. *Imagining Serengeti: A History of Landscape Memory in Tanzania from Earliest Times to the Present.* Athens: Ohio University Press.

Sinclair, A. R. E. 1995. "Serengeti Past and Present." In *Serengeti II: Dynamics, Management, and Conservation of an Ecosystem,* ed. A. R. E. Sinclair and P. Arcese, 3–30. Chicago, IL: University of Chicago Press.

Sinclair, A. R. E., and P. Arcese. 1995. *Serengeti II: Dynamics, Management, and Conservation of an Ecosystem.* Chicago, IL: University of Chicago Press.

Sinclair, A. R. E., J. G. Hopcraft, H. Olff, S. A. R. Mduma, K. A. Galvin, and G. J. Sharam. 2008a. "Historical and Future Changes to the Serengeti Ecosystem." In *Serengeti III: Human Impacts on Ecosystem Dynamics,* ed. A. R. E. Sinclair, C. Packer, S. A. R. Mduma, and J. M. Fryxell, 7–46. Chicago, IL: University of Chicago Press.

Sinclair, A. R. E., S. A. R. Mduma, and P. Arcese. 2002. "Protected Areas as Biodiversity Benchmarks for Human Impact: Agriculture and the Serengeti Avifauna." *Proceedings of the Royal Society of London,* Series B. *Biological Sciences* 269:2401–2405.

Sinclair, A. R. E., S. Mduma, and J. S. Brashares. 2003. "Patterns of Predation in a Diverse Predator-Prey System." *Nature* 425:288–290.

Sinclair, A. R. E., and M. Norton-Griffiths. 1979. *Serengeti: Dynamics of an Ecosystem.* Chicago, IL: University of Chicago Press.

Sinclair, A. R. E., C. Packer, S. A. R. Mduma, and J. M. Fryxell, eds. 2008b. *Serengeti III: Human Impacts on Ecosystem Dynamics.* Chicago, IL: University of Chicago Press.

Sitati, N. W., M. J. Walpole, R. J. Smith, and N. Leader-Williams. 2003. "Predicting Spatial Aspects of Human–Elephant Conflict." *Journal of Applied Ecology* 40:667–677.

Stelfox, J. G., D. G. Peden, H. Epp, R. J. Hudson, S. W. Mbugua, J. L. Agatsiva, and C. L. Amuyunzu. 1986. "Herbivore Dynamics in Southern Narok, Kenya." *Journal of Wildlife Management* 50:339–347.

Thirgood, S., C. Mlingwa, E. Gereta, V. Runyoro, R. Malpas, K. Laurenson, and M. Borner. 2008. "Who Pays for Conservation? Current and Future Financing Scenarios for the Serengeti Ecosystem." In *Serengeti III: Human Impacts on Ecosystem Dynamics*, ed. A. R. E. Sinclair, C. Packer, S. A. R. Mduma, and J. M. Fryxell, 443–470. Chicago, IL: University of Chicago Press.

Thompson, D. M., and K. Homewood. 2002. "Entrepreneurs, Elites, and Exclusion in Maasailand: Trends in Wildlife Conservation and Pastoralist Development." *Human Ecology* 30:107–138.

Thompson, D. M., S. Serneels, D. Kaelo, and P. C. Trench. 2009. "Maasai Mara—Land Privatization and Wildlife Decline: Can Conservation Pay Its Way?" In *Staying Maasai: Livelihoods, Conservation, and Development in East African Rangelands*, ed. K. Homewood, P. Kristjanson, and P. Trench, 77–114. London, U.K.: Springer.

Thornton, P. K., K. A. Galvin, and R. B. Boone. 2003. "An Agro-Pastoral Household Model for the Rangelands of East Africa." *Agricultural Systems* 76:601–622.

PART
IV

Law, Policy, and Organization

TO THE GENERAL PUBLIC, talk of land and biodiversity conservation commonly conjures up visions of natural scientists and intrepid explorers seeking to understand how to protect animals, plants, soils, water, mountains, rivers, lakes, and the like—individuals in the tradition of John Muir seeking the wisdom of the forest, or Rachel Carson uncovering the complex global threats of unregulated pesticides. Even Teddy Roosevelt, well-informed enthusiasts will remind you, was deeply motivated by his love of birds, his passion for hunting big game, and his irrepressible urge to explore wild and remote places. Such individuals, still showing up in the pages of *National Geographic*, continue to inspire us today.

However, the reality is that the work of land and biodiversity conservation is distinctly crossdisciplinary, engaging not only the skills of natural and social scientists and those who venture far into the wilderness. Large landscape conservation would be nowhere without the talents of lawyers, financiers, public policy advocates, organizational design specialists, and what we now in the digital age call networkers—people whose skill is convening the talents of a large, diverse, and geographically dispersed team toward a common goal. Universities, colleges, and research institutions around the world are some of our best sources of such professional talent. In this section, we look in depth at several initiatives, based at academic and research organizations, in which law, advocacy, policy making, policy implementation, and organizational skill are key factors of success.

In their thoughtful article, Fred Cheever of the University of Denver's Sturm School of Law and Nancy McLaughlin of the University of Utah's S. J. Quinney College of Law discuss the ways in which law schools continue to play a central role in the development of the conservation movement in the United States. They discuss how university law schools provide the foundation for conservation through (1) the work of environmental law clinics, which changes both law and conservation conditions on the ground, (2) factual research that reveals the realities of law and conservation, (3) conferences and other gatherings that draw together

229

stakeholders and bring them into meaningful conversation, and (4) the generation of ideas that shape the law of conservation. They make it clear that as we grapple with new challenges in the field—for example, the apparently unavoidable changes to land and water resources as a result of climate change—law schools will continue to play an essential role in the evolution of U.S. conservation policy and practice.

In the following chapter, Geoffrey Wescott of Deakin University in Australia writes of the development over a 40-year period of coastal zone planning and management practices along the Australian state of Victoria's exceptionally scenic and biodiverse coastline, and of the involvement of himself and his university, the state government, and the Victorian environmental community in bringing about these changes. Wescott continues by assessing how his university and similar institutions around the globe might improve their capacity to become drivers of conservation activity by encouraging academics aiming to serve as conservation catalysts to develop outstanding communication skills; a robust network of contacts in the public, nonprofit, and private sectors; and a willingness to actively and adaptively participate in public discourse. In turn, he notes, universities themselves will need to cultivate, reward, and promote such individuals, and modify their staff evaluation and promotion criteria to recognize outreaching achievements as well as traditional measures of teaching quality and research productivity.

Guillermo Donoso then looks in his chapter at the remarkable story of the creation of Karukinka, a highly distinctive natural sanctuary found in the Chilean Tierra del Fuego on the southern tip of South America. Karukinka was the brainchild of a team at the financial giant Goldman Sachs, which was able to set Karukinka's land base aside from the assets that Goldman came to own as part of a deal involving distressed corporate debt. Goldman donated the Karukinka reserve to the World Conservation Society (WCS), a New York-based nonprofit organization, and WCS then convened distinguished Chilean corporate and academic leaders in the Karukinka Advisory Council and tasked them with planning and managing the preserve. Members of this council helped to forge ongoing strategies and initiatives, including a plan to eradicate invasive beavers from the region, the successful effort to create a marine protected area in the ocean waters adjacent to Karukinka, and an ongoing binational effort to protect and monitor migratory bird habitat in both the Chilean and Argentinean Tierra del Fuego. In each of these cases, leading Chilean academics from a large number of universities have been in the past, and will be in the future, essential project advisors and implementers.

To round out this section, we have a piece by Karena Mahung, who recently completed her undergraduate degree at the University of the West Indies (UWI) at St. Augustine, Trinidad and Tobago (T&T). In her senior year at UWI, Karena was asked by her professor and academic advisor to prepare a paper outlining how the government of Trinidad and Tobago might use conservation easements to jump-start its own program of public–private collaboration on land conservation. Armed with the training she received at the Acadian Program in Maine during the summer between her first and second years at UWI, and at the Yale Conservation Finance Boot Camp during the subsequent summer, Karena tackled the job with impressive skill and detailed knowledge. The completed paper was submitted to the appropriate minister in the T&T government for consideration. Karena's essay is testimony to the power of undergraduates at institutions of higher learning to engage directly in meaningful policy dialogues. Given her impressive achievements to date, it is no surprise that Karena has recently been accepted to continue her studies in a master's program at the Yale School of Forestry and Environmental Studies.

11

Law as a Cornerstone of Conservation Policy: United States Law Schools as Conservation Catalysts

Federico Cheever and Nancy A. McLaughlin

In the United States and around the world, universities are almost universally committed to furthering the public interest. The University of Denver vision statement declares it will be "a great private University committed to the public good."[1] The University of Utah's mission statement indicates that its purpose is to "serve the people of Utah and the world through the discovery, creation, and application of knowledge."[2] Lawyers, as a profession, are committed to the integrity of the legal system and to providing legal services to those who need them.[3] The overwhelming majority of American Bar Association–accredited law schools in the United States are affiliated with universities. Law schools take their obligation to the public interest seriously. Most law faculty members are evaluated not only on their teaching and scholarship but also on their service to the community.

Law has played a central role in the conservation tradition of the United States, from the creation of the public domain, to the protection of migratory birds through conservation diplomacy, to the establishment of protected landscapes and the preservation of biological diversity. Activist and scholar David Sive said of environmentalism, "in no other political or social movement has litigation played such an important and dominant role. Not even close."[4] While Sive spoke of litigation, other

---

1. University of Denver. "Vision & Values: Graduating Citizens Who Will Make a Difference in the World." [Webpage]. http://www.du.edu/explore/visionandvalues.html.

2. University of Utah. "University Mission Statement." [Webpage]. http://admin.utah.edu/office_of_the_president/university-mission-statement.

3. American Bar Association, *Model Rules of Professional Conduct*, 2013, Rule 6.1. http://www.americanbar.org/groups/professional_responsibility/publications/model_rules_of_professional_conduct/rule_6_1_voluntary_pro_bono_publico_service.html.

4. Oliver A. Houck, *Taking Back Eden: Eight Environmental Cases that Changed the World*, Washington, DC: Island Press, 2010.

aspects of law, including regulation, taxation, and the definition and enforcement of property rights, have played an even more significant role in environmental protection.

Not surprisingly, university law schools have served as key players in conservation. Not only have they engaged in the essential work of organizing and rationalizing legal authority and instructing new lawyers, they have also acted more directly as conservation catalysts by creating environmental law clinics and developing legal insights and policy initiatives through research, seminars, conferences, and the convening of diverse stakeholders. Universities can also provide open access to legal research, analysis, and resources in a way that private businesses and interest groups cannot.

As our understanding of conservation problems grows, as those problems change, and as our tools to address them evolve, law schools will continue to play an essential role. This chapter describes some of the initiatives undertaken by law schools across the United States that illustrate the importance of these institutions as conservation catalysts.

ENVIRONMENTAL LAW CLINICS AND THEIR ROLE IN CONSERVATION

Since the beginning of the 20th century, law schools in the United States have established clinics in which law students, with supervision from faculty, represent members of the community in legal matters.[5] For more than a century, these clinics have served clients who otherwise might not be able to obtain legal representation. The clinics have also helped teach generations of new lawyers the skills of their trade.

Originally, most clinics focused on representing indigent clients in minor criminal and civil disputes. In the 1960s and 1970s, law school clinics began organizing around particular types of issues. In the early 1970s, the University of Oregon opened a clinic focused on environmental law.[6] At about the same time, the National Wildlife Federation established a similar clinic at the University of Colorado Law

---

5. For example, the clinical program at the University of Denver's law school was established in 1904. See University of Denver, Sturm College of Law, "Law School Clinical Programs." [Webpage]. http://www.law.du.edu/index.php/law-school-clinical-program.

6. Adam Babich and Jane F. Barrett, "Why Environmental Law Clinics?" 43 *Environmental Law Reporter* 10039, 10040, 2013.

School.[7] Since that time, the number of environmental law clinics at U.S. law schools has grown dramatically.

Scores of law schools in the United States now offer their students opportunities to work for environmental clients—ranging from national organizations to small local groups—on significant cases affecting the environment. Prominent environmental law clinics exist at Duke University,[8] Georgetown University,[9] Harvard University,[10] the University of Maryland,[11] Tulane University,[12] and Stanford University,[13] to name only a few. The law schools at the University of Denver[14] and the University of Utah[15] also operate environmental law clinics.

Environmental law clinics are best known for winning high-profile environmental cases, from the Georgetown Environmental Law Clinics toxic waste enforcement and National Environmental Policy Act work,[16] to the University of Denver's litigation against environmentally damaging timber sales on federal lands.[17] In some cases, these victories inspire

---

7. Ibid. See also Robert F. Kennedy Jr., "Environmental Litigation as Clinical Education: A Case Study," 8 *Journal of Environmental Law and Litigation* 319, 321, 1994.

8. Duke University, Duke Law, "Environmental Law and Policy Clinic." [Webpage]. http://law.duke.edu/envlawpolicy/.

9. Georgetown University, Georgetown Law, "Institute for Public Representation." [Webpage]. http://www.law.georgetown.edu/academics/academic-programs/clinical -programs/our-clinics/IPR/index.cfm.

10. Harvard University, Harvard Law School, "Emmett Environmental Law and Policy Clinic." [Webpage]. http://www.law.harvard.edu/academics/clinical/clinics/elpc.html.

11. University of Maryland, Frances King Carey School of Law, "Environmental Law Clinic." [Webpage]. http://www.law.umaryland.edu/programs/environment/clinic/.

12. Tulane University, Tulane University Law School, "Tulane Environmental Law Clinic." [Webpage]. http://www.tulane.edu/~telc/.

13. Stanford University, Stanford Law School, "Environmental Law Clinic." [Webpage]. http://www.law.stanford.edu/organizations/clinics/environmental-law-clinic.

14. University of Denver, Sturm College of Law, "Environmental Law Clinic." [Webpage]. http://www.law.du.edu/index.php/law-school-clinical-program/environmental -law-clinic.

15. University of Utah, S. J. Quinney College of Law, "Environmental Clinic." [Webpage]. http://www.law.utah.edu/clinic/clinic-list/the-environmental-clinic/.

16. Email from Hope Babcock, co-director, Institute for Public Representation, professor of law, Georgetown Law, to Federico Cheever, senior associate dean of academic affairs and professor of law, University of Denver Sturm College of Law (June 21, 2013, 10:12 a.m. MDT) (on file with author).

17. *Rocky Mountain Wild v. Vilsack*, 09-cv-01272-WJM (D. Colo. 2012).

highly public political attacks on specific environmental law clinics or environmental law clinics in general.[18]

Clinic cases can facilitate broader conservation efforts in a variety of surprising ways. In some instances, clinics rediscover legislation that appears to have been forgotten entirely by the agencies charged with enforcing it. The United States Energy Policy Act of 1992 contained provisions requiring the federal government to purchase alternative fuel vehicles, but many federal agencies simply ignored those provisions until a federal court ordered them to comply in a case filed by the University of Denver's environmental law clinic.[19] Eventually, more than a dozen federal agencies, including the Central Intelligence Agency, bought thousands of alternative fuel vehicles as a result of the clinic's litigation.[20]

Clinics have also pioneered the use of new enforcement and dispute resolution mechanisms. When the North American Free Trade Agreement came into effect, environmental law clinics were the first to work to protect natural resources through the North American Agreement on Environmental Cooperation (NAAEC), which is an "environmental side agreement" that was adopted to mitigate the effect of the treaty.[21] In 2004, the Center for Biological Diversity, Greenpeace Mexico, the Los Angeles Audubon Society, and a variety of other environmental groups represented by the University of Denver environmental law clinic submitted a petition pursuant to NAAEC asserting that Mexico had failed to enforce provisions of its own environmental legislation by permitting construction of a liquid natural gas regasification terminal adjacent to the Coronado Islands in Baja California. The islands are home to a breeding colony of endangered seabirds. The submitters asserted that the environmental impact assessment that Mexico approved was insufficient and did not adequately take into account, among other things, the impacts of light pollution on nocturnal seabirds, the risk of catastrophic

---

18. See Babich & Barrett, *supra* note 6, at 10040.

19. *Center for Biological Diversity v. Abraham*, 218 F. Supp. 2d 1143 (N.D. Cal. 2002).

20. Email from Jay Tutchton, general council, WildEarth Guardians, to Federico Cheever, senior associate dean of academic affairs and professor of law, University of Denver Sturm College of Law (June 20, 2013, 12:54 a.m. MDT) (on file with author).

21. Ibid.

explosions, and the risk of introducing rats onto the islands.[22] As a result of the petition, the Secretariat of the Commission for Environmental Cooperation of North America issued a determination requesting a response from Mexico, the first step in enforcement under the NAAEC. The developer subsequently dropped its plan to construct the facility near the Coronado Islands.[23]

Frequently, when clinic cases alleging violations of environmental laws are settled, the alleged violators agree to pay significant financial penalties. These penalty payments are often used for environmental projects designed to mitigate the damage done to human communities affected by the violations. In 2009, WildEarth Guardians, represented by the University of Denver environmental law clinic, filed suit against a major Colorado utility for Clean Air Act violations at a coal-fired power plant in Denver. In the 2013 consent decree settling the case, the defendant agreed to stop burning coal at the power plant by 2017 and to commit $447,000 to environmentally beneficial projects in the neighborhoods near the power plant.[24] Those projects include energy efficiency upgrades to homes in low-income communities, solar energy installations on public buildings, and green space improvements.

While many environmental law clinics remain primarily focused on litigation, some are also beginning to undertake transactional work. Indiana University's Conservation Law Clinic provides students with the opportunity to serve as interns in the Conservation Law Center, a public interest law firm.[25] With the assistance of these interns, the Conservation Law Center has structured public and private agreements to preserve land and resources; negotiated an indemnity clause that resulted in the addition of more than a thousand acres to a national wildlife refuge;

---

22. The petition alleged violation of Articles 78 to 83 of the Ley General del Equilibrio Ecológico y de Protección al Ambiente (General Law of Ecological Balance and Environmental Protection) and Article 5 of the Ley General de Vida Silvestre (General Wildlife Law). *Ibid.*

23. Diane Lindquist, "Chevron Gives Up on Building LNG Plant; Coronado Islands Plan Had Faced Opposition," *Baja Times*, April 2007 http://www.bajatimes.com/past /articles07/articles04_07/art3.html.

24. *WildEarth Guardians v. Public Service Co. of Colorado*, Consent Decree, April 30, 2013.

25. Indiana University Bloomington, Maurer School of Law, "Conservation Law Clinic." [Webpage]. http://www.law.indiana.edu/students/clinic/conservation.shtml.

prepared comments on permitting processes for proposed renewable energy facilities and on the United States Coast Guard's ballast water rulemaking (ballast water can introduce aquatic invasive species); and participated in the administrative law process to ensure that new Confined Animal Feeding Operations regulations adequately protect streams and lakes from pollution.[26]

Environmental law clinics across the United States will continue to bring important cases and otherwise further conservation efforts in many ways. Most clinicians would agree, however, that the greatest conservation benefit of environmental law clinics is the now extensive community of clinic alumni in the United States who are committed to public service, familiar with and trained to use environmental law, and aware of the benefits that the law can offer conservation.

LEARNING IN THE FIELD: RESEARCH-BASED LAW CONSERVATION SEMINARS

Although legal education has a strong theoretical component, it need not take place in an ivory tower. In 1995, when one of the authors of this chapter began teaching one of the first courses in private land conservation transactions offered at a U.S. law school, the best way he could find to teach the students about the subtleties of these transactions was to send them "into the field" to identify, analyze, and discuss specific transactions. By teaching this class off and on for many years, he developed an extensive library of papers analyzing private land conservation transactions. This body of student work charts the growing sophistication of land trust transactions in Colorado and around the United States. Its creation would not have been possible without the law school's support for experiential learning and the willing and patient cooperation of the land trust community in Colorado.

In 2011, professors at six U.S. law schools dramatically extended and systematized the basic concept of a legal field seminar focusing on

---

26. Conservation Law Center, "News Archive." [Webpage]. http://conservationlaw center.org/news_archive.php; email from W. William Weeks, director, Conservation Law Center, to Federico Cheever, senior associate dean of academic affairs and professor of law, University of Denver Sturm College of Law (June 26, 2013, 12:56 p.m. MDT) (on file with author).

private land conservation transactions. Professors at Stanford University, the University of Denver, Indiana University, the University of Wisconsin, the State University of New York at Buffalo, and the University of South Carolina, concerned about the effect of global climate change on land trusts across the United States, sent their students into the field in six states to gather evidence.

While instructors conducted the seminars in their own way, students systematically gathered information using four questionnaires developed by all instructors and employed consistently in all six seminars.

- The first questionnaire required the students to gather information regarding the bioregion in which their research would take place. That information included census data, election results, likely climate change impacts, and the identity of major public land use regulation institutions and major private land conservation entities, the latter of which could be nonprofit or governmental, depending on the jurisdiction.
- The second questionnaire required the students to gather information about the specific conservation entities that were the focus of their research. They were required to review the nonprofit tax returns or equivalent documentation for the entities, and to describe the staffing, history, and currently stated goals of the entities.
- The third questionnaire required the students to analyze the provisions of four conservation easements provided by each of the entities identified for purposes of the second questionnaire. This questionnaire included detailed questions about each conservation easement's location, the method of its acquisition (donated, partially donated, purchased, retained, or exacted), the land uses the easement allows on the property, the stated purposes of the easement, any wildlife species specifically identified, and a variety of other provisions. The goal was to provide a detailed summary of each conservation easement, its limitations, and its potential to respond to climate change.
- The fourth questionnaire required the students to interview a representative of each conservation entity that held the conservation easements analyzed for purposes of the third questionnaire. This questionnaire included questions about the experience and qualifications

of the land trust representative as well as her thoughts about the land trust and climate change.

As they completed the fieldwork, the students uploaded the information on the four questionnaires to a central database at the University of Wisconsin for subsequent analysis.

The 2011 Distributed Conservation Field Seminars generated a number of interesting conservation effects. First, the review of more than 300 easements in six states across the United States and interviews with dozens of land trust officials resulted in the creation of an extensive database of information that is now being used to generate policy white papers on land trusts and climate change. One of these white papers—*Private Land Conservation and Climate Change: Rethinking Strategies and Tools*—was presented at the Land Trust Alliance's Land Trust Rally in 2013. The authors hope that this white paper will inspire further discussion of climate change responses in the land trust community.

In addition, the process of gathering information needed to complete the questionnaires—in particular, the interviews required for the fourth questionnaire—inspired a broader conversation about each community's response to climate change. From personal knowledge, the information-gathering process inspired discussions among members of the Colorado conservation community about climate change. The act of asking the question appears to have been as important as the information gleaned from the response.

CONSERVATION EASEMENTS—ENGAGING STAKEHOLDERS

The United States public is investing significant funds in conservation easements through federal and state tax incentive and easement purchase programs.[27] In June 2013, the National Conservation Easement Database

---

27. See, e.g., Roger Colinvaux, "The Conservation Easement Tax Expenditure: In Search of Conservation Value," 37 *Columbia Journal of Environmental Law* 1, 2012, 9–10 (estimating total revenue loss of more than $3.6 billion from the federal charitable income tax deduction for individual conservation easement donations from 2003 through 2008; the figure would be larger if corporate donations were included); Office of the State Auditor, *Conservation Easement Tax Credit Performance Audit*, Denver, Colorado: Office of the State Auditor, September 2012 http://www.leg.state.co.us/OSA/coaudi tor1.nsf/All/5F733A628FCF979A87257A94007374E8/$FILE/2171%20ConserEasem

reported having gathered data on more than a hundred thousand conservation easements encumbering more than 19.8 million acres in the United States, but estimates that there are actually 40 million acres so encumbered, or an area more than eighteen times the size of Yellowstone National Park.[28] These conservation easements, many of which are drafted to protect the land they encumber "in perpetuity" or "forever," play a key role in integrating privately owned lands into large-scale landscape conservation initiatives.

For decades it was assumed that protecting land "in perpetuity" with a conservation easement meant that the land was permanently protected in accordance with the restrictions on development and use set forth in the easement, that modifications to or amendments of the deeds would be rare, and that termination of the easements, whether in whole or in part, would be rarer still. But as the number of acres protected by conservation easements has grown, conditions have changed, the subject lands have changed hands, and methods of farming, forestry, and ecological protection have evolved, the pressures to modify and even terminate these perpetual instruments have grown.

This, in turn, has raised a number of important legal and policy questions. For example, pursuant to what process and under what circumstances can these perpetual instruments be modified or terminated in order to, for example, respond to changing conditions or accommodate

---

TaxCredit%20092612%20KM.pdf ("Similar to other tax credits, the State 'pays' for the conservation easement tax credit by foregoing revenues from individual and corporate income taxes that it otherwise would have collected. Overall, for the 10-year period since the credit's inception . . . taxpayers have claimed approximately $639 million in tax credits resulting from approximately 3,200 conservation easement donations."); Department of Conservation and Recreation, *Calendar Year 2011 Land Preservation Tax Credit Conservation Value Summary*, Richmond, Virginia: Department of Conservation and Recreation, January 2013. http://leg2.state.va.us/dls/h&sdocs.nsf/By+Year/RD682013/$file/RD68.pdf (In the first 12 years of Virginia's tax credit program, landowners received $1.26 billion in state tax credits for conservation easement and fee-simple donations); Land Trust Alliance. "LWCF and Forest Legacy." [Webpage]. http://www.landtrustalliance.org/policy/public-funding/lwcf-and-forest-legacy (Federal funding for the U.S. Forest Service Forest Legacy Program was $79.5 million in 2010 and approximately $50 million for each of 2011, 2012, and 2013).

28. The Conservation Registry. National Conservation Easement Database. http://nced.conservationregistry.org; National Park Service. "Yellowstone Fact Sheet." [Webpage]. http://www.nps.gov/yell/planyourvisit/factsheet.htm. (The world's first national park consists of 2,221,766 acres).

the wishes of new property owners? How is the public interest and investment in these instruments and the conservation and historic values they are intended to preserve in perpetuity protected under the law? To what extent are the representations about perpetual land protection made by land trusts and government entities in solicitation, educational, and promotional materials and in easement deeds legally binding?[29] What respect must be accorded to the intent of conservation easement grantors, many of whom agreed to make charitable gifts of their conservation easements in large part due to the promise that their land would be protected in perpetuity according to the terms set forth in the easement deed? And what constitutional or other barriers might prevent the retroactive application of newly enacted state or federal laws addressing modification and termination to existing perpetual conservation easements?

While some of these issues have been discussed within the land trust community, a variety of other stakeholders with significant interests should also be part of the conversation.[30] Those stakeholders include:

---

29. See, e.g., Jackson Hole Land Trust, "Conserve Your Land," [Webpage] http://jh landtrust.org/land-protection/conserve-your-land/ ("Easements are donated or sold by the landowner to the land trust, which then has the authority and obligation to enforce the terms of the easement in perpetuity. When a parcel of land is placed under easement, the landowner still owns the property, which remains freely transferable, but the easement stays with the land forever."); Little Traverse Conservancy, *The Conservation Easement as a Land Protection and Financial Planning Tool*, http://www.landtrust .org/ProtectingLand/ConsEaseGuidebook.pdf ("The Conservancy accepts the easement with the understanding that it must enforce the terms of the easement in perpetuity . . . .A conservation easement ensures that property will be protected and cared for forever, regardless of who owns the land in the future."); Minnesota Land Trust, "Stewardship," [Webpage] http://www.mnland.org/stewardship/ ("Conservation easements are forever."); Vermont Land Trust, "Stewardship: A Perpetual Commitment to Conservation," [Webpage] http://www.vlt.org/land-stewardship ("we have promised to look after, or steward, the conservation protections placed on this land forever."); New York State Department of Environmental Conservation, "Conservation Easements," [Webpage] http://www.dec.ny.gov/lands/41156.html ("When the state accepts and holds a conservation easement it takes on the responsibility to monitor and enforce the terms of the easement in perpetuity [forever]"); Maryland Department of Natural Resources, Maryland Environmental Trust, "Conservation Easement Overview," [Webpage] http://www.dnr.state.md.us/met/land_conservation.asp ("the land is protected *forever*") (emphasis in original).

30. See, e.g., John M. Bryson, "What To Do When Stakeholders Matter," 6 *Public Management Review* 22, 23, 2004 http://www.hhh.umn.edu/people/jmbryson/pdf/stake holder_identification_analysis_techniques.pdf (discusses the dangers of not attending

- conservation easement grantors, many of whom, as noted above, intended to ensure the protection of specific properties;
- funders, including foundations, other charitable organizations, and individual donors who contributed funds for the purpose of acquiring conservation easements protecting specific properties;
- federal taxpayers, who are investing billions of dollars in perpetual conservation easements through Internal Revenue Code (IRC) § 170(h), which allows property owners to claim federal charitable income tax deductions for making charitable gifts of qualifying conservation easements;[31]
- state taxpayers, who are similarly investing significant sums in perpetual conservation easements through state and local tax incentives;[32]
- the Internal Revenue Service (IRS), which plays a key role in protecting the federal investment in tax-deductible conservation easements, which must be "granted in perpetuity" and the conservation purposes of which must be "protected in perpetuity;"[33]
- state attorneys general, who are charged with overseeing charities, protecting the public interest and investment in charitable and

---

to the information and concerns of stakeholders); Nadine B. Hack, "How Deeply Engaging Stakeholders Changes Everything," *Forbes*, May 3, 2011. http://www.forbes.com /sites/85broads/2011/05/03/how-deeply-engaging-stakeholders-changes-everything/ (discusses the benefits of engaging all stakeholders in the business context); U.S. Environmental Protection Agency, *Getting In Step: Engaging Stakeholders in Your Watershed* (2nd ed., 2013), http://cfpub.epa.gov/npstbx/files/stakeholderguide.pdf (emphasizes, in the context of watershed management, the need for support from all relevant stakeholders—"those who will make decisions, those who will be affected by them, and those who can stop the process if they disagree").

31. See *supra* note 27 (discussing the revenue loss from the deduction). Other federal tax incentives for conservation easement donations for which cost estimates are not readily available include Internal Revenue Code (IRC) § 2522(d), the charitable gift tax deduction; IRC § 2055(f), the charitable estate tax deduction; and IRC § 2031(c), the additional estate tax exclusion.

32. See Jeffrey O. Sundberg and Chao Yang, "State Income Tax Credits for Conservation Easements: Do Additional Conservation Easement Credits Create Additional Value?" 66 *State Tax Notes* 10 p. 728 December 3, 2012 (discusses state tax credit programs intended to encourage conservation easement conveyances); *supra* note 27 (discusses revenue loss from the credit programs).

33. I.R.C. §§ 170(h)(2)(C), (h)(5)(A). *See also* Treasury Regulation § 1.170A-14 (containing numerous requirements intended to ensure that the conservation purposes of tax-deductible conservation easements will be "protected in perpetuity").

public assets, and ensuring that charitable and government entities use the charitable gifts they solicit and accept for the purposes specified by the donors;[34]

- owners of conservation easement–encumbered lands, whether the easement donor or a subsequent owner, who must live with the perpetual restrictions on the use of the land; and
- community members, who both invest in conservation easements and benefit from the perpetual protection of land within their communities.

Law schools can play a key role in both facilitating a dialogue among such diverse stakeholders and in serving as independent sources of education and information available to all parties. Described below are two initiatives relating to conservation easements that illustrate how law schools can serve in these roles and, in the process, function as significant catalysts for conservation.

BROAD STAKEHOLDER ROUNDTABLES

In May 2012, the University of Utah S. J. Quinney College of Law and the Conservation Law Center, which is affiliated with Indiana University's Maurer School of Law, organized a Protected in Perpetuity Roundtable.[35] The primary purpose of the roundtable was to facilitate a dialogue among diverse stakeholders about legal and policy strategies for ensuring that the conservation purposes of federally deductible conservation easements will be "protected in perpetuity" as required by IRC § 170(h),[36] while at the same time acknowledging the need for flexibility to adapt to

---

34. See generally Marion R. Fremont-Smith, *Governing Nonprofit Organizations: Federal and State Law and Regulation*, Cambridge, MA: Belknap Press, 2004.

35. The 2012 Protected in Perpetuity Roundtable was sponsored by the Western Conservation Program of the Resources Legacy Fund; The Nature Conservancy; Conservation Partners, LLC; Cumming Foundation; The Nature Conservancy, Utah Chapter; the Law Office of Stephen J. Small, Esq., P.C.; Utah Critical Lands Alliance; Piedmont Environmental Council; the Humane Society Wildlife Land Trust; Conservation Resource Center; the Wallace Stegner Center for Land, Resources, and the Environment at the University of Utah's S. J. Quinney College of Law; the Conservation Law Center at Indiana University Maurer's School of Law; and the Montage Deer Valley.

36. *See supra* note 33 and accompanying text.

changing conditions. Many of the questions noted in the previous section were discussed during the course of the roundtable.

Given the constraints inherent in the facilitation of a productive group discussion, organizers limited the roundtable to 35 participants, who were chosen with an eye toward maximizing the number of stakeholders represented as well as ensuring geographic diversity. Participants included three representatives from the Internal Revenue Service, each from a different region; state attorney general representatives from ten states;[37] land trust representatives from national, regional, state, and local organizations; attorneys who specialize in conservation easement law from various states; institutional and individual donors; community members; academics; and an accountant. Given time constraints (the roundtable was a one-day meeting), the discussion was limited to perpetual conservation easements conveyed in whole or in part as charitable gifts and for which the donor claimed federal tax benefits. Purchased easements, and those exacted, acquired for mitigation purposes, or retained by a nonprofit or government entity upon sale of the subject land were not addressed.

Organizers gave roundtable participants background materials to read before the meeting. Participants arrived on a Friday evening and, following a short introduction by the organizers, were asked to introduce themselves and state what they hoped to gain from attending the roundtable. The following morning the roundtable opened with a short presentation on cases and controversies that involved modifications to or terminations of perpetual conservation easements to which some party objected.[38] Those cases and controversies helped ground the issues in

---

37. The states represented were California, Colorado, Illinois, Maryland, Massachusetts, Montana, New Hampshire, New York, Pennsylvania, and Wyoming.

38. See, e.g., Nancy A. McLaughlin, "Internal Revenue Code Section 170 (h): National Perpetuity Standards for Federally Subsidized Conservation Easements; Part 2, Comparison to State Law," 46 *Real Property, Trust & Estate Law Journal* 1, at 28–30, 2011, http://papers.ssrn.com/sol3/papers.cfm?abstract_id=1888689 (discussing the Myrtle Grove controversy), in which the Maryland attorney general filed suit objecting to a land trust's proposed amendment of a tax-deductible conservation easement to permit a seven-lot upscale development on the protected property; the suit settled with the easement remaining intact and the parties agreeing, among other things, that subdivision of the property is prohibited, any action contrary to the express terms and stated purposes of the easement is prohibited, and amending, releasing (in whole or in part), or extinguishing the easement without the express written consent of the Maryland

reality and make them less abstract. Most of the remainder of the day involved a professionally facilitated discussion of a variety of case studies involving complex amendment and termination scenarios. An implicit assumption underlying the discussions, evident in the Protected in Perpetuity Roundtable moniker, was that ensuring the permanence of the protection of land encumbered by a perpetual conservation easement is the main goal, and the flexibility to adapt to changing conditions must be balanced against the commitment to permanence. The roundtable discussions were purposely nonadversarial, and the case studies were hypothetical.

Objectives

The primary objectives of the roundtable were to facilitate a dialogue among the various stakeholders regarding both perpetuity and flexibility and to promote an understanding of the interests and obligations of—as well as the challenges faced by—the various groups represented. Participants were also asked to share their thoughts and ideas regarding next steps in terms of developing resources, strategies, and official or unofficial guidance that would be helpful to the various stakeholders.

Chatham House Rule

The roundtable was conducted under a modified version of the Chatham House Rule, which originated at the Royal Institute of International

---

Attorney General is prohibited, except that prior written approval of the Attorney General is not required for actions permitted under the terms of the easement.); ibid. at 30–31 (discussing *Bjork v. Draper*, 886 N.E.2d 563 (Ill. App. Ct. 2008), appeal denied, 897 N.E.2d 249 (Ill. 2008), in which an Illinois appellate court invalidated a "swap" and certain amendments that the land trust holder agreed to at the request of new owners of the protected land, explaining that to allow the changes would render meaningless the provisions in the easement specifying its conservation purpose, prohibiting structures and improvements on the protected grounds, and prohibiting the easement's termination or extinguishment, in whole or in part, without court approval); ibid. at 36–37 (discussing the Walmart controversy, in which two nonprofit organizations and a private citizen sued the owner of easement-protected land—a development corporation—and the holder of the easement—the city of Chattanooga—because they permitted construction of a four-lane access road to an adjacent Walmart in violation of the easement's terms; the case settled with the development corporation agreeing to convey a replacement parcel of land and $500,000 to the plaintiffs to be used for similar conservation purposes and to pay the plaintiffs' legal fees); ibid. at 39–42 (discussing *Salzburg v. Dowd*, in which the Wyoming attorney general filed suit objecting to a Wyoming county's termination of a tax-deductible easement at the request of new owners of the land; the suit settled with the termination being declared null and void and the easement remaining intact with minor court-approved amendments).

Affairs in London, also known as Chatham House, with the aim of providing anonymity to speakers to encourage openness and the sharing of information. The rule, which is used internationally as an aid to free discussion, states:

> When a meeting, or part thereof, is held under the Chatham House Rule, participants are free to use the information received, but neither the identity nor the affiliation of the speaker(s), nor that of any other participant, may be revealed.[39]

The Chatham House Rule thus permits public disclosure of the views expressed at the roundtable, but without attributing those views to any specific individual, agency, organization, or office, or group of individuals, agencies, organizations, or offices. By operating under the rule, participants were free to speak as individuals and express views that may not be those of the agency, organization, or office with which they are affiliated. Conducting the proceedings under the rule permitted the IRS and state attorney general representatives, in particular, to freely share ideas and explore concepts and solutions without concern that their comments would be attributed to them or to the agency or office with which they are affiliated. There were no members of the press or other media at the roundtable.

Outcomes

Based on the evaluations received, the response of roundtable participants was overwhelmingly positive, and the roundtable objectives were accomplished. With the help of a professional facilitator, the diverse stakeholders engaged in an in-depth but collegial and nonadversarial dialogue regarding what it means to protect land in perpetuity with a conservation easement as required by IRC § 170(h) and at the same time allow sufficient flexibility to adapt to changing conditions. Although there were differences of opinion regarding some details, there was a general consensus regarding the impermissibility or permissibility of certain actions with respect to many of the case studies.

Participants also gained a much greater understanding of the interests and obligations of and challenges faced by the various groups represented. For example, the land trust representatives heard directly

---

39. Chatham House, Chatham House Rule, http://www.chathamhouse.org/about/cha tham-house-rule.

about the interests and obligations of the IRS and state attorneys general (e.g., the obligation of the IRS to efficiently and equitably administer federal tax laws and the respective roles of the IRS and state attorneys general in the oversight of charities and the assets they hold on behalf of the public). In addition, the IRS and state attorney general representatives heard firsthand about the challenges land trusts face in administering perpetual conservation easements over the long term. Although no definitive conclusions were reached on either the case studies or the more general issues under discussion, the objective of the roundtable was not to resolve the issues but to begin the dialogue and educate the various groups about each group's respective role and perspective, and this goal was clearly accomplished.

The roundtable also led to greater collaboration and communication between and within the various participant groups regarding the issues discussed. For example, land trust representatives have felt more comfortable contacting IRS and state attorney general representatives, and state attorney general representatives have had increased communication and education within their ranks regarding the role of the attorney general in the oversight of the government entities and charities administering conservation easements on behalf of the public.

Given the success of the 2012 roundtable, the organizers intend to convene additional roundtables to continue the dialogue among the diverse stakeholders about the issues of perpetuity and flexibility, as well as other difficult and emerging issues.

EDUCATIONAL CONFERENCES

In February 2013, the Wallace Stegner Center at the University of Utah S. J. Quinney College of Law sponsored a half-day conference entitled "Perpetual Conservation Easements: What Have We Learned and Where Should We Go From Here?" The conference highlighted the extraordinary growth in the use of perpetual conservation easements in the United States over the last three decades and how uncertainties in the law and abusive practices threaten to undermine public confidence in and the effectiveness of these instruments as land protection tools. A diverse group of academics, practitioners, land trust representatives, and federal and state regulators examined (i) the history and legal underpinnings of this unique tool, (ii) the successes as well as problems that have arisen as a result of its widespread use, and (iii) proposed reforms and how best to deal with the increasingly difficult issues associated with the long-term administration of these perpetual instruments. The purpose of the conference was to pause for a moment and consider where we are, what we have learned, and where we should go from here, with the dual goals of minimizing abuses and ensuring that perpetual conservation easements will actually provide the promised conservation benefits to the public over the long term.

Highlights of the conference included a discussion by a former counsel to the U.S. Joint Committee on Taxation and now a professor of law of the exceptional history and exceptional enforcement challenges associated with the IRC § 170(h) deduction, as well as proposed reforms; a leading real property law scholar's recommendation that the perpetual conservation easement be given a new label—"perpetual conservation restriction"—to disentangle it from the potentially confusing and problematic common-law baggage that accompanies traditional easements; a comprehensive discussion of the laws governing charities and assets held for the benefit of the public by the leading authority on U.S. nonprofit governance issues; an assistant attorney general's overview of the attorney general's role in supervising charities and protecting charitable assets on behalf of the public, including the important educational, facilitative, and protective as well as a regulatory role that attorneys general play in the charitable sector; another assistant attorney general's description of her office's on-the-ground experience working with land trusts on amendment, termination, and enforcement issues; and concluding remarks by one of the founders and the executive director of a longstanding statewide land trust detailing the struggles, challenges, doubts, and triumphs she and the land trust experience in their quest to honor the promise of perpetual protection made to conservation easement grantors and the public in the face of inevitable pressures and an uncertain legal landscape.

The conference was streamed live and could be watched from any Internet-connected location. Videos of the various presentations are posted on the law school website, and articles written by speakers were published in the conference edition of the *Utah Law Review*.[40]

---

40. For video recordings of speaker presentations and links to articles published by speakers, see "Perpetual Conservation Easements: What Have We Learned and Where Should We Go From Here?" Nonprofit Law Prof Blog, March 20, 2014, http://lawpro fessors.typepad.com/nonprofit/2014/03/symposium-articles-on-perpetual-conserva tion-easements.html.

INTEGRATING PUBLIC AND PRIVATE LAND CONSERVATION LAW AND POLICY

In addition to the benefits discussed above, the core benefit of law schools for conservation has always been and remains the generation and development of important ideas. Over time, well-articulated ideas can reshape the landscape of conservation.

Of particular importance to this book is the role that universities and their law schools can play in broadening the perspective of current conservation actors. Law schools can help focus both public and private land conservation actors on the broad purposes of conservation, primarily the preservation of ecosystems, the species they host, and the services they generate for the benefit of diverse human communities. Law schools accomplish this sort of conservation catalysis by synthesizing information from different sources and pointing out necessary changes required for the integration of conservation regimes over broad landscapes—that is, on the national, international, and even global scale.

The most universal division in the conservation of landscapes is the division between public and private. Traditionally, legal systems impose different rules on land held by the government for the public good and land held by private parties. While this distinction is unlikely to disappear, large-scale landscape conservation requires integrating systems of conservation on public and private lands. According to the U.S. Department of Agriculture, 60 percent of at-risk species in the continental United States are associated with privately owned forestland.[41] Ninety-five percent of the plants and animals listed as endangered under the Endangered Species Act have at least some habitat on private land.[42]

In the United States, the professionals and the human communities associated with public and private land conservation are different. They operate in different political environments and are, in many cases,

---

41. Susan M. Stein, Mary A. Carr, Ronald E. McRoberts, Lisa G. Mahal, Sara J. Comas, *Threats to At-Risk Species in America's Private Forests: A Forests on the Edge Report*, General Technical Report NRS-73. Newtown Square, PA: U.S. Department of Agriculture, 2010.

42. Margaret A. Walls and Anne Riddle, *Biodiversity, Ecosystem Services and Land Use: Comparing Three Federal Policies*. Resources for the Future Discussion Paper 12-08, Washington, DC: Resources for the Future, February 2012. http://www.rff.org/Publi cations/Pages/PublicationDetails.aspx?PublicationID=21818.

subject to different legal rules. An important role university scholars can play is to help ensure that the conservation regimes on public land and the conservation regimes on private land are compatible.

One of the essential elements in ensuring compatibility between public and private conservation is durability. Public and private land conservation efforts need to create conservation mechanisms that will last for similar if not identical periods of time. In the vast majority of situations, that period of time has been defined—in both the public and private sectors—as perpetuity.

The tool of choice for private land conservation in the United States is the perpetual conservation easement, now authorized in some form by statute in forty-nine states and the District of Columbia,[43] and the acquisition of which is facilitated by generous federal and state tax incentives and appropriations to easement purchase programs.[44] As noted in the previous section, the National Conservation Easement Database has gathered data on conservation easements encumbering more than 19.8 million acres in the United States, and estimates that there are actually 40 million acres so encumbered.[45] Although these numbers are impressive, the vast majority of the acres appear to have been encumbered since the mid-1980s[46] and, despite the nominally "perpetual" nature of many conservation easements, the durability of these instruments remains unsettled.[47]

Federal public land management agencies in the United States, on the other hand, must manage the lands under their control consistent

---

43. See, e.g., Nancy A. McLaughlin, "Internal Revenue Code Section 170 (h): National Perpetuity Standards for Federally Subsidized Conservation Easements, Part 2, Comparison to State Law," 46 *Real Property, Trust & Estate Law Journal* 1 27 n. 89, 2011. (While all fifty states have enacted some form of legislation authorizing the creation and enforcement of conservation easements, North Dakota does not appear to permit the creation of perpetual conservation easements.)

44. See *supra* note 27.

45. See *supra* note 28 and accompanying text.

46. See National Conservation Easement Database, search "All States and All Easements," subsection "Easements by Acquisition Date." http://nced.conservationregistry.org/reports/easements.

47. See Nancy A. McLaughlin, "Perpetual Conservation Easements in the 21st Century: What Have We Learned and Where Should We Go From Here?" 2013 *Utah Law Review* 687 (discusses the surprising lack of certainty and consensus regarding what it means to protect land "in perpetuity" or "forever" with a conservation easement).

with broad, unchanging mandates that preserve those lands for future generations of Americans.[48] These agencies are subject to specific requirements that prohibit them from exchanging public lands for money payments or inferior lands. Public land management agencies can only accept exchanges if the public receives as good or better value in resources than the resources it transfers into the private sector.[49] In addition, federal public land agency decisions regarding land exchanges and land use under the broad mandates for land conservation are subject to review in court.[50] Most state land management decisions and decisions of public bodies regarding private land use are similarly subject to review in court.[51]

The independent and public nature of the United States court system makes it an excellent choice for resolving land use disputes. Under some circumstances, more informal, localized, and specialized tribunals may function efficiently. What is important, however, is that the reviewing entity is independent of the parties and as free from local economic, political, and other pressures as is practicable.

The channeling of significant public resources into private land conservation at both the state and federal levels supports compatibility between public and private land conservation. If we wish the public to continue to be willing to invest their tax dollars in private land conservation, we must ensure that such conservation transactions, like their public counterparts, are durable, transparent, and accountable to the public.

In the United States, the legal concept on which we rely most often to constrain public land management is the notion of public trust.[52] In many states, we impose a specific public trust on submerged lands and, in some cases, other lands subject to public influence.[53] In federal legis-

---

48. See, e.g., National Park Service Organic Act of 1916, 16 U.S.C. 1.

49. 43 U.S.C. 1716 (2006) (Exchanges can take place only if "the values and the objectives which Federal lands or interests to be conveyed may serve if retained in Federal ownership are not more than the values of the non-Federal lands or interests and the public objectives they could serve if acquired.")

50. Generally, all final federal land management decisions are subject to review under the provisions of the federal Administrative Procedure Act, 5 U.S.C. 706. In addition, a variety of federal resource laws, including the Endangered Species Act, contain specific citizen suit provisions. 16 U.S.C. 1540.

51. See, e.g., National Park Service Organic Act, 16 U.S.C. 1.

52. See *Illinois Central Railroad v. Illinois*, 146 U.S. 387 (1892).

53. See *National Audubon Society v. Superior Court*, 658 P.2d 706 (Cal. 1983).

lation, we consistently talk about the concept that federal public lands are held "in trust" for the people of the United States. The federal government has a general duty to manage the land in the best interests of the American people.

Talking about trust relationships in private land conservation provides the conceptual key to compatibility with public land conservation. This does not mean that conservation easements held by land trusts are or should be subject to all of the same standards as public conservation lands. However, nonprofit and government holders of conservation easements should have a fiduciary duty to manage the easements as their creators and funders intended, and for the benefit of the public. The value of private land conservation transactions lies in their local, grassroots, voluntary nature and the ability to tailor the terms of conservation easements to the particular characteristics of the land. It is not that such transactions should lack transparency or accountability or be any less durable than their public lands counterparts.

By bringing public and private conservation actors together and helping them explore the compatibility of the two approaches and the durability necessary for the protection of biological diversity, universities can act as significant catalysts for coordinated public and private action on behalf of the environment. That essential coordination can multiply our options for large-scale landscape conservation.

CONCLUSION

Universities and the law schools within them will continue to play an essential role in conservation in the United States. Law will remain a cornerstone of conservation policy, and as our understanding of the requirements of conservation change, law will change as well. Law schools catalyze conservation through environmental law clinics, research field seminars, stakeholder gatherings, educational conferences, policy formulation, and the provision of the public with open access to research, analysis, and other resources.

While no actor is ever completely disengaged from the endeavor in which he or she participates, law schools can act and lead as relative neutrals, capable of engaging parties who do not normally interact and championing new ideas whether or not they are currently popular.

12

A Walk on the Beach: Catalyzing the Conservation of Victoria's Coast

Geoff Wescott

In the late 1960s, a plant preservation group approached the local government council whose district encompassed the stunningly beautiful but increasingly popular Bells Beach in Victoria, Australia (figure 12.1). The group wished to become the community-based Committee of Management for the cliffs and heathland above the beach. Because Bells Beach is known as the home of the world's longest-running surfing competition, the group was concerned that the beach's increasing popularity and use by surfers was resulting in damage to its unusual heathlands in the coastal reserve.

The members of the local council presumably knew that decisions on committee appointments were not their responsibility. Because the area was public land, such authority fell to the state of Victoria's Minister for Crown Lands. However, instead of forwarding the plant group's request to the minister, the council applied to act as the committee itself. The council, unfortunately, was motivated by the prospect of personal gain, as it was primarily interested in exploiting the increasing popularity of the reserve for tourism and recreational purposes. Although the council was duly appointed the Committee of Management, the environmental deterioration of the reserve and the loss of habitat and plant communities continued unabated—indeed, it accelerated for the next decade.

The Bells Beach case was one of several dozen revealed by a Victorian Public Interest Research Group (VPIRG) study of coastal management in the state of Victoria, which was carried out by university students during the summer of 1973–1974 (VPIRG 1977).

At the time of the study, more than 120 Committees of Management operated along the coast, overseeing more than 20 percent of the Victorian coastline in foreshore reserves. Some of the committees were established within local councils, and some were composed of community members. The system and governance of the Committee of Management

FIGURE 12.1. Bells Beach Foreshore Reserve in 2013.

approach was chaotic; its administration was close to nonexistent. For example, the VPIRG study (1977) found that the majority of committees operating in subject study areas had not submitted required annual reports for many years. Furthermore, it was unclear how committee members had been appointed, by whom, when, for what term, and under what process.

Although Victoria had established a Port Phillip Authority (PPA) in 1966 (Sorenson 1997), to coordinate planning and management of the public foreshore reserves around the large embayment that has Melbourne at its head, the coastal management system for Victoria was clearly in need of repair. The VPIRG coastal study team recommended that a coastal authority be established in order to coordinate the planning and management of both public and private land in coastal Victoria. Eventually, an entity quite similar to such a coastal authority was established and was instrumental in significantly improving the management of coastal resources.

I was one of nine members employed by VPIRG on the coastal study team. With my involvement in that study, I was launched into a lifetime of direct involvement in improving the planning and management of this much-loved natural asset.

DESCRIPTION OF THE VICTORIAN COAST

The south-facing Victorian coast runs in a generally east-west direction and covers some 2,000 km (more than 1,200 miles). Its long stretches of sandy beaches are backed by substantial sand dunes, including some naturally bare dunes; there are also stretches of cliffs and bluffs with a considerable number of small estuaries. Farthest east is the Gippsland Lakes, a complex of freshwater and estuarine lakes; to its west and south is Corner Inlet near the iconic Wilsons Promontory National Park, established in 1898; farther to the west and north is the Western-port Bay, which features two large islands and a substantial opening to Bass Strait; and farther to the west and north, just separated by a thin peninsula from Westernport Bay, is Port Phillip Bay, the largest enclosed area of seawater in the southern hemisphere, on which sits the capital city of Melbourne, with a population of some 4 million people (Land Conservation Council 1993, Bird 1993, Wescott 1993) (figure 12.2).

Within a two-hour drive of Melbourne are most of the popular recreational beaches, including Bells Beach, only 104 km (64 miles) along

FIGURE 12.2. Geographical map of the state of Victoria, Australia.
Base map from wikimedia.org; place names added by James Levitt.

Great Ocean Road from central Melbourne. Great Ocean Road is considered by many to be one of the most beautiful coastal drives in the world.

The coastal vegetation strip is largely in public hands: More than 70 percent of the coastline lies within some form of protected area (including national, state, and coastal parkland) under the management of Parks Victoria. Fortunately, the growth of many coastal towns is limited by surrounding preserved parkland, most of which has been reserved in the last 25 years. This coastline experiences more than 90 million visits per year (Victorian Coastal Council 2008) and holds great economic and cultural value for Victoria and for Australia as a whole.

BECOMING A CONSERVATION CATALYST

My experience on the VPIRG study changed my life. I had earned undergraduate and master's degrees in science at the University of Melbourne and had entered a doctoral program, but the zoology research doctorate that I was pursing seemed increasingly to be too academic, too oriented toward pure science and divorced from the crucial work of protecting the marine environment. It was not clear how a study of marine hybridization and speciation in crabs was going to improve the world and save the coast. Accordingly, in 1978, I decided to discard my scholarship towards a Ph.D. in marine biology to complete a master's program in conservation at University College London, at my own expense. I had jumped from pure to applied science.

On returning to Australia in 1979, I applied for a position as executive director of the Conservation Council of Victoria (CCV; now Environment Victoria). It was the perfect opportunity to apply both the ecological and conservation advocacy knowledge I had acquired in my London studies, and it was much closer in spirit to the pioneering work in which I had been involved at VPIRG.

The CCV served as the umbrella body and coordinating council for more than 125 community-based nongovernmental conservation groups that had, in total, more than 125,000 members. In a period marked by rapid expansion in the number and area of national parks in Victoria, CCV directly lobbied the government, the opposition in the state Parliament, and senior decision makers for better conservation outcomes in the state. At the same time, various industrial development interests were proposing expansions of brown coal–fired power station operations in Victoria.

The late 1970s and early 1980s were heady times for environmental advocates. Industrial lobby groups seeking to extract and use brown coal and other natural resources were responding forcefully to what they perceived as a threat to their businesses—and to business as usual—from the new community-based conservation groups. In reality, the resource users had been able in the past to deal with governments behind closed doors and had free, or nearly free, access to publicly owned resources.

I learned two vital long-term lessons from my experience as executive director of the CCV. First, I came to understand the art of the briefing note, also known as the executive summary. It became critically important for me to be able to summarize and adequately communicate with politicians and policy makers about complex issues by using a brief note, press release, or pithy media statement—the so-called 30-second media grab. To tell a good story, the message had to be concise and explicit regarding the specific action being advocated.

Second, I learned the great value of leveraging credible partners, including universities, as conservation catalysts. It became clear to me that resource users had long cultivated their links at universities in order to obtain sponsored research that provided credible data in support of industrial projects and interests. This process was especially notable in areas such as forestry, for example, where the links between industry, program graduates, and university departments were very close. Similarly close ties were evident in engineering and applied science departments, which had connections to power generation and heavy secondary industry groups.

At that time, conservation advocates had few if any equivalent allies inside Australian universities. Very few university degrees in environmental studies and science were offered, and networked relationships among graduates, university staff and faculty, and professionals in the environmental field were sorely lacking. Conservationists had little opportunity at universities to find supportive research, or even appropriately trained researchers, to bolster their arguments. Few individuals were considered to be credible conservation experts across the public, NGO, and academic sectors.

In late 1981, now more cognizant of the utility of multisectoral expertise, I left the CCV as an employee (while remaining a volunteer officer) to begin a Ph.D. program in coastal policy at Deakin University on a Deakin Foundation full scholarship. My aim was to design an integrated planning and management system for the Victorian coastal zone.

In more general terms, I aimed to become a "pracademic"—or, as this book characterizes it, a "conservation catalyst"—whose academic research aided and abetted positive environmental reform by providing independent scientific data and well-informed policy proposals.

After 12 months as a full-time Ph.D. student, the opportunity arose to take up a position as a tutor in biology at a local community college. Over the following year, I started work as the first staff member of a new applied science degree in environmental policy and management at Victoria College in Melbourne. I also served on a number of NGO boards and advisory bodies as well as on the government's National Parks Advisory Council.

All the while, I continued working part time toward my Ph.D., which was finally completed at Deakin in 1989. By that time, I was fully equipped to continue as an academic educator focused on coastal management and the planning and management of private land; to offer my expertise as a qualified researcher with a Ph.D., numerous conference presentations, and a growing list of publications; and to contribute to policy forums and debates as a member of various government advisory councils and as an active member of several prominent NGOs.

FROM POLICY PROPOSALS TO A LEGAL FRAMEWORK FOR VICTORIAN COASTAL STRATEGY

Once I had earned my Ph.D. from Deakin, I was able to rework my thesis into a technical paper published by Victoria College (Wescott 1990). The rewriting yielded a hundred specific recommendations, each of which could be expanded upon for emphasis. The most significant recommendation echoed the VPIRG study published some 13 years earlier, calling for the creation of a state coastal commission.

By the early 1990s, it had become more evident that such an agency was necessary. There had been some reform of the laws relating to coastal management in the preceding decade: a Coastal Management and Coordinating Committee with little real power had been created; refined reporting roles and jurisdictions for Committees of Management had been established; and the government adopted a coastal policy in 1988 that offered a sound list of concepts and ideas but lacked means of implementation. At the time, there were still two major government agencies and more than 50 local councils that had to contend with approximately

59 acts of the Victorian parliament relevant to coastal planning and management (Wescott 1990, 1993).

In the absence of a coastal agency with consolidated responsibility and an implementation strategy, there was no central authority to oversee development proposals for a major aluminium smelter on coastal heathland in Portland in the far west of the state (which was eventually built) or proposals for nuclear power stations in Westernport Bay or along the west coast (which were never built).

I drafted, edited, refined, and rewrote recommendations for comprehensive reform into a format suitable for digestion by senior bureaucrats and politicians. I then presented the proposals, complete with a one-page summary, in person to both the minister for conservation and the shadow minister for conservation in 1991–1992. The documents emphasized that a governance framework and clear legislation was required that would allow sound principles to be not just considered, but implemented by the relevant regulatory agencies. This key idea inspired a phrase that characterized a common shortcoming of conservation management: Policy Without Implementation (for example, see Wescott 1993).

The Liberals, who were the opposition party at the time, adopted this proposed coastal policy in full for the 1992 election, advancing the idea of a coastal and bay management council as the lead agency. The Liberal/National Party coalition were then elected in Victoria, and by early 1994, the new government had produced a coastal discussion paper that included a proposed coastal strategy, as well as a coastal council and institutional arrangements, very similar to those proposed in the original presentations to the newly appointed conservation minister. The new Liberal government also appointed a Coastal and Bay Management Council Reference Group (CBMCRG) to consider submissions on the discussion paper and to make recommendations on coastal reform in Victoria. I was fortunate to serve as chair of this group.

In August 1994, the group published its report to the conservation minister (CBMCRG 1994), who accepted nearly all of its recommendations and introduced a coastal management bill in the Parliament of Victoria later that year. The Coastal Management Act was passed in April 1995. Figure 12.3 (Wescott 1998) illustrates the institutional arrangements and commitment to public participation incorporated in the act.

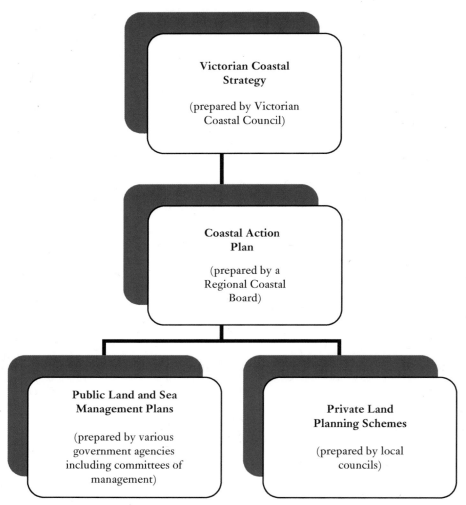

FIGURE 12.3. Diagram of the Victorian Coastal Planning and Management System.

The act centers on the implementation of integrated coastal zone management and the establishment of ecologically sustainable development principles. It calls for the production of a statutory strategy-planning document (the Victorian Coastal Strategy) prepared by the overriding advisory body (the Victorian Coastal Council) and adopted by the Victorian government.

I served on the first council, appointed late in 1995. The government completed and adopted the first coastal strategy document after substantial public participation, and some controversy, in 1997 (Victorian Coastal Council 1997).

Notwithstanding several changes in the Victorian government's ruling party, the Coastal Management Act has, as of this writing, been kept intact for nearly two decades. Labor governments, elected in 1999 and again in 2002, approved and published in 2002 the second Victorian Coastal Strategy document submitted by the council, characterizing the strategy as follows:

> The Victorian Coastal Strategy has been prepared by the Victorian Coastal Council and adopted by the Victorian State Government. The Coastal Management Act of 1995 established the Victorian Coastal Council as the peak body for the strategic planning and management of Victoria's 2,000 kilometres of coastline and marine environment. The Council provides advice on coastal issues to the Minister for Environment and Conservation (Victorian Coastal Council 2002).

Similarly, the Labor Government elected in 2006 published the third strategy document submitted by the council in 2008. And the Liberal/National government elected in 2010 is reviewing the draft 2013 Victorian Coastal Strategy document at the time of this writing. The coastal management system brought into being by the act could, like any other creation of public policy makers, fall victim to partisan politics if a new government at some time decides to make its mark with a major change in strategy. The system has, however, endured several cycles of change in government, and is currently an important component of participatory environmental management in Victoria.

BENEFITS FOR EDUCATION, RESEARCH, AND EMPLOYMENT

As with all policy-related processes, the development and implementation are only the first steps in a continuous cycle of review and refinement. The Victorian Coastal Strategy document has benefited from being the subject of courses taught at Deakin University, a measure that yielded continuous attention to and suggestions for refinement of the strategy process. It also trained a new generation of coastal zone managers who have contributed to strategy implementation over the course of nearly two decades.

For example, I had the opportunity to summarize the initial Victorian coastal strategy review process in an article in the *Environmental and Planning Law Journal* (Wescott 1995). In addition to producing a peer-reviewed paper, I was able to engage several undergraduate students in studying the creation and implementation of coastal strategy. Upon graduation, several were able to find employment in the field as executive officers of the Coastal Council, regional coastal boards, and community-based coast care programs. At present, the statewide coordinator of the coast care community education and outreach program is a Deakin Ph.D. graduate who studied coastal policy at the university.

The process also enriched ongoing undergraduate and postgraduate research at Deakin. Three Ph.D. students and a handful of honors students writing theses in their final year as undergraduates were able to focus on Victorian coastal policy. They prepared case studies and analyses on such topics as public committees of management, citizen science in the coastal zone, the development of related Marine Protected Areas (MPAs), and the integration of catchment zones and coastal management. A number of these studies have been published or referenced in publications (e.g., Cornish and Wescott 2004; Wescott 2006a).

During this period, a national Marine and Coastal Community Network (MCCN) was established to act as an information clearinghouse and honest broker in marine and coastal matters. Each state had a regional coordinator; in Victoria, the operation was closely tied to the Victorian National Parks Association (VNPA). I served at the time as the state and national chair of the community reference groups providing advice on VNPA research (see Binkley et al. 2006). This network played a vital role in stimulating public interest in coastal and marine matters (Wescott and Fitzsimons 2011).

Several other environmental projects arose during this period in connection with the establishment of the Victorian coastal strategy process. In the late 1990s and early 2000s, the Victorian Coastal Council, the MCCN, and several other conservation organizations supported the creation of MPAs in Victorian coastal waters (Wescott 2006b). In November 2002, the Australian government established a system of "no-take" national parks and sanctuaries covering 5.6 percent of Victoria's coastal waters. As part of the system's creation, MCCN earned a grant, which was passed on to Deakin University, for AU $1.2 million to carry out mapping of the marine habitats around these MPAs.

Deakin also obtained funds from Parks Victoria (the manager of the MPAs) to research the establishment of a citizen science program for MPA monitoring (see Koss et al. 2009, for an overview). The research officer leading the process completed a Ph.D. on stewardship at Deakin University as part of this project (Koss et al. 2005). A number of other MPA-related projects resulted in academic and professional publications (e.g., Porter and Wescott 2004; Blayney and Wescott 2004). Many of these outcomes were reported at the first International Marine Protected Areas Congress (IMPAC 1), which was held on the Geelong campus of Deakin University in 2005.

ASSESSMENT OF STRENGTHS, WEAKNESSES, OPPORTUNITIES, AND THREATS

Evidence of the strength and success of the effort, based in part at Deakin University, to help establish and then maintain an integrated coastal zone management system, is apparent in its framework: the normalization of concepts that were incorporated into the initial legislation, and the persistence of coastal institutional arrangements that have been in place continuously for 19 years.

The other clear marker of success has been the integration of the teaching, learning, and research of coastal and marine management issues within Deakin. University-based research led to a system that was then modified and adopted by the state. Students were able to witness firsthand the development and implementation of the coastal management system as an example of policy processes. The incorporation of real-world research into education led directly to employment for graduates in coastal management and to other students carrying out coastal research at the undergraduate honors (fourth-year-thesis–based) and Ph.D. levels. In turn, the outcomes of this research were fed back into the system, which has improved as a result.

Academically, scores of peer-reviewed papers related to Victorian coastal management were published and substantial research grants were obtained, enhancing the institution's research performance profile. Less easy to measure was the institution's enhanced reputation (and probable student recruitment benefits) from its visible, direct involvement in public affairs and the hosting of a major conference.

The effort has also exposed weaknesses. First, the central role of one person (myself) throughout most of these initiatives may become a vulnerability if no one emerges to take over the effort. Second, there is no formalized policy or procedure for carrying on once the founder has entirely stepped aside. There are no memoranda of understanding, no contracts, and no written confirmation of the informal organic relationships that have emerged between the university and its partners in this effort. The university also lacks an evaluation system that recognizes and rewards such external community service; like many institutions of higher learning, Deakin focuses its staff evaluations on the traditional areas of research and teaching. Only certain types of service—on-campus administrative and professional association service—are recognized for evaluation purposes.

The latter weakness represents an opportunity to develop institutional processes that internally recognize university-based projects and longer-term efforts that provide durable, strategically significant benefits to the community. The creation of such policies, as well as the establishment of incentives for faculty to provide such community benefits, could transform a number of academic careers at Deakin.

The most obvious threat to this effort is the loss of key individuals from the project. However, the possibility of political or institutional change always exists. It is hoped that such change will not simply emerge from a misplaced desire for perpetual newness in the political system or within the academic institution, regardless of outcomes in the real world.

LESSONS LEARNED AND THE WAY FORWARD

An academic who strives to be a conservation catalyst needs be able to translate and interpret complex research results into comprehensible community outcomes. In a complementary fashion, such an individual also needs to be able to reach inward, translating real-world experience into research projects that equip students, as they graduate, to contribute their talents to ongoing work in the general community.

A conservation catalyst needs to have strong communication skills to interact with politicians, decision makers, and the media; strong connections to NGOs, government, and advocacy and community groups; and a commitment to social benefit and social discourse as well as to the production of papers and articles for their academic peers.

Universities, if they seek to cultivate such practitioner–academics, need to better understand the necessary skill set required to reach both inward and outward, offer positive incentives to faculty and staff who are striving to cultivate such skills, and align internal staff promotion frameworks to reward faculty and staff who can ably serve the university community as well as the community at large.

If universities are able to consistently reward and promote such individuals, both the academy and society will benefit. In the process, the significant potential for social advancement, sometimes locked behind the walls of academic institutions, may be productively harnessed.

REFERENCES

Binkley, M., A. Gill, P. Saunders, and G. Wescott. 2006. "Community Involvement in Marine and Coastal Management in Australia and Canada." In *Towards Principled Ocean Governance*, ed. D. Rothwell and D. L. VanderZwaag, 249–279. London and New York: Routledge.

Bird, E. C. F. 1993. *The Coast of Victoria: The Shaping of Scenery*. Carlton, Victoria, Australia: Melbourne University Press.

Blayney, C., and G. Wescott. 2004. "Protecting Marine Parks in Reality: The Role of Regional and Local Communication Programs." *Australasian Journal of Environmental Management* 11 (2): 126–128.

Coastal and Bay Management Council Reference Group. 1994. *Recommendations on the Establishment of the Coast and Bay Management Council*. Melbourne, Australia: Victoria Department of Conservation and Natural Resources.

Cornish, A., and G. Wescott. 2004. "Implementing Integrated Coastal Zone Management Through the Use of Coastal Action Plans: Lessons from Victoria, Australia." *Australasian Journal of Environmental Management* 11 (4): 300–304.

Koss, R., P. Gilmour, K. Miller, A. Bellgrove, J. McBurnie, G. Wescott, and A. Bunce. 2005. *Sea Search: Community-Based Monitoring of Victoria's Marine National Parks and Marine Sanctuaries*. Parks Victoria Technical Series Number 19. Melbourne, Australia: Parks Victoria.

Koss, R. S., K. Miller, G. Wescott, A. Bellgrove, A. Boxshall, J. McBurnie, A. Bunce, P. Gilmour, and D. Ierodiaconou. 2009. "An Evaluation of Sea Search As a Citizen Science Programme in Marine Protected Areas." *Pacific Conservation Biology* 15 (2): 116–127.

Land Conservation Council. 1993. *Marine and Coastal Special Investigation Descriptive Report*. Melbourne, Australia: Land Conservation Council.

Porter, C., and G. Wescott. 2004. "Recreational Use of a Marine Protected Area, Point Lonsdale, Victoria." *Australasian Journal of Environmental Management* 11 (3): 201–211.

Sorenson, J. 1997. "National and International Efforts at Integrated Coastal Management: Definitions, Achievements and Lessons." *Coastal Management* 25:3–41.

Victorian Coastal Council. 1997. *Victorian Coastal Strategy*. East Melbourne, Australia: Victorian Coastal Council.

———. 2002. *Victorian Coastal Strategy 2002*. East Melbourne, Australia: Victorian Coastal Council.

———. 2008. *Victorian Coastal Strategy 2008*. East Melbourne, Australia: Victorian Coastal Council.

Victorian Public Interest Research Group (VPIRG). 1977. *A Coastal Retreat*. Melbourne, Australia: Monash University.

Wescott, G. C. 1990. *Victorian Coastal and Marine Planning and Management*. Melbourne, Victoria: Victoria College.

Wescott, G. 1993. "Policy Without Implementation: Victorian Coastal Zone Management in 1992/1993." *Environmental and Planning Law Journal* 10 (2): 87–96.

———. 1995. "Victoria's Major Review of Coastal Policy: The Establishment of a Coordinating Coastal Council." *Environmental and Planning Law Journal* 12 (3): 1–8.

———. 1998. "Reforming Coastal Management to Improve Community Participation and Integration in Victoria, Australia." *Coastal Management* 26 (1): 3–15.

———. 2006a. *The Future of Victoria's Greatest Asset: The Coast. An Independent Review of the Coastal Management Act 1995 After Ten Years of Operation*. Melbourne, Australia: Deakin University.

———. 2006b. "The Long and Winding Road: The Development of a Comprehensive, Adequate and Representative System of Highly Protected Marine Protected Areas in Victoria, Australia." *Ocean and Coastal Management* 49 (12): 905–922.

Wescott, G., and J. Fitzsimons. 2011. "Stakeholder Involvement and Interplay in Coastal Zone Management and Marine Protected Area Planning." In *Marine Resources Management*, ed. W. Gullett, C. Schofield, and J. Vince, 225–238. Chatswood, Australia: LexisNexis Butterworths.

13

Karukinka: A New Model for Conservation

Guillermo Donoso

In 2008, as a result of growing conservation concerns in the Tierra del Fuego region of Patagonia, the Chilean and Argentinean governments signed a binational agreement pursuant to the 1992 environmental treaty and the wildlife protocol shared by the two nations. Under the terms of the binational agreement, these two governments prepared a strategic plan for the eradication of beavers in Tierra del Fuego, a step seen as essential to the restoration of southern Patagonian ecosystems that have come under severe threat from this introduced and invasive species. The two nations did so with the assistance of a full complement of national and regional partners, including government agencies, local and national universities, and the Wildlife Conservation Society (WCS), which owns and manages Karukinka, a vast nature reserve in the region. Since then, the binational environmental management effort that has carried out the plan, informed by strategic recommendations of advisory boards engaging academic and private-sector advisors, has earned wide praise in the region as a model of interdisciplinary and international conservation collaboration.

In August 2011, local officials in Tierra del Fuego Province announced that, based on in-depth scientific biodiversity research conducted by the Wildlife Conservation Society in conjunction with Chilean universities and government agencies, commercial salmon fishing would be banned off the province's coast. The decision was taken in recognition of the value of regional marine biodiversity to tourism and the development of a sustainable local economy.

And on April 10, 2012, WCS and Chile's Ministry of Environment signed a memorandum of understanding committing both parties to cooperate in the management of protected areas on Tierra del Fuego, including Karukinka and the Bahía Lomas Ramsar site. The memorandum describes a relationship in which WCS provides conservation science, research, and technical expertise to support conservation management activities while working with the Chilean government to extend conservation outreach and environmental education initiatives throughout Chile. As a result of the memorandum, private conservation efforts in Karukinka have become more directly aligned with national priorities (WCS 2012a).

These notable achievements in collaborative, cross-sectoral national and international conservation would have been unlikely in the southern cone of South America some twenty years earlier. They have been realized in part due to the Karukinka advisory council's engagement, conservation science insight, and technical expertise. The board's members comprise academics from several of Chile's leading post-secondary institutions, including the Universidad de Chile, the Pontificia Universidad Católica de Chile, the Universidad Austral de Chile, and the Universidad de Magallanes. By incorporating viewpoints from the private, civil, and academic sectors through the advisory board process, the Karukinka reserve offers an important precedent for the management of large landscape conservation initiatives in the southern cone of South America.

Currently, Chile has almost 300 private protected areas comprising 1.3 million hectares, or 9 percent of the area protected by public reserves; these lands are estimated to provide ecosystem services worth at least US $421.1 million per year (Pliscoff 2009, Figueroa et al. 2010). Recent analyses of biodiversity conservation in Chile have emphasized the increasingly significant role of civil society and the private and academic sectors in achieving long-term conservation objectives. These sectors are especially important because they can advance conservation in parts of the country, including the Mediterranean zone in central Chile and Tierra del Fuego in the far south, in which private and institutional land ownership have traditionally represented a large proportion of the total.

In addition, there is a growing consensus that participants from a diversity of economic sectors can strengthen the work of the state in establishing workable environmental and biodiversity conservation policies (CONAMA 2003, 2005, 2006; OCDE 2005; Luebert and Becerra 1998; Luebert and Pliscoff 2006); developing sustainability mechanisms for conservation initiatives (CONAMA 2003, 2005, OCDE 2005); strengthening scientific research (CONAMA 2003, Centro de Análisis de Políticas Públicas 2000); and enhancing environmental education in the field of biodiversity conservation (CONAMA 2003).

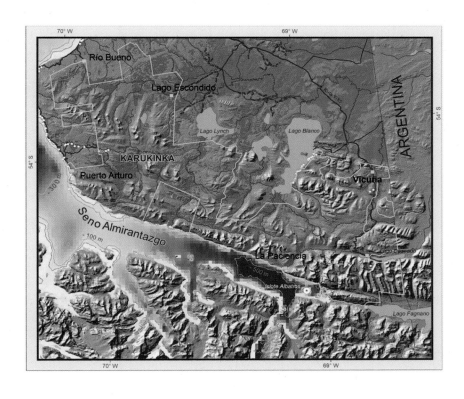

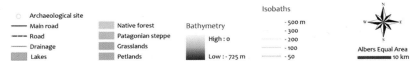

FIGURE 13.1. Geographic Location of Karukinka.
Source: Map used with permission from WCS-Chile.

In this context, Wildlife Conservation Society's (WCS) Karukinka conservation initiative in the southwest tip of Tierra del Fuego in Chile (figure 13.1) is a particularly compelling case.

UNLIKELY BEGINNINGS

The story of Karukinka begins with what at the time were unusual and fateful circumstances. In February 2002, the U.S.-based investment bank Goldman Sachs (GS) decided to acquire certain defaulted bonds of the

Trillium Corporation, a U.S.-based forestry company, at a highly dis-counted price. Among its other holdings, Trillium owned a significant amount of land in the Chilean Tierra del Fuego. With the attention and interest of Larry Linden, a senior GS executive with a deep interest in environmental conservation, as well as of Henry Paulson, GS's CEO and president, avid birder, and a member of the Board of Governors of The Nature Conservancy (Sellers 2004, Saavedra et al. 2011), the company sought to better understand the biological and cultural value of the Karukinka landscape. With some staff reconnaissance, Paulson and Linden quickly learned that the land had a wide variety of remarkable geographic, biological, and cultural attributes.

Goldman Sachs, recognizing the high local and global value of the resources in Karukinka, decided to create a nature reserve from two of the parcels of land it had acquired in December 2003 in the course of Trillium's bankruptcy. To implement this decision, GS selected an inter-nationally recognized U.S.-based conservation organization, the Wild-life Conservation Society, to receive 272,000 hectares in the two parcels and to take the lead in creating a nature reserve. This donation took place in the Chilean city of Punta Arenas in September 2004. For donating this valuable conservation land, GS received a tax benefit in the United States (Saavedra et al. 2011). The resulting property donation represented one of the world's most significant private land conservation donations to date, and the largest in Chile (Saavedra 2006, Saavedra et al. 2011). Subsequent additions to Karukinka that connect its parcels and provide ocean frontage have increased the reserve's total area from 272,000 to 297,665 hectares, or about 735,000 acres (Saavedra et al. 2011).

Having given the land to WCS, GS followed through with a finan-cial gift to WCS to support initial operations at Karukinka and then established a trust fund to sustain Karukinka in perpetuity. The gifts garnered the attention of leading global media sources, including BBC News, which reported, "WCS President Steve Sanderson says the do-nation marked a watershed in conservation policy, not only because Goldman Sachs gave the land away, but also because it pledged around $12 million of its own money to ensure the land's protection for years to come" (Long 2009).

Goldman Sachs's Karukinka model of using private funds to sup-port ambitious conservation efforts is being emulated and replicated else-where in Chile. For example, the Chilean subsidiary of Hewlett-Packard committed to providing financial support for the project within the framework of its national policy of social responsibility (Saavedra 2006). And in 2013, The Nature Conservancy (TNC) announced that BHP Billiton, the global mining group with major copper mining operations in Chile, had made a substantial gift totaling US $20 million to retire debt associated with the purchase of TNC's Valdivian Coastal Reserve in Chile's Los Ríos region and to create an endowment fund for site steward-ship (The Nature Conservancy 2013).

A RICH LEGACY OF BIODIVERSITY AND CULTURE

Karukinka's land encompasses ecologically significant areas of subant-arctic and temperate forests as well as peatlands, grasslands, and high mountain meadows. In addition to providing habitat for various species of native plants and animals, many of them endemic, the property holds significant cultural value as the historic home to ethnic groups such as the Selk'nam (figures 13.2–5).

The wealth of biodiversity and ecological value found in Karukinka is truly astounding. The reserve's cathedral forests represent the largest subantarctic temperate forests south of the 54th latitude and remain one

FIGURE 13.2. Karukinka encompasses some of the largest stands of lenga beech forests in Patagonia.
Source: Photo used with permission from WCS-Chile.

FIGURE 13.3. Karukinka is home to globally important peat bogs.
Source: Photo used with permission from WCS-Chile.

FIGURE 13.4. Large guanaco populations make Karukinka their home.
Source: Photo used with permission from WCS-Chile.

of the world's purest and best-preserved subantarctic ecosystems. Despite their ecological importance, few global conservation efforts have focused on these forests compared to the enormous attention devoted to their tropical counterparts.

Additionally, Karukinka contains impressive peatbogs that cover 25 percent of its area. Especially in the face of climate change, Karukinka's peatbogs are vitally important conservation targets, as they are responsible for the capture and sequestration of more than 300 million tons of carbon dioxide each year, thereby preventing significant negative impacts of global warming. Peatbogs also regulate hydrological cycles that sustain nearby forests, conserve large reserves of fresh water, and act as a natural filtration system that reduces sediment transport into Karukinka's groundwater. The peatlands are host ecosystems for a variety of insect, fish, flora, lichen, and microorganism species, which often cannot exist outside of peat's characteristic low-oxygen, low-nutrient environment and peatland flooding conditions. It is imperative that conservation efforts address the area's peatlands, as they are increasingly threatened by extraction activities for use as a soil substrate and fertilizer.

Karukinka as a whole is home to a remarkable array of wildlife: the area has at least 99 animal species, including at least 17 mammals, 77 birds, and 5 fish. The reserve hosts several endemic and endangered species such as the guanaco; it is estimated that Tierra del Fuego has the largest population of guanacos, with more than 60,000 living in one location. Off the coast of Karukinka are several marine mammal and cetacean species, along with various species of shore birds that in many cases are threatened in the long term.

FIGURE 13.5. Members of the now-extinct Selk'nam culture lived in what is today known as the Karukinka reserve.
Source: Photo used with permission from WCS-Chile.

In addition to animal species, researchers have recorded 416 species of vascular plants, including 6 tree species that are considered vulnerable, in the Magallanes region of Chile where Karukinka is located. In the bogs surrounding Karukinka's forests, there is an additional wealth of flora, including 49 native species of orchids specific to Chile and various carnivorous plants.

CHALLENGES FACING KARUKINKA

Despite its isolation and its rich endowment of biological and cultural attributes, Karukinka faces significant challenges to its integrity. Indeed, all of Tierra del Fuego has been affected by human activities since pre-Hispanic times.

In particular, the region has been significantly altered by beavers, which were introduced in Tierra del Fuego in the 1950s. Because the area lacks natural predators that would limit beaver populations, the impacts of beaver activity on Karukinka's subantarctic temperate forests have been devastating. With their voracious dam building and tree harvesting, beaver populations are creating a progressively fragmented landscape marred by dead trees. They have destroyed a significant proportion of Karukinka's forest stands, which play a critical role in the maintenance of water and hydrological cycles in the reserve's basins. Beavers are therefore one of the greatest threats to biodiversity in Tierra del Fuego, and beaver remediation is at the core of conservation efforts in the region, as demonstrated by the 2008 binational agreement for the strategic removal of beavers in both the Chilean and Argentinian Patagonia regions.

In addition to beavers, muskrats, minks, foxes, rabbits, and wild pigs, about 50 other species of exotic and invasive plants currently threaten the delicate balance of sustainability in Karukinka. The recently introduced breeding colony of red deer represent a new invasive species threat to the area.

While the large beaver population stresses Karukinka's forests, the prolific Patagonian coast suffers additional pressures of its own from overfishing and uncontrolled tourism. Karukinka's coast offers protection to seals, elephant seals, and albatrosses, which depend both on land and sea for their sustenance and reproduction.

Furthermore, the growing commercial demand for peat as an organic soil enrichment substance has significantly increased the commercial attractiveness of Karukinka's peatbogs. Mining the peat in large quantities would clearly present a significant threat to the ecosystem.

With such extensive physical challenges to its ecological integrity, the gift of Karukinka as a haven for biodiversity in the first decade of the 21st century came with a major management and financial burden. It became clear that, to maintain the treasured biodiversity at Karukinka, the land would have to be intensively managed over many decades. Without such management, the place could be overrun by invasive species, peat miners, tourists, and fishing outposts.

Due in part to the controversies associated with the establishment by U.S. business magnate Douglas Tompkins of the Pumalín Reserve in northern Patagonia, it became clear that any conservation plan devised to address these challenges would have to be accepted by a Chilean populace that had become uneasy with the idea that large portions of their national territory would be managed by foreigners.

BRINGING CHILEAN LEADERSHIP AND CULTURE TO KARUKINKA

Having accepted the gift of the property and the associated endowment fund, WCS had to act deliberately to create a conservation model unique to Karukinka. From early on in the process, WCS pledged to make Karukinka an initiative that emphasizes a Chilean national identity. Perhaps the most significant step towards this goal was the establishment of the Karukinka Advisory Council, composed mainly of Chileans who are leading representatives in the nation's academic and private sectors. Each council member brings diverse input to the Karukinka conservation model.

As a first and highly significant step in giving the reserve a Chilean identity, the council's first agreement was to baptize the new park Karukinka, a Selk'nam word meaning "our land." The Selk'nam people, who once had indigenous settlements in the region, are now extinct as an ethnic group. Today their culture survives only in place names, ethnographies, memoirs, and dramatic photographs of their people in ceremonial costume.

Since their first meeting in September 2005, the members of the Advisory Council have worked to reconcile vastly different philosophies about how conservation efforts should be pursued in Chile. These disparate points of view have, for example, been represented in various discussions by entrepreneurs and businessmen such as Eliodoro Matte,

Pedro Ibáñez, and Mark Tercek (the former Goldman Sachs environmental markets expert who became president of The Nature Conservancy in July 2008); notable attorneys Kathleen Barclay and Laura Novoa; and professors from Chile's leading universities, including ecosystem scientist Javier Simonetti from the Universidad de Chile, environmental economist Guillermo Donoso from the Pontificia Universidad Católica de Chile (the author of this article), forest ecology expert Antonio Lara from the Universidad Austral de Chile, Juan Carlos Castilla, the internationally distinguished marine scientist based at the Estación Costera de Investigaciones Marinas (ECIM) within the Universidad Católica, and Mateo Martinic, the prominent Magellan historian and a professor emeritus at the Universidad de Magallanes in Punta Arenas.

Although Advisory Council members often had differing motivations and agendas, the council created a cohesive and thorough conservation strategy for Karukinka that incorporates the viewpoints of a widely diverse Chilean constituency. Through a long-term process of collaboration and cooperation, the array of backgrounds represented on the council has over time led to a conservation vision in which business and environmental priorities can harmoniously coexist, rather than be at odds with one another. After various deliberations, the council agreed that Karukinka's primary task is conservation but that financial sustainability must be an essential element of the project. Although at times the council's diverse makeup led to conflicting opinions regarding how best to manage Karukinka, its interdisciplinary nature proved valuable when members addressed the wide variety of challenges that arose.

In 2012, WCS, with strategic input from the Advisory Council, articulated a vision for Karukinka that emphasizes both conservation and sustainable economic development. Key excerpts from that plan follow below.

> Working with partners, we will achieve the following conservation objectives to realize our vision in the next ten years:
>
> • Effective stewardship ensures persistence of the world's largest block of subantarctic old-growth forest.
> • Peat bogs and the ecological processes that support them are recovered and maintained.
> • Admiralty Sound's colonies of black-browed albatross and elephant seals are sustained.

- A functional population of guanacos is sustained.
- Culpeo fox populations in Karukinka are stable and increasing.

WCS's strategy for Karukinka will yield a new model for regional conservation in the 21st century: protecting biodiversity and supporting the prosperity of local people through innovative public–private partnerships while offering new insights into the global effort to adapt to climate change. Our vision will be achieved when:

- Science-based land-use policies in Chile and Argentina allow old-growth forest ecosystems to recover throughout Tierra del Fuego.
- Chilean law and policy protects Karukinka's peatlands from mining.
- The Government of Chile establishes a protected area in Admiralty Sound that benefits marine resources and supports local fisheries and tourism.
- A Public-Use Plan is adopted in Karukinka that allows local people, visitors, managers, scientists, and students to benefit from and have safe access to the spectacular protected land and seascapes.
- Effective management and sustainable finance programs are in place for the Karukinka reserve (WCS 2012b, pp. 8–9).

Another step taken by the advisory council toward strengthening the Chilean identity of this conservation initiative was to encourage the hiring of Chilean staff at the local, regional, and national levels. Barbara Saavedra, a Chilean biologist who earned her Ph.D. at the Universidad de Chile and has served as director of WCS in Chile since 2005, is now the president of the Ecological Society of Chile and directly oversees the Karukinka effort. With Saavedra in a leadership position, Karukinka has hired and trained a largely Chilean staff to undertake administrative, park ranger, and scientific research work at the site.

The advisory council has also taken a role in shaping Karukinka's communications strategy. Since its establishment, the council has recognized that the Karukinka project had to be presented so that Chile's citizens, government, and armed forces would view it in a positive light. In this context, the council helped establish a communication plan that considered the possible negative reactions to conservation efforts and took the steps necessary to transform conservation into a source of Chilean pride and national identity. It has been particularly encouraging of efforts to reach some 2,000 schoolchildren in the region with environmental education materials that highlight the magnificent natural and cultural resources to be appreciated in the far southern section of Chile.

THE ROLE OF THE ADVISORY COUNCIL IN SCIENTIFIC RESEARCH

One of the most significant roles played by the members of the advisory council—particularly the council's academic members—has been in the design, execution, and analysis of scientific research at Karukinka. Such scientific research has led to important management practices for the reserve and has informed important public policy decisions about both Karukinka and surrounding areas.

Ocean Policy

Advisory council member Juan Carlos Castilla's foundational work on ocean conservation is widely recognized as having laid the groundwork for many of the marine conservation initiatives now ongoing in Chile. It is worth noting that marine researchers in the Chilean academic sector have led the drive to apply insights from their disciplines to the hard work of creating national marine reserves. A report from Advanced Conservation Strategies, a U.S.-based environmental consulting firm active in Chile, described this dynamic:

> Chilean academics have played a critical historical role in
> marine management and conservation. It was academia that
> first proposed the need for marine biodiversity protection
> and a holistic, science-driven approach to establishing a
> national network of protected areas. University academics
> are actively working on applied marine issues across ecological, social, and economic disciplines. Researchers have
> played strong roles in impact studies, biological and ecological studies, spatial planning, fisheries biology, economics,
> governance, and social psychology. (Advanced Conservation
> Stategies 2011, p. 3)

Indeed, Castilla has served just such a role, advocating strongly within the advisory council for the creation of a marine program focused on marine environments in, adjacent to, and proximate to Karukinka. Once the program was created, Castilla went on to champion the idea that WCS, in association with a broad coalition of Chilean academic and public-sector research organizations, help lead the effort to compile a baseline survey, present it to the regional government as part of a comprehensive marine resource protection plan, and assist in achieving long-term resource conservation outcomes. As described by Barbara Saavedra, Javier Simonetti, and Kent Redford (2011) in a recent paper on the subject, the effort has already yielded significant results.

> The creation of Karukinka's marine program allowed WCS to actively participate in the coast zoning process that took place in the Magallanes region in 2009. Intended to provide the regional government with scientific and up-to-date input, WCS, together with WWF, led an exercise to identify the marine High Conservation Value Areas (HCVA) in the Magallanes region. This process started with the organization of a general workshop in September 2009 for all national experts on the Magallanes coastline that applied systematic planning methodologies to identify and prioritize conservation targets as well as threats and actions to alleviate these threats.
>
> A total of 74 objects for conservation were identified, and the geographic distribution of 46 of them could be defined (e.g., areas used by Peale's dolphin, fjord bottoms with glacier influence, presence of hydrocoral or submarine canyons, penguin colonies). Twenty-three threats to marine biodiversity were identified, including habitat destruction, overexploitation of biological resources, poor salmon farming–related practices, contamination, litter, and unregulated tourism (Vila et al. 2009). Using a planning algorithm widely used in conservation (Marxan), potential protected area distribution scenarios were analyzed and selected, maximizing, at the same time, the representation of conservation objects and minimizing the implementation costs.
>
> The analysis identified a 28-HCVA portfolio for the Magallanes Region that covered 26% of the region's coast and protected 46 marine conservation objects, including submarine mounts, fish feeding areas, sandy beaches, areas

containing native seaweed forests, reproductive colonies, and areas used by cetaceans, among others (Vila et al. 2010).

This portfolio was submitted to the Regional Government of Magallanes as input to the zoning process underway and provided an important scientific perspective to this process. We hope this work will help generate effective planning, allowing a balance between fishing, tourism, salmon farming activities, and conservation of biodiversity.

Engagement with the Government in the planning exercise had one significant conservation outcome which was its decision to ban salmon farming in Tierra del Fuego Province on grounds that the coast is better suited to tourism, an industry that is not compatible with salmon industry farming (Besnier, Governor of Tierra del Fuego; pers. comm.) (p. 379).

An August 24, 2011, press release announced the news: "The Wildlife Conservation Society (WCS) today commended local Chilean officials for keeping salmon farms from the fragile coastal waters of Tierra del Fuego Province due to environmental concerns. The officials also reduced salmon farming in nearby Antarctica and Magellanes Provinces along the Patagonian coast" (WCS 2011).

Peatland Mining Policy

Experts in Karukinka are currently developing tools and guidelines for sustainable peatland extraction. Through the consultation of academics, lawyers, advisory council members, and interdisciplinary collaborators, various alternatives to current peatland extraction practices are being pursued. With a financial commitment of $185,000 each year over the next ten years, WCS and council members will continue to investigate alternatives to peatland extraction as well as protection mechanisms that work in tandem with conservation efforts (WCS 2012b).

Several council members have played central roles in the research and implementation process associated with cohesive peatland mining policy for Karukinka. Indeed, much of their work would not have been possible without the council's range of interdisciplinary expertise. In examining specific alternatives to current mining practices in Karukinka's peatlands, reviewers identified options ranging from a potential ban on all mining in the reserve; promoting peatlands as a potential site for mitigation of the effects of climate change; and marketing the large stores of carbon held by the peatlands in either voluntary or regulatory carbon offset markets. Laura Novoa, a council member and a highly regarded Chilean lawyer who specializes in contractual, mining, and natural resources matters for mining companies, has helped evaluate several of these alternatives from a legislative standpoint (Saavedra et al. 2011).

The participation of council member and professor Guillermo Donoso (the author of this chapter) also contributed to peatland protection and stewardship through his contribution to an economic study on the feasibility of financing further peatbog conservation through carbon offsets. Additionally, council member and professor Javier Simonetti's research on the ecological basis for peatbog protection has provided ample justification and context for peatland mining alternatives.

Finally, Steve Sanderson, the CEO of WCS until his retirement in July 2012, was exemplary in his efforts to understand and act upon the long-term advice and suggestions of various experts within the council regarding peatland mining policy.

CONCEIVING A BINATIONAL STRATEGIC PLAN FOR BEAVER ERADICATION

More than half of the riverine forests in Tierra del Fuego have been lost as a result of beaver impacts on the local ecosystem (Skewes et al. 1999, Baldini et al. 2008). Beginning in 2006, WCS and the advisory council initiated a new vision for Karukinka that would address the restoration of riverine forests in the face of severe damage from beavers. They decided to investigate how beaver eradication might be accomplished throughout their unchecked range in southern Patagonia. After an initial analysis of control efforts made to date, a review of relevant international information about appropriate management techniques for exotic species, and confirmation of the threat to biodiversity and the economy of the southern part of the southern cone (Saavedra et al. 2011), WCS committed strategically and financially to beaver eradication as a primary conservation strategy in Karukinka (Menvielle et al. 2010).

In 2008, council leadership defined a new protocol to achieve this strategic commitment. Initially, WCS decided to contribute staff time and financial resources to a study cofunded by the Chilean and

Argentinian governments that convened international experts to further evaluate the potential impacts, both negative and positive, of a new beaver eradication agenda (Parkes et al. 2008). These experts found that eradication was both feasible and the most cost-effective management tool through which WCS could restore ecosystems in southern Patagonia. Although the long-term vision would prove to be highly complex and costly, the study found that the effects of inaction towards invasive species in Karukinka would be catastrophic to local ecosystems.

With the scientific backing of the 2008 study and the support of advisory council members, the Chilean and Argentinian governments moved forward to sign a binational agreement, or strategic plan, committing their countries to the restoration of native ecosystems in southern Patagonia through beaver eradication as a response to invasive species damage (Saavedra et al. 2011). This unique agreement was a huge step toward cross-border collaboration to manage and conserve natural resources across the breadth of Tierra del Fuego.

Council members were active in the effort to define, coordinate, and implement the binational strategy, contributing to the development of pilot areas where WCS-Chile could introduce management interventions, provide technical support (such as GIS technology) as the foundation of eradication operations, create a business plan containing the financial mechanisms for beaver eradication and the build-up of technical capacity (that is, a group of professional trappers), as well as administrative, governance, and management capacities to implement beaver eradication over the long term (Saavedra et al. 2011).

From the beginning, WCS and the advisory council have been essential players in the advancement of beaver eradication strategies in Karukinka. An allocation of $310,000 in WCS funds each year over ten years has been dedicated to pursuing land-use policies in Chile and Argentina that promote eradication of beavers as well as other critical invasive species from Tierra del Fuego, provide technical assistance to restore degraded forests, control hunting, and limit livestock access to Karukinka's forests (WCS 2012b). Chile's Ministry of the Environment has also made beaver eradication a national priority and expects to contribute financially to the implementation of pilot beaver eradication sites through GEF funds (Saavedra et al. 2011).

COLLABORATION OF WCS AND THE GOVERNMENT OF CHILE AT THE BAHÍA LOMAS RAMSAR SITE

Near the eastern mouth of the Straits of Magellan, about 160 km (100 miles) to the north of Karukinka on the Isla Grande de Tierra del Fuego, is Bahía Lomas (Lomas Bay), an internationally significant wetland complex. The government of Chile, which in 1981 became a signatory to the Ramsar Convention (initially created in Ramsar, Iran, in 1971 to help protect globally significant wetlands and wetland habitats), agreed in June 2004 to add the 58,946-hectare (145,660-acre) Bahía Lomas site to the Ramsar list, thereby committing to the bay's long-term protection and sustainable management.

The extensive tidal plain at Bahía Lomas sees some 7 km of tidal variation every day. The site, often hosting frigid temperatures and high winds, is a wonderland for certain migratory shorebirds. The Western Hemisphere Migratory Shorebird Network (WHRSN) website describes it as follows:

> Bahía Lomas hosts almost 50% of the Red Knot (*Calidris canutus rufa*) population; the area is the most critical wintering ground for this species in South America (Morrison & Ross 1989; Morrison et al. 2004; Niles et al. 2008). Similarly, is the second most important site for Hudsonian Godwit (*Limosa haemastica*), a migratory Nearctic shorebird; 10,000–12,000 birds have been recorded during the winter season (Morrison & Ross 1989; Morrison et al. 2004; Niles et al. 2008).
>
> Additionally, this bay is also an important wintering ground for *Calidris fuscicollis* and *Charadrius falklandicus* (Matus, Blank & Espoz, in prep.). Adding up the population densities for these two species plus those recorded for *Haematopus leucopodus* (around 4,000 individuals), *C. canutus* and *L. haemastica*, the area hosts more than 20,000 shorebirds per year (WHSRN 2014a).

It is important to know that Bahía Lomas and nearby birding sites in Argentina serve as seasonal homes for an avian celebrity: a red knot named B95 whose travels have been followed for nearly two decades by a remarkable team of ornithologists. The seasonal pilgrimage of B95 is described in a document prepared by WHSRN, which is hosted at the Manomet Center for Conservation Sciences, a Massachusetts-based organization that maintains a bird observation center near Bahía Lomas.

> The famous migratory shorebird B95—named for the code on his orange leg flag—has made the arduous journey from wintering grounds in southernmost Argentina to breeding grounds in the Canadian Arctic, and back, at least 20 times. The oldest rufa red knot known to science, B95 has become the international face of shorebird conservation and quite the rock star to those who follow him.
>
> In early December 2013, we joyously breathed a sigh of relief when he was seen again in Río Grande, Tierra del Fuego, Argentina, amid a flock of some 110 red knots. For scientists Patricia González and Luis Benegas of Argentina, and Allan Baker of Canada, the resighting was also a happy reunion; all three were on the team that first banded B95 in Río Grande some 19 years ago! (WHSRN 2014b).

In April 2012, WCS expanded its presence at Bahía Lomas with the ongoing support of members of the Karukinka Advisory Council. Javier Simonetti was particularly active in advancing the ideas expressed in the memorandum of understanding (MOU) about Bahía Lomas signed by WCS and the government. A WCS press release described the MOU as follows:

> The two parties will cooperate in the management of the protected areas on Tierra del Fuego, including Karukinka and the Ramsar site, Bahía Lomas.
>
> • WCS will provide conservation science and technical expertise to support the management of conservation throughout the nation in wetlands and in terrestrial and marine areas.
> • WCS will provide research and assist with strengthening the capacity of key stakeholders needed in maintaining biodiversity.
> • WCS and the government will work together to extend conservation outreach and environmental education.
>
> "We expect this MOU will further efforts of WCS sharing its knowledge on conservation planning with the government," said Dr. [Barbara] Saavedra. "With this public–private

cooperation, WCS's efforts will be more directly aligned with
national priorities. We will bring our conservation scientific
expertise to support the government of Chile. WCS is a
global conservation organization and can bring the latest
tools from around the world to Chile. At the same time, the
world can learn from Chile's example."

WCS has a strong conservation program in Chile,
including owning and managing Karukinka—a
294,999-hectare (728,960-acre) protected area on the island
of Tierra del Fuego (WCS 2012a).

In effect, WCS's success in bringing respected university scientists onto
the Karukinka Advisory Council and into on-the-ground scientific collaborations with the Chilean government is now being replicated at
similarly significant sites in Tierra del Fuego and elsewhere in Chile.
It is reasonable to expect that, should this collaboration succeed in its
goals, similar collaborations will arise at additional important natural
sites in Chile.

KARUKINKA AT PRESENT

Thanks to the special partnership between WCS and Goldman Sachs,
Karukinka today represents a new model for the conservation of biodiversity based on public—private and local—global interactions. Over
the past decade, Karukinka has fostered the participation of national
and international researchers and conservationists in developing effective and transferable mechanisms to support economic and ecological
sustainability.

FACTORS IN THE PROJECT'S SUCCESS

Several elements have contributed to the success of Karukinka Natural
Park. First, it is important to highlight the foresight of the global financial institution Goldman Sachs, without which this entire project would
not have been possible. The company's decision to establish a reserve
under the WCS, together with the creation of a trust fund to sustain the
park in perpetuity, catalyzed the development of what Karukinka is today: a new model for biodiversity conservation.

Secondly, the alliance with Wildlife Conservation Society (WCS), founded in 1895 with the mission to save wildlife and wild places across the globe, has been essential to the long-term success of this project. The involvement of a U.S.-based conservation organization gave Karukinka clout and placed it on an international stage from its conception, stimulating greater support and willingness to participate among key players. Furthermore, the continuous outreach efforts of WCS staff in Chile encouraged collaboration and communication among multiple partners from diverse public and private backgrounds at both the local and global levels.

Lastly, the establishment of the Karukinka Advisory Council, composed mainly of Chilean academics and business leaders, has positioned Chilean-based conservation on a global stage. The council has provided a platform from which to discuss and propose conservation guidelines that are relevant and transferable to similar initiatives throughout the world. The participation of academics from several prestigious universities has also allowed for the application of their academic knowledge and know-how to Karukinka's conservation challenges. More importantly, these experts have called for the establishment of funds to support graduate research on the reserve's priority topics, thereby ensuring further collaboration between the academic sector and Karukinka conservation work in the future.

HAS IT WORKED?

Karukinka's situation at present indicates that it has been possible to conserve the ecological and cultural legacy of this land in an interdisciplinary effort that involves both the public and private sectors, emphasizes local and global conservation goals, and incorporates binational partnership with Argentina. WCS Chile has established an effective protection of the donated land, generated mechanisms for economic sustainability, and carried out scientific research and education efforts that have culminated in the conservation of Patagonian biodiversity.

WHAT BARRIERS AND OPPORTUNITIES ARE IN THE PARK'S FUTURE?

The main barrier going forward is the need to find additional funding. Despite the great generosity of Goldman Sachs, WCS is still seeking new funds to pay for ambitious research, education, and stewardship programs.

In 2012, WCS announced that it is seeking $14 million in additional funding for Karukinka (WCS 2012) over 10 years.

The long-term success of this project will also depend, at least in part, on the continued participation of universities in this initiative. An impressive list of partnering organizations, including government, academic, and private-sector participants, illustrates the remarkable reach of the Karukinka initiative (WCS 2012). Participating institutions of higher learning and research include the following (and more are joining the effort on a regular basis):

Centro Austral de Investigaciones Científicas (CADIC)
Centro de Estudios Avanzados en Ecología y Biodiversidad (CASEB)
Centro de Estudios del Cuaternario, Fuego-Patagonia y Antártica (CEQUA)
Centro de Estudios del Hombre Austral
Comisión Nacional del Medio Ambiente (CONAMA)
Explora: Programa Nacional de Divulgación y Valoración de la Ciencia y la Tecnología
Fundación Senda Darwin
Groupo de Estudios Ambientales (GEA), Universidad de Magallanes
Instituto Antártico Chileno (INACH)
Instituto de Ecología y Biodiversidad (IEB)
Instituto de Fomento Pesquero (IFOP)
Instituto de Investigaciones Agropecuarias (INIA)
Instituto de la Patagonia (IP)
Landcare Research, New Zealand
National park services of Chile and Argentina
Pontifica Universidad Católica de Chile
Red de Alta Dirección de la Universidad del Desarrollo
Servicio Agrícola y Ganadero (SAG)
Universidad Austral de Chile
Universidad Católica del Norte
Universidad de Chile
Universidad de Concepción
Universidad de Magallanes
Universidad Técnica Federico Santa María
Universidad Santo Tomás
University of California Santa Barbara
University of California Santa Cruz

The time dedicated to this project by the academic members of the advisory council is not recognized in their academic evaluations and often falls outside of their job descriptions. Much of their participation in this project has been motivated by passion alone, and has relied on the generous donation of extracurricular time on the part of individuals. In the future, it is imperative for academic authorities to recognize the dedication of academic researchers to the Karukinka conservation initiative, either financially or by establishing institutional support for the project. We hope that additional academic partners will become involved in Karukinka conservation work if sufficient incentives are made available.

To date, graduate student researchers have proven best able to consistently report back to their home institutions on the progress of the project. It is important to continue to find funds to underwrite and give proper credit to these developing professionals for their efforts. We also hope to see greater involvement of undergraduate students in land conservation initiatives associated with Karukinka, preferably by establishing curricular activities that recognize and incentivize younger students to engage with vital sustainability issues.

CONCLUSION

Karukinka is emerging as one of the most important conservation initiatives in the southern cone of South America. This is due in part to the remarkable generosity of Goldman Sachs and other private and philanthropic funders; the steady and professional management provided by the Wildlife Conservation Society and its collaborators in the public, civic, and academic sectors; the sometimes critical advice and involvement of the Karukinka Advisory Council; and the broader engagement of a wide spectrum of public agencies, academic institutions, and nongovernmental and private sector organizations, as well as a broad and diverse spectrum of citizens, university students, and even schoolchildren.

Ongoing stewardship of Karukinka's cultural heritage and biodiversity will require both scientific and technical foundations on which to base management decisions as well as philanthropic and public support for the actions to be undertaken. Trained and competent professionals in biodiversity conservation are scarce in Latin America in general and in Chile in particular, and public understanding of environmental issues remains at a very basic level.

As a model of biodiversity conservation and sustainability, Karukinka aims to provide a venue for promoting a level of conservation awareness and literacy in the region by providing the necessary elements for citizens to make informed decisions on the use and preservation of biological resources. It will strive to continue establishing a precedent in this area for many years to come.

REFERENCES

Advanced Conservation Strategies. 2011. *A Coastal-Marine Assessment in Chile.* A report prepared for The David and Lucile Packard Foundation. Midway, UT: Advanced Conservation Strategies.

Baldini, A., J. Oltremari, and M. Ramirez. 2008. "Impacto del Castor (*Castor canadensis*, Rodentia) en Bosques de Lenga (*Nothofagus pumilio*) de Tierra del Fuego, Chile." *Bosque* 29 (2): 162–169.

Centro de Análisis de Políticas Públicas. 2000. *Informe País: Estado del Medio Ambiente en Chile—1999.* Santiago, Chile: Centro de Análisis de Políticas Públicas, Universidad de Chile.

Comisión Nacional del Medio Ambiente (CONAMA). 2003. "Estrategia Nacional de Biodiversidad." Santiago, Chile: CONAMA.

———. 2005. "Plan de Acción de País para la Implementación de la Estrategia Nacional de Biodiversidad 2004–2015." Santiago, Chile: CONAMA.

———. 2006. "Sistema de Áreas Protegidas (SAP)." Santiago, Chile: CONAMA.

Figueroa, E., S. Valdes, R. Pasten, M. Aguilar, M. L. Pineiros, P. Reyes, J. Rojas, and N. Joignant. 2010. *Valoración Económica Detallada de las Áreas Protegidas de Chile.* United Nations Development Program (UNDP), World Bank–Global Environmental Facility (GEF), and Ministry of the Environment, Chile, eds. Santiago, Chile: Salecianos Impresores S.A.

Long, G. 2009. "Saving Chile's Southern Wilderness." *BBC News,* February 25. *http://news.bbc.co.uk/2/hi/7853076.stm*

Luebert, F., and P. Becerra. 1998. "Representatividad Vegetacional del Sistema Nacional de Áreas Silvestres Protegidas del Estado (SNASPE) en Chile." *Ambiente y Desarrollo* 14:62–69.

Luebert, F., and P. Pliscoff. 2006. *Sinopsis Bioclimática y Vegetacional de Chile.* Santiago, Chile: Editorial Universitaria.

Menvielle, F., M. Funes, V. Malmierca, D. Ramadori, B. Saavedra, A. Schiavini, and N. Soto. 2010. "American Beaver Eradication in the Southern Tip of South America: Main Challenges of an Ambitious Project." *Aliens: The Invasive Species Bulletin* 29:9–16.

The Nature Conservancy. 2013. "Companies We Work With/BHP Billiton/Protecting Critical Lands Around the World." *www.nature.org/about-us/working-with -companies/companies-we-work-with/bhp-billiton-1.xml*

Organización de Cooperación y Desarrollo Económicos (OCDE). 2005. *Evaluaciones del Desempeño Ambiental: Chile.* Santiago, Chile: Comisión Económica para América Latina y el Caribe (CEPAL).

Pliscoff, P. 2009. "Análisis de Representatividad Ecosistémica de las Áreas Protegidas Públicas y Privadas en Chile." In *Creación de un Sistema Nacional Integral de Áreas Protegidas para Chile: Documentos de Trabajo,* ed. W. Asenjo, 25–108. Santiago, Chile: CONAMA, PNUD, GEF.

Saavedra, B. 2006. "Karukinka, Nuevo Modelo para la Conservación de Biodiversidad." *Revista Ambiente y Desarrollo de CIPMA* 22 (1): 21–27.

Saavedra, B., J. Simonetti, and K. Redford. 2011. "Private Conservation: The Example that the Wildlife Conservation Society Builds from Tierra del Fuego." In *Biodiversity Conservation in the Americas: Lessons and Policy Recommendations,* ed. E. Figueroa. Santiago, Chile: Ocho Libros Editores Ltda.

Sellers, P. 2004. "Hank Paulson's Secret Life." *Fortune,* January 12. *http://money.cnn .com/magazines/fortune/fortune_archive/2004/01/12/357911/*

Skewes, O., F. Gonzalez, L. Rubilar, M. Quezada, R. Olave, V. Vargas, and A. Avila. 1999. *Investigación Aprovechamiento y Control de Castor* (Castor canadensis) *en las Islas Tierra del Fuego y Navarino. Informe Final. Servicio Agrícola y Ganadero (SAG) XII Region, Magallanes y Antártica Chilena.* Santiago, Chile: SAG.

Western Hemisphere Shorebird Reserve Network (WHSRN). 2014a. "About Us: Bahía Lomas." Web page. *www.whsrn.org/site-profile/bahia-lomas*

———. 2014b. "Red Knot Reunions." *WHSRNews,* February 7. Online newsletter. *www.whsrn.org/news/article/red-knot-reunions*

Wildlife Conservation Society. 2011. "Chile Says No to Salmon Farming Off of Tierra del Fuego." Press release. August 24. *www.wcs.org/press/press-releases/chile-salmon -farming.aspx*

———. 2012a. "WCS and Government of Chile Sign Sweeping Conservation Agreement." Press release. April 11. *www.wcs.org/press/press-releases/wcs-chile-conservation -agreement.aspx*

———. 2012b. *Wildlife Conservation Society's Best of the Wild 2012. Karukinka: A Ten-Year Vision.* Bronx, NY: Wildlife Conservation Society.

14

Conservation Easements as a Land Conservation Strategy in Trinidad & Tobago

Karena Mahung

Around the globe, the shared challenge presented by unsustainable land use has inspired the creation of multiple strategies that have proven successful in various countries and regions. Conservation easements are one such strategy, born from the need for private land conservation in the United States but explored in other regions of the world, including in Latin America and the Caribbean.

As described by Korngold (2011) and Fishburn et al. (2009), conservation easements are tools that allow private landowners to voluntarily render over their property's development rights, thus ensuring perpetual protection of the land's conservation values. The voluntary legal contract stipulates restrictions on the property that ensure the preservation of the natural integrity of the land, including its ecological, environmental, and scenic features (Korngold 2011). This mechanism enables the continued use of the property for sustainable timber harvest, farming, habitation, or other appropriate uses with the simple condition that easement restrictions will be upheld by current and future owners in perpetuity (Fishburn et al. 2009).

Several economic, social, and environmental features of Trinidad and Tobago—the most species-rich Caribbean island (Kenny et al. 1997)—validate the need to explore new strategies in order to tackle the country's natural resource management challenges. Biodiversity plays an important role in the provision of ecosystem services that support human well-being, including the provision of freshwater, food (e.g., fisheries products, crops, livestock), shoreline protection, flood regulation, and erosion control (Government of Trinidad and Tobago 2010). Unique ecosystems such as the Nariva Swamp, Trinidad and Tobago's largest wetland, are recognized nationally and internationally for their ecological significance (Government of Trinidad and Tobago 2010).

As the Caribbean's most industrialized nation, Trinidad and Tobago has experienced several decades of economic growth driven by its energy sector (Ministry of Planning and the Economy 2012). The impetus towards economic stability and development, however, has often come at the expense of the environment. Changes in land use and land cover have been identified as direct causes of the country's biodiversity loss (Ministry of Housing and the Environment 2010). Compounding these threats is the fact that Trinidad and Tobago is a Small Island Developing State (SIDS) with limited land space, finite natural resources, and fragile ecosystems, vulnerable to external environmental and economic shocks (Ministry of Planning and the Economy 2012). Combined with a lack of effective governance and implementation of environmental laws and policies (Ministry of Housing and the Environment 2010), these factors greatly exacerbate negative environmental impacts. There is an urgent need for assessment of ineffective land management strategies and for the exploration of the feasibility of new strategies that can provide more appropriate tools for tackling these environmental challenges.

CONSERVATION EASEMENT FRAMEWORK

Several fundamental financial, legal, and management elements play critical roles in the success of conservation easements. These elements can be viewed as some of the basic prerequisites for the application of this land management tool (figure 14.1).

Financial Requirements

Government Actors: Financial Incentives This particular characteristic of conservation easements has had a profound influence on their proliferation over other land management strategies. In the U.S. model, as explained by Korngold (2007), easements donated in perpetuity to a qualified nonprofit organization for the purpose of conservation are eligible for federal tax deductions. In addition, land burdened by a conservation easement is subject to a lower property value and therefore reduced federal estate tax.

Private Actors: Less-than-Fee Interest Through this arrangement, nonprofit organizations receive a "less than fee" interest in the land, which is a nonpossessory right that nonetheless enables them to enforce re-

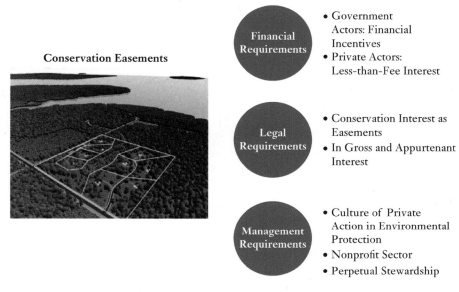

FIGURE 14.1. Key Elements of Conservation Easement Use. Diagram and photo by K. Mahung.

strictions while the landowner retains fee ownership of the property. In other words, easements held by nonprofits, whether through owner donation or other means, do not convey full ownership of the property, and nonprofits are not required to pay the property's full value. Thus conservation easements are often cheaper and more effective than, for example, outright land acquisition (Korngold 2011).

Legal Requirements

In Gross vs. Appurtenant Easements It is important to distinguish between two types of conservation easements: in gross and appurtenant. Easements in gross refer to those in which the owner does not or is not required to own land next to the burdened property (Korngold 2007); this means that there are no geographical or physical limits as to where the nonprofit can hold easements. Appurtenant easements, on the other hand, involve two properties that are in most cases adjacent to one another, with one as the dominant property and the other the servient property (Cope 2005). This latter arrangement generally limits the use and geographical distribution of easements for conservation purposes, as nonprofits are required to own property adjacent to the land to which they want to apply easements.

Conservation Interests as Easements The use of the term *easement* for the U.S. conservation tool is actually a misnomer. Traditionally in law, easements ensure the right to do something on the land of another; conservation easements, by contrast, restrict the activities of a landowner on the servient property and are thus more accurately a covenant. In a case of "semantic sleight-of-hand" (Korngold 2007, 20), the latter type of arrangement was termed an easement in order to avoid the restrictions linked to covenants under U.S. common law. In 1981, the Uniform Law Commission approved and recommended the Uniform Conservation Easement Act for all U.S. states, which circumvented the major hurdles posed by traditional common law and set off the first significant wave of conservation easement creation (National Conference of Commissioners on Uniform State Laws 1981).

Management Requirements

Culture of Private Action in Environmental Protection A distinguishing feature of conservation easements is their reliance on a landowner's understanding of his or her property's conservation values and the role private property owners can play in preservation. Conservation easements are voluntarily pursued by landowners—not mandated by governments—who seek to benefit from an arrangement that allows them to preserve the natural integrity of the land in perpetuity while still productively using the land.

Nonprofit Sector The involvement of the nonprofit sector, and particularly the land trust movement, has been a critical factor in the success of the U.S. model. Nonprofit organizations provide the stewardship that maintains the conservation benefits enjoyed by society. Because the public invests in conservation through the tax benefits that accompany the creation of such easements, nonprofits must in effect be accountable for the investment of public funds.

Perpetual Stewardship The restrictions placed on the property in order to preserve its natural integrity may be for a specified period of time or in perpetuity. It is important to note that many of the financial incentives offered by the government only apply when landowners place restrictions on their property in perpetuity, making these forms of conservation easements more popular.

ASSESSING THE POTENTIAL OF CONSERVATION EASEMENTS IN TRINIDAD AND TOBAGO

Financial Requirements

The financial incentives associated with easements have played a major role in their success and proliferation as a conservation strategy in the U.S. Elsewhere in the world, however, the provision of these financial incentives has been a challenge. In Latin America, many countries have been unable or unwilling to take such measures, especially during the recent financial crisis; the only country in the region that has been able to offer and maintain substantial financial incentives for conservation easements is Costa Rica (Environmental Law Institute 2003). Belize has drafted policy and legislative frameworks to support conservation easements and private protected areas, but the government cites its inability to provide financial incentives due to the country's poor economic situation as one of the factors holding back the formalization of this process. Although there is an ongoing initiative to formalize and legislate an incentive scheme to encourage conservation by private landowners (Ministry of Natural Resources and the Environment 2010), the lack of a financial structure leaves the effort at a great disadvantage.

Trinidad and Tobago's economic situation places it in a unique position in the region with respect to this prerequisite. Unlike Belize, and despite the absence of a policy and legislative framework to support conservation easements, Trinidad has a financial structure in place that could potentially be used to promote easement creation: the Green Fund, established by the government in 2001 under the Miscellaneous Taxes Act. This structure accumulates funds by a 0.1% Green Fund Levy imposed on gross sales or receipts of companies carrying on business in the country. The fund was established with the purpose of financially supporting remediation, reforestation, and conservation activities undertaken by local organizations and community groups; as of January 2012, an estimated TT$2.7 billion had been made available for these purposes. The policies guiding the use of this fund include the National Environmental Policy, the Medium-Term Policy Framework 2011–2014, and other relevant international and regional environment and development commitments such as the UN Millennium Development Goals (Laydoo 2012).

As a part of a National Biodiversity Assessment currently underway in Trinidad and Tobago, a legislative review of policies and laws related to biodiversity management and protection has found that a particular stipulation within the National Environmental Policy supports the "provision of economic incentives to private landowners to establish and maintain private forests and agro-forestry, especially in critical watershed areas, and reforesting of degraded forest land with ecologically compatible tree species" (National Biodiversity Committee 1998, 19). This stipulation suggests that the use of the Green Fund to provide financial incentives to private landowners who use conservation easements to achieve biodiversity protection and the maintenance of ecosystem services on private lands is a policy-supported option.

Despite the obstacles to meeting this prerequisite, Trinidad and Tobago can learn from nearby success stories when considering ways to enact their own conservation easements. Costa Rica's payment for ecosystem services program, PSA (*Pagos por Servicios Ambientales*), offers landowners market-based incentives that play an essential role in (1) the maintenance of globally significant biodiversity, and (2) the protection of lands adjacent to protected areas or in biological corridors that are under private ownership (Sánchez-Azofeifa et al. 2007). As part of the program, landowners have the option of entering into one of three types of contracts that creates legal easements that remain with the property even if it is sold. Rights to the greenhouse gas–mitigation potential of the property are transferred over from the private landowner to the government, which is then able to trade these abatement units on the international market (Sánchez-Azofeifa et al. 2007). The three types of contracts provide varying degrees of financial incentives (all in the form of monetary payments) based on the level of conservation activities on the property: forest conservation, reforestation, or sustainable forest management. Through the use of elements of both conservation easements and ecosystem service payments, Costa Rica's PSA program demonstrates how these tools can be applied within Latin America and the Caribbean in modified forms to suit the local culture of natural resource management.

Legal Requirements

In the United States, clear and strong legal support has been critical to the success of the conservation easement movement. The passing of the

Uniform Conservation Easement Act in 1981 precipitated a sharp increase in the growth of land trusts and the use of conservation easements. Within Latin America, the lack of a secure legal framework to support private conservation programs has been a primary challenge to implementation of this system. The fact that the U.S. model operates under common law, whereas most Latin American countries operate under the European civil code, poses a unique set of difficulties.

Despite the lack of any national law that recognizes the use of perpetual easements for conservation purposes or the creation of in gross easements that involve an independent third party, countries have still found ways to use these instruments (Environmental Law Institute 2003). Environmental nonprofits have been creatively using traditional appurtenant easements under the civil code to form easements with conservation-minded landowners. Costa Rica pioneered the use of traditional laws to facilitate the creation of easements in 1992, and these efforts have now spread to other Latin American countries (Swift et al. 2004). However, in the Latin American model, easements are limited to traditional appurtenant easements between two neighboring estates, with the exception of three states in Mexico—Nuevo León, Quintana Roo, and Veracruz—in which statutory laws enable in gross easements (Environmental Law Institute 2003).

Environmental law groups in Latin America have made progress in seeking legislative reform that allows for in gross easements that can be held by third-party entities such as nonprofits in order to provide the necessary support for effective private land conservation in the region (Environmental Law Institute 2003). Countries such as Chile, Costa Rica, and Ecuador have introduced proposed laws authorizing in gross easement.

Chile's efforts to amend its civil code in order to create a new type of conservation category that would be similar to conservation easements in the U.S. model marks a breakthrough for the future of private land protection in Latin America. Rather than borrow an instrument from another legal system, this tool has been created to serve as a functional, flexible, and enforceable legal instrument especially for private conservation initiatives in Chile (Levitt 2010). Because it is adaptable to any nation with a Napoleonic legal system, it is under review by countries such as Argentina, which has large tracts of privately owned land requiring protection. This instrument, Derecho Real de Conservación, was passed in March 2012 by Chile's Chamber of Deputies (the lower house of the bicameral legislature) and has been forwarded to the Senate (Patagonia Sur Workshop Group 2012).

In Belize, representatives from environmental management organizations have drafted a framework that would provide legal support for an existing system of private protected areas and private landowner initiatives to conserve land. The Conservation Covenant Act and National Park Systems (Amendment) Act, both presented in 2009, currently await approval by the national Cabinet. The amendment to the National Park Systems Act would provide legal recognition to private protected areas, and the Conservation Covenant Act would assist private landowners who want to place restrictions on their land for conservation purposes. Although termed a covenant rather than an easement, most of the fundamental elements of the act are taken from the U.S. model of legal support for conservation easements; unlike most other Latin American countries, Belize operates under common law. The bill permits in gross easements for (1) the conservation of biological diversity; (2) the protection of aesthetic or scenic values; and (3) support of recreational use, open space use, environmental education, or research and scientific studies. The binding agreement creating the covenant would be made between current and future landowners of the property with an entity that commits to be the holder of the easement contract, either a government or conservation nonprofit organization.

The efforts underway in Belize provide a window of opportunity for Trinidad and Tobago, another country that operates under common law, to analyze Belize's draft legal and policy frameworks and assess their suitability for adaptation.

Management Requirements

As previously highlighted, the importance of a culture of private action in environmental protection and a strong nonprofit sector able to support perpetual stewardship are critical factors in the success of conservation easements. In the management of this conservation tool, the private landowner, the nonprofit sector, and the government all have very clear roles that require a high degree of commitment to ensure success and proliferation. In examining the potential for application of this model in Trinidad and Tobago, natural resource managers as well as policy and decision makers need to determine whether the essential management prerequisites are suited to the local culture of conservation.

CONCLUSION

Conservation easements require private landowners to voluntarily enter into a contractual agreement with a nonprofit or government entity that places restrictions on their property that will limit some forms of development for the purpose of maintaining the natural integrity of the land. Landowners willing to place these restrictions on their ownership usually have a strong connection to the property (for example, a long history of ownership or family ties to the property) and an awareness that its aesthetic and conservation values (including biodiversity and environmental services) benefit not only themselves but their communities as well. Easements also require that there be a nonprofit sector that is either already versed in or willing to develop the technical capacity to undertake the legal and management responsibilities associated with conservation easements. Just as important, the government must provide the legal and financial structures necessary to ensuring the success and proliferation of this tool.

Unlike the other Latin American and Caribbean nations under discussion in this chapter, Trinidad and Tobago finds itself in a position to align most, if not all, of the major prerequisites necessary for the application of easements. Already mandated by the National Environmental Policy is the provision of economic incentives to private landowners for the purposes of conservation, specifically forest protection. The Green Fund, a financial structure guided by this same policy, was created for the purpose of supporting remediation, reforestation, environmental education, and conservation activities, and its funds are only accessible by specific categories of Trinidadian nonprofit and community groups.

Although all the countries analyzed above lack one or more crucial pieces of the easement framework, key groups of landowners, nonprofit managers, and policy makers are still in pursuit of the goal of formalizing the conservation easement model in Latin America and the Caribbean. The instrument is, in fact, already being used in many places despite the lack of formal financial incentives.

REFERENCES

Cope, J. 2005. *The Conventional Wisdom on Conservation Easements in Latin America*. San José, Costa Rica: Centro de Derecho Ambiental de Costa Rica (CEDARENA).

Environmental Law Institute. 2003. *Legal Tools and Incentives for Private Lands Conservation in Latin America: Building Models for Success.* Washington, DC: Environmental Law Institute.

Fishburn, I., P. Kareiva, K. Gaston, and P. Armsworth. 2009. "The Growth of Easements As a Conservation Tool." *PLoS ONE* 4 (3): e4996.

Government of Trinidad and Tobago. 2010. *Fourth National Report of Trinidad and Tobago to the Convention on Biological Diversity.* Port of Spain, Trinidad: Government of the Republic of Trinidad and Tobago.

Kenny, J., P. Comeau, and L. Katwaru. 1997. *A Survey of Biological Diversity: Trinidad and Tobago.* Port of Spain, Trinidad: United Nations Development Program.

Korngold, G. 2007. "Solving the Contentious Issues of Private Conservation Easements: Promoting Flexibility for the Future and Engaging the Public Land Use Process." Case Research Paper Series in Legal Studies, Working Paper 07-24. Cleveland, OH: School of Law, Case Western Reserve University.

————. 2011. "Globalizing Conservation Easements: Private Law Approaches for International Environmental Protection." *Wisconsin International Law Journal* 28:585.

Laydoo, R. 2012. "The Green Fund." First Workshop on Forest Financing in Small Island Developing States, April 23–27. PowerPoint presentation. Port of Spain, Trinidad: Ministry of Housing and the Environment.

Levitt, J., ed. 2010. *Conservation Capital in the Americas: Exemplary Conservation Finance Initiatives.* Cambridge, MA: Lincoln Institute of Land Policy.

Ministry of Housing and the Environment. 2010. *National Report of Trinidad and Tobago to the Convention on Biological Diversity.* Port of Spain: Government of the Republic of Trinidad and Tobago.

Ministry of Natural Resources and the Environment. 2010. *IV National Report to the United Nations Convention on Biological Diversity.* Belmopan, Belize: Ministry of Natural Resources and the Environment.

Ministry of Planning and the Economy. 2012. *Working for Sustainable Development in Trinidad and Tobago.* Port of Spain, Trinidad: Ministry of Planning and the Economy.

National Biodiversity Committee. 1998. *Belize National Biodiversity Strategy.* Belmopan, Belize: Ministry of Natural Resources and the Environment.

National Conference of Commissioners on Uniform State Laws. 1981. *Uniform Conservation Easement Act.* Chicago, IL: National Conference of Commissioners on Uniform State Laws.

Patagonia Sur Workshop Group. 2012. *Patagonia's Potential: Climate Change Mitigation in the Private Conservation Context: A Feasibility Study for the Patagonia Sur Foundation.* New York: School of International and Public Affairs, Columbia University.

Swift, B., V. Arias, S. Bass, C. Chacon, A. Cortez, M. Gutierrez, V. Maldonaldo, M. Milano, L. Nunes, M. Tobar, V. Sanjines, P. Solano, and V. Theulen. 2004. "Private Lands Conservation in Latin America: The Need for Enhanced Legal Tools and Incentives." *Journal of Environmental Law and Litigation* 19 (1): 85–140.

PART
V

The Contribution of the Humanities

IN HIS TREATISE *Rhetoric*, Aristotle famously explained that a persuasive argument requires three essential elements: *ethos*, or the credibility or authority attributed to the presenter; *logos*, or the logic or apparent truthfulness of the argument; and *pathos*, or an effective appeal to the passions of the listener.[1] The first four sections of this book have provided abundant ethos and logos: authors from some of the world's best-known universities explain in detail the ways and means by which they have achieved remarkable large landscape conservation outcomes. But conservationists working to advance these initiatives must appeal to the hearts as well as the minds of their audience of policy makers, budget allocators, and the general public. This is where the humanities—both arts and letters—can be so powerful.

The first chapter of this section offers the transcript of Alex Suber's wonderfully engaging short film about the expedition of two Colorado College (CC) alumni from the headwaters of the Colorado River in the Rocky Mountains to the cracked mud flats spread out along its dried-up delta, south of the U.S.-Mexico border. The film (created by Suber when he was a college freshman) and expedition (completed by Will Stauffer-Norris and Zak Podmore) were made as part of Colorado College's 2011–2012 State of the Rockies program, focused that academic year on the fate of the great river of America's southwest and Mexico's northwest. Student policy recommendations made as part of the State of the Rockies program added momentum to the many voices calling for the reform of policy regarding allocation of water to the delta in Mexico. Remarkably, those voices were eventually heard by senior policy makers on both sides of the border, leading to the eventual amendment of the U.S.-Mexico water treaty. The amended treaty now allows for more water to reach Mexico and the vital estuaries leading to the Sea of Cortez. Audiences from Waterville,

---

1. Aristotle. Circa 350 B.C.E. *Rhetoric.* Translated into English by W. Rhys Roberts. Available at http://classics.mit.edu/Aristotle/rhetoric.1.i.html. See Part II for paragraph on credibility, truthfulness, and passion.

303

Maine, to Valdivia, Chile, have cheered the film and its hopeful message that the informed voices of a new generation can indeed contribute to dramatic change in the management of natural resources.

Next is the text of Caroline Harvey's impassioned slam poetry creation, "Body of Bark," a piece that she performed live for the participants of the Conservation Catalysts meeting held in Cambridge, Massachusetts, in the spring of 2013. Ms. Harvey, an assistant professor in the Department of Liberal Arts at Berklee College in Boston, preaches what she practices as the coach of the school's award-winning Slam Poetry Team. Caroline's performance, centered around the connection she formed with an old beech tree growing in the backyard of her childhood home, served to remind each of us at the 2013 Cambridge meeting of the deep and enduring connection that each of us formed with the natural world at some formative period in our respective lives—a connection that we must allow 21st-century youth to form with the natural world if our plans for the success of landscape-scale conservation initiatives are to earn widespread popular support.

The third chapter of this section was written by Blair Braverman, an exceptionally talented young author and graduate of Colby College and the University of Iowa's master's program in nonfiction writing. After earning the trust of deer hunters in rural Iowa and working as a dogsled guide and naturalist in Alaska, Norway, Colorado, and Wisconsin, Blair offers insights into our ability to live with nature on a day-to-day basis that are fresh, eloquently expressed, and challenging to conventional wisdom. She gives her readers ample reasons to pause for thought, to question their own motivations, and to seek new working balances with the sometimes cold—even frigid—realities of the natural world.

For sheer charm and disarming earnestness, however, it is hard to beat the letter penned by 10-year-old Alice Van Evera that concludes this volume. Alice and her friends Lily Georgopoulis and Mari McBride, at the Estabrook Elementary School in Lexington, Massachusetts, decided that they needed to act to protect the world they love, and formed a group called Save Tomorrow. The girls proceeded, with uncommon pluck, to appear before Lexington's Town Meeting to advocate for a new residential solar energy ordinance, invoking the wisdom of *The Lorax* by Dr. Seuss and earning a standing ovation from the typically reserved assembly. The girls were subsequently moved to speak out for the protection of historic trees in their neighborhood, and they continue to brain-storm about ways that they can act to protect the planet. It is Alice and her friends, and children like them speaking out in nations around the globe, whom we will depend on to keep the fires of enduring conservation innovation going for many generations to come.

15

Colorado College's Large Landscape Conservation Strategy to Save the Colorado River Basin

A film by Alex Suber, Colorado College Class of 2015

In 2011, Colorado College freshman Alex Suber made a film describing the journey of Colorado College graduates Zak Podmore and Will Stauffer-Norris along the length of the Colorado River, from its headwaters in Utah to its delta in Mexico.

The film, made to illuminate the work of Colorado College's State of the Rockies project, details both the physical journey of the two young adventurers and the engagement of a team of Colorado College students in the effort to transform the river delta from its tragic present condition—largely dry, caked mud flats—into a future in which the river is reborn as one of the most vibrant and significant estuaries in North America. The short film can be seen in its entirety on the Internet at www.ConservationCatalysts.org.

At the Students as Catalysts for Large Landscape Conservation conference held at Colby College in Waterville, Maine, in March 2013, Suber's film was recognized as an outstanding contribution to conservation by an arts and humanities student. The transcript of the film's narration follows below. The film was subtitled for a viewing at the Tenth Congress on Latin American Protection of Private and Indigenous Lands held in Santiago, Chile, in August 2013. The audience of conservationists from across South America gave the film a standing ovation.

TITLE: Colorado College's large landscape conservation strategy . . . to save the Colorado River basin.

NARRATOR: How creative an approach to large landscape conservation can undergraduate students discover?

NARRATOR: During 2011 and 2012, Colorado College's State of the Rockies project—now in its 10th year—has chosen to address one of the largest landscape conservation issues in North America: the Colorado River basin.

NARRATOR: We chose to address the increasingly complicated issues of water supply and demand in the basin by melding traditional research and report aspects of the project with new approaches.

NARRATOR: The task for our student researchers and explorers, large in a geographic sense, has become even more immense considering the perspective we are trying to imbue in the project's research.

NARRATOR: What voices can and should the younger generation have in protecting and managing this huge river basin and its iconic Grand Canyon?

NARRATOR: While employing the traditional aspects of the project, including student—faculty collaborative research and the publishing of our annual State of the Rockies report card, the project has also pursued new avenues of research and outreach.

NARRATOR: Engaging Rockies citizens—particularly the youth—through social media and incorporating an adventure and exploration science dimension into the project have changed our approach to conservation work and proven successful in engaging young and old alike to address the complex system of one of the United States' largest rivers.

NARRATOR: Colorado College's long history with the Rocky Mountain west, since 1874, coupled with its unique one-course-at-a-time block plan and location at the base of Pike's Peak in the Rockies, laid the groundwork for the State of the Rockies project nearly 10 years ago.

NARRATOR: Today, the Rockies project is still leaning on this history with the Rocky Mountain west while also trying to incorporate the young and adventurous spirit that has defined the student body of our small liberal arts college.

SUBTITLE SCREEN: The Colorado College State of the Rockies Project. Research. Report. Engage.

NARRATOR: It was mid-October, and Zach and I were starting our journey from source to sea, going 1,700 miles down the Green and Colorado rivers.

NARRATOR: We'd heard the Colorado River didn't reach the ocean anymore, but we were determined to see for ourselves.

BACKPACKING STUDENT 1: And we're going to try to follow whatever this is over here, um, 1,700 miles to Mexico. That's the plan.

BACKPACKING STUDENT 2: Which way is Mexico?

NARRATOR: Just as we had made it to the source, our first speaker-series event was starting. It was time to start a large-scale conversation about the Colorado River basin and its management.

STUDENT SPEAKER 1; Speaker Series Event, October 17, 2011: The State of the Rockies project for 2011 and 2012 seeks to present information regarding the current issues in the basin, highlight the implications of changing climate as a variable to the current system, and incorporate the perspective of future generations.

LARRY MACDONNELL, PROFESSOR OF LAW; Speaker Series Event, October 17, 2011: I think the challenge before us is substantial. We have reached a point in our uses of the water of the basin where the Bureau of Reclamation has now acknowledged that we are fully consuming every drop of water that the basin produces.

LARRY MACDONNELL, PROFESSOR OF LAW; Speaker Series Event, October 17, 2011: We have already reached that point, and the question is: how do we then move ahead with the continuing demands and needs and interests of all of the seven states, the republic of Mexico, the many Indian tribes that have reservations within this area, and all of the diverse interests we have in the water and the rivers, and how can we meet those different interests?

LARRY MACDONNELL, PROFESSOR OF LAW; Speaker Series Event, October 17, 2011: I think that tells us that we don't really have a lot of time to just assume that this is not a problem, that we'll deal with it when we need to. I think we need to start today.

NARRATOR: Back on the river, we were enjoying the magnificent wilderness and beautiful canyons of the Colorado. But at the same time, we realized the scale of human impact on the river.

BACKPACKING STUDENT 1: So I'm standing here at the first point where water is taken out of the Green River. So, you can see behind me there is a big diversion ditch, and a lot of this water is being funneled into that irrigation canal. Just when we thought we were going to have enough water to start kayaking, a bunch of it gets sucked out.

JENNIFER PITT, ENVIRONMENTAL DEFENSE FUND, NOVEMBER 7, 2011: I spent a great bit of my career at Environmental Defense Fund focusing on the river where it's not really a river anymore. The latter picture there is the Colorado River sinking into the sand between the state of Arizona and Baja California, so actually the Colorado River is drying up on American soil.

JENNIFER PITT, ENVIRONMENTAL DEFENSE FUND, NOVEMBER 7, 2011: If I have any thoughts for a conclusion—it's sort of a depressing picture that I laid out, except that I think this growing recognition that we live in an age of limits, that water from the Colorado River is not endless, that we cannot keep just using more, and we have been until this point, but we cannot do that anymore. That in that series of decisions and compromises and agreements and conversations, we might also be able to right some of the wrongs that have been done on this river and prevent future inadvertent problems that we don't really want to have to live with. Thank you very much.

NARRATOR: As we kayak down the river covering about 20 miles a day, the sheer immensity of the Colorado revealed itself in a way that no map ever could.

NARRATOR: We started wondering how this finite resource could meet the needs of a growing population. As Jennifer Pitt said, "We live in a world of limits, and the Colorado River is no exception."

NARRATOR: What were we losing in the process of transforming the river?

NARRATOR: We were about to embark through one of the largest landscape alterations the United States has ever seen: Lake Powell.

BACKPACKING STUDENT 1: Oh God, so many houseboats. It's insane.

BACKPACKING STUDENT 2: We've been paddling across Lake Powell for about six days now. I keep reminding myself as we're out here that there is a canyon below us and a river that is no more, and if we start from the belief that a river has a right to be itself, to flow, and a canyon has a right to not be 500 feet under water, then there is something terribly wrong here.

BACKPACKING STUDENT 1: Bald eagle and coal plant.

NARRATOR: These massive dams are the most obvious impact on the Colorado River system. But a growing concern is the effect of climate change on the water supply in the basin.

JEFF LUKAS, WESTERN WATER ASSESSMENT, DECEMBER 5, 2012: It's a real pleasure to be here in the springs and here at Colorado College and contributing to the State of the Rockies project. Anthropogenic climate change is part of what I call the climate risk portfolio.

JEFF LUKAS, WESTERN WATER ASSESSMENT, DECEMBER 5, 2012: Here I'm showing an ensemble of 34 projections from 16 models, multiple runs from a few of those models. Every single one of them is forecasting a warmer future for Western Colorado—for the region and, for that matter, globally.

NARRATOR: After over 100 days of the paddling down the river, we hit the US–Mexico border. There, at Morelos Dam, the riverbed is completely dry, and the entire flow of the Colorado River is diverted into irrigation ditches.

BACKPACKING STUDENT 1: So I'm here at the riverbed, the old riverbed, of the Rio Colorado, we just took a walk over here from the irrigation canal. And this is it. This is what happens to the Colorado River. Just bone dry, old tire.

NARRATOR: This is the worst place I've ever paddled. Once I accidentally splashed a few drops into my mouth. My mouth burns.

NARRATOR: In the once-lush Colorado River delta, we were forced to hike across cracked mud flats. In areas where you could once paddle a canoe, we were forced to bushwhack through tamarisk.

NARRATOR: Finally, after 113 days of traveling, we made it to the Sea of Cortez. It was time to travel back to the State of the Rockies conference and share what we had seen on the river.

JOHN TUBBS, DEPUTY ASSISTANT SECRETARY FOR WATER AND SCIENCE, CONFERENCE CALL WITH SOURCE TO SEA PADDLERS AND U.S. DEPARTMENT OF THE INTERIOR, FEBRUARY 3, 2012: Having just come off of the river, what are some of your top takeaways that you've really learned on your experience?

BACKPACKING STUDENT 1, CONFERENCE CALL WITH SOURCE TO SEA PADDLERS AND U.S. DEPARTMENT OF THE INTERIOR, FEBRUARY 3, 2012: When we planned the trip, we didn't really know where the river ended up; we spent a lot of time in the wilderness sections of Utah and Colorado kayaking and rafting; we heard that the river didn't reach the sea, but we didn't know what that meant until we came here and saw it, and it means that there are hundreds of thousands of acres that once had water flowing through them and all of that is dry now except for a select few parts, less than 10 percent of the original wetlands.

BACKPACKING STUDENT 2, CONFERENCE CALL WITH SOURCE TO SEA PADDLERS AND U.S. DEPARTMENT OF THE INTERIOR, FEBRUARY 3, 2012: You can really see the difference between the places that have even just a little bit of water, and there's so many birds, and then there's these areas that we hiked through with just mile after mile after mile of tamarisk, which is an invasive species, and that contrast is so striking that even that tiny amount of agricultural wastewater basically can make that big of a difference in restoring the delta.

SUBTITLE SCREEN: **The voice of a younger generation.**

STATE OF THE ROCKIES REPORT CARD SERIES EVENT, INTRODUCTORY SPEAKER: Challenges are tall and they abound, but they are not unsolvable. As part of the concluding section of this year's State of the Rockies report card, our five student researchers have laid out five separate actions to ensure a healthy and viable river basin for the next generation. Now I'll turn it over to them to quickly cover their research focus of the last year and their actions regarding the future of the Colorado River basin.

STUDENT SPEAKER 1, STATE OF THE ROCKIES REPORT CARD SERIES EVENT: My section focused on dam diversions and water use. So currently there is a serious supply and demand imbalance in the Colorado River system.

STUDENT SPEAKER 2, STATE OF THE ROCKIES REPORT CARD SERIES EVENT: I focused on the law and policy of the river. The law of the river is comprised of over 30 independent pieces of legislation and court opinions, making it one of the most highly regulated rivers in the world.

STUDENT SPEAKER 3, STATE OF THE ROCKIES REPORT CARD SERIES EVENT: I looked to answer the question wondering if America's playground is under threat. So I was looking at the relationship between recreation and water and the future of recreation in the basin.

STUDENT SPEAKER 4, STATE OF THE ROCKIES REPORT CARD SERIES EVENT: The current situation of decreasing water supply and increasing water demand in the Colorado River basin really requires a fundamental shift in our discourse so that we provide new ways of thinking about water supply strategies that don't jeopardize environmental needs.

STUDENT SPEAKER 5, STATE OF THE ROCKIES REPORT CARD SERIES EVENT: My section focused on the effects of climate change on the Colorado River basin. As you can see on this slide, the Colorado River basin will have significantly less surface water available by the mid-21st century. This is primarily due to warm temperatures affecting the snowpack that provides 80 percent of the water of the Colorado River.

GOVERNOR OF COLORADO, JOHN HICKENLOOPER: Thank you, Dr. Hecox, you should be very proud of the whole program and the work that those students have done, it's very very impressive . . . we know we aren't going to develop our way out of this crisis any more than we can completely conserve our way out of this crisis. In other words, you saw the pictures of the dam that Zak and Will described, where just south of there, there is clearly no water, so bigger and better dams aren't going to be the ultimate solution. They might help us manage the problem, but they're not the solution.

NARRATOR: The governor was listening. We may not have been able to make the decisions ourselves, but we were influencing those who did: the secretary of the interior, Ken Salazar; the director of the USGS, Marcia McNutt; and the governor of Colorado, John Hickenlooper.

NARRATOR: They were listening to our voice. The voice of a younger generation speaking out for their future who were making a stand to sustain and conserve the future of the Colorado River, and we aren't done.

NARRATOR: In the summer of 2012, we launched one of the first solar rafting expeditions. We're mapping out where all the water is going; we're still researching, still reporting, and still engaging. Because it's the conservation efforts of today that will shape tomorrow.

EPILOGUE: *On November 20, 2012, the United States and Mexico signed an agreement to allocate water to the Colorado River Delta.*

CREDITS:

Director and Editor: **ALEX SUBER**

Footage: **ALEX SUBER, ZAK PODMORE, WILL STAUFFER-NORRIS, CARSON MCMURRAY, DAVID SPEIGEL**

Original Score: **ELIOT GOLDMAN**
Additional Music: **PANEYE**
Voiceover: **BRENDAN BOEPPLE, WILL STAUFFER-NORRIS, ALEX SUBER**
Supported by: **MARINE VENTURES FOUNDATION; THE COLORADO COLLEGE STATE OF THE ROCKIES PROJECT – RESEARCH, REPORT, ENGAGE; NRS; THE OCEAN FOUNDATION**
Translations: **EMILY NARANJO-STURZENEGGER**

16

Body of Bark

Caroline Harvey

This is the body I live in. My skin, the smooth bark stretching over bones
that grow and break and heal and grow.
This mouth and tongue, the rattle of leaves that warn of storm and wind,
my voice calling out into the middle of the night blue air
of summer, shouting into the cold brittle of winter when the silence
is as loud as grief.

We did not ask to be born, to be these animals of industry, but
here we are. The earth did not beg for us
to stand here, to dig our feet into the dirt, but this is where we
become, where we build our brick houses,
child after child, our families growing, breaking, healing. The beech tree
in upstate New York

that looms over the sledding hill of my childhood home, it did not ask
for me to climb it. But I did. That smooth grey bark,
how it shined luminescent in my favorite dusk light, how when I tried
to sleep its leaves would sound their shimmer
like the sweet sirens of seductive legend. How it called to me, tempting me
out into the starlit night

of deep purple August, how in my bare feet and hand-me-down T-shirts
I would strut like a quick and quiet peacock, scamper
to the top of the hill and find her—this beech tree—unafraid of the shadows.
So sturdy. So grounded and still in contrast to the
inside ocean of my own turmoil. I knew her knots in the dark, would hook
my tiny pink hand

onto that first hitch in her trunk, swing my right leg over the low branch,
then my left foot finds that one irregular notch,

and I pull myself higher, and then higher again, until I can lay my
body out flat, my toes dangling over the side and
combing the air, my head a pile of wild hair nestled into the
fork where she spreads out

underneath me, wide as a bed fit for a god. These are the moments we adore:
the trees we climbed, the mud pies we made for the mothers
who tolerated our follies, the flowers that amazed us, the moon that
never abandoned. These are the moments
when we do not feel ourselves as separate from the land, when nature
swallows us whole and we can revel

in our smallness, in our indisputable, bone-deep connection to the places
we call home. And now, how to grow up into cities? How to
strap our feet into shoes and strut, not to the climbing trees, but to the office,
to the computer screens, to the briefcases and to the
four-door sedans that carry us so swiftly over the dirt that we can no longer
feel the cool stones we once so fully loved.

But look again at your mouth. Tell me it is not still filled with beech leaves,
Tell me that your skin is not still the glow of sun's dusktime fade.
That your carefully chosen grown-up words are not still, sometimes, just the
shimmer of a branch in spring. We cannot pretend,
even though we move with radical and fumbling urban speed, that our bodies
are not still made of bark.

So we are called
called
to the work:
to the work of the growth and the break
and the heal and the growth and the break
we are called
to the trees, to the trails
to the break and the break and the healing
to the Big Sur cliffs, to the Massachusetts mountains
to the Guatemalan volcanoes
to the growth, to the break, to the healing
to the rivers in Thailand

the glaciers, to the ice, to the breaks,
to the temples in India
we are called
to the heal
to the places where the dirt knows us by name
where we can dig our feet in
and sweat through one more season
of heal, of growth
of change.

Once, in the winter, home for a holiday, I hiked through the snow
to that shining beech tree. I was young. I felt
daring. The sun was bright in the noontime sky and I launched myself onto
a newer, slimmer branch. I will not ever
shake off the sound of that limb cracking. How in my foolishness,
the tree that I loved

split in two. I clamored to keep my body from tumbling to the ground, but
watched the poof of powder as that splintered branch
settled into the snow beneath me. How I mourned for that branch. Felt the
guilt grow in my body like a weed. My sister told me then
how the strength of things changes over time, how in the cold
of winter's grief

the tree holds less water, and therefore less resilience. We tried
to fuse it together using rope and duct tape.
All afternoon we tried to give the tree back its broken arm. We failed,
but we were better for the trying, better
for the knowing that sometimes even the things we most love
break.

I haven't been to that house in five years, haven't climbed that beech in ten,
but last month my mother sent me a photo.
The beech leaves blooming huge in the ripe beginning of spring. The light,
just how I remember it: a little bit of silver
and a dash of gold, the ground not quite green, but trying,
becoming, almost, again.

I cannot see in the photo how the broken limb healed, if it grew again, or if it rotted
and fell. But in the morning, dressing myself for the work of living this
adult life, buttoning down my collar and pouring myself into
slacks the color of duct tape, I try and remember to feel
that cool bark stretching itself across
these small hands
these tiny hands
that refuse
to quit.

17

The Drowning Fish: Large Landscapes and the Burden of Significance

Blair Braverman

I went deer hunting recently in northern Wisconsin, which is perhaps surprising given that I am a young vegan environmentalist, also surprising given that most of my companions were men twice my age. But I was curious, and they welcomed me, and for several days we walked in the woods together. We combed the underbrush in silent lines, and although twice when I saw deer I pretended to try to shoot them, the only real shots I fired were to communicate my location to the others during a brief period of geographic disorientation. I appreciated that: the fact of being lost less than the fact that I *could* get lost in the expansive northwoods. The others ended the week with freezers full of meat, and I ended it with a stockpile of a rather different form of nourishment.

Typically, when I've gone to the woods with other American environmentalists, we plan ahead of time. We go hiking or backpacking or canoeing, making sure to bring a field guide and a camera, and perhaps as the canoe drifts silently over the glassy water someone sighs out, "This is exactly what I needed," at which point we agree that yes, this *is* what we needed, what we *all* needed, and we thank the person who suggested the trip, and agree that we should do this much more often.

But I'm resistant to the sense of significance that permeates such a trip, the expectation that it contains meaning. I don't mean to imply that there is something the matter with finding nature significant, but rather to note that environmentalists (perhaps in an unconscious effort to validate our own decisions to devote time, resources, and even lives to the protection of nature) carry a constant awareness of that significance; and the danger, I've begun to suspect, is that the sustained weight of this significance can come to feel like a burden.

A sense of significance can also, ironically, reveal a kind of distance from nature. One of my personal goals is to make the most important things in my life as unremarkable as possible, by doing them so regularly that they become commonplace. And so I want to be able to enter a landscape without needing the experience to be sacred. I love a healthy dose of wonder, but there's a limit to the wonder that a person can feel on a daily basis, and so when I go outside and feel overcome with wonder—as I did, regrettably, on the deer hunting trip—it's generally a sign that I haven't been outside enough lately.

For evidence of environmentalists' expectation that time in wilderness requires, or is enriched by, a sense of significance, we can look to nature writing. As David Gessner (2005, 6) laments, nature writing is perennially "quiet"—*quiet* being a common if rather anemic compliment applied to such work—and quiet also, I'd argue, in the way that a person can lower his voice at the dinner table and thereby suggest that his words deserve more attention than they've actually earned.

After all, language will always fail to replicate nature, so nature writers fall back on what language does best, which is interiority—emotion. Nature writers insert meaning; they insert wonder; they add value to the product, so to speak. The whole genre is biased by the strengths and limitations of its medium, and then *we* are biased by the genre, and rather than expecting annoyance, or discomfort, or any of the other million experiences we could have in nature, we anticipate meaning.

Here's news, fresh from my iPhone: a cowboy is moving to Montana. He's 70, maybe, or older—one of the last men in the country who logs with draft horses, and after half a century of seasonal ranching work he's finally moving west for good. He called to explain why I won't see him over the holidays, but also to share his excitement. "I'm going to drive cattle and hunt mountain lions for the rest of my life," he said. "Montana is the closest to heaven that I'll ever get."

I'm not much of a lion hunter myself, but I couldn't help but feel wistful as he described it to me. I like a landscape where I can turn a corner and not know what's coming, and I've been feeling myself lately that I could use some Big Sky Country, or some Big anything. Country music on the radio and a long horizon, and look at me now, getting nostalgic for a red-state fantasy I never knew in the first place. I get along with cowboys and hunters, dogsled drivers and bush pilots, and even when I have serious problems with their politics or methods I can romanticize their lifestyles as far as all get-out: where people know their place in the scheme of things, in a place that can swallow them whole.

I've sometimes struggled against this attraction (to what—resource use? Rural living? Right-wing sentimentality?), because it's not how an environmentalist is "supposed" to feel. And it's true that there are certainly instances where the two inclinations are at odds. "You can't have this job and call yourself an environmentalist," a coworker at a heliport told me once, and although I did not yet identify strongly as an environmentalist, the statement bothered me, and stuck in my mind like a burr. First, because I thought at the time that it was probably true, and second, because I didn't like hearing that I could not appreciate certain aspects of seemingly conflicting worldviews. Now it seems obvious to me: of course these ideas can overlap, even if the practices (flying helicopters versus conserving fossil fuels) don't, and for my coworker to write off environmentalism as incompatible with his lifestyle means only that he's setting himself up for a poverty of ideas. Environmentalists do the same when we write off hunters, snowmobilers, even Republicans. "A good cause has to be careful of the company it keeps," Rebecca West (1942) reminds us, and environmentalists should be careful of associating too much with just ourselves, if we want to build understanding and open communication with the people we are trying, after all, to win over.

I wore a dress to hunter safety class, sat at a folding table in the Izaak Walton League headquarters of Ottumwa, Iowa, amid a sea of Carhartt jackets, and kicked myself for not planning ahead to blend in better. That first day, one of the instructors asked me, "Why are you here?" and when I said I was planning to go hunting over Thanksgiving, he nodded a lot and said okay, that sounded great, he'd just been curious. And as class discussion turned from the importance of gun rights to the importance of wildlife identification, I relaxed. By the end of the third and last day I was kicking back with the instructors after class, and one of them said to me, "We've been glad to have someone of your obvious appearance here." What did he mean? "Someone like you, you'll go back to your liberal university town, and if you tell people what you learned about hunters and our perspective, they'll actually be open to it. But if we tried to talk to them?" They all laughed. "People will listen to you," he said. Then he said he had a secret recipe for dry rub for venison, and that he'd send me some in the mail so that I could use it on my first deer.

So now I'm back in my city apartment, smearing Grub Rub on my tofu, thinking about my assumptions: that hunters are the ones who won't listen to conservationists, rather than vice versa; that an environmental consciousness, as we typically interpret it, implies a somehow more valid connection to nature. If the men that I hunted with don't use the same language that I do to describe nature, then they have their own language, equally precise. Hunter Craig explained deer to me in a country bar one night; he pointed the fingers of his right hand to show how a buck can slide its hooves along the ground, walking silently even in crunchy leaves. "Deer are genius," he said, shaking his head. Then he glanced over at me: "—at what they do. They're genius at what they do."

"What do they do?" I asked.

"Survive."

I almost missed it—the subtlety with which he revised his statement mid-sentence, his glance and hesitation in qualifying the word *genius* with "at what they do." Where a nature writer might have played up the praise in effort to fit the typical lavish wonder of the genre, Craig, in his restraint, expressed his admiration in a way that felt honest and, for me at least, rare. And his insight, his point, is succinct and incisive—the kind of insight about the natural world that I would wish for a child, for any young environmentalist, or for myself.

I started this essay with a formula in mind: Tragedy = Awareness > Power. Tragedy in literature, according to German philosopher Karl Jaspers, occurs where awareness exceeds power, and particularly when a character encounters a situation where "awareness of a major need exceeds the power to satisfy it" (1953, 17). Well, stop me if that doesn't describe your life exactly. We are all of us tragic figures then, and environmentalists hold a unique awareness of some of the world's major needs.

Knowledge of that tragedy is another weight we carry into wilderness, a weight more visible—if not actually heavier—than the weight of expectation of significance, and most of us recognize that for children, at least, such a burden can be counterproductive. One Norwegian schoolteacher didn't talk to her class about climate change because doing so would "[take] nature away from the children" (Norgaard 2011), and those words recall a certain David Sobel maxim drilled into me during a brief stint as a naturalist educator: "No tragedies before fourth grade" (1996, 27). Let kids have their nature before we tell them it's ruined; let them enter landscape without a sense of urgency or despair. Which is wise, I think, if never fully possible. But what about us adults? Where in the world should we get our comfort, our solace?

I for one am regularly horrified by the frequency with which I am encouraged to take my solace from nature. Thank you for the reminder, Gretel Ehrlich, Kathleen Dean Moore, and all the other thinkers and writers whose writings have suggested the same. It's not that there's a problem with taking solace from nature; it's just that these works, and others, construct an expectation that to do so is somehow virtuous and right, adding even further weight to the burden of what one ought to feel, or be able to feel, in the outdoors.

Every tragic figure needs a tragic flaw, and sometimes I suspect this is ours: that, as environmentalists, our relationship to landscape is forever colored, first by anger and guilt over that landscape's destruction, secondly by external pressure to display a personal relationship to that landscape, and thirdly with a sense that we should find solace for our anger and guilt from the very same landscape that inspired them. We are always owing something to the landscape, and wanting something from it.

My wish for young environmentalists is that we take a lesson from outdoorsmen—*outdoorsmen* being the sexist (if often apt) term for hunters, fishermen, snowmobilers, cowboys, and other highly competent users-of-nature who, while they may be involved in specific conservation efforts to protect their resource of interest, are often unattached to the environmental community as a whole—or, often enough, are considered to be at odds with it. But what many outdoorsmen have, and what I want for myself and my peers, is a neighborly relationship to landscape, an understanding that time in nature is as likely to be unpleasant, frustrating, or boring as it is to be exciting or restorative, and an ability to take it for granted in the way that we in weaker moments take for granted our closest loved ones—precisely because they are so close, so present and continuous in our lives. Short of a rural life, the best way to develop this relationship is to spend time, real time, in big spaces, preferably with a job to do—collecting food, building shelters, maintaining trails, anything that keeps a person distracted and gets them tired. Manual labor, I suspect, is the cure for *significance*, and is part of the reason that anyone who enters nature with a task—be it lion hunting, cattle driving, or pulling up invasive plants—will be hard put to romanticize that particular landscape, much as they might come to know and appreciate it.

So here's my take on large landscape conservation, if I may come at it from a distinctly human perspective: large landscape conservation is the protection and preservation of an expanse of wild land so big, with such a tiny nature-to-human ratio, that anyone who enters it with expectations will soon realize the absurdity and arrogance of entering nature with any human expectations at all.

My neighbor the rocket scientist tells me that when the first fish returned from outer space, they drowned. Having learned to make do by gulping air from the small bubbles that drifted about their tank in zero gravity, they could not remember how to get oxygen from the bountiful expanse of the water's surface. Similarly, I'm afraid that we urban humans compensate so well with small landscapes—parks and ponds and gardens—that we no longer know how to be in big spaces, or how to be comfortable with them, which is the only way we can really be open to accepting any meaning or insight they might offer—and open, also, to accepting that there may be none.

REFERENCES

Gessner, D. 2005. *Sick of Nature*. Lebanon, NH: Dartmouth College Press.

Jaspers, K. 1953. *Tragedy Is Not Enough*. London, U.K.: Victor Gollancz.

Norgaard, K. M. 2011. *Living in Denial: Climate Change, Emotions, and Everyday Life*. Cambridge, MA: MIT Press.

Sobel, D. 1996. *Beyond Ecophobia: Reclaiming the Heart in Nature Education*. Great Barrington, MA: Orion Society.

West, R. 1942. "World of Books: The Greek Way." *Sunday Times* (London, England), August 23.

18

A Letter from Alice Van Evera

Alice Van Evera
24 Demar Road
Lexington, Massachusetts

Dear Mr. Jim Levitt,

Save Tomorrow is an organization made up of fourth graders at Estabrook School. We started Save Tomorrow because for a long time we had been very concerned about climate change. The most active members are Lily Georgopoulos, Mari McBride, and myself, Alice Van Evera. We are all 10 years old.

So far, we have worked on two main projects: helping a solarization project for the public buildings of Lexington, and helping stop the deforestation of our town.

We helped the solarization project by speaking at Town Meeting in favor of changing town laws in ways that helped make Lexington greener. Town Meeting and audience members are not allowed to clap, so it was exciting when they broke into applause for us. However, it was more exciting when the article passed unanimously.

We are helping stop the deforestation of our town by creating a petition with at least 44 signatures from kids at our school. Mari and I brought the petition to a meeting that helped decide whether the deforestation happens or not. (It is still undecided.)

We have two more projects in mind for the future: help environmentalist Lynne Cherry make a movie about Save Tomorrow and work against the use of palm oil in food and other products. The reason that we stand against the use of palm oil is that people take down many trees to get the oil and it ruins the animal habitats.

Thank you for listening to our story.

Signed, Alice Van Evera ☺

The work of Alice Van Evera and her friends was reported in *Pilgrim's Progress*, the newsletter of the Pilgrim Congregational Church in Lexington, Massachusetts. Alice and her family are members of that church. The account follows below.

PILGRIM ENVIRONMENTAL GROUP

Did You Know? . . .

That in March at Lexington's Town Meeting, three fourth graders spoke up to support one of the warrant articles? Alice Van Evera and two of her friends had been wondering how they could do something to help protect our planet from pollution and global warming. They discussed their plans with Alice's dad, Steve. He suggested they consider supporting one of the Town Warrant Articles, the one that would allow the town to place solar panels on town buildings. They asked several people how this could be done and then they began their own research.

Each of the girls wrote her own statement of why it was important to save energy and stop polluting. Steve drove them to Town Meeting on the evening that "their" Warrant Article was to be discussed and introduced them to the Town Meeting moderator, Deborah Brown. She showed them where they would stand when it was time to speak. At the appointed time, they each read their pieces into the microphone in the balcony. When they had finished, they quoted together from *The Lorax*, a book by Dr. Seuss. It reads:

"Unless someone like you cares a whole awful lot, nothing is going to get better. It's not."

After that, the Town Meeting burst into applause and gave them a standing ovation (normally not allowed). The warrant article passed unanimously.

About the Authors

Mark Ashton is the Morris K. Jesup Professor of Silviculture and Forest Ecology and director of the Yale Forests at the Yale School of Forestry & Environmental Studies. Email: mark.ashton@yale.edu.

Blair Braverman is a nonfiction writer currently based in northern Wisconsin. Email: blairbraverman@gmail.com.

Perry Brown is the provost and vice president for academic affairs at the University of Montana in Missoula. Email: provost@umontana.edu.

Richard Campbell is the former manager of the Yale Forests. He is currently with Save the Redwoods League.

Federico Cheever is professor of law at the University of Denver's Sturm College of Law, where he teaches environmental, natural resources, and property law. Email: fcheever@law.du.edu.

Lisa Cloutier is senior program manager in the Department of Planning and Urban Form at the Lincoln Institute of Land Policy. Email: lcloutier@lincolninst.edu.

Christopher S. Cronan is a professor in the School of Biology and Ecology at the University of Maine. His areas of expertise include biogeochemistry, plant ecology, ecosystem ecology, and land use planning. Email: chris.cronan@umit.maine.edu.

Steven Cumming holds a Canada Research Chair in Boreal Ecosystems Modeling at the Département des Sciences du Bois et de la Forêt at Université Laval. Email: steve.cumming@sbf.ulaval.ca.

Brian Donahue is environmental historian at the Harvard Forest and professor of American environmental studies at Brandeis University. Email: bdonahue@brandeis.edu.

Guillermo Donoso is a professor of agricultural and resource economics in the Department of Agricultural Economics at the Pontificia Universidad Católica de Chile. Email: gdonosoh@uc.cl.

Joe J. Figel is a graduate student completing his Ph.D. as a member of the Reed F. Noss Science and Planning in Conservation Ecology Lab at the University of Central Florida. Email: jj.figel@knights.ucf.edu.

Karl Flessa is professor of geosciences at the University of Arizona in Tucson. Email: kflessa@email.arizona.edu.

David Foster is an ecologist and director of Harvard University's Harvard Forest. Email: drfoster@fas.harvard.edu.

Matthew Fried was a student in the master's class of 2013 at the Yale School of Forestry & Environmental Studies. He is currently with the U.S. Forest Service.

Kathleen Galvin is a professor in the Department of Anthropology and director of Sustainable African Ecosystems and Societies under Global Change, a research group at Colorado State University. Email: Kathleen.Galvin@colostate.edu.

Isabella Gambill is a research assistant at the Lincoln Institute of Land Policy. Email: isabella.gambill@gmail.com.

Douglas Givens worked in the development office at Kenyon College for 28 years; he retired from the vice presidency in 2000 to serve as the founding managing director of the Philander Chase Corporation, a position he held until 2011. Email: givens@kenyon.edu.

Caroline Harvey is a poet, performer, and educator who currently teaches at Berklee College of Music in Boston. Email: charvey1@berklee.edu.

Clarisse Hart is outreach and development manager at the Harvard Forest. Email: Hart3@fas.harvard.edu.

Michelle L. Johnson earned her Ph.D. in 2014 from the University of Maine's School of Forest Resources and now works for the U.S. Forest Service in New York City. Email: michelle.l.johnson@maine.edu.

Dickson Kaelo, Maasai pastoralist, is currently the CEO of the Kenya Wildlife Conservancies Association as well as a Ph.D. student at the University of Nairobi. Email: olekaelo@yahoo.com.

David Kittredge is forest policy analyst at the Harvard Forest and professor of forestry in the Department of Environmental Conservation at the University of Massachusetts. Email: david.kittredge@eco.umass.edu.

Meg Krawchuk is an assistant professor and lead of the Landscape and Conservation Science Research Group at Simon Fraser University. Email: meg_krawchuk@sfu.ca.

Patti Kristjanson is leader of the Linking Knowledge with Action theme for the Research Program on Climate Change, Agriculture, and Food Security (CCAFS) in Nairobi, Kenya. Email: p.kristjanson@cgiar.org.

Kathy Fallon Lambert is science and policy integration director at the Harvard Forest. Email: Klambert01@fas.harvard.edu.

Shawn Leroux is an assistant professor of ecosystem ecology in the Department of Biology at Memorial University of Newfoundland. Email: sleroux@mun.ca.

James N. Levitt is director of the Program on Conservation Innovation at the Harvard Forest, a fellow at the Lincoln Institute of Land Policy, and a senior fellow at Highstead. Email: james_levitt@waverleyresources.com.

Robert J. Lilieholm is the E.L. Giddings Professor of Forest Policy in the School of Forest Resources at the University of Maine, where he teaches and conducts research in natural resources economics, policy, and management. Email: robert. lilieholm@maine.edu.

Kim Lisgo is manager of the BEACONs Project and has studied and coordinated research on the effects of industrial development on the ecology of a variety of boreal wildlife. Email: kim.lisgo@ales.ualberta.ca.

Matthew McKinney is the director of the Center for Natural Resources and Environmental Policy at the University of Montana. Email: matt@cnrep.org.

Nancy A. McLaughlin is the Robert W. Swenson Professor of Law at the University of Utah's S. J. Quinney College of Law, where she teaches federal income tax, trusts and estates, estate planning, private land conservation, and courses on conservation easements. Email: nancy.mclaughlin@law.utah.edu.

Karena Mahung is from Belize and is a student in the Master of Environmental Management program at Yale University. Email: karena.mahung@yale.edu.

Patricia Martin is the central Florida conservation director for the Florida chapter of The Nature Conservancy (TNC). Email: tmartin@archbold-station.org.

Spencer R. Meyer earned his Ph.D. in 2014 from the University of Maine's School of Forest Resources and is now a postdoctoral researcher at Yale University's School of Forestry & Environmental Studies. Email: spencer.meyer@maine.edu.

David Nkedianye, Maasai pastoralist, was recently elected the first governor of Kajiado County, Kenya, and leads policymaking for almost a million people in Maasailand. Email: d.nkedianye@cgiar.org.

Dave Owen is a professor at the University of Maine School of Law. Owen specializes in environmental law, and his research interests range from ecosystem restoration to climate change. Email: daveowen@usm.maine.edu.

Robin Reid is a professor in the Department of Ecosystem Science and Sustainability and directs the Center for Collaborative Conservation at Colorado State University. Email: Robin.Reid@colostate.edu.

Mohammed Said is a research scientist with the International Livestock Research Institute in Nairobi, Kenya. Email: m.said@cgiar.org.

Fiona Schmiegelow is a professor of conservation and landscape science and director of the Northern Environmental and Conservation Sciences Program at the University of Alberta. Email: fschmieg@ualberta.ca.

Alex Suber is a filmmaker and student at Colorado College. Email: alex.suber@coloradocollege.edu.

Hilary M. Swain is executive director of Archbold Expeditions, an independent nonprofit research, education, and conservation center in south-central Florida. Email: hswain@archbold-station.org.

Gary M. Tabor is a senior fellow at the Center for Natural Resources and Environmental Policy at the University of Montana and executive director of the Center for Large Landscape Conservation in Bozeman, Montana. Email: wildcatalyst@gmail.com.

Mary Tyrrell is the executive director of the Global Institute of Sustainable Forestry at the Yale School of Forestry & Environmental Studies. Email: Mary.tyrrell@yale.edu.

Alice Van Evera lives and attends school in Lexington, Massachusetts.

Geoff Wescott is an associate professor of environment in the School of Life and Environmental Sciences at Deakin University in Melbourne, Australia. Email: wescott@deakin.edu.au.

Stephen Woodley is co-chair of the WCPA-SSC Task Force on Biodiversity and Protected Areas; the WCPA (World Commission on Protected Areas) and the SSC (Species Survival Commission) are the two largest of the six commissions of the International Union for the Conservation of Nature (IUCN). The IUCN was founded in 1948 as the first global environmental organization and is today the largest professional global conservation network, with more than 1,200 member organizations (including more than 200 government and 900 nongovernmental organizations). The IUCN's six commissions unite nearly 11,000 volunteer experts from a range of disciplines and some 160 countries. The commissions assess the state of the world's natural resources and provide the union with sound know-how and policy advice on conservation issues.

Index

Abbey, Ed, 57
Aboriginal title and associated rights, 115
Abrahamson, Warren, 82–83
Academic collaboration, Wildlands and Woodlands Initiative and, 10–12
Academic community, attributes of, 40, 40(table)
Academic institutions: bringing stakeholders together, 37; as catalysts in large-landscape conservation, xvii–xx; collaborative rationality approaches and, 38; lack of confidence in role and relevance in solving environmental problems, 38–39; role in creating alternative energy future, xvi–xvii; role in Wildlands and Woodlands Initiative, 24–25. *See also* Universities
Academic scientists: classification of, 56–57; role of, 56–57
Acadia National Park, 171, 195
Acadian Internship in Large Landscape Conservation and Stewardship, 195–196
Acadian Program in Regional Conservation and Stewardship, 138, 231
Acipenser brevirostrum (shortnose sturgeon), 173–174
Acquisition and Restoration Council (Florida), 76–77
Adaptive management areas and active management, 107
Administrative Procedure Act, 252n50
Advanced Conservation Strategies, 280
Advanced Silviculture Prescription course, 160(fig.)
Africa. *See* Mara-Serengeti ecosystem; Savanna, conservation of
African district council game reserves, 211
Ahearn, Jack, 9
Albatross, 278
Allagash River canoe way, 177
Allen, Joel A., 129
Allen David Broussard Catfish Creek Preserve State Park, 76

Alternative energy, role of academic institutions in evolution of, xvi–xvii
Alternative futures modeling, lower Penobscot River watershed, 175, 183–193, 197, 199; future development scenarios, 191–193, 192(fig.); identifying areas of potential conflict and compatibility, 188–191, 189(fig.), 190(fig.); stakeholder-derived land suitability modeling with Bayesian belief networks, 186–187, 188(fig.); study goals and objectives, 185–186
Amenity-based economic development, 180–182
American Bar Association, 233
Animals, scrub, 80(fig.)
Anti-regulatory environment, land-use planning and, 198–199
Aphelocoma californica, 65
Aphelocoma coerulescens (Florida scrub-jay), 65
Appalachian Trail, 197
Appurtenant easements, 295–296
Archbold, Richard, 66, 67
Archbold Biological Station, 61, 63, 67, 92; establishment of, 66; fire management and, 81; Florida black bear study, 86; Florida scrub-jay study, 85; K-12 education program, 89; Lake Wales Ridge project and, 75, 77; private funding of land acquisition and, 77; workshop on Ridge ecosystem at, 74
Archbold Board of Trustees, 67
Archbold Expeditions, 66
Archbold Research Station, xix
Argentina, 300; beaver eradication plan and, 283–284
Aristotle, 303
Arthropods, Florida scrub and, 67, 72
Ashton, Mark, 156, 161
Atlantic Multidecadal Oscillation, 85
Atlantic salmon *(Salmo salar)*, 173, 174
Australia. *See* Victoria (Australia), coastal conservation in
Avon Park Bombing Range (Avon Park Air Force Range), 73, 81, 87, 88(fig.)

ABOUT THE
Lincoln Institute of Land Policy

The Lincoln Institute of Land Policy is a private operating foundation whose mission is to improve the quality of public debate and decisions in the areas of land policy and land-related taxation in the United States and around the world. The Institute's goals are to integrate theory and practice to better shape land policy and to provide a nonpartisan forum for discussion of the multidisciplinary forces that influence public policy. This focus on land derives from the Institute's founding objective—to address the links between land policy and social and economic progress—which was identified and analyzed by political economist and author Henry George.

The work of the Institute is organized in three departments: Valuation and Taxation, Planning and Urban Form, and International Studies, which includes programs on Latin America and China. We seek to inform decision making through education, research, policy evaluation, demonstration projects, and the dissemination of information through our publications, website, and other media. Our programs bring together scholars, practitioners, public officials, policy makers, journalists, and citizens in a collegial learning environment. The Institute does not take a particular point of view, but rather serves as a catalyst to facilitate analysis and discussion of land use and taxation issues—to make a difference today and to help policy makers plan for tomorrow. The Lincoln Institute of Land Policy is an equal opportunity institution.

LINCOLN INSTITUTE
OF LAND POLICY

113 Brattle Street
Cambridge, MA 02138-3400 USA

Phone: 1-617-661-3016 or 1-800-526-3873
Fax: 1-617-661-7235 or 1-800-526-3944
Email: help@lincolninst.edu
Web: www.lincolninst.edu